CW00724263

David

with thanks and
best wishes

Stephen

# SEXUAL SLANDER IN NINETEENTH-CENTURY ENGLAND

*Defamation in the Ecclesiastical Courts, 1815–1855*

S.M. WADDAMS

# Sexual Slander in Nineteenth-Century England

*Defamation in the Ecclesiastical Courts, 1815–1855*

UNIVERSITY OF TORONTO PRESS
Toronto Buffalo London

© University of Toronto Press Incorporated 2000
Toronto Buffalo London
Printed in Canada

ISBN 0-8020-4750-5

Printed on acid-free paper

---

**Canadian Cataloguing in Publication Data**

Waddams, S.M., 1942–
  Sexual slander in nineteenth-century England : defamation in the
  ecclesiastical courts, 1815–1855

Includes bibliographical references and index.
ISBN 0-8020-4750-5

1. Libel and slander – England – History – 19th century.
2. Ecclesiastical courts – England – History – 19th century.   I. Title.

KD1960.W32 2000      346.4203'4      C99-932819-0

---

University of Toronto Press acknowledges the financial assistance to its publishing
program of the Canada Council for the Arts and the Ontario Arts Council.

This book has been published with the help of a grant from the Humanities and
Social Sciences Federation of Canada, using funds provided by the Social Sciences
and Humanities Research Council of Canada.

University of Toronto Press acknowledges the financial support for its publishing
activities of the Government of Canada through the Book Publishing Industry
Development Program (BPIDP).

Every Person or Persons who utter, publish, assert, or report ... reproachful, scandalous, or defamatory Words, to the Hurt and Diminution of the good Name, Fame, and Reputation of another Person, contrary to good Manners and the Bond of Charity, are and ought to be admonished, constrained, and compelled to the reclaiming and retracting of such reproachful, scandalous, and defamatory Words, and to the restoring of the good Name, Fame, and Reputation of the Person thereby injured; and that for the future they refrain from uttering, publishing, or declaring any such reproachful, scandalous, or defamatory words; and are and ought to be canonically punished and corrected ...

Extract from a libel for defamation (Hereford, 1826)

# Contents

TABLES

APPENDICES

*Illustrations follow page 144*

# List of Illustrations

# Preface

The ecclesiastical courts in the first half of the nineteenth century had exclusive jurisdiction over three classes of case that had nothing directly to do with ecclesiastical matters, namely, probate of wills, matrimonial disputes, and certain kinds of defamation. In these matters the ecclesiastical courts exercised jurisdiction over the whole population, and administered, to the extent of their jurisdiction, the general law of the land. Ecclesiastical law in these areas was more legal than ecclesiastical, though in some respects both.

This is a study of the defamation jurisdiction in the last forty years before its abolition in 1855. This jurisdiction was an important part of the English law of defamation. The cases, all involving sexual slander, are also of potential importance and interest to those concerned with many aspects of social relations, especially sexual reputation. Yet, despite the attention that has been given to nineteenth-century sexuality, these documents have been neglected, both by legal and by social historians. No published study has hitherto made any use of the defamation cause papers in this period. I have placed them here in their legal context in order to make them accessible and useful to historians of all kinds.

A great advantage to the student of ecclesiastical court records is that the evidence was taken in writing. Most of the depositions have survived, enabling us to see the evidence in precisely the form in which it was read by the judge. The depositions supply a wealth of detail not accessible in respect of other courts, and record the statements of persons not accustomed to put their opinions into writing, and whose perspective is therefore normally lacking. Slander is injury by spoken words, and with no kind of legal injury are background and context so important to its social impact and effect.

This is a legal study in that the questions addressed are questions about the law, but it goes beyond what might be called an internal legal study. I have asked, first, what was the law, and, secondly, how was it administered? These questions turn out to be not at all as simple as they seem, and have required assessment of the archival evidence. I have also asked, in part III, what was the nature of the injury complained of, how effective in practice was the legal remedy, and what was the effect of the law on attitudes and behaviour? Where possible I have illustrated the practical effects of the law from the cause papers themselves, not for the sake of the inherent interest of the illustrations, though this is considerable, but because the cause papers offer the best evidence of how the law operated: what the law is cannot in the end be divorced from what the law does.

Modern historians, legal, social, and ecclesiastical, looking at the defamation cases through the eyes of the nineteenth-century reformers, have tended to see them as curious relics surviving among the ruins of a crumbling ecclesiastical jurisdiction. The picture that emerges from a study of the court records is both more complex and more interesting. The defamation jurisdiction, despite its defects, protected important social and individual interests that were highly valued as much by the reformers as by conservatives.

We are accustomed to think of nineteenth-century reform as tending uniformly in the direction of improving the legal and social position of women. The abolition of the defamation jurisdiction scarcely fits this pattern. This was a jurisdiction that tended in practice to protect the interests of women rather than men: 90 per cent of the cases were brought by women. Moreover, it was a jurisdiction that put a certain amount of power directly into women's hands, even where social status and financial resources were lacking.

This study is based principally on the records of the ecclesiastical courts in the various dioceses of England, Wales, and the Isle of Man. The records consist in most cases of record books, called court books or act books, recording the formal business of the courts, and cause papers, that is, the pleadings and the depositions of witnesses. These records have survived in somewhat varying forms for most dioceses, with a few gaps. Most of them have never been systematically studied, and the cause papers in many dioceses are uncatalogued and unsorted.

Among the papers there is sometimes to be found the correspondence of proctors, the ecclesiastical lawyers. In most dioceses these are occasional and sporadic, but there is an important exception. The papers of a nineteenth-century proctor, William Askwith, have survived and are preserved at the Borthwick Institute in York. These papers include correspondence and drafts of pleadings for cases of all classes within the court's jurisdiction. They are unsorted, and intermingled with other papers, but since draft pleadings and letters between lawyers usually include the names of the disputing parties, it has proved possible to identify papers relating to nineteen defamation cases (Askwith acted in forty-nine defamation cases between 1815 and 1855). These supplement the official records in a way that is invaluable for a study of this sort. The papers include letters from attorneys giving instructions to Askwith and explaining the clients' objectives, and letters in reply in which Askwith explains points of ecclesiastical law unfamiliar to common lawyers, discusses alternative strategies, and advises on litigation tactics. Details of ecclesiastical law and procedure are difficult to discover: Askwith's letters supply first-hand evidence on many points of law and practice, and on the expectations of the parties and their reaction to the legal system.

One of the remarkable characteristics of the defamation cases is their variety: they are hard to classify in social terms, and they do not lend themselves readily to any all-embracing or overarching explanation; on the contrary, they invite caution. Generalizations are often useful to historians and sometimes necessary, but attention to legal records reminds us that every generalization is composed of particulars, and that to every generality there are many exceptions. Divisions by time period or by social class are necessary for some historical purposes, but the records of these cases (Regency to Victorian in date, lower to upper-middle class in social status of the parties) suggest that there were no sharp discontinuities in either respect.

In quoting from manuscript documents, I have usually retained original spellings, even where irregular, but I have occasionally altered capitalization and punctuation and I have expanded some abbreviations, for the sake of readability.

I am very grateful to the archivists of the English county record offices, of the National Library of Wales, of the Manx Museum, of the Greater London Record Office, of the Guildhall Library, and of the Lambeth Palace Library for generous access to the documents in their custody. I would like to thank St Deiniol's Library, Hawarden, and Clare Hall, Cambridge, for visiting fellowships. I am particulary grateful to the Department of History and to the Borthwick Institute of Historical Research at the University of York, where I held a visiting fellowship in 1996. Without the generous access allowed me to the documents at the Borthwick Institute, this study could not have been accomplished in its present form.

I am grateful to the University of Toronto for allowing me a generous leave of absence, to the Social Sciences and Humanities Research Council of Canada for providing research funds, and to many friends who kindly read the typescript and made helpful suggestions.

S.M. WADDAMS

# Abbreviations

| | |
|---|---|
| B & C | Barnwall and Cresswell's Reports |
| B & S | Best and Smith's Reports |
| Co Rep | Coke's Reports |
| Crim LR | Criminal Law Review |
| Deane | Deane's Reports |
| Eccles LJ | Ecclesiastical Law Journal |
| F & F | Foster and Finlason's Reports |
| GLRO | Greater London Record Office |
| H & N | Hurlstone and Norman's Reports |
| HLC | House of Lords Cases |
| Hag Con | Haggard's Consistory Reports |
| Hag Ecc | Haggard's Ecclesiastical Reports |
| HO | Home Office (PRO) |
| LJQB | Law Journal Reports (Queen's Bench) |
| Ld Raym | Lord Raymond's Reports |
| LPL | Lambeth Palace Library |
| Mod | Modern Reports |
| Notes of Cases | Notes of Cases in the Ecclesiastical and Maritime Courts |
| PCB | Proctors' Cause Book, Borthwick Institute, York |
| Peake | Peake's Reports |
| Phil | Phillimore's Ecclesiastical Reports |
| PP | Proctors' Papers, Borthwick Institute, York |
| PP (followed by date) | Parliamentary Papers |
| PRO | Public Record Office |
| QB | Queen's Bench Reports |

| Swab  | Swabey's Admiralty Reports |
|-------|----------------------------|
| Taunt | Taunton's Reports          |

Diocesan records (letters and numbers identifying documents refer respectively to the classmarks used by the following archives):

| Bangor         | National Library of Wales, Aberystwyth                   |
|----------------|----------------------------------------------------------|
| Bath and Wells | Somerset Record Office, Taunton                          |
| Bristol        | Bristol Record Office, Bristol                           |
| Carlisle       | Cumbria Record Office, Carlisle                          |
| Chester        | Cheshire Record Office, Chester                          |
| Chichester     | West Sussex Record Office, Chichester                    |
| Durham         | University Library, Durham                               |
| Ely            | University Library, Cambridge                            |
| Exeter         | Devon Record Office, Exeter                              |
| Gloucester     | Gloucestershire Record Office, Gloucester                |
| Hereford       | Hereford and Worcester Record Office, Hereford           |
| Lichfield      | Lichfield Joint Record Office, Lichfield                 |
| Lincoln        | Lincolnshire Archives, Lincoln                           |
| Llandaff       | National Library of Wales, Aberystwyth                   |
| London         | Guildhall Library, and Greater London Record Office      |
| Manchester     | Central Library, Manchester                              |
| Norwich        | Norfolk Record Office, Norwich                           |
| Oxford         | Oxfordshire Archives, Oxford                             |
| Peterborough   | Northamptonshire Record Office, Northampton              |
| Richmond       | West Yorkshire Archive Service, Leeds                    |
| Ripon          | West Yorkshire Archive Service, Leeds                    |
| St Asaph       | National Library of Wales, Aberystwyth                   |
| St David's     | National Library of Wales, Aberystwyth                   |
| Salisbury      | Wiltshire Record Office, Trowbridge                      |
| Sodor and Man  | Manx Museum, Douglas, Isle of Man                        |
| Winchester     | Hampshire Record Office, Winchester                      |
| Worcester      | Hereford and Worcester Record Office, Worcester          |
| York           | Borthwick Institute of Historical Research, York         |

SEXUAL SLANDER IN NINETEENTH-CENTURY ENGLAND

# Introduction:

# 'Grievous and oppressive to the subjects of this realm'

In 1853 a quarrel occurred between neighbours in Merthyr Tydfil, in the course of which Charlotte Jones was supposed to have said to Louisa Roberts, 'You are a whore, and a damn whore too.'[1] These words, common in more than one sense, had an uncommon effect, for they led directly to the abolition of a branch of English law that had been in force for more than six hundred years.

In September 1853 instructions were given to Mr J. Huckwell, a proctor (ecclesiastical court solicitor), to commence proceedings in the Consistory Court of the Diocese of Llandaff, and on 17 September a citation (summons) was issued and served personally on Charlotte Jones, requiring her to appear in the court to answer to Louisa Roberts for slander. On that occasion she was reported to have said, 'I don't care for the Llandaff court. She [Louisa Roberts] is a bloody whore.'[2] Charlotte Jones did not appear on the day named in the citation, nor on the three following court days. On 28 December, pursuant to a direction of the judge, a formal notice was served on her, warning her that she would be imprisoned for contempt if she did not appear. She still did not appear in court, but, according to Huckwell, she went to his office with a friend, where it was explained to her, in English and in Welsh, that she would be imprisoned if she did not appear in court or agree to sign an apology and pay Roberts's costs. She did none of these things, and in April 1854 she was arrested and imprisoned in Cardiff jail.[3]

It may probably be assumed that Charlotte Jones did not have much general interest in the curious history of the English law of slander that extended jurisdiction in such matters to the ecclesiastical courts, but her case was taken up by someone who did. William Simons was a solicitor in Merthyr Tydfil, who was determined to attack the power of the ecclesiastical courts. In February 1855, when Jones had been in prison for ten months, he prepared a petition for her to Parliament, elaborating the case in a printed pamphlet.[4] The petition, published in a local newspaper, the *Star of Gwent*, on 3 March, with a letter to the editor from Mr Simons, was in forceful language. It asserted that, though 'some hasty words were spoken on both sides' in the original dispute with Louisa Roberts, Charlotte Jones 'did not use towards her any sort of slanderous expression or insinuation.' The petition went on to say that she had attempted to raise the necessary money for the costs by borrowing a pound from neighbours. On finding this to be insufficient, she organized 'what at Merthyr is called a "tea party", to which guests pay 1s. each for admission,' and sold some tickets, but was compelled to use the money for expenses caused by accident and sickness in her family. The petition said that she was unwilling to take the oath required 'to obey the lawful commands of the ordinary [i.e., the bishop],' because this was an official 'of whose dignity, authority and discretion I am ignorant,' a point elaborated at some length by Simons in his pamphlet, where he wrote that the only 'ordinary' known to most people was to be found in their tavern on market days. Jones's petition went on to assert that she was the mother of fourteen children, of whom the eldest was fourteen years old, and that one of her children had fallen asleep from over-fatigue after doing the housework and had burned herself severely. She asserted the respectability of her family, and prayed that Parliament would 'abolish the jurisdiction of the ecclesiastical courts in matters of slander.'[5] She signed it by mark (X), and it may be assumed that its language owes more to Simons than to herself.

Simons, in his covering letter to the newspaper, described this as a 'melancholy tale.' He accused the bishop of contemplating the suffering of Charlotte Jones, which Simons called a flagitious wrong, with 'stoical indifference.' He added that 'it makes the blood run cold to see men affecting the garb of Christianity looking calmly on at the long imprisonment of the poor, and tacitly supporting dread acts of tyranny and punishment for trifling, venial, and accidental failings.'[6] The leading article in the same issue of the newspaper echoed Simons's views and style in a way that must have been gratifying to him, describing the incident as an act of unmitigated cruelty perpetrated under the sacred name of law, and calling on Parliament to step in and break up 'the whole system of our abominable ecclesiastical laws.' The writer went on to refer to the Crucifixion and the Inquisition as evils similarly perpetrated by ecclesiastical power, concluding by describing the ecclesiastical courts as 'tyrannical, merciless, and implacable.'[7]

Huckwell wrote a letter, addressed to the editor of a conservative newspaper, the *Cardiff and Merthyr Guardian*, in which he sought to defend his conduct, and that of the judge, on conventional legal grounds: the proceedings of the court were duly authorized by law, and Charlotte Jones was in prison 'in consequence of her own contumely.'[8] As might have been anticipated, this provoked a further attack from Simons, who did not mince his words:

> Charlotte Jones has been Mr Huckwell's prisoner for more than a twelve month. He chuckles and pronounces this to be all right. I say that some people have strange notions of propriety. Well, but Mr Huckwell is not alone in his glory. The bishop smiles benignantly and sanctions the imprisonment. He puts Mr Huckwell under his episcopal apron and heeds not the throes of the wretched prisoner. Were they heeded he would have done something towards her relief; and yet, I dare say, that Mr Huckwell and the bishop call themselves Christians.[9]

Huckwell thereupon seems to have retired from the public debate.

Facts asserted in petitions are not always subjected to rigorous proof, and perhaps it is not surprising that John Roberts, Louisa's husband, had a somewhat different reaction to Charlotte Jones's petition. 'She [Jones] is of the worst of character,' he wrote to Huckwell, 'and also some of her children – one of them was imprisoned for 1 month for felony since Charlotte Jones has been to Cardiff. She is only the mother of 5 – only 4 living – and neither of the children was burnt since her imprisonment. 2 of the children are married and they and the workmen made a subscription some time back to enable them to pay the costs, but instead of doing so they spent the money.'[10]

It happens that there is an independent source of information on one of these discrepancies. The census records reveal that, on 30 March 1851, Charlotte Jones had four children, then aged twenty, twelve, nine, and three.[11] It is likely therefore that the statements in the petition that she had fourteen children, and that the eldest was aged fourteen, are in error. It need not be concluded, however, that anyone was guilty of fraud. It is probable (though not certain) that Charlotte Jones did not read or write,[12] and the undoubted enthusiasm of Simons, and his desire to make the strongest possible case, combined with some difficulties in communication, might have produced the petition in its final form.

On 21 December 1854 a proctor, instructed by Simons, did enter an appearance for Charlotte Jones, but he refused to undertake that she would purge her contempt, saying that he was not instructed to do so. Huckwell offered to forgo his fees and secure Jones's release, providing that she submitted to the rules of the court, but, according to Huckwell, this proposal was declined by Simons, who said that he would pay no fees, but would effect her liberation by other means. Her proctor then refused to act further for her, as Simons 'would accede to no terms.' Huckwell concluded, with some justification it would seem, that 'it is Mr Simons who subjects his client to an unnecessary lengthened imprisonment by refusing to take the proper steps for her liberation and choosing rather to await the passing of a statute for removing the jurisdiction of defamation causes from the ecclesiastical courts!!'[13]

In February 1855 a bill was introduced in the House of Commons to effect just this purpose, and strenuous efforts were made in Cardiff by the officials of the court to secure Jones's release. On 12 March the judge himself (the chancellor, the Revd Hugh Williams) took the exceptional step of visiting her in jail, telling her that the proctors were willing to forgo their fees, and that if she could raise £6 for the sheriff's fee she would be released immediately.[14] Williams took the even more exceptional step of offering to contribute personally to the cost. In a letter to her husband, written on the same day, perhaps at Williams's suggestion,[15] Jones said that Williams had told her that 'if you collect two or three pounds yourself, he Mr Chancellor Williams and his friends would make the deficiency up.' Her letter said, 'On the whole I consider Chancellor Williams's proposition kind and liberal' and added 'Now I hope that Mr Simons will concur in this opinion as I long to be at home.'[16] Apparently Simons did not concur, for Charlotte Jones remained in prison, even after the enactment of the statute abolishing the courts' jurisdiction.[17] She signed a recantation and apology on 7 July witnessed by an attorney's clerk and by the turnkey of Cardiff jail (see plate 1).[18] This document, which presumably led to her release,[19] headed 'In the Consistory Court of Llandaff,' must be the last apology for slander enforced by an ecclesiastical court.

When lawyers undertake reform causes, it sometimes happens that political interests do not coincide precisely with the personal interests of their clients. Lord St Leonards said, when the bill was debated in the House of Lords, that 'undoubtedly the case of Charlotte Jones was one of those to which relief would be given [under a clause providing for release of those in prison at the time the statute should come into force]; but he believed that there never was a case that was less entitled to their lordships' attention; ... every reasonable proposition was made to spare her; but some persons were determined to be made martyrs, and so a great outcry was raised about that particular case.'[20] There is, it will be seen, truth in this assessment to this extent, that if Simons's principal object had been to secure the release of Charlotte Jones, the object would have been effected some months earlier. Nevertheless the thrust of Simons's complaint was unanswered: Jones had spent an inordinate amount of time in prison for what was, at worst, a trivial offence.

The bill to abolish the jurisdiction of the ecclesiastical courts in defamation cases was introduced in the House of Commons on 27 February 1855, by Robert Phillimore, a distinguished ecclesiastical lawyer (later a judge). He was a known friend of the ecclesiastical courts,[21] who had himself argued, in a pamphlet published a few years before, in favour of preserving the defamation jurisdiction, but without the power of imprisonment, saying that he thought it very proper that those who slandered their neighbours should apologize to them in the parish church.[22] Phillimore, an Anglo-Catholic churchman who tended towards a romanticized view of the medieval antecedents of the Church of England, was inclined to favour the idea of penance. By 1855 he had evidently been persuaded that penance enforced by law was not practicable in the nineteenth century. Perhaps he thought that if the ecclesiastical jurisdiction must go, it was better that the blow should be struck by a friendly hand: there is a strong note of nostalgic regret in the preamble to the statute, which recites that 'the jurisdiction of the ecclesiastical courts in suits for defamation has ceased to be the means of enforcing the spiritual discipline of the Church, and has become grievous and oppressive to the subjects of this realm.'[23]

Lord Brougham, who had presented Charlotte Jones's petition to the House of Lords, said in the course of debate on the bill, 'It often happened that a woman in some brawl, possibly a squabble in an alehouse, was overheard, unhappily, by some practitioner of the law to use defamatory expressions; and a suit was instantly commenced, undeniably for the purpose of obtaining costs. The poor woman paid a little, and being unable to pay the rest, she went to prison.'[24]

The words chosen by Lord Brougham – and similar language was used by others in arguing for abolition of the jurisdiction – have the effect of trivializing the cases, especially the references to 'some brawl,' 'squabble,' 'alehouse,' and 'poor woman.' There is an implication that such matters could be assumed by Lord Brougham's hearers to be of little consequence. The reference to overhearing by a lawyer suggests that no plaintiff had any genuine interest in commencing the suit herself. It would be possible to suppose, from such arguments, that the law operated mainly against women and that the cases consisted entirely of petty quarrels in which no legitimate or even substantial interest was concerned. As we shall see, this is very far from being an accurate picture. The majority of defendants were men. Ninety per cent of the plaintiffs were women, and often interests were at stake that were perceived by the plaintiff, and by her friends, to be very important to her. Many of the cases involved not direct insult, but the spreading of rumour, with consequent serious damage to the plaintiff. Even in the cases of direct insult, there is often evidence that the plaintiff was seriously hurt by it. There is evidence in many cases that the plaintiff, or her relatives and friends, and not legal practitioners, constituted the moving force that led to the institution of the suit. Defamation cases were not, in general, a principal source of professional income to the proctors, who depended largely on testamentary work. Their spokesmen would willingly have sacrificed the defamation work in exchange for preservation of the testamentary jurisdiction (this too was lost to them in 1857). A very different set of circumstances appears in another case, approximately contemporary with that of Charlotte Jones, and where also the defendant was imprisoned. Some of the defamatory words in this case were, as it happens, spoken in an alehouse, but they were not the less harmful on that account. The purpose of this second introductory illustration is not to suggest that Lord Brougham was mistaken in his conclusion – there were many good reasons why the jurisdiction could not continue as it was – but to suggest that the picture he presented was incomplete: he never ceased to be an advocate, and, as good advocates always do, he painted a picture that suited his case.

Sarah Sharpe, an innkeeper's daughter, unmarried at the age of forty-one, was engaged to be married to Thomas Fowler, aged forty-five, who gave his profession as 'contractor' and was described as a 'gentleman' in the libel (statement of claim). Evidence in the ecclesiastical courts took the form of written depositions, discussed more fully in a later chapter,[25] and the depositions of six witnesses were given in support of the plaintiff's case. Joseph Rea, also an innkeeper, said that Thomas Dauncey, the defendant, had observed to him that, if the intended marriage took place, 'Fowler would not have a very prudent girl.' Dauncey had said that this was a common report in the village (Stonehouse, Gloucestershire), and that he himself had 'been with her' several times (taken to imply sexual intercourse) and could tell Rea the day. Dauncey had said that it was reported that an eighteen-year-old girl, Elizabeth, who had lived with Sarah Sharpe and her parents until her recent death, though supposed to be Sharpe's niece, was really her own illegitimate child. Dauncey, who was a shoemaker, said that he had often made shoes for Elizabeth, and that Sarah Sharpe had always paid for them. He also said that she had had a miscarriage in consequence of her association with a man called Blanche. Rea repeated all this to Fowler, and two weeks later, when Fowler and Dauncey met at Rea's inn, Fowler asked Dauncey to go into another (presumably private) room, where Dauncey repeated the allegations, adding that Sharpe was 'anything but a virtuous woman.' Fowler himself gave evidence and said that he had decided to break the engagement on account of the rumours about Sharpe's chastity, though this was not, he said 'wholly in consequence of the defendant's statements: I have heard things from other quarters quite sufficient to induce me not to marry the promoter [plaintiff], whatever my intentions might once have been.' He said that he thought Sarah Sharpe's character was injured by the defendant's words, but added that 'her character was spoken lightly of, as far as I can now learn, previously to the commencement of this suit.' Rea thought that her character was not injured by the defendant's words, which suggests either that her reputation was already damaged, or that Dauncey was not credible.

Evidence was also given by four near relatives of Sarah Sharpe. Her brother John, on hearing that Dauncey had defamed his sister's character, sought him out and demanded an explanation. Dauncey, according to John's evidence, at first refused to answer the questions but then said that John 'had better let the matter drop, else there would be a damned sight more come out, and he [Dauncey] would expose the whole buggering family.' He added, 'She is a damned thundering whore, and damn me if I have not got down the day of the month when I made her a whore.' According to John Sharpe, Dauncey said that he would have married her himself 'if it had not been for the character he had heard of her and of her general bad conduct.' Another brother, Edward, and his wife gave evidence, saying that they were Elizabeth's true parents, though not giving any very persuasive explanation of her having resided from the age of three with her aunt and grandparents. These witnesses were supported by a sister, Mary Hadley, who claimed to have been present at Elizabeth's birth. All four witnesses said that Elizabeth was Edward Sharpe's daughter, and the last three said that they had seen the plaintiff at frequent intervals throughout her adult life, and had never known her to be pregnant.[26]

Not everything that appears in legal records can, of course, be taken at face value. Some of the documents are formulaic: the libel (plaintiff's statement of claim) was an elaborate document consisting usually of three or four manuscript pages largely of assertions that were not required to be proved, and sometimes that were known to be false. Witnesses' statements in the depositions may often be influenced by favour to one of the parties or hostility to the other. But where witnesses speak of matters not in dispute between the parties, their evidence tends to be highly reliable, and gives a view of day-to-day events from persons who often were not accustomed to record their observations, and whose perspective, therefore, is usually not available from other sources. Moreover, the making of a statement or assertion may be significant, regardless of its truth.

Thus, curiously enough, it is on the questions on which they might seem most reliable – the disputed matter sworn to on oath – that the records are the least valuable to a historian. For matters not in dispute, however, the records offer excellent historical evidence. We shall probably never know whose daughter Elizabeth was, or whether Sarah Sharpe had had a miscarriage. But the depositions establish convincingly how important to an unmarried woman, and to her relatives, was her reputation for chastity, and how strong was her interest in a good marriage. Thomas Fowler took it for granted that if she had been imprudent, as alleged by Dauncey and others, she would not be a suitable wife. John Sharpe evidently considered it his duty to confront Dauncey on behalf of his sister and to remonstrate with him about the injustice of defaming her. He did not consider it surprising that Dauncey, as well as Fowler, should have broken off engagements on account of rumours of his sister's unchastity. The case also illustrates the different attitude to a man's reputation for chastity: Dauncey was not reticent, nor expected to be so, in acknowledging his own part in Sarah Sharpe's unchastity. Such unconcern with a reputation for chastity was quite common among men, but by no means universal, as we shall see when we examine the cases in which men were plaintiffs.[27]

The court records usually do not indicate the reasons for the ultimate decision, but in this case it is recorded that the judge expressly rejected the evidence of four of the witnesses, while accepting that of Rea and John Sharpe as proving that the defamatory words had been spoken, and gave sentence against Dauncey, with costs fixed at £12. From this it can be deduced that the judge found that Dauncey had accused Sharpe of unchastity on the two occasions deposed to by Rea and John Sharpe. We cannot know what the judge thought about Sarah Sharpe's former conduct: truth was not a complete defence, and the rejected depositions may have been considered irrelevant.[28] The allowance of costs at the figure of £12 supports this hypothesis, as this would be about the appropriate level of costs for a case involving two witnesses only. Twelve pounds is a substantial sum, and by no means suggests, as a very low award of costs might do, that the judge thought that the defendant's conduct was in any degree justified, or that the plaintiff was undeserving.[29]

Sentence for the plaintiff usually included a requirement that the defendant should appear in the vestry room of the plaintiff's parish church and make a formal apology, known in various dioceses as penance, recantation, reclamation, retraction, or declaration. In many cases, successful plaintiffs did not insist on actual performance of this ceremony, but Sarah Sharpe did insist, at considerable length,[30] and Dauncey, refusing to perform the penance or to pay the costs, was imprisoned for contempt of court.[31] After six months he was released on a writ of habeas corpus (a common law process for reviewing the legality of imprisonment). The ground for the issue of the habeas corpus is not recorded in the ecclesiastical court records. The common law court which granted the writ must have found a procedural irregularity, or that the ecclesiastical court had exceeded its jurisdiction,[32] perhaps because Sharpe, having alleged the loss of her marriage in consequence of the slander, could have brought an action at common law.[33] As we shall see, the ecclesiastical court theoretically lacked jurisdiction in any case that was actionable at common law, and the common law courts sometimes seized on technical deficiencies to justify a writ of habeas corpus.[34]

The case of Charlotte Jones would not have had the effect that it did unless public confidence in the ecclesiastical courts had already been eroded. These courts had been under attack on several fronts since 1830, and in many respects their structure, jurisdiction, and procedure were out of tune with prevailing opinion.[35] The problems were identified in 1832 in the report of a royal commission on the ecclesiastical courts.[36] The reformers favoured a centralized professional judiciary,[37] but there were many small local ecclesiastical courts with practically no business, and, therefore, no experienced judges or practitioners. Most of the judges lacked professional legal training, and there were important differences in substance and procedure from one diocese to another. Only in London and York were there any advocates (corresponding to barristers at common law), and in York only one who was active. In many dioceses there were so few active proctors that competition and public choice were severely restricted. Many of the offices were sinecures, the duties being exercised by deputies. The restricted jurisdiction in probate matters created constant problems of conflict with other courts that had jurisdiction to interpret wills. Family relationships among court officers were common. This was a constant complaint in Doctors' Commons, in London.[38] In Chester the evidence to the Commission revealed that the judge was the son-in-law of the registrar, and that two of the five proctors were the registrar's sons.[39] The exclusion of oral evidence, with consequent restriction on cross-examination, was regarded as a grave defect. There were problems of substantive law: the law that permitted the levying of a tax (church rate) on the whole population for the support of the parish church was a substantial grievance, and the law of divorce was in urgent need of reform.

These were matters of acute political controversy, and the institution of the ecclesiastical courts bore the brunt of objections to the substantive law. A sentiment that grew rapidly between 1830 and 1855 was that it was offensive to religious liberty that Church of England courts, with episcopally appointed judges, however competent they might be, should determine important civil rights of all citizens.[40] The sole method of enforcement of orders of the courts was imprisonment for contempt, which was a very blunt instrument apt to lead to oppressive consequences, as in the case of Charlotte Jones. There were more particular objections to the defamation jurisdiction: penance was obsolete as a punishment, and often did nothing to restore the plaintiff's good name; truth was not a complete justification, and this was objectionable as a restraint on free speech. Increasing mobility of population put further strains on the diocesan court system, and on the defamation jurisdiction in particular. Jurisdiction was based on the defendant's residence, but frequently words were spoken in one diocese by the resident of another; witnesses might reside in a third diocese. Even if the process could have been fully secularized, the notion of an enforced apology to the plaintiff in her local community had come to seem obsolete: a public apology in the market-place, for instance, would have been more medieval in some respects than penance in the vestry room of the church. By 1846, the Society for the Abolition of Ecclesiastical Courts declared its object 'to emancipate the jurisprudence of our country from the ecclesiastical interference which now renders it opposed to the civil liberty of British subjects, a source of oppression and hardship, and a national dishonour, because a moral wrong.'[41]

The Ecclesiastical Courts Commission, in its report in 1832, said, of defamation suits, that

> The proceedings in these suits have occasioned much odium to the Ecclesiastical Jurisdiction; Imprisonment having in several instances taken place; either from the obstinacy of the party proceeded against, or his inability to obey the sentence of the Court by payment of costs.[42]

Of the sixty-eight persons imprisoned by the ecclesiastical courts between the beginning of 1827 and the end of 1829, thirty-four were imprisoned in consequence of defamation suits,[43] a disproportionately large number, considering both the number of defamation suits, and the seriousness of the offence. The Commission recommended that 'the cognizance of such causes should be wholly withdrawn from the Ecclesiastical Courts.'

Interestingly, the Commission proposed a substitute:

> We do not think, however, that persons, aggrieved by Defamation, should be left wholly without a remedy; for many cases may occur, in which the fame and character of an individual may be almost as deeply affected, by words charging incontinency, as by a written libel; and, therefore, we humbly suggest that it may be expedient, under restrictions to prevent abuse, to permit the parties aggrieved to resort to the Magistrates at the Petty Sessions, who may be invested with a power to punish such offences by fine and imprisonment to be limited.[44]

Several of the witnesses who appeared before the Commission had agreed with such a proposal. One of them was Granville Vernon, the chancellor of York, who was quoted as saying, in a defamation case in 1833, with obvious reference to this recommendation, that 'he hoped he should get rid of such cases as these in this court as they would be much better disposed of by a Justice of the Peace fining the offending party in a penalty of 5s.'[45] This recommendation, in effect to create a new crime of sexual slander, presented many difficulties: it would have been a serious restraint on freedom of speech, and would not have been welcomed by complainants, who, instead of having control over proceedings in which they could not be competent witnesses, would find that they were competent and compellable witnesses in a proceeding over which they had perhaps no control, and subject to public cross-examination.

The proposal was never implemented, but the fact that it was favoured by the Commission (which included several common law and ecclesiastical law judges) and by Vernon and other witnesses shows clearly how the question of sexual slander was then regarded by the professional elite. The prevailing view was that the ecclesiastical jurisdiction, though cumbersome and obsolete in many respects, was yet serving a necessary social purpose by punishing conduct that, properly viewed, was a social nuisance deserving of summary but not excessive punishment. For these objects the ecclesiastical jurisdiction was very poorly adapted: the procedure was expensive and cumbersome, and the punishment, which took the form of an obligation to pay the plaintiff's costs, was excessive. Costs in a disputed case could easily amount to £20 or £30, a penalty wholly disproportionate to the seriousness of the misconduct, and far beyond the means of most litigants. Moreover, the only method of enforcement was imprisonment for contempt, again unduly harsh as a punishment of misconduct. As late as 1848 it was said in Parliament that 'the use of such language as formed the subject of these suits was, undoubtedly, unjustifiable' but with the addition that 'it was monstrous to inflict such heavy penalties upon persons of a humble class in life, for a comparatively trivial offence.'[46] One reason why the defamation jurisdiction lasted until 1855 was that reformers could not agree on a substitute.

There were many attempts, between 1832 and 1855, to reform various aspects of the ecclesiastical court system,[47] but the intertwining of substance and procedure with institutional reform, as well as the highly controversial nature of church rates and divorce made comprehensive reform impossible. Eventually the separate heads of ecclesiastical jurisdiction that affected the population at large were taken away one by one. In 1857 matrimonial and probate jurisdiction was transferred to newly created secular courts.[48] In 1860 jurisdiction to punish brawling (rowdy conduct on church premises) was abolished,[49] and compulsory church rates in 1868.[50] But the defamation jurisdiction had been the first to go, precipitated, as we have seen, by Charlotte Jones.

**Part I**

**THE LAW**

# 1

# The Common Law

In English law there was, and still is, an important distinction between libel and slander. Libel (in general, defamation by written words) was actionable in a common law court, and could lead to an award of damages. It was also a crime, and criminal prosecutions for private (i.e., non-political) libels were not uncommon throughout the nineteenth century.[1] Slander (defamation by spoken words) was not a crime, nor was it actionable without proof of special damage, i.e., generally speaking, actual loss capable of measurement in money. There were three exceptions: words imputing a crime punishable at law by imprisonment or by some other corporal punishment, words tending to disparage the plaintiff in an office, trade, or profession, and words imputing a loathsome disease (including, but not limited to, venereal disease).[2] In those three kinds of case, an action lay (i.e., was admissible or sustainable) without proof of special damage. There was no exception in English law for slander imputing unchastity, until such an exception was introduced (for women only) by statute in 1891,[3] thirty-six years after the end of the ecclesiastical jurisdiction. Thus, spoken words imputing unchastity and not causing monetary loss were not actionable at common law.

The ecclesiastical courts were courts of limited jurisdiction, controlled by the common law courts through the writ of prohibition. The earlier wide defamation jurisdiction of the ecclesiastical courts[4] had been steadily eroded, and by the nineteenth century it was established that the ecclesiastical courts had jurisdiction only over imputations of conduct that constituted a crime at ecclesiastical law, a rule summarized, from the point of view of a practitioner in the ecclesiastical courts, as 'only such defamatory words cognizable here which impute an offence that would be punishable here.'[5] Punishment of fornication and adultery had practically ceased in England and Wales[6] by the nineteenth century, but the theoretical power to punish those offences ('crimes' in ecclesiastical law) remained significant in that it defined the defamation jurisdiction. A further restriction was that no ecclesiastical suit could be brought in respect of words actionable at common law.

Putting together these rules, we can see that the defamation jurisdiction was narrow. The only significant conduct that constituted a crime in ecclesiastical law but not at common law was sexual misconduct (fornication, adultery, and incontinence in the language of the ecclesiastical courts), and the defamation jurisdiction was therefore effectively confined to imputations of such misconduct.

The jurisdictional limits are well illustrated by a Peterborough case in which an opinion was sought from Dr Stephen Lushington, himself judge of the London Consistory Court, and, interestingly, still giving private opinions after ten years in that office. William Dix, a surgeon and apothecary, was travelling in a gig (a light two-wheeled carriage) with a companion, when he was overtaken by Henry Scarse, also a surgeon and apothecary, on horseback, who slackened pace and rode for nearly a mile beside the gig. Some quarrelsome words were exchanged, and Scarse said (among other insults), 'you came out without your horns this morning; you are a cuckold,' taking off his hat repeatedly and pointing significantly to it. He added, 'You do keep a bawdy house.' Lushington gave as his opinion that calling Dix a cuckold, if proved by the necessary two witnesses, would enable a suit to be brought, but not by Dix himself. It was his wife, not he, who was impliedly accused of adultery, and she only was entitled to bring the suit. Secondly, all reference to keeping a bawdy house ought to be omitted from the libel, because keeping a bawdy house was an offence punishable at common law, and if these words were included, the proceedings would be vulnerable to a prohibition:

> I am of opinion that a suit may be instituted in the ecclesiastical court for these expressions and that if the evidence should prove the fact that they were spoken the suit must be successful. The suit must be brought in the name of the wife ... for she is the person defamed. The words of ecclesiastical cognizance are the calling [Dix] a cuckold & the expressions 'coming out without your horns' should form the charge. Not the other expression, for the charge of keeping a bawdy house is of temporal cognizance & if laid in the libel would be cause for prohibition.
>
> Gt George St, Aug 2, 1838                                        Stephen Lushington[7]

This advice was taken, and the suit, in the name of Eliza Dix, was successful. Scarse appeared in court, confessed that the libel (statement of claim) was true, and performed a reclamation (formal apology) in open court, paying costs of £6.5s.[8]

In some cases complaints of accusations of common law offences did appear in the libels. Often these were rejected by the ecclesiastical court judge. In a Norwich case in 1834, Charlotte Harvey complained that Robert Campling had said, 'You damned old cat of hell, you blasted old cat of hell, you don't come by your house honestly. Blast you, you don't come by anything honestly.'[9] The judge rejected the libel, commenting that the first accusation (cat of hell) was too vague ('void of any sense or satisfactory explanation'), and that the second was outside the court's jurisdiction ('actionable and punishable in the common law courts'), and that a prohibition would lie. He added, by way of consolation, 'In rejecting the libel I confer a benefit on the plaintiff. Costs must follow of course but were the libel admitted and the suit persisted in they would be much greater.'[10]

Libels were rejected for similar reasons in other dioceses.[11] In a York case in 1820, Frances Etty complained that Robert Kneeshaw had called her a whore, but, in his defence, Kneeshaw said that the words he had used were that 'she harboured nothing but whores.' Askwith, the defendant's proctor, wrote to his instructing attorney that these words 'will not sustain the plea as they only amount at most to charging her with keeping a disorderly house and are not actionable in the Spiritual Court.'[12] The case was dismissed, but without costs, reflecting the judge's view that, though the words proved were not within the strict jurisdiction of the court, the use of such words did no credit to the defendant, and was to be discouraged as far as possible. As Askwith put it, the judge thought that Kneeshaw

> did not come into court with very pure hands, for altho' he [the judge] could not give credit to the testimony of Etty's witnesses, still enough was shewn that Kneeshaw had used very improper language during the squabble, not to be entitled in the discretion of the court to Costs.[13]

It was, of course, very common for abusive words, particularly when spoken in the heat of a quarrel, to include accusations of several kinds of wrongdoing. Insults addressed to women commonly added the opprobrious word 'whore' to another insult. If the other insult was actionable at common law, the ecclesiastical courts were deprived of jurisdiction.

This rule, denying jurisdiction in cases of 'mixed' spiritual and temporal slander, had anomalous consequences: a woman called a whore, or a bitch and a whore, could sue in the ecclesiastical court, but if she was called a thief and a whore, she could not. At York the correspondence of William Askwith makes it clear that the jurisdictional limitation was taken seriously. William Page, an attorney at Scarborough,[14] wrote to Askwith in 1825 instructing him to issue a citation against a woman for calling Page's client 'whore, thief and other bad names.'[15] Askwith's reply was as follows:

> You state the words to be *whore and thief* and other bad names. The Eccl Court cannot sustain a suit for mixed words of temporal & spiritual cognizance and the word thief is clearly not actionable in our court but at law and therefore shd it appear in the progress of the cause either by the cross examination of our own witnesses or by the defendant's proofs, that the words whore and thief were spoken by the deft at the same time, it would be fatal to the suit & subject your client to costs ...[16]

In a York case ten years later, where the defendant shouted abuse outside the plaintiff's house, calling her whore and thief, the case was dismissed, without costs, though whether want of jurisdiction was the reason, or the only reason, for the disposition is not recorded. The case was a serious one, and might have been expected to attract a mark of the judge's disapproval had he felt able to give it, as the abuse was repeated,[17] and the plaintiff was actually confined to her room at the time, lying in for childbirth.

Granville Vernon, the York chancellor, was a barrister, and no doubt was anxious to avoid being subjected to a writ of prohibition. Furthermore, he was hostile to the defamation jurisdiction, and open therefore to arguments that restricted it. Judges in other dioceses, many of them clergymen without formal legal training, were not so particular on the point. In a Carlisle case, for example, in 1832, the plaintiff obtained sentence on proof that the defendant had said 'Thou's a damned whore and a damned thief.'[18] A prohibition was actually granted by the Court of Queen's Bench in a Welsh case of 1841, one of the comparatively rare cases in which the plaintiff was a man. The Revd Thomas Gwyn complained that Mary Evans had accused him of having committed, while intoxicated, what amounted to an indecent assault on her on a highway, 'attempting [Evans said] to throw me and my horse into the ditch; also put his hand under my safeguard [an outer riding garment] and then shoved it up under my petticoat until it reached my knee. I struck him with my whip and galloped off.'[19] Gwyn sued successfully in the ecclesiastical court,[20] but Evans obtained a writ of prohibition to quash the sentence, on the ground that though the ecclesiastical court had jurisdiction over the accusation of intoxication against a clergyman (because a clergyman could be punished for it by the ecclesiastical court),[21] it had no jurisdiction over the accusation of indecent assault, that being a crime at common law.

It has often been pointed out that abuse directed at men was less likely to involve allegations of sexual misconduct than abuse directed at women: where a man might be called a rogue and a villain, a woman would be called a whore.[22] Whether the use of the opprobrious word implied actual misconduct or was mere vulgar abuse, the choice of a sexual insult is significant, and its usual absence in the case of abuse of men is an aspect of the double standard of sexual behaviour. There was, however, one word of sexual abuse commonly directed at men, namely, 'bugger.' This very rarely appears in the ecclesiastical court records for reasons that will now be clear: buggery, or sodomy, was a common law crime, and so the word, whether intended as an actual accusation of crime or as a casual insult, did not give rise to an ecclesiastical lawsuit. I found only one case in which a suit was brought on such grounds. Jeremiah Stead complained of what was evidently a real accusation of homosexual conduct. The witnesses deposed that the defendant had said, 'he is a man's man and likes man better than woman ... You may go upstairs and tell Stead he is a bugger and I can prove it.'[23] It is fairly clear that the court lacked jurisdiction, but sentence was given for Stead, with £14 costs.[24] It is not surprising that such suits were rare. Bringing an ecclesiastical lawsuit in such circumstances was a hazardous enterprise, for the probability must have been that the suit would be dismissed for want of jurisdiction, leaving the plaintiff with liability for two sets of costs, a reputation further damaged, and perhaps an increased risk of prosecution at common law. But where husband and wife were both abused, the husband might obtain some measure of redress indirectly, by means of a suit in his wife's name. In a case of 1846, arising in the diocese of Canterbury, but heard in the Arches Court in London, Daniel Swaffer said, 'My brother Jack is an old bugger and his wife is a buggering old whore.' The suit was brought by Sarah Swaffer, Jack's wife. She obtained a sentence, and penance was duly performed by Daniel Swaffer.[25] Similarly, in a Norwich case, the complaint was that the defendant had said to a woman, 'You married a sodomiting old bugger that could not get children and had to hire old Peel to get them for you.' The suit was commenced jointly by the wife and husband, but the libel (statement of claim) was in the name of the wife only.[26] A man could not sue for being called a bastard, but, theoretically, his mother could.[27] No case was found that succeeded solely on the basis of a man's being called a bastard.[28]

Accusations of having or imparting venereal disease were actionable at common law.[29] Nevertheless, accusations of this sort appear often in the ecclesiastical cause papers, and plainly the judges in several dioceses were ready to admit them. In a York case a clergyman complained of the words 'John Kelly had got the bad disorder, that he had got a burnt arse.' Askwith, who was acting for the defendant, sought an opinion from an advocate, who advised that the libel was not admissible. The advocate's notes include this: 'Charging pox not in Eccl Court – Actionable,' with a reference to a common law decision of 1699 granting a prohibition. However, the libel was admitted, and the advocate advised an appeal. A note in Askwith's hand reads

> He [the advocate] thinks the libel in Kelly v. Batty was shamefully & scandalously admitted; has turned the thing in his mind & it ought to be appealed.

These notes demonstrate that practitioners were conscious of this limit on the court's jurisdiction, but that judges did not always observe it.[30]

It was common for abusive expressions to include reference to venereal disease, as in 'bloody clapped whore,'[31] 'nasty poxy old whore,'[32] 'pox'd bitch,'[33] and 'pox'd arsed whore.'[34] In some cases this was mere vulgar abuse, but in other cases specific accusations were intended,[35] and in this context the cause papers record the use of very coarse language by both men and women.[36] Occasionally proof was attempted of the truth of the accusations. The most extensive example of this is a Somerset case of 1832, where depositions of thirteen witnesses were taken.[37] Susan Dorney was the daughter of a tollgate-keeper, Thomas. Mary Webb, whose husband, a baker, had been accustomed to give rides on his cart to Susan Dorney, but had recently refused to continue the practice, accused Susan Dorney of having communicated venereal disease to Mary Webb's stepson, John. Thomas Dorney, Susan's father, came immediately to demand an explanation, and Mary Webb said 'that the reason they did not choose to haul his daughter Susan was because her son-in-law John had got the bad disorder of her ... upon which ... Thomas Dorney told her ... that he would put her into Wells court.' Witnesses were produced on both sides to test the truth of the accusation. Susan Dorney went the next day to be examined by a surgeon, who deposed that he 'did not discover any appearance of venereal disease' – an inconclusive diagnosis, since, as is now known, the disease is often asymptomatic.[38] John Webb deposed that he had contracted, from the effect of intercourse with Dorney, 'the disease commonly called "the clap" and which his medical attendant called a gonorrhoea,' and another man gave similar evidence. Sentence was given for Dorney, but with reduced costs.[39] In a later case, in the same county and diocese, the defendant was proved to have said, 'How do you get your dresses, you stinking whore, by laying on your back. You have been salivated twenty times and I know the surgeon perfectly well and I'll make you walk in wet sheets again.'[40] A dispute between two women in Chester in 1823 gave rise to two suits. Ann Prescott was accused of saying, 'You heard what she said, that I had got the pox, but it is not me that has it but her; if she was as clear of the pox as me she would be clear indeed, for I never deserved it.' A suit and a counter-suit ensued.[41]

Keeping a bawdy house was a crime at common law: hence Dr Lushington's advice that an accusation of keeping a bawdy house ought not to be included in a libel for defamation in the ecclesiastical court. Not all proctors, however, followed this advice punctiliously. A Lincoln libel of 1823 complained of the words 'She is a stinking whore and keeps a disorderly house and a bawd house and keeps two girls as whores for the purpose of prostitution.'[42] In other cases, the accusation was omitted from the libel, but appeared in the evidence of the witnesses. Though this might be said to reveal a 'mixed' case, beyond the jurisdiction of the ecclesiastical court, many judges were not so strict as to dismiss cases on this ground. In a Welsh case of 1852 the defendant was proved to have said to a woman and her daughter, 'You are a whore and a couple of whores and you keep a bawdy house';[43] in a case of 1838 the words were '[she] is a whore and keeps as big a bawd house as any body in Wellington and her looses young men in the house all hours in the night.'[44] In each case the plaintiff obtained sentence. It must have seemed to many judges unduly strict for the plaintiff to lose her case because she proved that she had been doubly insulted, and provided the words imputing unchastity were not spoken in the same breath as those imputing the common law crime, it would appear that the proofs could be separated, and the words of ecclesiastical cognizance taken as proved.

Defamations commonly took various sorts of written forms, but few were the subject of litigation in the ecclesiastical courts, because libel (written defamation) was actionable – and indeed indictable – at common law. But, as with almost every rule applicable to the ecclesiastical courts, there were exceptions. In a York case of 1841 a housekeeper complained that her former employer had written letters asserting that she had entertained men for sexual purposes in his house without his knowledge, and that he had sent the letters to a friend, intending the friend to communicate their contents to the plaintiff's current employer.[45] The case proceeded to the stage of depositions on the plaintiff's behalf, and a very extensive defensive allegation (seventeen pages). It seems clear that this suit was beyond the court's jurisdiction, and an action at common law had in fact been commenced and abandoned, but no judicial determination was made on the point because the defendant died and the suit abated. In a Lincoln case, however, where a man complained of a letter accusing him of intercourse with a prostitute, the defendant confessed, and sentence was given for the plaintiff.[46] This may perhaps have been a case where the plaintiff was satisfied with sentence in the ecclesiastical court, and the defendant had no interest in forcing the matter into a (much more expensive) common law court.

Abusive words scribbled on notices or chalked on walls were not uncommon, as the evidence shows in several cases, but they did not usually form the actual subject of suits, for the jurisdictional reason mentioned. But there is one such case in which Mary Bach complained that Hans Engstrom had written and displayed two notices, crudely inscribed 'Bach's wife is a whore and he a liar,' and 'Bach's wife is a brutal whore and he a liar for ever' (see plate 2).[47] The disposition of this case is unknown, but it would appear to have been beyond the court's jurisdiction.

# 2

# The Ecclesiastical Law

## Sources of Law

The details of the ecclesiastical law as it related to defamation are surprisingly difficult to discover, and can often only be deduced from a study of the court records, with the help of such unofficial sources as proctors' correspondence and advocates' opinions, where these survive. There was practically no relevant statute law, and judicial reasons were not reported until the nineteenth century. There are only ten defamation cases reported in all (four during the period of this study). The commentaries on ecclesiastical law adopt a style that can best be described as desultory: they jump from one narrow point to another equally narrow and often unrelated point. The reader searches in vain for sustained analysis relating the general to the particular, or theory to practice, or reconciling conflicting principles.

The statutory and quasi-statutory sources of law date from the thirteenth century. A Constitution of the Province of Canterbury of 1222 provided for excommunication of those who, for the sake of gain, hatred, favour, or any other cause maliciously impute a crime to anyone whereby he is defamed in the eyes of good and respectable persons and for which he might be liable to purgation or other burden.[1] A statute of 1285 confirmed the jurisdiction of the ecclesiastical courts over defamation 'where money is not demanded, but [it is] a thing done for the punishment of sin,'[2] and defamation cases were common enough in the fourteenth century to be mentioned by Chaucer as a part of the archdeacon's jurisdiction.[3] An annotated eighteenth-century collection, in two folio volumes, of statutes, canons, and constitutions includes a few references to defamation.[4] A number of books of ecclesiastical law and practice, mainly derived from a sixteenth-century work of Francis Clerke,[5] contain a few pages each on defamation.[6] Use of these books is not made easier by the fact that the printed edition of Clerke's work is based on a corrupt manuscript text.[7] Two digests published in the nineteenth century offer a few pages on defamation, largely duplicative of earlier works.[8] Most of these works were available to nineteenth-century judges, registrars, advocates, and proctors. Professor Helmholz found manuscript copies of Clerke's work in various record offices where they were transferred, mainly in the twentieth century, from cathedral registries. The copy of Conset's *Practice* now in the Borthwick Institute, York, is inscribed on the flyleaf with the name of the York registrar, 'Joseph Buckle, 1844.' William Askwith, the York proctor, when asked by a common law attorney to recommend a book on ecclesiastical court practice, recommended J.T. Law's *Forms of Ecclesiastical Law*, a translation of part of a Latin work of 1728, not an easy book to read, and certainly not an accurate guide to the law or practice of the nineteenth century.[9] The attorney, however, was not misled by it, because it was out of print and unobtainable.[10]

The records show considerable variations among ecclesiastical courts in different dioceses.[11] They differed in terminology, in the manner in which they kept their records, and in important points of practice. Some appear to have been more concerned than others with avoiding prohibitions from the common law courts. The award of costs, a crucial factor in a defamation suit, was almost entirely within the discretion of the judge. A judge hostile to defamation suits could effectively discourage them by awarding only nominal costs to a successful plaintiff, and several judges said openly that this was their policy.[12] On many points of law and practice there was uncertainty. Practically no legal rules were established in the important areas that common lawyers call justification and privilege. Sometimes the correspondence of proctors, where it survives, reveals a settled practice,[13] but on some points it shows that even experienced proctors were unsure. Askwith, for example, was uncertain, in what must have been the quite common case of words spoken in one diocese by a person resident in another, which diocese had jurisdiction. He issued the citation in one such case initially in the wrong diocese and wrote to London for an opinion on the question.[14]

**The Nature of the Suit**

The thirteenth-century constitutions and statutes mentioned above, on which the defamation jurisdiction was founded, imply that the purpose of a defamation suit was punishment for sin. This would seem to put it in the category that ecclesiastical lawyers called 'criminal.' Unlike most criminal suits, however, which were brought in the name of 'the office of the judge,' defamation suits were generally, and by the nineteenth century almost always, brought in the name of the person defamed.[15] They shared some of the characteristics of criminal suits, being theoretically *pro salute animae* (for the health of the soul) and for the correction of manners, but they were not called 'causes of correction,' and were considered as 'mixed' (i.e., both criminal and civil in nature). The Ecclesiastical Courts Commission of 1832 said that defamation 'is of an anomalous character.'[16] The proceedings, if successful, led to an order for performance of penance and costs, but not to any award of direct financial benefit to the plaintiff; to that extent the proceedings were criminal. But they were commenced by 'libel' (statement of claim), not by 'articles' (the equivalent of a criminal indictment), and they were in the name of the plaintiff, required her consent for commencement, were entirely under her control, and could be settled by her at any time; in these respects they were civil in nature.

**Defences**

A successful plaintiff had to show that the words complained of imputed an ecclesiastical crime, that is, adultery or fornication. In a number of cases it was argued that the words alleged or proved to have been used by the defendant were ambiguous or uncertain in meaning, or too vague or, while precise, did not impute actual commission of the ecclesiastical offence.

It was common for the libel (statement of claim) to state that the defendant had called the plaintiff a whore, but it was not necessary for the plaintiff to prove that 'whore' was the actual word used. It was well established that any form of words would suffice to subject the defendant to the court's jurisdiction, but it was essential that they should clearly impute fornication or adultery.[17] Thus, a woman could, with impunity, be called 'damned stinking bitch, drunken bitch, good for nothing faggot, and stinking baggage,'[18] 'damned old cat of hell,'[19] and 'dirty slut.'[20] In a letter to an instructing attorney, William Askwith advised against pursuing a case on the basis of the use of the word 'hussy':

> The word *Hussy* it is true means a bad woman, but then it is often used ludicrously in slight disapprobation; and if the court should so view it and even admit the libels I am pretty confident after proving the words to that effect the decree would be *without costs.*[21]

In another York case, brought by a man, the defendant was proved to have said that the plaintiff had been 'too intimate' with his niece, a common enough euphemism for unchastity, like 'too kind,'[22] but the judge thought that it fell short of what was necessary, 'as the plaintiff might have been too intimate with his niece and yet not have accomplished that which alone would bring the case in the jurisdiction of the court.'[23] But he gave no costs, suggesting that he thought it a borderline case. Also near the borderline was a case in which again the plaintiff was a man, a Baptist minister, who was said to have 'gone a-whoring.' There was considerable evidence discreditable to the plaintiff, who had been temporarily suspended from his ministry on allegations of sexual misconduct, and so the judge may perhaps have been glad of a reason to dismiss the suit (though without costs): the reason he gave was that the words imputed only an intention to commit adultery, and not actual accomplishment of it.[24] Askwith, the defendant's proctor, had not anticipated this result.[25] Somewhat surprisingly again, a defendant could safely say that a woman was 'not much better than a common prostitute,'[26] since this was not actually to say that she *was* a prostitute. In a case in Bath in 1852, a clergyman was accused of saying to a father that his daughters were 'as bad as common prostitutes of the town' and 'no better than common prostitutes.' The two eldest of the four daughters (aged sixteen and fifteen) brought suits, which were, however, dismissed for the reason just mentioned.[27]

On the other hand the *mitior sensus* principle (preferring the milder sense) was not taken to the extremes sometimes seen at common law.[28] Courts were generally aware that words take their meaning from their context, and plaintiffs in several cases achieved success on the basis of words which in context implied fornication – though taken separately they would have seemed insufficient.[29] Everywhere and always there have been in use a number of colloquial synonyms for sexual intercourse, and these were generally held to suffice.[30] Where a defendant said that 'Sykes has done every daughter that Abraham Sheard has,' Lavinia Sheard sued successfully for defamation,[31] though it is obvious that, in another context, the words might be innocent. In one of Askwith's cases in York, his client was accused of saying to another person, 'You ride Pearson's wife.' Askwith, in correspondence with the instructing attorney, and in observations for use of the advocate, strenuously pressed the argument that to 'ride' a woman did not necessarily have a sexual connotation, referring to an incident he said he remembered of a strong woman who used, on a wager, to offer to run fifty yards with a man on her back against any challenger running a hundred yards. It will seem to modern readers that Askwith was straining a little here, and so it seemed also to the judge, who admitted the libel, 'observing that words the meaning whereof are understood by persons of ordinary understanding to have an incontinent allusion are considered actionable.'[32] In a case in the following year, where the words 'kept mistress' were in issue, Askwith expressed the view, rightly no doubt, that the judge would probably come to a similar conclusion.[33]

In a number of cases the defendant's accusation was of specific sexual misconduct that fell short of sexual intercourse, or 'criminal' intercourse, as sexual intercourse outside marriage was usually called. These cases could not give rise to a successful suit in the ecclesiastical court even though grave damage might ensue from the accusations. In one case the plaintiff was a cook, aged thirty-one, accused by a woman lodging in the same house of having been found on a sofa in the embrace of a fifteen-year-old boy (a fellow servant). The plaintiff's livelihood was at stake, and she was greatly aggrieved by the accusation (one witness said that 'she raved like a mad woman') and offered to go to a doctor to be examined, but the defendant said, 'you may save yourself that, for I have not accused you of any thing criminal.' The case was dismissed, for the accusation of 'something criminal' was essential to the court's jurisdiction.[34]

It was not essential, however, that the accusation should be seriously intended, and there are very many cases in which the context shows that the defendant's intention was abuse, rather than accusation of actual misconduct. Provided that words were used that on their face imputed the necessary offence, the defendant was liable. (The usual word was 'whore' but 'strumpet'[35] was also common, and so was 'bawd'[36] – strictly speaking, a procurer.) In a London case of 1819, Susannah Tuck, according to the libel, stood outside Catherine Roles's door and addressed her as follows: 'Oh you whore, you mother of whores, you bitch, you bitch of a whore, you bawd,' adding, after Roles shut the door, 'You, I mean you at number 11.' Many of the cases already mentioned, and to be mentioned, are of this sort, and it is needless to multiply examples. The ecclesiastical law differed on this point from the common law, where mere vituperative abuse was not actionable.[37]

It was not necessary that the plaintiff's name should have been used, but it was essential that she should have been clearly identified. Thus, where a witness heard the words 'she's a whore' addressed to the plaintiff's husband, but could not be sure of whom they were spoken, the suit was dismissed.[38] Reasonable inference was permitted, however, as in a case where the defendant was heard to speak the defamatory words and the plaintiff was immediately afterwards heard crying.[39] It was also necessary, of course, to prove that the defendant was the speaker of the opprobrious words. This was not usually in question, but in one case involving a matrimonial dispute, the suit was dismissed on ground of mistake of identity. Elizabeth Harrison, in dispute with her husband, John, thinking that he was about to abscond with the furniture, went to the house and said, 'Harrison I am come to claim my thirds [a wife's one-third interest in her husband's property].' According to Elizabeth's two witnesses, a friend of her husband's, William Leetham, said, 'Bess you are a whore, get out, you are a bitch of a whore,' to which Elizabeth Harrison replied,

'Dog, I'll make thee pay for calling me a whore.' She was, her proctor wrote, 'a woman of spirit & no wonder that she expressed herself warmly on the occasion.'[40] The defence was that her husband, but not Leetham, had called her a whore, and the judge accepted this and dismissed the suit. William Askwith, who was proctor for the plaintiff, was not happy with the result, writing to his instructing attorney:

> How far he [the judge] is right in this opinion the parties present best know, but I must continue to think Mrs Winter and Elizabeth Arundell [the plaintiff's witnesses] could not be mistaken in the person.

No costs were awarded, and Askwith sought to console himself (and his correspondent and their client) by adding, 'At all events Leetham has not much to boast of on the occasion inasmuch as his expenses must be greater than those of Mrs Harrison.' Askwith's bill was £27.11.0.[41] There is another interesting feature of this case. If the judge thought that the plaintiff's witnesses were honestly mistaken, the words 'Dog, I'll make thee pay for calling me a whore' must have been addressed by Elizabeth not to Leetham but to her husband, and the judge must have characterized the case in his mind as a kind of surrogate matrimonial dispute. A suit by a wife against her husband for defamation was, it seems, possible (a wife could sue her husband in the ecclesiastical court in a matrimonial cause), but very rare. I found only one example, and this was settled before witnesses were produced.[42]

It was, of course, a defence that the words had not been spoken at all, but this defence, though often attempted, rarely succeeded. The reason for the lack of success of this line of defence had to do with the method of proof, which was by written deposition.[43] A judge who did not personally see or hear the witnesses had a natural tendency to weigh all depositions equally, and, if possible, to reconcile conflicting accounts of events without accusing any witness of actual perjury.[44] Thus, where the plaintiff produced two witnesses who positively swore that the offensive words had been spoken, and the defendant produced, say, four witnesses who swore that they had been present but had not heard the words, the natural tendency of the judge, unless the plaintiff's witnesses were independently discredited,[45] was to conclude that the words had been spoken, but that the defendant's witnesses had not heard them, or had forgotten them. This tendency was actually elevated into a rule of law in a decision of the Arches Court, the appeal court for the Province of Canterbury, in 1821:

> [T]he rule of law is that one affirmative witness outweighs several negative witnesses, because both may be true. ... The words may have been spoken, and some

one present not hear or recollect them. There were six ladies and one gentleman present: there was much talking; there might be two conversations going on at the same time. ... there is no inconsistency in some hearing [the defendant] and others not. ... There is no reason not to believe the two witnesses examined on the libel: they must be guilty of the grossest perjury, if what they say is not true.[46]

William Askwith's correspondence shows how these considerations affected his practical advice in the conduct of litigation. Writing to an instructing attorney, Askwith advised against production of defence witnesses, on several grounds, the first of which was:

It can only be in the nature of proving a negative. No justification can be set up as a good defence for libellous words, and all that Winter's witnesses are likely to prove besides is that they were present at the times of quarrel but did not hear the defamatory words spoken, and were so situated that had they been spoken believe they must have heard them. This may be true, yet if Wharton's witnesses have sworn positively to the speaking of the words, such testimony in contradiction I fear would avail little or nothing.[47]

A line of defence often attempted was that the defendant had spoken words similar to those deposed to by the plaintiff's witnesses, but which, upon close scrutiny, turned out to fall short of actually making a defamatory accusation. Such a defence succeeded in a York case of 1835, where the defendant was alleged to have said that William Atkins, who was a tailor by trade, had measured Ann Hauxwell, the plaintiff, 'below the apron strings.' The defendant successfully proved that he had merely said that Atkins 'has been wanting to measure Hauxwell's wife six inches below her apron strings but she would not let such a pug-nosed monkey-faced devil have any concern with her.'[48] In an unusual case transferred to the Arches Court from Lichfield, John Hampden complained that Joseph Eyton had accused him of seducing Eyton's wife. The defence was that Hampden had been systematically harassing Mrs Eyton, 'intruding himself into her society without her invitation and consent, and following her about the streets.' Sir Herbert Jenner Fust, giving reasons for admitting the defensive allegation, considered that it was most improbable that a husband, while still living with his wife, should publicly accuse her of adultery.[49] He thought that Eyton must have meant, 'You are endeavouring to seduce my wife as much as is in your power to do.'[50] In another case the defendant attempted to show, at inordinate length (by nine witnesses), that he had not, as alleged, actually said that the plaintiff was 'Hoddy's whore,' but had merely addressed to her the questions, 'Whose whore art thou? Hoddy's?'

The defensive allegation asserted that the plaintiff had abused the defendant and his wife, calling him a rogue and a rascal and her an old whore; there then followed a replicatory plea, supported by seven witnesses, reasserting the plaintiff's original case. The judge, with evident irritation directed at both parties, dismissed them both without costs, saying that 'it was of no public advantage or benefit to enter into the details of the evidence.'[51]

There were a few other defences: the defendant had to reside within the jurisdiction of the court,[52] and suit had to be commenced within six months of the time when the words complained of were spoken.[53] Reconvention (counter-accusation of defamation) was theoretically a defence, but was very rarely used. Coote, writing in 1847, said that reconvention was 'now obsolete.'[54] The consequence of a successful reconvention was that both parties were dismissed, without costs, though the judge had power, of his own motion, to order *both* to perform penance.[55] A suit by reconvention was almost as expensive as a separate counter-suit, and committed the defendant to prove his case at the same time as the plaintiff, offering no opportunity of a sentence requiring the plaintiff to pay the defendant's costs. On the other hand, from the defensive point of view, if the plaintiff had used defamatory or abusive words to the defendant, almost equally good results could be expected from proving this by interrogatories to the plaintiff's witnesses (comparatively inexpensive), or by the defendant's own witnesses. Even if the proof fell short of what would support a counter-suit, it might lead the judge to dismiss the case,[56] or, at worst, to give sentence for the plaintiff but without costs, a more or less equivalent disposition from the financial point of view. The preferred defence strategy was, therefore, almost always not to reconvene, but to cross-examine the plaintiff's witnesses, reserving the options of filing a defensive allegation[57] and (within six months of the speaking of the words) commencing a counter-suit. William Askwith, writing to instructing attorneys, expressed his assessment of these considerations as follows:

> Cases of defamation are very little encouraged or countenanced by the judge of our court, so that if it could be shewn on the cross-examination of plaintiff's witnesses that the parties were one as abusive as the other, or that the plaintiff was the aggressor, when the words are charged to have been spoken ... I think at any rate the judge would not condemn defendant in costs, though on that point I cannot speak with any degree of certainty, as costs of course fall within his discretion.[58]

In a Norwich case one of the plaintiff's witnesses said that he 'heard the plaintiff and defendant call each other whores.' Among the papers is a note, perhaps by the registrar addressed to the judge:

In the depositions published in this cause it appears by the evidence ... that the plaintiff called the defendant 'a whore.' The court therefore it is presumed will dismiss this cause without costs, the plaintiff and defendant appearing by the evidence in the cause both amenable to ecclesiastical punishment in the same degree.[59]

Whoever may have been the author of this note, the judge did not conform precisely to the prediction in it, because sentence was given for the plaintiff, though without costs.[60]

In the Isle of Man, which, though not part of England, constitutes a diocese of the Church of England, ecclesiastical court procedure was highly informal.[61] There were no proctors or advocates. Cases were commenced by petition addressed to the judge. In 1821 Ann Creer complained that Isabella Christian had accused her of having had an illegitimate child eighteen years previously. Sentence was given for Creer, requiring, incidentally (contrary to English practice at this date), performance of penance by Christian in public and in penitential habit.[62] Isabella Christian commenced a counter-suit, complaining that, as she was passing Creer's house,

Ann Creer made use of the most abusive provoking and slanderous words towards your petitioner by repeatedly calling her a cursed whore and also saying that your petitioner was a whore unto a man for several years, and many other such expressions very unseemly to be uttered by one of her sex, and if your petitioner gave her any answer it was after she was provoked to the height of passion.[63]

The judge, in response to this petition, actually rescinded the earlier sentence, ordering each party to pay her own costs,[64] thereby recognizing, in effect, a defence of recrimination, though without the English procedure of reconvention.

**Truth**

In one of his letters, just quoted, Askwith said, 'No justification can be set up as a good defence,' and this was, subject to important qualifications about costs and penance, the general state of the ecclesiastical law in this period.[65] In one of the few reported cases, Sir Herbert Jenner Fust said, 'Proof of the fact of fornication or adultery has never been admitted by these courts ... as a justification or even extenuation.'[66]

It is difficult to be certain of how the law worked in practice because of the wide judicial discretion to remit costs and penance. Jenner Fust's words 'or even extenuation' are misleading in respect of many dioceses where costs were refused or reduced and penance remitted if the words spoken were shown to be true. Thus a defendant who proved the truth of what he had said might, in some dioceses, expect to escape an order for costs or penance. This, even where it was a settled practice, was not equivalent to recognition of truth as a complete defence, because the defendant might be admonished not to repeat the slander and would not be entitled to costs against the plaintiff. Such a practice, however, might be perceived as recognition, in effect, of a partial defence, and it would certainly tend to discourage the institution of a suit where the plaintiff and her proctor anticipated this result.

Askwith's opinion was that a showing that the words were true was not a defence but might be expected to reduce the punishment (by which he meant costs and penance). The evidence confirms that his view of the practice at York was accurate. In France v. Aaron (not one of Askwith's cases), for example, where the defendant proved that the plaintiff had borne an illegitimate child, and where sympathy with the defendant was strong on account of gross provocation, the defendant was admonished and ordered to pay £5 costs – a lenient disposition certainly (when compared with full costs and penance), but by no means equivalent to a complete defence.[67]

Askwith several times had to explain the law to incredulous common law attorneys. One attorney, acting for a male defendant who had asserted that the plaintiff was a whore, and that he and other men had, as the attorney put it, known her carnally, wrote to Askwith saying that the truth of the assertion could be proved: 'The plaintiff was a prostitute in Hull before she was married & her husband knew it, & knows that she has been very common since.' He added, 'We suppose if defendant does prove plaintiff to be the woman described the court will dismiss the case.'[68]

It fell to Askwith to explain that this supposition was erroneous: 'I think the bad character of the plaintiff is inadmissible as a defence to this suit, & would not justify the court in dismissing the defendant without some degree of punishment.'[69] He added his understanding of the reason for the rule:

In a criminal prosecution for defamatory words, I am afraid the court cannot allow the defendant to set up a justification of himself by pleading & proving the plaintiff to be a whore &c, for supposing her to be such a character, she is liable to answer for her misconduct before a proper tribunal and is not to be abused & called with impunity by any one that may think fit.[70]

The exclusion of the defence of justification, though different from the rule in a common law civil action, was not without parallels, or wholly without the support of informed contemporary opinion. The criminal law of libel did not admit truth as a defence, and was only partly altered in this respect by statute in 1843.[71] Scottish law did not admit truth as a justification, and this aspect of Scottish law was defended by the author of the leading book on the subject.[72] A select committee of the House of Lords, under the chairmanship of Lord Campbell, recommended an integration of the civil and criminal law and of libel and slander, admitting a defence of justification only when it could be shown that publication was in the public interest.[73] This would have had the effect of greatly enlarging the reach of the civil law of defamation, and was objectionable to some for this reason as infringing upon freedom of speech. The report was partly implemented in 1843[74] in respect of criminal libel only, but the opinions expressed in it, and the evidence given by witnesses, show that there was a substantial body of opinion against admitting justification as a defence. The hypothetical example most frequently chosen to support the argument is one close to the theme of this study: the case of a respectably married woman who, having had the misfortune to bear an illegitimate child many years earlier in a distant place, is exposed by an enemy acting maliciously, or with worse motives.[75] This was by no means a fanciful example: the court records show that many of the cases that came into the ecclesiastical courts involved allegations that a married woman had had an illegitimate child before her marriage.[76] No one doubted that malicious exposure of such ancient misdeeds was morally objectionable, anti-social, and very damaging to the woman and to her family; many thought that it should be punished. Another aspect of the matter was that, if justification were a defence, there would be 'open season' to abuse and insult a woman on account of her earlier misfortune, which could make her life intolerable – substantially the point made by Askwith in the letter just quoted.[77] The ecclesiastical law, therefore, was not wholly out of sympathy with contemporary opinion on this point. The quasi-criminal nature of the suit was significant in this context: there might be good reason why an undeserving plaintiff should not receive damages, but there was good reason also why a defendant should be punished for anti-social conduct.

Joseph Phillimore, the chancellor of Worcester, wrote to his deputy registrar, who had sent him the papers in a pending cause, giving instructions by that means to his surrogate:

The proceedings in the defamation suit seem correct, as I judge of them from the minutes of the court. I am of opinion that the libel is admissible but I think ... that the words following within the parentheses vizt 'who was & is a person of good reputation & character' should be expunged, as it would not be competent to the adverse party to plead bad character in reply. I do not trouble Mr Wheeler [the surrogate] with a letter as I write so fully to you. You will have the goodness to shew him this letter.[78]

This shows that Phillimore plainly did not regard truth as a defence. It also shows the high degree of uncertainty and variation in practice in the ecclesiastical courts, and the possibility of a misunderstanding of the formal recitals in the documents. The libels in most dioceses did include the words to which Phillimore objected, and a common practice, as we have seen, was to permit the defendant to prove the plaintiff's bad character in mitigation of costs and penance.

Though truth was not a complete justification in the ecclesiastical courts, many people, even lawyers, erroneously thought that it was. Askwith's common law correspondent, mentioned above, is a case in point. There are many indications in the cause papers that lay persons thought the same. In the Somerset case of Dorney v. Webb, John Webb, the defendant's stepson, said to Thomas Dorney, the plaintiff's father, that 'he could not hurt him for he only spoke the truth,' and in a Carlisle case of 1854 a witness said to the defendant that Mr Salkeld (the plaintiff's husband) was going to have him up for slander, to which the defendant replied, 'How could he when it was true?'[79] In a London case of 1824 the defendant accused her own husband of adultery with the plaintiff, and invited a defamation suit, thinking that it would give her an opportunity to prove the adultery. 'They have threatened me with law and I wish they would do so. She has weaned your affections from me,' she said to her husband, 'and I only want to be brought up to a court of justice and I can prove it.' Having learned of the legal position, she said that 'she knew the law must take its course but that it was a very hard thing against her that she might not open her mouth to say what she had seen and knew.'[80] Sentence was given against her with costs.[81] In this case, as in some others,[82] a defamation suit may have offered an opportunity to air a matrimonial dispute.

In a later case in the same diocese, a defendant was actually imprisoned for refusing to retract his words and refusing to perform the penance ordered by the court. In a petition addressed to the judge from Chelmsford Gaol, and supported by a letter from his curate, he said that 'he was not aware that on setting forth the truth (for the statement he positively avers to be true) he was liable to punishment.' The petition is marked in pencil, perhaps by the registrar, 'Judge can do nothing – the penance must be performed.' The judge, Dr Stephen Lushington, who was a member of Parliament, mentioned the case in a debate there, saying that he regretted having had to imprison the man, and that he knew not 'by what law parties, so imprisoned, can be liberated.'[83] Eventually, after a year in prison, the defendant did perform the penance, and was released, the plaintiff's proctor waiving the costs.[84]

Although truth was not a complete justification, a successful attack on the plaintiff's reputation might, as we have seen, reduce the costs payable by the defendant, or lead to remittal of the penance, and such attacks are quite often found among the cause papers.[85] But such a strategy, as Askwith wrote in the letter already quoted, could only be pursued 'by entering into a tedious & expensive litigation.'[86] This comment could not be better illustrated than by the Somerset case of Dorney v. Webb.[87] Two witnesses initially deposed to the defamatory words, as was required for all cases. But a defensive allegation was then filed, supported by four witnesses, asserting that Susan Dorney was a woman of 'ill fame and of a very disorderly life and conversation who had been delivered of a bastard child.' A defensive allegation opened the door to a further allegation on behalf of the plaintiff, and Susan Dorney filed one, supported by no fewer than seven witnesses, including the father of Dorney's child, who had been arrested at Dorney's instance under the bastardy law, and compelled to pay child support.[88] He appeared to bear no grudge on this account, and deposed that Dorney was of good reputation, 'save and except as to what may be thought of her by her having allowed him to take liberties with her and by which she became with child,' a convincing but not discourteous demonstration of the double standard of sexual behaviour in men and women. Dorney sought to show that she had been courted in an open and honourable manner, and seduced under promise of marriage, circumstances amounting to misfortune – and often so called by way of euphemism – rather than crime.[89] The judge gave sentence for Dorney, but altered the form of it so as to omit the usual clauses asserting that the words had been spoken 'to the infamy hurt and diminution' of her 'good name fame and reputation.'[90] The defendant was ordered to pay £25 towards costs. Had this been a York case, and had Askwith's advice been sought and followed, questions about the child would have been included in the interrogatories to Dorney's witnesses, but there would have been no allegation on either side, with consequences that would have been less costly to both. When a case of this sort is decided for the plaintiff, it is often impossible to know whether or not the judge accepted the attack on her character; in Dorney v. Webb, the deliberate alteration of the usual form of the sentence shows plainly that the judge thought that Webb had convincingly demonstrated Dorney's bad character, but that this was nevertheless no excuse for speaking the defamatory words. The award of costs, though it must have fallen considerably short of covering Dorney's actual expenses, was by no means a trivial sum.

In a Bristol case where a wife accused her own husband of adultery it appears that the truth of the accusation may have had some influence on the disposition of the case. The cause papers contain a collection of fifteen love letters written by Prudence Payne, a widow, to Thomas Rowley, a married man, and include a poem elaborately decorated with lace and pressed flowers (see plate 3). Several of the letters included the instruction that they should be burned – sound advice, as events showed. When Mary Rowley, Thomas's wife, discovered the letters, she sought out Payne's brother, a surgeon, even interrupting him when he was about to bleed a patient, to denounce his sister and her own husband, producing the letters from her bag. Prudence Payne instituted a defamation suit, and Mary Rowley filed a defensive allegation to which she annexed the letters, the allegation asserting not that the defamatory words were justified, but that they had been spoken 'from excitement and anger' after discovering the letters, a defence that might be expected, at best, to reduce costs. However, the case was dismissed, probably on the ground that the speaking of the defamatory words was insufficiently proved,[91] a conclusion that might possibly have been assisted by judicial sympathy for the defendant. The defamation suit seems in this case to have offered Mary Rowley an opportunity to carry on a sort of shadow matrimonial suit,[92] accusing her husband in a judicial forum, without going to the length of instituting a matrimonial suit; adultery might not have been provable in a divorce (separation) suit, and in any event she may not have desired a separation. Possibly she wished to preserve the letters for future use in a divorce suit, and, if so, she found a very effective way of doing so, at the same time putting them effectively beyond her husband's reach.

Occasionally it happened that the truth of the defamatory words might be proved by way of discrediting a witness, as in a Norwich case of 1846.[93] The brothers William, Frederick, and Henry Youell, prominent nurserymen and florists in Yarmouth,[94] dismissed their foreman, William Hussey, accusing him of an improper association with a married woman, Elizabeth Craske. Craske brought a suit against two of the brothers, and Hussey gave evidence denying the association. A witness for William Youell then deposed that Craske and Hussey had been in the habit of meeting in the witness's house, engaging in improper familiarities: 'when they met she flew to him and they kissed'; she was seen sitting on his lap with his hand in her bosom; they were alone together in the bedroom, and the bed was disarranged. Craske and Hussey also met at another house, 'not once,' the judge said in his reasons, but 'so often that ... [the householder] could not recollect how many times.' It was alleged that they met by accident 'but he [the judge] put no faith in such accidental meetings.'[95] The truth of the defamatory words was here established not, ostensibly, as a justification, but, on the contrary, to suggest, by discrediting the plaintiff's witnesses that the words were not proved to have been spoken at all. Hussey was an unreliable witness because immoral, because he had lied about his association with Craske, because he had an interest in the suit, and because he bore a grudge against the Youells. Establishing the truth of the words would not ordinarily assist a defence that the words were never spoken at all, but in this case the defence succeeded, and the judge's reasons (which, unusually, were reported at some length in a local newspaper)[96] show that his sympathies were strongly with the defendants. Justification appears in this way to have been, to a degree, unofficially recognized.

## Prior Report

The prior existence of a defamatory report did not excuse a person who repeated it.[97] The law was that 'those who propagate such reports assist in the injury, and are parties to the defamation.'[98] In an opinion on a Winchester case in 1824, Dr Lushington, later judge of the London Consistory Court, wrote: 'Tho' the libel only charges the party with repeating what he said he had heard, I think that the offence of defamation was committed.'[99] In a Norwich case of 1846 the plaintiff's husband, father, and brother-in-law called together on the defendant to complain that she had spread a report that the plaintiff had lived in adultery before her recent marriage. The defendant (very rashly from a legal point of view) agreed to see the three men and readily admitted what she had said, adding 'that she had heard the statement from a great many persons – that it had been commonly talked of at her dinner table.' Evidently she thought that her conduct was perfectly reasonable, but sentence was given against her with costs and penance.[100]

There was a common law rule, in effect until at least 1829, that a person accused of slander could excuse himself by revealing the source of his information.[101] This common law rule was very widely known, and assumed by many to apply as well to sexual slander. So it often occurred that the plaintiff, or her friends, demanded that the defendant 'give up his author,' i.e., reveal the source of his information,[102] and it was often supposed, by both sides, that doing so would excuse the defendant from further liability.[103] In a Worcester case of 1845, Ann Collis repeated a rumour about Caroline Bate, a fifteen-year-old girl,[104] that she had been made pregnant by one of her father's servants, and had been delivered of a child, adding that 'my servant girl has told me this' having heard it one Sunday after church from a servant in Bate's household. Collis offered to produce her servant to 'confront' Bate's servant in order to determine the source of the rumour, and such a meeting actually took place, with considerable formality, in an attorney's office. Collis evidently thought that this was the most she could reasonably be expected to do, but Thomas Bate, Caroline's father, instituted a suit, and obtained a sentence. Collis appealed unsuccessfully to the Arches Court of Canterbury, where Sir Herbert Jenner Fust said, distinguishing the common law rule,

> The distinction between this case and the cases referred to by Dr Bayford [Collis's advocate] is that they were civil actions. In an action for damages, if the defendant gives up the original author of the slander, or the person from whom he heard the words, it is sufficient. But this is not an action for damages but for character.[105]

Sometimes a defendant offered spontaneously to give up her author. Proof of this was apt to hamper the defence. In 1830 Elizabeth Christie was alleged to have said that Ann Morton 'had left a bastard child in the East Indies.' Two defence witnesses deposed that the words used were 'I know nothing about that, but I can give up my author.' This was not helpful. As the defending proctor wrote to his instructing attorney, 'why should Mrs Christie say, I am very willing to give up my author, if she had not said plumply that Morton had left a bastard child &c.' He added, gloomily, 'this must be got over as well as we can, but I fear the result must be private penance and costs.'[106] His prediction was accurate: sentence was given for the plaintiff, with penance and costs.[107]

## Privilege

Every system of defamation law must recognize that, in certain circumstances, defamatory words may be spoken in good faith and for a legitimate purpose: this is the defence known to common lawyers as privilege. Almost nothing is to be found on this subject in the books on ecclesiastical law, but there are indications that in practice a defence of privilege was sometimes afforded. A notorious defamation suit, still much discussed thirty years after its termination, had ended in 1812 with a decision of the High Court of Delegates, then the court of last resort, dismissing the suit, leaving each party to pay his and her own costs, which, on the estimate of the plaintiff's proctor, amounted to £600 to £700 on each side.[108] The defendant, William Bentham, had warned his wife and a young lady 'under his protection' against association with the plaintiff, Ann Russell, on the ground of her past sexual misconduct.[109] The High Court of Delegates gave no reasons, and even the plaintiff's proctor was unsure whether the case had been dismissed because the words were not proved to have been spoken, or on the ground of justification (privilege). He thought the latter, because if the words had not been spoken at all he would have expected costs to be awarded to the defendant. This decision hardly amounts to a clear assertion of a legal defence of privilege, but it seems to have been understood as recognizing such a defence. In a case of 1844, from the diocese of Lichfield but heard in the Arches Court, Sir Herbert Jenner Fust said:

> *Russell* v. *Bentham* was a case of a very different description, because the party was allowed to go into the particulars of the charge and proof of the report for this reason: if there were such report there would be no malicious defamation, and on that ground he was allowed to go into proof to justify the caution he had given to the ladies, and it amounted to a privileged communication, in the relation in which he stood towards the young person: it was a justification of the caution and a foundation for the caution.[110]

Jenner Fust rested the defence of privilege on the concept that privileged words were not spoken maliciously, and this echoed the fifteenth-century comment of Lyndwood, who, glossing the word 'maliciously' in the Provincial Constitution of Canterbury of 1222, wrote that one making an accusation in the course of criminal proceedings, and proving it, would not himself be liable to punishment for defamation.[111] The principle here was that, since it was in the public interest that crime should be punished, it would be wrong to punish for defamation those who assisted in the prosecution of crime. This was rarely put to the test in the nineteenth century, because criminal proceedings for adultery and fornication, except against clergymen, were extremely rare. The point did arise, however, in a Norwich case of 1820. Frances Freeman made an accusation against a clergyman, Nathan Todd, of incest with his own daughter, Mary Anne. Freeman asked to see the churchwardens, and told them that she, evidently while resident as a servant in Todd's house, had seen Todd and his daughter in bed together, and that she had heard Nathan Todd say 'My dear, come on to me' and had heard Mary Anne say 'Pray, Father, don't.'[112] A suit, brought jointly in the names of Nathan and Mary Anne Todd, was dismissed.[113] No reasons were given, but it seems likely that the judge found that the words (deposed to by the two churchwardens) were spoken, and the probable ground of dismissal, therefore, was privilege. Specific provision was made in the canons of 1603 for the protection of churchwardens (but not mentioning their informants),[114] showing that there was then no general defence of privilege, or at least that its scope was doubtful.[115]

In several cases where clergymen were defendants, rather than plaintiffs, questions of privilege arose. In a Hereford case of 1828, a clergyman, William Gilpin, speaking to one of his parishioners, Elizabeth Roberts, was supposed to have said, 'I have heard that you have had connexion with Mr Bright, and been naught with your husband.' Roberts bought a suit against Gilpin but herself stated in an affidavit that 'she did not suppose that Mr Gilpin intended to do her harm, but merely to tell her what he had heard as her fault,' evidently considering that he had merely been about his duties as her clergyman. The suit was dismissed (without costs), though whether on account of privilege, or because the words were not proved, cannot be certain.[116] In a Norwich case, the Revd Arthur Taylor told John Daveney, in reply to pressing questions, that he had heard a report that Daveney's niece, Emily, had eloped with Lord Hastings. A suit was instituted in Emily's name by her father (she was eighteen years old), but John Daveney himself (the uncle), giving evidence for the plaintiff, said that 'I considered that the defendant did only his duty as a clergyman and a friend of mine and the family to make the communication to me,' and that he considered the suit 'most unwarrantable and unjust.' It was dismissed, this time with costs.[117] Again, however, we cannot be certain of the reason, as the evidence of the second witness was very weak, and the case may have been dismissed for want of proof.

The clergy enjoyed no immunity from this branch of the ecclesiastical law. No case was found in which a clergyman was actually ordered to perform penance, but one Hereford case was settled on terms whereby a clergyman paid the plaintiff's costs. He and his wife had been sued for saying that the plaintiff, Sarah Bates, 'was gone off in the family way.' In an effort to avert liability Mr Williams, the clergyman, wrote:

> Mr Williams has to inform Miss S. Bates that a *report* to her disadvantage has been current in town & country for a considerable time – & that neither Mr nor Mrs Williams ever stated that you went off in the way you mention.

As we have seen, it was no defence that the defamatory rumour was already current, and the suit was compromised on terms favourable to the plaintiff, the defendant paying the plaintiff's taxed costs (£24.11.1).[118]

Officials other than clergy might have occasion, in the course of their duties, to comment on the sexual reputation of others. In a Somerset case of 1834, Robert Churches, overseer of the poor, was sued by Isabella Stroud, an unmarried woman, for saying that she had suffered a miscarriage. Churches appeared in person in court and admitted that when the plaintiff had applied to him for parish relief, he said that he had been told that her illness had been occasioned by her having miscarried. In the interrogatories, the plaintiff's mother, who gave evidence of hearing the words, was asked 'whether the whole of the conversation ... did not arise out of his being obliged in the performance of his duty as overseer to make enquiries as to the state of health of the said Isabella Stroud before he could relieve her.'[119] The disposition of this case is unknown, but the inclusion of this question shows that considerations that would by common lawyers have been discussed under the heading of privilege were not alien to the thinking of the ecclesiastical courts.

In a York case of 1833, Robert Gypson, in the course of giving instructions to a bailiff to levy a distress against a man called Bowes Humble, made disparaging remarks about his wife, Sarah Humble. The bailiff was asked whether the words were not spoken in confidence and were not intended merely 'as a caution to you to take care ... as they were dangerous bad people.' The defensive allegation did not include this line of defence, and it is doubtful whether it could have excused Gypson's words, which were proved to have been expressed in 'very coarse language,' including the assertions that Sarah Humble was a 'great whore' and that 'I have fuck'd her many times.'[120]

Employers often took an interest in their employees' lives and conduct that might from various perspectives be described as protective, paternalistic, or meddlesome. In a Chester case of 1815 an altercation occurred when John Crook attempted to persuade his apprentice to leave his drinking companions at an inn. He was proved to have said to the plaintiff, who was present on the occasion, 'Damn you for a whore; you have been a whore all the days of your life and I can prove you one.' Crook's defence was that he was merely acting the part of a good employer in looking after the morals of his apprentice; he said that his apprentices had previously been convicted by the magistrates of misconduct at the inn, and that he (Crook) had entered a recognizance for their future good behaviour. His own account was that, without alluding to the plaintiff in particular, he had told the company that his apprentices 'should not stop there among a parcel of whores and rogues.' This intervention, putting the best construction on it, must be judged deficient in subtlety and tact. Crook paid heavily, for he suffered two broken ribs at the hands of the plaintiff's husband, and sentence was given against him in the ecclesiastical court.[121]

The employer fared better in the case of the Yarmouth florists, Craske v. Youell.[122] The complaint was that the Youell brothers had objected to an improper association between their foreman, William Hussey, and the plaintiff. William Youell, in his defence, asserted that 'if any defamatory words were spoken they were spoken as his [Hussey's] master by way of remonstrance caution or warning.'[123] The judge dismissed the suit, but not on the ground of privilege: in fact he expressly stated in his reasons that 'if the words were used they would amount to defamation, as they were more than a warning.'[124] A tactful admonition, in private, it seems, might have been defensible; public accusations were not. It seems, therefore, that a limited defence of privilege, or its equivalent, was in practice recognized by the courts, but that it was ill defined, and that in many cases where a decision might have been rested on privilege, the judge sought another ground for dismissal of the suit.

## Malice

The libel (statement of claim) often included the assertion that the words had been spoken 'maliciously and with intent to defame,'[125] and the formal sentence of the court usually contained an assertion that the defendant 'did ... publicly and maliciously' speak the defamatory words,[126] but actual malice was not required to be proved. Lyndwood had said that malice might be presumed,[127] and this was the rule also in the nineteenth century. Sir Herbert Jenner Fust said, in 1846, 'If I find the words were uttered without justification, I must be of opinion that they were uttered with malice, unless a reasonable cause is assigned.'[128] The possibility of displacing the presumption of malice thus enabled the courts to allow for the defences known to common lawyers as justification and privilege. That the defendant was drunk, or that he spoke in the heat of anger or distress, were not defences, but proof of these facts was often attempted, in some cases with success. The wife who discovered love letters written to her husband claimed in her successful defence that she spoke in 'excitement and anger.'[129] Generally the best that could be expected was a reduction of costs, if the defendant could show that the slander was 'at the worst, a mere unpremeditated sally of passion.'[130] Such a defence was offered in a York case, where also the defendant was 'not perfectly free from liquor and much vexed and irritated' by the plaintiff's having insulted his wife. Sentence was given for the plaintiff, but with costs of £5 only. Askwith, the defendant's proctor, considered this a favourable result, writing to the attorney: 'As the defamation was certainly proved, Dickinson [the defendant] ought to think himself well off, for no doubt the expenses of the plaintiff will be more than he has to pay in the whole.'[131] In a somewhat similar Gloucester case the defendant, according to a witness, 'was so aggravated that he did not know what he was saying more than a child.' Sentence was given for the plaintiff, with costs of £10.[132]

In a York case of 1841, it was argued in mitigation that the defendant was a former sailor, 'one of a class of men by whom vulgar language was frequently bandied about, without really meaning what they said.' It was also proved that he was intoxicated. The plaintiff's advocate replied that 'The plea that the defendant was a sailor would avail him nothing; as well might an experienced thief plead in mitigation, on a conviction for felony, that he had been brought up among thieves and had been accustomed to steal.' The judge gave sentence for the plaintiff, with full costs, commenting that he 'did not consider that this was a case arising accidentally from heated blood, or from a mere propensity to vulgarity.' This shows that such considerations might have had some weight in an appropriate case, though not in this one, where the judge found that the defendant had deliberately set out to damage the plaintiff.[133]

## Provocation

The commonest ground alleged in mitigation was provocation. The chancellor
of York, Granville Vernon, considered provocation as characteristic of the typical case. He said, in the course of his evidence to the Ecclesiastical Courts
Commission, 'I have usually found it necessary to terminate these causes by
admonishing the party to refrain from using any such language in future, and
leaving the costs to fall upon each party separately; the sense of which has
been that I have felt both parties were equally in fault, that there was provocation enough to have accounted for the words, though not matter to justify
them.'[134] It was clear enough that provocation was not, legally speaking, a
defence,[135] but a sentence for the plaintiff without costs and without any order
for penance, such as Vernon was in the habit of giving, was almost tantamount
to a dismissal. It is not surprising, therefore, that provocation was often
alleged. The letter from William Askwith, the York proctor, quoted above,
shows that he thought it very definitely to the defendant's advantage to prove,
if possible, that there was abusive language on both sides.[136] 'Unless we can
establish,' he wrote in another case, 'that [the words] were uttered by the
defendant under great provocation, in a moment of irritation &c &c I am
afraid the decree will be ultimately against us.'[137]

There are many cases in which plaintiffs were alleged to have abused defendants with words, commonly, in the case of women defendants, impugning
their chastity.[138] Women might be harassed throughout their lives by allegations of this sort: in a York case of 1838, transcribed in appendix A, below, the
plaintiff was shown to have been in the constant habit of taunting the defendant with a single instance of alleged misbehaviour that had occurred twenty-
four years previously, before her marriage, by which taunts she and her family
were eventually driven out of the neighbourhood.[139] In a Somerset case, in the
course of a quarrel between two women, the plaintiff called the defendant a
'rafty whore,' adding that 'when thee was out of town thy husband brought
home a whore and made a bawdy house of the room and gave her sixpence.'
The defendant, according to the plaintiff's witness, 'made a laugh at it, and
said he gave her half a crown,' though she was sufficiently irritated to call the
plaintiff, in return, a 'rotten whore' and (according to another witness) to say,
'you was a whore before you were married.' The case was dismissed, each
party paying her own costs.[140]

In the case of men, the most common accusations were that they were
villains, rascals, thieves, rogues, robbers, and buggers,[141] or that they were
infected with venereal disease.[142] Imputions against men of mere unchastity
occur occasionally,[143] but a man might more often be insulted by an assertion

that his wife was a whore,[144] or by plain incivility to his wife,[145] or by a suggestion that his daughter was a 'nasty dirty stinking bitch,'[146] or that his sister was a 'nasty bitch.'[147] It is clear that a man's reputation depended in part on the good repute of his female relatives. In one case a man was provoked by an accusation that he had beaten his wife,[148] and in another that he had neglected his wife and children,[149] evidence that such behaviour, though it may have been common, was not respectable. Very frequently, especially when the defamatory words arose out of a quarrel between two men, the provocative words were spoken by the plaintiff's husband.[150] Sometimes the provocation might be a deliberate attempt to entrap the defendant: in one case a witness was asked, 'Did not [plaintiff] call [defendant] rogue and by many other and what opprobrious names on purpose to enrage and provoke him ... to speak some defamatory words with a view intent and design of bringing a suit against him?'[151]

It was often suggested and alleged by defendants that the plaintiff was 'troublesome, quarrelsome and litigious,'[152] and of 'violent temper and character,'[153] and in many cases proof was offered of abusive words.[154] Provocative conduct of various sorts was also alleged. In one case the plaintiff had stood on a wall overlooking the outoffices (latrines) in the neighbouring yard, evidently while they were in use by men, inducing the defendant to say, 'Are you got upon the wall to shew your arse you nasty bitch? You had better shew your cunt. Will you see my prick? You have seen it and have had it many a time and shall again. I wish you had one in you now as thick and as long as my arm.' He was not excused, despite his proctor's argument that the plaintiff's conduct was indecent and provocative.[155] In a Chester case the plaintiff annoyed the defendant by taking his hat as security for a disputed debt for drink at a public house.[156] In several cases it was suggested, alleged, or proved that women plaintiffs had used actual violence against defendants, or defendants' spouses or children.[157]

In many of the cases just mentioned the provocative words or behaviour were not actually proved by witnesses: suggestions in interrogatories were not required to be proved, and assertions in defensive allegations did not always proceed to the stage of proof; nor did witnesses always tell the truth. Nevertheless, the recurrence of such suggestions and assertions is significant, and shows that the conduct alluded to was plausible, and that it sometimes occurred, even though it cannot be said to have been proved in each individual case. Moreover, the desire of defendants to prove that plaintiffs were immodest or aggressive is evidence of the prevailing expectations of behaviour. Thus the significance of these cases lies not so much in a demonstration that women were sometimes immodest and aggressive (though they sometimes were) as in a demonstration that immodest and aggressive women, especially when 'troublesome quarrelsome and litigious,' were departing from contemporary standards of propriety.

# Part II

# THE COURTS

# 3

# The Courts and Their Officers

## The Courts

In 1835 there were twenty-six dioceses in England and Wales, four of which (the four northern dioceses), together with Sodor and Man (the Isle of Man), constituted the Province of York; the other twenty-two dioceses formed the Province of Canterbury (see plate 12). In 1836 the refounded diocese of Ripon (formed from parts of Chester and York) and in 1848 the diocese of Manchester (from part of Chester) were added to the northern province. The principal episcopal court in each diocese, generally called the consistory court, had full jurisdiction over all ecclesiastical causes, including defamation. The Ecclesiastical Courts Commission of 1832 collected figures showing the numbers of each kind of case in the ecclesiastical courts in the years 1827, 1828, and 1829. The summary table prepared for the Report[1] (reproduced below in table 1) shows that the kind of business, and the number and proportion of defamation cases, varied very substantially from one diocese to another. In Gloucester, for example, in those three years, defamation cases formed the largest class of business, exceeding even testamentary cases; in other dioceses there were no defamation cases in the three-year period. Some reasons will be suggested later to account for the differences.

The consistory court sat usually in a corner or transept of the cathedral, divided from the rest of the church by partitions, and furnished with a raised seat for the judge and a large table for the proctors. One such space remains, as it was in the nineteenth century, at Chester (see plate 4). There were some exceptions to the use of cathedrals: Doctors' Commons, in London, had its own courtroom (see plate 5); the Ely court sat in the university church in Cambridge, and the Peterborough court in a church in Northampton.

Sessions of the courts were held generally every two or three weeks during term, with extra sessions when needed. There were four terms, and usually four sessions in each term, so there might be fifteen or twenty sessions in a year. With the consent of the proctors, business might be done at other times and places, before a surrogate judge. Towards the end of the period under study, business declined steeply, and in some courts a year or more might pass without a single session.

The principal kinds of cases heard in the consistory courts were testamentary, matrimonial, defamation, tithes, church rates, disputes over seating in church, faculties (licences for alterations to church buildings), brawling (quarrelsome conduct on church premises), and clergy discipline. Of these, the first three (testamentary, matrimonial, and defamation) affected the population at large, and had nothing to do with the affairs of the institutional church. They constituted the general English law on the aspects of these matters that fell within the courts' jurisdiction. The table prepared by the Ecclesiastical Courts Commission of 1832 (table 1, below) shows that, in 1827, 1828, and 1829, defamation cases constituted just under one-quarter of the business of the consistory courts, and were the second largest class of business after the testamentary cases.

Brawling cases were sometimes substitutes for defamation suits, as in a Norwich case where a quarrel had taken place between two women as they were leaving church, in the course of which the defendant denied that she had committed a theft, and added, 'I never received love letters from other peoples husbands neither.' This would not support a defamation suit, for it did not impute adultery, but, because the words were spoken in the churchyard, the defendant was found guilty of brawling. She could not be made to perform penance, but she was obliged to pay costs, amounting to £24, and was committed to prison for non-payment of them. According to one of the witnesses, the defendant's primary motive was to injure the promoter's (complainant's) reputation, because when the witness suggested that the churchyard was an inappropriate place for such accusations, the defendant replied, 'It is the right place to come to let people know it.'[2]

There were a number of courts below the level of the consistory courts which exercised jurisdiction in defamation causes. The bishop could appoint a commissary to exercise episcopal jurisdiction in a limited area of the diocese, and there were fourteen such commissaries in 1830. The only one with substantial business, however, was in Richmond,[3] which, though in the county of Yorkshire, was until 1836, by a quirk of ecclesiastical geography, in the diocese of Chester but very remote from the see city. The Richmond court had its own proctors, and conducted its procedure and kept its records in the manner of the consistory courts. It became the court of the diocese of Ripon when this diocese was refounded in 1836, though the York court continued to exercise jurisdiction over those parts of the diocese of Ripon that had formerly been in the diocese of York. The commissary courts exercised episcopal jurisdiction, and were inferior to the consistory courts only in the sense that the jurisdiction of the commissary was limited geographically. The Richmond court was by far the most active of the commissary courts, with fifty cases in the three-year period of the Commission's survey. The six commissary courts in the diocese of Lincoln had practically no business.[4]

Most dioceses were divided into (usually two or three) archdeaconries, and the archdeacons had jurisdiction over ecclesiastical causes, including defamation. The exercise of this jurisdiction varied widely, being most active in the two southwestern dioceses (Exeter, and Bath and Wells). The archdeacon's court of Wells, for example, had thirty-seven causes in the three-year period just mentioned, and that of Cornwall forty-nine. Most archidiaconal courts, however, had ceased business altogether.[5] Account must also be taken of numerous courts for areas exempt from episcopal jurisdiction (called peculiars). There were no fewer than 237 of these, theoretically with defamation jurisdiction, but most with no business of any description in the three-year period examined by the Commission of 1832.[6] On the other hand, a few of these courts did hear occasional defamation cases, usually employing the officers of a nearby consistory court to conduct the proceedings.[7] These courts all had effective power to imprison for contempt.[8]

The records of the archidiaconal and peculiar courts are not uniformly preserved. An estimate can be made, however, of the number of defamation cases heard in these courts. Returns to a parliamentary inquiry in 1828 show that the number of defamation cases in the inferior courts between 1824 and 1826 (inclusive) was 38, compared with 384 in the consistory courts,[9] and it may therefore be estimated that the number of defamation causes heard in the courts of inferior jurisdiction was about one-tenth of the number heard in the episcopal courts. Probably this is an overestimate for the whole period under study, as it is likely that the business of the inferior courts declined more sharply than that of the consistory courts after 1830.[10]

## Judges

The presiding judge of each consistory court was styled the chancellor, and represented the bishop, who, in his judicial capacity, acted exclusively through the chancellor.[11] The chancellors were episcopally appointed, but acted judicially, and so not necessarily in accordance with the bishop's personal wishes in particular cases.

In 1836 the chancellors of the twenty-six dioceses in England and Wales included eight lay persons (i.e., non-clerical) of whom six were civilians, that is, doctors of civil law and members of Doctors' Commons, and one was a barrister.[12] The remaining eighteen chancellors were clergymen.[13] By 1844, the courts of ten dioceses were presided over by civilians, probably reflecting the better communication at that date between London and the cathedral cities in southern England.[14]

Judicial duties might be delegated to surrogates,[15] who, outside London, were usually clergymen.[16] The chancellor of Lichfield, the Revd J.T. Law, said in a book published in 1831 that, on his appointment, he 'found the business of the court conducted by an experienced principal surrogate,' and that he contemplated leaving the business in his hands; some chancellors did this, holding the office of chancellor as a virtual sinecure.[17] Joseph Phillimore, the chancellor of Worcester, adopted an intermediate practice, which cannot have been wholly satisfactory to those practising in the court, appointing a surrogate but then interfering with his decisions by correspondence. In a letter to the registrar, quoted in the last chapter, he directed amendment of a libel, asking for the letter to be shown to the surrogate.[18] Several entries in the Worcester Act Book record decisions made by the surrogate 'under the chancellor's direction,' and there is a letter from Phillimore written from London pinned to a page in the Act Book, addressed to the registrar, in which Phillimore wrote, 'I am *startled* by the proceedings last court day in the defamation suit,'[19] and directing a particular decision in a testamentary case.

A more common function of surrogates was to perform administrative (rather than strictly judicial) duties – for example, administering oaths to witnesses and others. Large numbers of surrogates were appointed for this purpose in some dioceses. In York over one hundred names are listed in a single entry.[20] In Chester there were eighty-seven in one archdeaconry.[21] In some places, however, there were too few. In a case of 1848, witnesses who had travelled sixteen miles to Gloucester found that they had wasted their journey because no surrogates were available to administer the oath.[22]

By one of the Canons of 1603, the judges were required to be 'learned in the civil and ecclesiastical law ... and reasonably well practised in the course thereof.'[23] Learning in ecclesiastical law and practice, even defenders of the system were compelled to admit, was often lacking. William Ward, the deputy registrar of Chester, in giving evidence to the Ecclesiastical Courts Commission, was asked about the training of the judge, who was, incidentally, Ward's son-in-law. Ward's rather feeble answers were that he was not trained, but had read some books (three were named),[24] and that he read the ecclesiastical court reports. In answer to another question, Ward said, 'I must acknowledge that he has not yet had much practical knowledge.'[25]

Further evidence of the sometimes total absence of judicial knowledge and experience comes from the preface to the book mentioned above, published in 1831 by the Revd J.T. Law. The book is an annotated translation of the first part of Thomas Oughton's *Ordo Judiciorum* (1728), Law's avowed purpose being to improve the public image and reputation of ecclesiastical law.[26] In the course of his preface, he revealed that he was appointed chancellor without any legal knowledge or experience. He found the business of the court conducted, as already mentioned, by an experienced principal surrogate 'and by an admirable deputy registrar.' He could, if he had chosen to do so, have left the business in their hands, but decided to exercise jurisdiction personally:

> And when I did take upon myself the active discharge of the business of the Court, the vast experience and intense application of the deputy registrar caused matters to be so regularly conducted, and so clearly exhibited before me, that I scarcely felt any weight of responsibility, or the necessity for much exertion.

If his purpose was, as he injudiciously said in his preface, to resist 'the reform mania which is now rapidly spreading like the cholera morbus,'[27] his words could scarcely have been worse chosen, for this picture, of a wholly untrained and inexperienced local judge, first contemplating that he might hold office as a sinecure, and then relying so much on his registrar as not to feel the need of exertion, was the very opposite of the prevailing ideal of what was proper to the judicial role. Law made his case worse by adding that he found himself, on the sudden death of the registrar, 'all at once left at the head of the Consistory Court of Lichfield ... without that experience or knowledge which was desirable.' His was not a unique case: even the chancellor of York, who was a barrister, said that 'the great evil is that we have nothing to keep us straight in points of practice.'[28] Consciousness of his deficiencies led Law to read and then to translate and annotate Oughton's work, but the result is a book very difficult to read and understand, with practically no explanation of or commentary on what parts of Oughton's work were obsolete, and what parts were still considered applicable in nineteenth-century practice.

On disposing of a case, the judge usually gave brief oral reasons.[29] From the beginning of the century, regularly published reports appeared of ecclesiastical cases, but reasons in defamation cases were rarely reported, probably because law reporting was centred in London, where there were few cases, and few defamation cases went to the appeal level. Four defamation cases only, decided during the period of this study, were reported.[30] Occasionally reports appear in local newspapers, but these are sporadic, and usually severely abridged. In two or three instances, written reasons of judges are found among the cause papers.

The canon also required judges to be 'well affected and zealously bent to religion.'[31] Religious zeal, it must be said, was even less evident than legal learning. Charles Dickens, who had been a shorthand reporter in Doctors' Commons, depicted the proceedings there as a 'cosey, dosey, old-fashioned, time forgotten, sleepy headed little family party.'[32] Zeal, of any kind, is conspicuous by its absence from this picture. The judges, including those who were clergymen, perceived their role as legal, rather than religious: much of their business concerned proof of wills and administration of intestate estates, and the practitioners were all legal professionals, and not clergymen. It is true that the ecclesiastical courts were linked with the church, but so were many purely secular institutions at this date: any kind of moralistic zeal would be more likely to be found in a magistrate (many of whom, incidentally, were clergy) administering the ordinary criminal law, than in an ecclesiastical court judge. This was one point on which, despite their departure from the canon, the ecclesiastical courts were not criticized in their own time. Neither the reformers nor the conservatives of the nineteenth century thought that the administration of the ecclesiastical courts would be improved by addition of religious zeal.

The remuneration of the judges was derived from fees, and varied widely from one diocese to another. Dr Stephen Lushington, appointed to the London court in 1828, received an annual income of about £300.[33] He continued to supplement his income by practice as an advocate until his appointment to the High Court of Admiralty and the Judicial Committee of the Privy Council, in 1838. Lichfield, it may be noted, the diocese in which the Revd James Law, whose preface was quoted above, was chancellor, was one of the more remunerative, with an annual income of over £900. The chancellor of Chester was also well remunerated, with an income in 1828 of £1,290.[34] Defamation suits were not particularly profitable: the Carlisle judge received 14s. 8d. for a decree in a defamation case, and that only in cases where a decree was actually made.[35]

Several judges actively discouraged defamation suits, and openly said so. William Askwith, the York proctor, wrote that 'cases of defamation are very little encouraged or countenanced by the judge of our court,'[36] and he wrote to the same effect on several other occasions.[37] His view was confirmed by Granville Vernon, the judge, who was quoted in a newspaper to the effect that 'he would gladly be relieved of [defamation cases] altogether'[38] and that 'he hoped he should get rid of such cases as these in this court as they would be much better disposed of by a Justice of the Peace fining the offending party in a penalty of 5s.'[39] He said in his evidence to the Ecclesiastical Courts Commission that it would be very desirable to get rid of the jurisdiction entirely, and that 'I have usually found it necessary to terminate these cases by admonishing the party to refrain from using any such language in future, and leaving the costs to fall upon each party separately.'[40] In his reasons for deciding a case in 1838, he was quoted as saying that he found that the defamatory words were spoken, but that he thought it 'very unneighbourly and improper to put the defendant to so much expense.'[41] No costs were given. This was turning the theory of the jurisdiction on its head, for it was supposed to be the guilty defendant who was unneighbourly. Other judges held similar views. The deputy registrar of Chester (incidentally the diocese with most cases, though not the most in proportion to population) said that 'the court discourages [defamation suits] as much as possible.'[42] The chancellor of Salisbury said that defamation cases 'used to be frequent, but I think I have stopped the worst of them, by giving only a nominal sum for costs.'[43] The Commission recommended that the jurisdiction should be abolished, but that there should be substituted a new minor criminal offence of sexual slander. The report of the Commission, and the evidence published with it, would certainly have been known to the officers of all the ecclesiastical courts. A copy of the report in its original blue paper cover is now in the Borthwick Institute at York, where it was transferred from the archdiocesan registry.[44]

The actual manner in which the judge conducted the proceedings in defamation cases must have varied widely with the personality of the judge and with local practices, and direct evidence is usually wanting. Occasionally, however, evidence comes to light, as in two connected York cases, where the defendants, a father and son, appeared in person. A scuffle had occurred on a highway, in the course of which Jeremiah and Samuel Proctor were proved to have called Ellen Hutchinson 'a nasty trashy Irish whore,' and she was proved to have scratched their faces. Jeremiah and Samuel Proctor were arrested the same evening at Hutchinson's instance (or her husband's), and taken before the magistrates the next morning, where they were acquitted of assault after a summary hearing. Hutchinson then commenced a suit in the ecclesiastical court, and the Proctors (father and son) appeared in person, and asked the judge, 'What ha' ye agane us?' Evidently they expected an expeditious hearing similar to that before the magistrates, but they were disappointed. They were given copies of the libels (statements of claim), and withdrew into a corner of the room to peruse them. They then came forward and said they hoped the judge would hear what they'd got to say for themselves. The judge asked them whether they admitted or denied the charge, to which they replied that 'they'd never said aught of the sort about Mrs Hutchinson as were set down int' paper, and they hoped they might be heard what they'd got to say.' The judge said he had no power to hear them, and they left (according to the newspaper report) muttering about tardy justice.[45] It is evident from this account that the judge was sympathetic and courteous, although he could not do what the Proctors wished. Their appearance may not have been wasted, for it evidently attracted the judge's sympathy: this is the case of 1838 mentioned above in which the judge, though finding that the words were spoken, thought it unneighbourly on the plaintiff's part to have brought the suit, and refused costs.[46]

It is evident from Askwith's correspondence that Vernon (the York chancellor) was in the habit of giving intelligible reasons for his decisions, and Askwith often commented on those reasons in his correspondence with instructing attorneys. In one such case, where Askwith was acting for the plaintiff, a sentence was obtained, but without costs (a quite common disposition at York, as we have seen). Askwith wrote, 'we ran so very near the wind in the proof of the charge that he [Vernon] thought the justice of the case deserved nothing more than admonition – the party having, he considered, sustained no great injury as the defamatory words were at first spoken privately, and not with a view to defame the plaintiff publicly.'[47] The impression given, in this as in other cases, is of a conscientious judge, seeking to reach just results, whose reasons were understood and respected by Askwith even when they were not favourable to his client.

Askwith was not always uncritical. In a case in 1823, where again he was acting for a plaintiff, and again he obtained a sentence but without costs, he wrote, 'The reason assigned for not condemning the defendant in costs was his minority which appears to be an indulgence in favor of youthful depravity.'[48] The defendant in that case was a seventeen-year-old boy, who was proved to have said that the plaintiff was rumoured to entertain men for three shillings and sixpence a night, and to have called out at her in the street, evidently thinking it a joke, 'three and sixpence.'[49] One can sympathize here with the plaintiff, and with Askwith, in losing their costs, and yet see the point of view of the judge, who evidently thought it a case for moderate correction rather than heavy punishment, perhaps considering that costs, even if awarded, would probably not fall on the defendant personally.[50] He was required to perform penance (i.e., to make a formal apology), and did so.[51]

## The Registrar

It will be seen from the preface to Law's *Forms of Ecclesiastical Law*, quoted above, how important was the office of registrar, the duties of which were often performed by a deputy (the office itself being held, in that case, as a sinecure). It appears from what Law says in his preface that, when he first took office, the court was managed to everyone's satisfaction by the deputy registrar, and that it was only the unexpected death of this officer that induced Law for the first time to read a book of ecclesiastical law. The office was usually held by a former proctor who had practised in the court. The registrar kept the records of the court, contacted the proctors when necessary, and was available to the judge at every stage of the proceedings for consultation. When it is added that very often it was the registrar who examined the witnesses, and subsequently advised the judge on the appropriate sentence, it will be seen that, in many courts, his influence must have been enormous. Remuneration was by fees, payable to the registrar on various classes of business.[52] Defamation cases were not remunerative.[53]

## Advocates

There were two branches of the profession of civil law, namely, advocates and proctors, corresponding, theoretically, to barristers and solicitors at common law. However, only in London and York were there any practising advocates, and at York there were only two in 1830, of whom one was ill. Vernon, the York judge, said that in consequence of the shortage of advocates it was his practice to admit barristers as counsel, only requiring the signature of an advocate to the formal papers.[54] In the other dioceses proctors generally argued the cases.[55] In the case of a diocese within reach of London, the employment of an advocate from Doctors' Commons could be contemplated, but this was expensive, and might not even be advisable. In a letter to a Winchester proctor, the instructing attorney wrote:

> I am not on sufficiently good terms with Messrs Minchin [the opposing attorneys] to apply to them for information as to whether they mean to bring Dr Phillimore down to propound before the Chancellor in this matter but I am much inclined to think it is not the case. If however such is their intention it argues most favorably for us, as if they thought their case a good one they would scarcely incur the enormous expense of bringing down Dr Phillimore to support it. My client has not the means of retaining a civilian if such was his wish, but as you are so well acquainted with all the points of his case I think you perfectly competent to undertake his defence, and shall therefore leave him entirely in your hands.[56]

The cost of employing an advocate was considerable. In York and London the advocate had to be retained at the beginning of the case, and had to settle (approve) and sign all the pleadings, as well as actually argue the case if it came to a hearing. Needless to say, charges were made for the advocate (and his clerk) at every step as in the bill of costs transcribed in appendix A, below.[57] In another *uncontested* suit, the costs associated with the advocate amounted to £3, nearly half the total bill.[58]

The restricted number of advocates in York evidently constrained client choice. In a case of 1829, when the advocate first retained fell ill, Askwith suggested engaging a barrister visiting York for the assizes, writing that 'there is no counsel resident in York to whom I think it can be safely entrusted.'[59] In 1833, when the only two practising advocates were William Blanshard and Eustachius Strickland, Askwith wrote to his instructing attorney, 'Mr Blanshard is the plaintiff's advocate and consequently Mr E. Strickland, the only other advocate of the court must be employed for the defendant.'[60] In a later case in the same year, Askwith wrote that he would recommend retaining Blanshard, 'who I should prefer to our other advocate, Mr Strickland.'[61] It again turned out, however, that Blanshard had been retained by the other side, and Askwith had to settle, reluctantly, for Strickland.[62] In this case Strickland amended the defensive allegation over Askwith's objection, Askwith predicting (correctly) that the amended allegation would be rejected by the judge. Eventually the case was settled.[63] Proctors were often as competent as advocates, and more competent than barristers. Vernon said in his evidence to the 1832 Commission that 'the proctor is usually better informed than the ablest barrister in the common law courts.'[64]

Advocates were often employed, in courts of every diocese, to give opinions. Opinions were comparatively rare in defamation cases, because the issues at stake rarely justified the expense. But there are some examples. Two opinions of Dr Lushington's have earlier been quoted in cases in the courts of Peterborough and Winchester. Lushington's opinion was sought also in Norwich[65] and Gloucester cases,[66] and there are several examples of opinions of other advocates in defamation cases.[67] Lushington's reputation was high in this field, as in others. In a Winchester case a London proctor wrote to the Winchester proctor:

I therefore recommend you at once to submit a case for the opinion of Dr Lushington as to the best mode to be adopted and I will retain him to defend your client on your authorizing me so to do. This had better be done immediately for if the promoter should by any accident discover that it is your intention to appeal the cause in all probability he would at once avail himself of the eminent talents of that civilian.[68]

**Proctors**

There were about 230 proctors, over half of them in London, where there was a large testamentary business. York had eight proctors, and most other dioceses had fewer than eight. In the large diocese of Chester there were five proctors, two of them, as we have seen, sons of the registrar and closely related also to the judge.[69] Some proctors combined their practice with that of a common law attorney.[70]

The proctors were specifically required by one of the canons of 1603 not to act in any cause without the express consent of their clients,[71] and most of the written proxies (consents to act) are preserved among the cause papers. The proctor advised the client at all stages of litigation, either directly or through an instructing attorney, drafted the pleadings, interviewed the witnesses (unless this was done by an attorney), appeared on the client's behalf at every session of the court while the case was pending, and (except in London and York) argued any points that arose on the client's behalf.[72] Practice varied, however, on this as on almost every point, and in some dioceses the proctors made written rather than oral argument.[73]

Remuneration was by fees. The most satisfactory kind of case, from the financial point of view, was certainly a prolonged testamentary dispute with costs out of the estate. Defamation cases were not, in general, very remunerative, and the proctors in Doctors' Commons would have been glad to abandon the jurisdiction in exchange for retention of the testamentary work. In some dioceses outside London, however, the defamation cases were more important to the proctors. In Chester the deputy registrar, in answer to the question whether the business was sufficient to afford the proctors a decent maintenance, said 'Yes, pretty tolerable, but if the defamation cases are removed, that would reduce them. I am sorry to say that a considerable part of the emoluments have been derived from them.'[74]

This apologetic note was sounded even by practising proctors. In an Exeter case of 1828, the plaintiff's proctor, addressing argument to the judge, wrote that 'no persons are more disposed to discountenance suits for defamation than the persons who have the honor to represent the plaintiff but [this case is] a base act of foul mouthed calumny.'[75] The apologetic phrase no doubt represents what was known to be the judge's attitude to defamation cases ('a very unpleasant description of suit')[76] as much as the proctor's own opinion. William Askwith, the York proctor, referred to a defamation case as 'trumpery business.'[77]

Askwith did not encourage his clients to prolong litigation. On the contrary, he frequently recommended settlement, in order to avoid 'tedious, expensive, and doubtful litigation.'[78] When acting for defendants he several times advised prompt submission,[79] and frequently advised against prolonging proceedings by filing a defensive allegation.[80] He could not be accused, therefore, of multiplying his fees, but he was not indifferent to the collection of fees that were due to him. In one case, where he had been instructed by an attorney, and there was reason to doubt the client's willingness to pay, he declined to proceed further until his bill was paid.[81] In another case, he wrote that 'in matters of defamation where the parties apply to me personally I make it a rule not to prosecute any such suit for them without having money advanced to meet the expences for after the business is ended let the result be what it may I have too often been left unpaid.'[82] On another occasion he commented drily that 'poverty is no very desirable opponent in matters of defamation.'[83] Where his own client was impecunious, and where he was not instructed by a professional attorney, he did not expect to recover more than had been paid in advance: 'I conclude from the account which Matthew Trattles gives of his poverty that I must suffer the excess beyond the £10 paid.'[84]

Askwith was not indifferent, either, to the potentially oppressive nature of defamation suits. In a case where the defendant had been imprisoned for non-appearance,[85] Askwith, acting for the plaintiff, wrote to his instructing attorney, showing considerable sympathy with his client's opponent: 'The defendant's husband and her proctor have just been with me wishing to know the amount of the whole costs herein, that the poor woman may be released from captivity forthwith.'[86]

## Attorneys

As we have seen in several cases, proctors quite frequently dealt directly with their clients, and this was encouraged in one case by an attorney 'as the least expensive mode.'[87] However, if the client lived in a place distant from the court, it was common for the client to use an intermediary, usually a common law attorney. It is apparent from the references to attorneys in the cause papers that they varied widely in quality and respectability. One witness was asked, with reference to the plaintiff's attorney, 'Is the said Bowdler a regular attorney, or is he a hackney writer or bailiff's follower?'[88] Questions like this show why pressure was mounting that eventually led to strict regulation of this branch of the profession, together with the abandonment of the discredited title of 'attorney' for the more respectable one of 'solicitor.' Informal legal advice was common; a person who wrote letters for and gave advice to his neighbours was known to one witness as 'the counsellor,' and to others as 'the village lawyer' or 'glass of ale lawyer.'[89]

In a York case in 1836 the plaintiff, a Baptist minister, employed an attorney named Hodgson, who improperly altered a compulsory (summons to witness, or subpoena) by adding a witness's name to it, and induced the witness to make what turned out to be a futile trip from Gisburn to York. Askwith, acting for the defendant, wrote, 'The attorney has served her with a false subpoena to get her here today for which he was reprimanded by the court but I am afraid without much effect for he appeared to have an unblushing front.'[90] The defendant's attorneys wrote to Askwith in very disparaging terms about Hodgson, saying that he had acted 'in a blackguard and brutal manner'[91] and that he was 'extreme poor, mostly without certificate and picks up a scandalous living by the dirty and dishonest practice of his profession.'[92] They said that 'we are not a whit surprised at Mr Hodgson's altering the subpoena; it is a practice with him by no means infrequent to serve papers purporting to be copies of summons from the Wapontake [sic] Court and copies of writs from the superior courts when in fact no process has issued.'[93] These accusations look rather incautious from a lawyer; perhaps the writer was conscious of the fact that in a libel action at common law (unlike the ecclesiastical law, as he had just been informed by Askwith) truth was a defence.

Askwith had trouble with one of his own instructing attorneys in a case of 1826. Letters were not answered, appointments not kept, a misleading account of the facts was given, letters were written in discourteous language, there were misunderstandings and unreasonable requests made of Askwith. To add to the difficulties, the attorney was actually imprisoned for debt while the suit was pending, and wrote to Askwith a letter dated from York castle ('I have had the misfortune to be lodged here some time ...') asking for Askwith's bill.[94] Whether it was paid is not recorded. The other attorneys with whom he dealt (there were ten others whose correspondence survives in defamation cases) appear to have given satisfaction.

Two of Askwith's instructing correspondents were not attorneys but clergymen.[95] Both were plainly conversant with legal questions, and wrote in a businesslike manner. Mr Bromby, vicar of Hull, opened the correspondence in one case with this sentiment: 'Your services are required in promoting the ends of justice,'[96] striking a somewhat more lofty note than the opening letter in another case, in jocular professional style, from an attorney: 'These two ladies are determined to give us a little employment.'[97] It appears that clergymen acting in this capacity expected their expenses to be covered, but not fees for their services. In sending his bill in one case (for £11.5.6) to the Revd James Andrew, Askwith wrote that he did not expect to be paid beyond the £10 already received by Mr Andrew, and that Andrew should first deduct 'what you have paid for postage &c.'[98] However, in another case, which was agreed to be arbitrated on terms favourable to Askwith's client, and where his client had expressly told Askwith to be generous in his bill, Askwith allowed the sum of two guineas for Mr Bromby's (the clergyman's) services in addition, apparently, to some deductions for expenses. Bromby was surprised, and wrote to Askwith:

> Of course I did not refuse it. But I should like to know by what right I received any portion of that which belongs to you. In former business of a similar kind I have regarded this deduction which you allowed me to make from your bill as an indication that it was what I ought to receive for my trouble, & have consequently charged no more, except for what I have directly advanced. In future, I find, it will be to my interest to refer the matters of charge to you. As my conscience smites me in this deduction you must satisfy it.

Askwith probably did not lose much by his generosity, for Bromby added that he hoped that Askwith had received safely a barrel of oysters from London.[99]

Instructing attorneys would know more than the proctor about the facts of their cases, and it was Askwith's regular practice to invite comment from the attorney at all stages where it might be useful, particularly in drafting the interrogatories to witnesses, in drafting allegations, and in preparing observations for the use of the advocate at the hearing.[100] Whenever the client lived at a distance from the court, attorneys (or solicitors as they came increasingly to be called) usually made the necessary connecting link with the proctor.

Attorneys were far more numerous than proctors, but it was proctors who played the crucial role. They alone (apart from advocates where these were employed) had right of audience in the ecclesiastical courts and it was they who attended each session of the court, moving the litigation a step forward, or seeing it adjourned or otherwise disposed of as circumstances required.

# 4

# Patterns of Litigation

The numbers of defamation cases varied markedly from one diocese to another during the period under study (see table 2, below). There were 703 cases in the diocese of Chester, and none in Ely. In assessing the figures, account must be taken of the population of each diocese (listed as in 1835). From these it will be seen that the dioceses in which defamation cases were most frequent per person were Carlisle, Llandaff, and Gloucester. These figures have no obvious correlation with the strength of the Church of England (as measured either by church attendance, or by the comparative strength of dissent). This is not surprising: as has been said, those making use of the ecclesiastical courts did not usually perceive their function as closely related to the interests or activities of the church.

So long as costs were regularly awarded to the successful party, a plaintiff could litigate at little risk: there were very few defences, and, provided the necessary two witnesses were forthcoming to prove that the words had been spoken, the plaintiff could expect to win, and the plaintiff's proctor could accept the case in the confident expectation of recovering his costs from the other side. In the nineteenth century several judges, as we have seen, set out deliberately to deter plaintiffs by refusing to award costs to the successful party. This meant that a plaintiff, even with a strong case, had to be prepared to risk her own resources, or those of her husband or friends, and probably to pay her proctor in advance. Since there was no prospect of recovering damages, this was not, financially speaking, a profitable speculation.

Where defamation cases were frequent, that very fact had to some degree a self-sustaining effect. A plaintiff who had been slandered would know at once of the possibility of a suit, or she would immediately be informed of it by her friends and relatives. The mere existence of a legal remedy itself put pressure on the plaintiff and her friends to make use of it. There is considerable evidence, as we shall see, of plaintiffs feeling bound to institute a suit, lest by failing to do so they should appear to acquiesce in the accusation made against them. So long as a defamation suit was perceived as a normal and probable consequence of sexual slander, the perception tended to sustain the litigation, and the litigation in turn sustained the perception. In Carlisle, for example, where there was one case (in the period under study) for every 774 persons, almost everyone must have known – or have known of – someone who had been personally involved in a defamation suit, either as party, witness, or relative of a party or witness.

On the other hand, in districts where suits were very rare, there would be practical obstacles to instituting a suit: few plaintiffs would know of the possibility, or be advised of it; no one would think the worse of the plaintiff for not suing; attorneys, if consulted, would not think naturally of referring the plaintiff to a proctor; proctors who had never handled a defamation suit would be reluctant to undertake the work, and registrars and judges, unfamiliar with the process, and not anxious to encourage it, would be obstructive. In Ely, for example, there were no cases in the consistory court. The two defamation cases from the diocese were transferred to the Arches Court by a procedure called 'Letters of Request.' In one of these cases (which led to a notorious and riotous public performance of penance in a church near Cambridge, to be described in a later chapter)[1] the parties and the witnesses lived very near to Cambridge, where the Ely court sat, and so there was no obvious reason for transferring the case to London. It is probable that the plaintiff (a clergyman's wife) found it impossible to institute the suit in the Ely court, and was told that, if she insisted, her only course was to transfer it to London.[2] The Letters of Request in the other case from Ely recite that the transfer 'will be of advantage to the parties on both sides for the better assistance they can obtain of advocates and proctors in the ... Arches Court of Canterbury.'[3] This reason has nothing to do with the particular case, and suggests that the Ely court refused as a matter of general practice to entertain defamation cases.

Defamation suits declined after 1835, though not uniformly in all dioceses, as is shown in table 3, below. It is likely that the report of the Ecclesiastical Courts Commission, of 1832, was influential in this respect. The report included many disparaging remarks by judges and other officers of the courts about defamation suits, and indicated an almost unanimous opinion in the profession that they should be abolished, and that they were responsible for bringing the whole of ecclesiastical law into disrepute: 'the proceedings in these suits have occasioned much odium to the ecclesiastical jurisdiction.'[4] Publication of the report made these opinions widely known: it was practically an appeal to ecclesiastical judges and lawyers to do all they could to discourage defamation suits. It is not surprising that the report, together with the underlying reasons that supported its conclusions, had effect. The whole profession of ecclesiastical law was under siege at this time and there must have been strong pressure on proctors from judges, registrars, and fellow proctors not to encourage defamation suits, which then appeared to be the least defensible part of the business of the ecclesiastical courts, and of little financial value compared with probate.

The attitude of the judge was crucial: if he were known to be hostile to defamation suits, proctors could be effectively deterred from instituting them. In a draft statement defending his own conduct and that of the court in the Llandaff case of Louisa Roberts against Charlotte Jones, Huckwell, Roberts's proctor, explained that her friends had forwarded to the judge a certificate of her good character, 'fearing the court would not entertain the Cause (it being a direction from the judge to the proctors not to take up common defamation causes).'[5] A direction of this sort would be bound to have a dramatic impact on rates of litigation, considering the very small number of proctors in most dioceses and their need to maintain the judge's good opinion. Though there is no direct evidence of such express orders in other dioceses, it is probable that judges let their views be known to the proctors. Askwith wrote, of York, 'causes of defamation are very little encouraged or countenanced by the judge of our court.'[6] The judges could not absolutely prohibit defamation cases, but the varying strength of their hostility to them goes far to explain the varying numbers of cases in the different dioceses.

The consequence of such a variation was that the law effectively differed from one diocese to another, a feature that was disagreeable to the centralizing tendencies of prevailing legal opinion.[7] Jurisdiction depended on the residence of the defendant, the underlying concept being that the defendant ought to be corrected by the ecclesiastical authority to which he owed obedience. This concept of ecclesiastical obedience, obsolete in the nineteenth century, made the variation among dioceses doubly anomalous, because the same words spoken in the same place by two persons might have different legal effect if one happened to reside across a diocesan boundary.

It might be supposed that defamation suits would be most common in small communities, but the records reveal more urban cases than might be expected on the basis of population. In Norwich, for example, the three largest towns, with about 16 per cent of the population, accounted for 37 per cent of the defamation cases. (See table 5, below.)[8] Dr Morris, in her study of defamation cases in the diocese of Bath and Wells, also found that litigation occurred proportionately more often in places with populations over two thousand.[9] It is probable that in small villages most disputes were settled locally, perhaps by clergymen, though not acting as officers of the court (most were not),[10] and that the lack of ready access to legal advice discouraged litigation.

Litigation was predominantly among neighbours. In Norwich, for example, of 121 cases where the residence of both parties is given, 106 (88 per cent) involved parties of the same town or parish, and a further 9 (7 per cent) parties resident in parishes separated by less than five miles.[11]

In matters of procedure there were considerable variations among the dioceses. In a brawling case in 1828 in the Arches Court, Sir John Nicholl said:

> it is well known that the different dioceses have their peculiar usages, and those usages, in respect to the exercise of jurisdiction, constitute pretty much the law in the particular case, unless they be contrary to the general policy of the law, and to justice.[12]

An element of local flexibility, though not quite of autonomy, was a long-established feature of ecclesiastical law.[13]

Terminology varied markedly. The plaintiff, generally so called in this study for the sake of convenience, was known in various dioceses as the complainant, promoter, promotrix, promovent, promotent, impugnant, party agent, and actor. The defendant was variously called the respondent, party impugn, party promote, party promoted, and (confusingly) in Bangor, impugnant. The penance, or formal apology required of the losing defendant, was variously called a declaration, recantation, retraction, and reclamation. The performance of the penance might occur in the vestry room of the church, in the clergyman's house, or in open court. In some dioceses it was common to dispense with the penance and substitute an admonition. The manner in which the records were kept, and the names given to the record books, also varied. So did the rules governing various aspects of procedure, such as the time allowed for filing the libel (statement of claim), and how promptly contempt of court was punished by imprisonment.

Nevertheless, except in the Isle of Man, the general pattern of litigation was similar everywhere. A suit commenced with a citation (summons). Normally this was served personally, but if the defendant could not be found, a citation 'by ways and means' (substituted service) was issued, which could be served by nailing a copy on the door of the defendant's last known address,[14] or on the church door.[15] Service of citations was not always without incident: in one case the defendant put the citation into the fire; when the apparitor (court officer) returned three days later, she said 'she perfectly understood their contents but was not going to Norwich for any one and that as many citations as might be sent she would burn them all.'[16] A significavit (order for imprisonment) was issued.[17] Apparitors were not used in every diocese. In York, for example, Askwith wrote to his instructing attorney, 'Your clerk or any other indifferent person may serve the [citation].'[18]

The citation required the defendant to appear, personally or by a proctor. If the defendant conducted the litigation in person, as sometimes happened, he was ordered to appear on each successive court day while the case was pending.[19] The plaintiff filed a libel (statement of claim), and the defendant was called upon to give an affirmative or negative issue, i.e., to confess the charge or to dispute the case. This was an important point of decision for the defendant, and many cases ended here. Prompt submission meant that the defendant would be required to pay a sum of costs, varying from about £3 to £6, and to perform penance. To give an affirmative issue was to pay a premium (the costs, and inconvenience of the penance) to insure against the risk of much larger costs if the case were disputed and lost, and quite likely the same even if it were disputed and won, for cases were often dismissed without costs. The London court encouraged an affirmative issue by awarding a small conventional sum only (called style of costs) of three guineas – later reduced to £2 – in all such cases. This practice certainly had effect: 32 of a total of 103 cases were terminated by affirmative issue, a far higher proportion than in other dioceses.[20] Insurance is much more attractive if the premium is certain: a known figure of £2 was superior in this respect to 'taxed costs.'

All courts had procedures for dismissing cases for want of prosecution, but several courts had special rules requiring the libel in a defamation case to be filed promptly. In several dioceses the plaintiff's proctor had to be ready with the libel on the very day of the return of the citation.[21] Other courts were a little more flexible. In Norwich the rule was that the proctor paid a money penalty if not ready the first court day (presumably after the return of the citation), and the cause was dismissed if he was not ready on the second court day. Causes other than defamation were allowed an additional court day.[22] In York, the libel had to be filed on the next court day after the return of the citation.[23]

The dilemma faced by the defendant on the giving in of the libel can be appreciated by considering the advice given by Askwith to his client at this stage of a case. He wrote (to the attorney):

> The effect of admitting the words charged in the libel will put an end to the suit and oblige your client to perform the usual penance, and also to pay taxed costs ... Upon the whole as your client has instructed you to settle the suit and you seem to apprehend that witnesses will be found to swear to the words I think if you cannot settle with the plaintiff's attorney on or before the 23d inst, the most prudent course to be pursued, and the least expensive would be to confess the words, per-

form penance & pay taxed costs. In case we should offer any defence & ultimately fail the expences would be ten times greater than by putting an end to the
matter by an affirmative issue; even causing the plaintiff merely to prove the
words by witnesses it would more than double the present costs.[24]

These are weighty considerations in favour of submission, especially when
combined with a warning (as was given in this case) that truth was no defence
and that the defence that the words were not spoken was rarely successful. The
great majority of all cases were settled, and it may be deduced that when settlement occurred at this stage it was on terms that the defendant paid a large
part of the plaintiff's estimated taxed costs, together probably with making
some kind of apology.[25] In Carlisle, where defamation cases were most frequent by population, it is often recorded that 'the cause was dismissed, no
proctor having appeared for the defendant,'[26] signifying that the defendant had
settled on terms satisfactory to the plaintiff's proctor.

There must have been many defendants who settled on such terms while
privately denying that the words had been spoken, and there is direct evidence
of this in several cases. In a Llandaff case a letter was written to a proctor
objecting, on behalf of a defendant, to the pressure put on him to settle 'while
he denies that he said anything which would subject him to punishment.'[27] In
a Salisbury case of 1827, a letter to the registrar on behalf of a defendant said
that he denied defaming the plaintiff (though mentioning also, somewhat
inconsistently, that the defendant was intoxicated and was provoked).[28] The
defendant gave an affirmative issue, and was required eventually to pay costs
of £2 only, after another letter in his support from a clergyman.[29] Occasionally
the judge facilitated a settlement between the parties in the courtroom.[30]

If a negative issue was given, the next step was for the plaintiff to prove her
case by witnesses; at least two were required. The witnesses were examined in
private, and could be required to answer interrogatories (written questions)
prepared by the defence. The defendant was also entitled to give in a defensive
allegation (statement of defence), which then had also to be proved by at least
two witnesses, and which opened the door to a further allegation on the plaintiff's side, supported by further witnesses. An important tactical question for
the defence was whether to rely on the interrogatories, or to give in a defensive
allegation. This crucial decision had to be made in ignorance of what the
plaintiff's witnesses had sworn. Askwith wrote, on this point,

Before copies of the examinations in chief of Wharton's witnesses or their cross-
examinations can be obtained we must plead & examine our witnesses in defence;
hence you will perceive the difficulty of advising correctly in such a case.[31]

If the crucial facts could be elicited by interrogatories this was the superior strategy, because interrogatories were cheaper than an allegation, they did not give the plaintiff an opportunity of filing a further allegation, and evidence damaging to the plaintiff was most effective from the mouths of the plaintiff's own witnesses, but of course all this depended on the witnesses' knowing the relevant facts and being honest enough to disclose them. In one case Askwith wrote, 'If the answers are given fairly and in truth to the interrogatories there can be no need for Gypson [the defendant] to be at the expense of pleading any thing in defence.'[32] Gypson, however, insisted on a defensive allegation, which Askwith drafted, but wrote that it 'must be very doubtful as to any good it will do, equivalent to the risk of the certain expense attending it.'[33] The draft allegation was amended on counsel's advice, and Askwith again advised that it should be withdrawn as 'best for the interest of Gypson in every point of view.'[34] But the attorney replied that 'this defendant will never believe he has had justice done him unless he has his witnesses examined and therefore the allegation must be supported.'[35] The allegation was rejected in part by the judge, as Askwith had predicted, and the case was eventually compromised. In another case Askwith went so far as to say 'it would be in vain attempting to plead in contradiction to an action for defamatory words; everything will I trust be brought out by the interrogatories.'[36]

A contested case, even with diligence on both sides, could not be disposed of in less than about six months,[37] and many cases took a year, or even longer, in marked contrast to a minor criminal case, which might be disposed of by the magistrates on the morning after the alleged offence. In a York case of 1823, Askwith's client (the plaintiff) complained of delay. The citation had been returned on 12 June 1823. On 6 January 1824, Askwith explained that the delay was not his fault:

On the 12th of December last the court admitted Miss Foster's libel and assigned Stubbing's proctor to give a negative or an affirmative issue thereto on the 5th of February next, after which day, in case of a negative issue being given, arrangements must be made for examining the plaintiff's witnesses, and as I understood from Miss Foster when here that none of her witnesses would attend without being compelled, you will please to obtain and let me have the names and proper descriptions of all the persons that are to be produced for examination, that compulsories may be issued against them to enforce their attendance when required. Miss Foster complained to me of the delay herein, and I am sorry to say the little that has been done since she made such complaint is no way calculated to remove her uneasiness. But you may safely assure her it is 'the law's delay' not mine.[38]

The case was finally disposed of on 14 October 1824.[39] The court had rules to prevent undue delay, and they were taken seriously by the proctors. In a York case Askwith wrote to his instructing attorneys, who had to decide whether to file a defensive allegation, 'Pray let me have an answer herein yea or nay by return of post for after Thursday next we shall not be allowed to file any pleading on behalf of the defendant.'[40]

The system of entering the names of the cases in the court books helped to control delay. In most courts the names of pending cases with the names of the responsible proctors were entered in advance of each session into the Act Book, with space left to record the steps taken at the session. An example is transcribed in appendix A, below. The book was not only a record of the proceedings, but also functioned as an assignation (appointment) book recording the proctors' responsibilities. The system was cumbersome and could only work with a comparatively small number of cases, but it had the merit of reminding the judge as well as the proctors at each session of what cases were pending. The entry of the proctors' names in the book was an order of the court requiring them to appear and to do something: they had to take a step forward in the case, or expressly to seek an adjournment, or to announce its termination.

After publication of the depositions, the opposite party was permitted to file what was called an exceptive allegation, in order to prove that the witnesses had given false evidence. Exceptive allegations were rare in defamation cases, and the courts were generally reluctant to admit them because of the very real danger of being sidetracked by collateral issues. For example, a witness might say in answer to an interrogatory that he had not committed a certain alleged theft, and the opposite party might attempt to establish that in fact he had done so. In two connected cases a witness was accused of the theft of, curiously enough, half a hundred red herrings. A constable was produced as a witness on the exceptive allegation, together with the owner of the herrings, to prove the complaint, and the discovery of the herrings at the witness's house.[41] A further exceptive allegation was admissible, because it was open to the opposite side to impeach the credit of the witnesses on the first exceptive allegation, and there are some examples of this.[42] Inquiries into such collateral questions could stray far from the actual subject matter of the suit.[43] No absolute rule was possible, however, excluding exceptive allegations, because all judges could imagine some cases, or could remember some, where impeachment of a witness's credit was legitimate and necessary.[44]

A dramatic instance of the effect of successive exceptive allegations occurred in a London case of 1831, which ended in death and disaster for the plaintiff and her husband. The defendant had asserted that Thomas Rose, the porter at Symonds Inn (a place of residential accommodation for lawyers),[45] was not legally married to the woman he lived with, Catherine. Catherine Rose brought a suit, in the course of which she produced a witness (Sarah Lewis, her aunt) to swear that she (Lewis) had been present at the marriage of Thomas and Catherine on a certain day before they moved to the inn. The defendant excepted to the evidence of Sarah Lewis, producing witnesses to show that Lewis had not been there, and the plaintiff gave in a counter-allegation, supported by a witness calling himself Harry Child, who swore that he had also been present at the ceremony and had seen Lewis. The defendant then brought in another exceptive allegation, proving that the witness calling himself Child, whose real name was Throp, had not in fact been present at the ceremony. Throp was arrested, and so was Thomas Rose on a criminal charge of procuring false evidence, and both were committed in custody for trial at the Old Bailey. The cause papers include a petition from Catherine Rose, whose proctor had declined to act further for her, asking for a postponement of the defamation case until after her husband's trial, but shortly afterwards she died. The cause of death is not known, but she was only twenty-six.[46]

Multiple suits and counter-suits often arose out of connected events. In a Chester case a quarrel occurred in the street between Robert Latham and his sister Margaret, on the one hand, and Joseph Meakin and his wife, Charlotte, on the other, in the course of which Charlotte and Joseph Meakin were both said to have called Margaret Latham a whore, and Robert Latham was said to have replied, addressing Joseph Meakin, 'Damn thee, I have not done as thou hast done – thou'st married thy wife out of a pusling school [bawdy house] in London.' Three suits were instituted.[47] In Norwich in 1841, four suits arose from a single conversation.[48] Often counter-suits arose from a quarrel between two women, in which each was alleged to have defamed the other,[49] but sometimes the counter-suit was against the husband,[50] or against another relative, as in Meakin v. Latham,[51] or against a friend of the original plaintiff, or by a relative or friend of the original defendant.[52] Occasionally the counter-claimant was a man.[53] Sometimes the evidence for the counter-suit actually arose out of discussion of the original suit; in one case the plaintiff in the original suit was incautious enough to say of her opponent, 'I have put the bloody whore in Llandaff court' – at any rate this was the evidence of a witness against her in the counter-suit.[54]

Ecclesiastical procedure made provision for the parties to be compelled to answer allegations on their personal oath; this applied to both parties, so the defendant could be required to answer the libel, and the plaintiff could be required to answer a defensive allegation. These personal answers were rare in defamation cases, because a party could not be obliged to answer incriminating questions. A London proctor wrote, 'In cases of this description the personal answers of the party on oath are not required, it being a criminal prosecution.'[55] Nevertheless, there are some examples, but they show that answers were rarely of any use to the party demanding them, because the party required to answer either answered in terms favourable to his or her own case,[56] being handed a free opportunity to give evidence in her or his own behalf (otherwise impossible) – and, moreover, evidence untested by interrogatories[57] – or else returned purely formal answers, carefully worded to avoid contempt.[58]

For a period of about twelve years following 1821, Gloucester, in what appears to be a unique venture, adopted a summary procedure in defamation cases, receiving oral evidence, contrary to the general practice of other dioceses. Written depositions were resumed in 1834, and oral evidence was not again received until authorized by statute in 1854.[59] The reason for adopting the summary procedure was presumably the desire to save time and expense. The reason for resumption of the general practice is not recorded: perhaps the use of the summary procedure was for some time consented to by the proctors, but then consent was withdrawn.[60] There were evidently practical problems in attempting to marry summary and plenary procedures in a contested case of any complexity. For example, the libel, when given orally, was transcribed word for word into the Act Book,[61] presumably because the defendant had the right to know the case against him, and a detail such as the date at which the words were alleged to have been spoken was often crucial. This might have saved some time and expense to the parties, but not to the officers of the court.

Most cases (about two-thirds) were settled without production of witnesses, probably on terms favourable to the plaintiff – or at least on terms favourable to the plaintiff's proctor. In the remaining approximately one-third of cases where witnesses were produced, sentence was usually in favour of the plaintiff. In Norwich, for example, of forty-three cases in which witnesses were produced, the plaintiff obtained a sentence in thirty-two, and the defendant in seven. Figures showing the disposition of cases at various stages of litigation in the diocese of Norwich are given in table 6, below.

An appeal lay from the consistory court to the Arches Court of Canterbury or to the Chancery Court of York (in the case of the northern province), and from those courts to the High Court of Delegates or (after 1833) to the Judicial Committee of the Privy Council. Appeals were rare in defamation cases, for the reason that large sums of money (as in testamentary cases) or vital interests of status (as in matrimonial cases) were not at stake. Litigation, however, can gather a momentum of its own: costs were at stake, and submission might involve loss of reputation as well as loss of face. The notorious case of Russell

v. Bentham in 1812 went to the High Court of Delegates at a cost to each side of over £600.[62] In the period under study there were nine appeals to the Arches Court, of which two were allowed, three dismissed, three abandoned, and one abated by a party's death.[63] There was one appeal only in the northern province, from a peculiar court to the York Chancery Court, on a point of costs, which was allowed.[64] One case only went to the High Court of Delegates,[65] and two to the Judicial Committee of the Privy Council.[66]

Enforcement of the orders of the court was by imprisonment for contempt. Defendants were imprisoned for non-appearance, and for refusal to perform penance; either party (but it was usually the defendant) might be imprisoned for refusal to obey an order to pay costs; witnesses could be imprisoned for refusal to testify. It has sometimes been supposed that the ecclesiastical courts had no power to imprison, but only to excommunicate or admonish. Suppositions like this owe their origin to differences between theoretical and practical powers and to several potentially misleading features of procedure and nomenclature. In the nineteenth century the position was this: the courts did not (except in the Isle of Man) imprison as *punishment* for an ecclesiastical offence, but they had effective power to imprison for contempt (refusal to obey court orders). Before 1813, an order for imprisonment had to be preceded by excommunication, but a statute of that year[67] did away with the necessity of prior excommunication.[68] Although the words 'monish' and 'monition' were sometimes used, like 'admonish,' to refer to informal warnings, 'monition' was also the name of a formal written peremptory order of the court.[69] The process of imprisonment required a 'significavit,' a document issued by the ecclesiastical court to the Court of Chancery in London certifying that the person named 'hath been duly pronounced guilty of manifest contumacy and contempt of the law and jurisdiction ecclesiastical.'[70] The actual warrant for the arrest was issued by the Cursitors' Office of the Court of Chancery, but this was an administrative, not a judicial act, and followed as of course upon the filing of the significavit.[71] Thus it is true only in a technical sense to say that the ecclesiastical courts lacked power to imprison. In practice they had effective power to enforce their orders by imprisonment, much as when Chaucer had written 450 years before:

Of cursing [excommunication] oghte ech gilty man him drede [to fear] ...
And also war him [beware] of a significavit.[72]

Imprisonment was not infrequent: 68 persons were imprisoned between 1827 and 1829 pursuant to orders of the ecclesiastical courts, 34 in defamation cases.[73] The numbers of significavits preserved in the Public Record Office suggest that imprisonment occurred in about 12 defamation cases a year between 1815 and 1839.[74] In the diocese of York, significavits were issued in 15 per cent of all defamation cases (38 of 241), during the period 1815–55.

Habeas corpus was available to test the legality of the imprisonment, and it is probable that in some cases hostility to the defamation jurisdiction increased the willingness of the common law court to discern a technical deficiency in the ecclesiastical court process.[75] This possibility was recognized in an advocate's opinion on the validity of a significavit for non-payment of costs in the diocese of Winchester. Noting that the monition had failed to state to whom the costs were to be paid,[76] he advised: 'I think that a Significavit issued in the above form (at least without reference to the Monitions) will be binding," but he added cautiously, 'if it is examined by a Court of Common Law in connexion with the Monitions, I cannot answer for the result. On the whole however it may be ventured, in my opinion.' It is rather extraordinary that the monition, full as it was of cumbersome verbiage and unnecessary repetitions, still managed to omit something crucial. The documents are transcribed in appendix A.

The advocate's last sentence illustrates the mixture of wariness and respect with which the ecclesiastical courts viewed the common law, as well as the unpredictability of its interventions. Evidently the advocate's opinion was sound in this case, at least from the plaintiff's perspective, for a significavit was issued and the defendant spent three months in prison.[77] Habeas corpus proceedings must have been beyond the means of many litigants, and even when proceedings were brought, there was certainly no guarantee that the common law court would interfere. In a Peterborough case, the defendant defied the ecclesiastical court, was imprisoned, applied unsuccessfully for a habeas corpus, and then submitted to the ecclesiastical court.[78]

In some dioceses it was the practice for the court to require a warning letter to be sent to the defendant before issuing a significavit,[79] but this was not required by law and it was not the general practice. In the Winchester case of the defective monitions, the advocate expressed the opinion that the immediate issue of the significavit had been 'somewhat hasty,' but valid.[80] In a Chester case of 1833, a woman was served with a citation, but refused to accept a copy. She was not aware of any proceedings until she was informed that a writ was in the hands of the sheriff to take her to jail. By the assistance of her friends she paid the amount of the proctor's demand (£8.5.5), and petitioned the court to take it into account in awarding costs. She alleged that she had been provoked, but confessed the defamation, and was ordered to pay further costs of £3.[81] In other dioceses, rules of practice restrained the over-hasty issue of significavits. In a York case where the defendant had not appeared,

Askwith wrote that 'the business was obliged to be continued [adjourned] to the 28th of July [the next court day] the Court never decreeing a party contumacious on the return of the original process.'[82] In a Bristol case a decree for a significavit was reversed on proof that the defendant had come to the court in response to the citation but 'went away through ignorance before she was called.'[83]

Some defendants submitted without going to prison, as in the Chester case mentioned above, and some submitted within a short period afterwards, appearing in the court in custody,[84] or in the diocese of Norwich at a session of the court actually held in Norwich Castle (the prison).[85] Others spent long periods in prison. Nine persons were imprisoned in defamation cases by the Chester court between 1827 and 1829, of whom one died in custody and another spent six months in prison, the average length of imprisonment being one hundred days. There are no complete records of time spent in prison because the cases usually dropped out of the ecclesiastical court records on the issue of the significavit, but it is known that long periods of imprisonment sometimes occurred. In a case in the diocese of London, a man who refused to perform penance on the ground that what he had said was true spent a year in prison.[86] In a York case, a woman was signified in contempt in February 1822,[87] and was still in custody in March 1824.[88] In a late York case near the end of the court's jurisdiction, William Jackson was imprisoned for non-appearance in February 1853. The plaintiff's proctor had given up practice, and apparently everyone had forgotten about Jackson until, in October 1854, another proctor found out about the case and wrote a letter to the plaintiff's attorney in Scarborough asking what his intentions were. No reply was received, and the proctor addressed the court on Jackson's behalf, saying that he was ready to obey the orders of the court, but had no money to pay the costs. A proctor then appeared for the plaintiff[89] and gave in a Bill of Costs, which the registrar taxed at £11.12.0. The unfortunate Jackson was still in prison in January 1855.[90] These cases were oppressive. It was the lengthy imprisonment of Charlotte Jones that led to the abolition of the defamation jurisdiction in the same year (1855).

In an extraordinary case in Somerset in 1843, Jane Board sued Mary Hill, who brought a counter-suit against Jane Board's husband, Frederick. Both were imprisoned, one for non-payment of costs after sentence, and the other for non-appearance. After they had been in prison 'upward of seven months' they addressed a joint petition to the court for their release, which was granted.[91] Relief was available to some defendants under the Insolvent Debtors Act,[92] and occasionally it is recorded that persons had been released under this statute.[93] Hill and Board made reference to it in their petition, saying that, whereas other debtors had been relieved, the Act did not apply to them, perhaps because Hill was a married woman and Board was imprisoned for non-appearance, not simply for debt.

In the Isle of Man, a sentence bound not only the defendant but third parties also, and apparently for an indefinite period. The sentence included a provision that 'neither [the defendant] nor any other person should renew this slander under penalty of fine and imprisonment,' and the sentence could be enforced against anyone who revived the slander.[94] Since procedure was in any event informal, it would no doubt have been said, in defence of the process, that the defendant was no worse off faced with a petition to enforce a former sentence than he would have been with a fresh petition to punish the renewed slander directly.

One of the most striking features of the defamation jurisdiction, as we saw earlier, is the variation in numbers of cases from diocese to diocese. The primary explanation is more likely to be institutional than social. It is not likely that the frequency of defamation, or its social effects, varied with the crossing of a diocesan boundary. But it is very probable that the indifference and in some dioceses the outright hostility of the court officers operated as a deterrent to litigants.

# 5

# Evidence

## Oral Evidence

One of the principal criticisms of the ecclesiastical courts was that they did not receive oral evidence. With the exception of Gloucester during the twelve-year period mentioned,[1] and the Isle of Man, evidence in defamation cases took the form of written depositions. Only at the very end of the court's jurisdiction was a statute enacted that permitted the use of oral evidence, and some use was made of this in 1854 and 1855.[2]

There were certain points to be made in favour of the system of written depositions. It was convenient for witnesses, who could make an appointment with the examiner at a mutually suitable time, and did not have to wait, perhaps away from home, while the trial proceeded.[3] Where the witness could not travel, evidence might be taken by commission at any convenient place.[4] Since witnesses did not have to be accommodated during the trial, some observers thought that the ecclesiastical procedure was cheaper, but against this consideration had to be set the actual cost of preparing and copying the depositions. More substantively it was argued that, particularly on delicate matters of matrimonial law, a witness was less frightened[5] and embarrassed,[6] and more likely to reveal the truth, when examined in private. In one matrimonial case a witness was told, 'You need not be at all afraid, for you will not have to appear personally in court, but your evidence will all be taken down in writing in a private room.'[7] Cross-examination in open court, it was said, was more a test of the advocate's skill than of the reliability of the witness:[8] a sensitive and experienced examiner could discover the truth in private more effectively than a common law advocate in the adversarial atmosphere of the courtroom. It was also said that the ecclesiastical courts, not having power to commit for contempt in the face of the court, would find it difficult to maintain order and decorum in hearing oral evidence.[9]

But the arguments against the system of written depositions were over-whelming, and eventually they prevailed. Too much depended on the attitude and ability of the examiner, which varied greatly. Some examiners merely read the allegation or interrogatories to the witness, but others explained and rephrased them,[10] and put questions of their own in order to probe for the truth.[11] Some deliberately refrained from reading the libel or allegation, for fear of leading the witness;[12] others considered that there was little point in worrying about leading, since the witness would usually have come directly from the proctor's office, and would have heard the libel or allegation read there.[13] The difference between sympathetic and unsympathetic questions could obviously affect the answers,[14] and since neither the judge[15] nor the proctors were present at the examination, there was no effective way of assess-ing the tone in which the questions were asked and answered, or the de-meanour of the witness. Evidence was often taken down in the third person, so that the precise words of the witness were not recorded, and it was therefore difficult to tell, in cases of a non-answer ('and further to this article the witness knoweth not to depose'), whether, if untrue, it was a matter of contempt (for refusal to answer) or perjury (for giving false evidence). Perhaps most impor-tant, not all the words could be recorded: hesitations, rephrasings, repetitions, questions asked by the witness, introductory speech, and intermediate conver-sation were all omitted, so that the end result was not so much the witness's written evidence as a partial record of an oral examination.

The system of written interrogatories was a very inferior mode of cross-examination, because all the questions had to be framed in advance, in igno-rance of what evidence the witness was to give in chief, and in ignorance of answers to previous questions.[16] Daunting complexities could arise, as the drafters attempted to take account of possible variant answers by posing con-ditional questions, such as

> If the witness states her knowledge or belief that the Ministrant did allude to the
> report interrogate, let her be further required to state at whose house and in whose
> presence the ministrant so alluded to the said report.[17]

The effectiveness of interrogatories depended entirely on the examiner, who might or might not press the witnesses for pertinent answers. Thus Askwith complained in one case, 'The witnesses ... by some means have evaded giving Answers to the Interrogatories in some material points ... When they are speaking of the utterance of the defamatory words they swear point blank; but when they are pushed as to the particulars they answer they know not or they cannot say.'[18]

There was a real danger of gross error, because the examiner might not know the details of the case, and there was no one present to set him right. In the evidence to the Ecclesiastical Courts Commission of 1832 the case was mentioned of a witness who had deposed in a testamentary case to the execution of entirely the wrong codicil.[19] In another testamentary case in Norwich, the witness was deaf, and misunderstood the deposition when read over to him, only realizing that it was erroneous in crucial respects when he happened to see a copy of it three months later, after publication.[20] Another weakness was that general denials were often permitted of specific allegations. For example, in a Chester case the whole of the witness's answers to quite specific interrogatories was, 'She saith that referring to what she has deposed she can only further answer & depose in the negative to each and every matter interrogated.'[21] In another case in the same diocese a witness's full answer was 'that she cannot depose as to any matter or thing thereby interrogated.'[22] Proctors framing interrogatories attempted to guard against this sort of answer by including such directions as 'let the witness be most strictly interrogated as to the above facts,' or 'the Registrar is respectfully requested to obtain a clear and distinct answer to the latter part of these interrogatories, as the answers thereto may be the subject of a criminal proceeding hereafter.'[23] The inclusion of such requests itself indicates that the proctor had no effective control over what occurred in the examiner's office. Bentham criticized the ecclesiastical court procedure on the more general ground that the public interest was better served by publicity than by secrecy.[24]

## Preparation

It was necessary for the plaintiff to produce two witnesses who had heard the defamatory words, and there is evidence, particularly among middle-class plaintiffs, of the plaintiff's friends forming a kind of small committee and formally demanding an interview with the defendant. In Marsh v. Travers (Norwich, 1846), Lady Travers had, in private conversation, mentioned a rumour then current to the effect that Elizabeth Marsh had lived for several years in adultery with a man she later married. Marsh's husband, her father, and her brother-in-law called on Lady Travers, demanding that she should 'give up her author' (i.e., reveal the source of her information). She was rash enough to agree to an interview, in the course of which she supplied the necessary evidence for the suit.[25] This kind of semi-formal inquiry was evidently quite familiar in higher social circles. In another Norwich case, the plaintiff was a surgeon who complained of an allegation that he had seduced one of his women servants. He made a formal call on the defendant, accompanied by two friends, one of them a Congregational minister, demanding an apology, and that the defendant should give up his authority. Everyone involved was conscious of a third motive: to collect the evidence necessary for a suit in the ecclesiastical court. The defendant thought so, for he said, 'I know what you mean; you have brought my friend Mr Taylor [the minister] and Mr Brook, and if I say anything you intend to have your remedy at law. Time will shew, for we understand these little matters.'[26] Not well enough, however, for he had already said too much, and sentence was given on the evidence of Taylor and Brook.[27]

In a Hereford case, the suit was against a clergyman for defaming one of his women parishioners. The plaintiff's friend (incidentally also the man with whom she was accused of committing adultery) asked the parish clerk to join him in a call upon the clergyman, but the clerk, not wishing to be compelled to testify against his clergyman, was wily enough – or well enough advised (his wife begged him not to go) – to refuse, though he did stand at a distance and heard part of the conversation. He gave in an affidavit, but was not produced as a witness for the plaintiff.[28]

Before being produced for examination, a witness would be informally examined by the plaintiff's attorney (if there was one) and by her proctor. It was Askwith's habit to ask for the witnesses to be sent to his office before their examination,[29] and, though 'drilling' or 'coaching' was improper, it was evidently considered acceptable for the proctor to prepare the witnesses to some extent for their examination, and to learn what they proposed to say. A Gloucester bill of costs includes the items 'Journey ... 4 miles to see witnesses' and 'Attending witnesses previous to being sworn and examined,'[30] and in some dioceses it was customary to speak of 'pre-examining' witnesses.[31] In a York case, when witnesses came to see Askwith before their examination, he concluded that what they had to say would not be helpful, and he sent them home without producing them.[32] Sometimes he, or the attorney, suggested that the plaintiff should accompany the witnesses when they came to be examined, and no doubt this would often have the effect of reminding them of what was expected.[33]

Since neither the parties nor their proctors were allowed to be present during the examination, they did not learn precisely what the evidence was until publication (after all the evidence on both sides had been taken – save exceptive allegations).[34] Witnesses sometimes failed to fulfil expectations: in one such case Askwith wrote to the attorney that the evidence turned out to be 'not quite so strong as your instructions for the libel represented.' Sentence was nevertheless obtained, but without costs; this is the case where Askwith said that 'we ran near the wind' on the question of proof.[35]

In Foster v. Stubbing,[36] in which a seventeen-year-old boy had called out at Mary Foster in the street, 'three and sixpence,' Askwith was very nervous about the quality of the proof. He found that one witness contradicted himself in successive interviews, and wrote, 'there is every thing to fear for the result,'[37] even going so far as to suggest that Mary Foster should find herself another proctor.[38] The delicate distinction between preparation and coaching of a witness was evidently not quite clear to Foster, who had, Askwith wrote, 'hinted very strongly her dissatisfaction because I did not *make* her witnesses swear what she expected and wished them to do.' Askwith added, to his correspondent Mr Bromby, 'To you I trust no comment is needful upon such an insinuation.'[39]

Witnesses were often reluctant to give evidence, declaring that 'they never would attend unless compelled.'[40] A witness in a Hereford case said that he was asked to give evidence by the plaintiff's father without being cited by the court, 'and I refused to do so lest it should injure me in my business to interfere with other persons' broils' (he was an innkeeper).[41] The reluctance may in some cases have been more affected than real. In a London case a witness actually called on the defendant while on her way to Doctors' Commons to give evidence, in order to apologize for giving evidence against her, saying that 'she was sorry she was obliged to do so.' She did not, however, confer much of a favour on the defendant by this visit, because she went on to give damaging evidence of a repetition by the defendant of the slander in the ensuing conversation.[42]

## Procedure

The examiner normally put questions to the witness in private, writing down the answers as the witness spoke. When the examination was over, the witness waited while a fair copy was made, and then signed the deposition by name or mark. This procedure lent itself to possible collusion between witnesses after examination and before signature. An examiner gave in a declaration about an incident in a Hereford case that allows a rare opportunity to see the procedure in operation, as well as to identify several of its weaknesses:

After having examined ... Ann Gundy ... I went with [her] into my clerk's office where the other witness Catherine Protheroe was then sitting, for the purpose of having the examination ... fair copied by my clerk ... I had previously read over the same to Ann Gundy who said that the same was correct and true ... Upon looking over the deposition of Catherine Protheroe again I observed that the two witnesses disagreed respecting the time when the defamatory words alleged were spoken ... I mentioned this circumstance to the said Ann Gundy and ... the said Catherine Protheroe prompted or dictated to the said Ann Gundy the manner in which she should account for such variance in evidence, namely that she must either have misunderstood my questions or that I must have misunderstood her reply ... I several times in the course of my questions put to the said Ann Gundy was interrupted by the said Catherine Protheroe and at last threatened to turn her out of the office unless she desisted ... The said Ann Gundy persisted that the defamatory words were spoken at the time now mentioned in her written deposition, and the draft thereof was accordingly altered to such time.[43]

In several cases there is evidence that examiners permitted some short cuts in the drafting of depositions. In two cases brought by the same plaintiff against a father and son, arising out of a single incident, several of the witnesses gave identical evidence in the two cases. The depositions differ only in the defendants' names, and pencilled interlineations in one set of depositions indicate that one set was copied from the other.[44] The witnesses must have been allowed to say that their evidence in the second case was (except for the name of the defendant) identical with that in the first. In some Peterborough depositions, more significantly, the evidence of different witnesses is in almost identical language, suggesting either over-efficient coaching or depositions prepared in advance.[45] In another case in the same diocese, the deposition is unsigned, dated with month only and no day, again suggesting that it was prepared in advance of the examination.[46]

One of the weaknesses of the system of written depositions was that the precise words of the witness were not recorded. Many depositions are in the third person ('witness deposeth that ...'). In his evidence to the Ecclesiastical Courts Commission, the deputy registrar of Chester, William Ward, said that he recorded the answers 'as nearly as possible in the witness's own language, but sometimes it is absolutely necessary to vary it a little.'[47] One case from his own diocese which Ward may have had in mind, though he was not the examiner in it, was Crabtree v. Hardy (1824), where the deposition records a conversation between the plaintiff and the defendant in these terms:

The promovent Martha Crabtree asserted that she could obtain work when the party promote Henry Hardy could not, upon which the said Henry Hardy in the grossest language that can be supposed but which is unfit to be repeated intimated that her means of doing so was by having criminal conversation with the person by whom she was employed.[48]

A very grave weakness of this method of recording evidence is that it is not possible to be absolutely certain whether it was the witness or the examiner who thought that the defendant's words were unfit to be repeated, but since the witness signed the deposition by mark (X), it is highly improbable that he selected the expression 'having criminal conversation' as a synonym for whatever 'gross' word may have been used by the defendant. Nor is it likely that he referred to the parties as 'promovent' and 'party promote.' More likely the examiner here gave his own paraphrase of the witness's words; this was unsatisfactory, because there might be a dispute over precisely what words the defendant had used, and whether or not they did impute fornication or adultery, and these ought to have been questions for the court, not for the witness or for the examiner. For these reasons most examiners evidently encouraged witnesses to report the precise words used by the defendant, and made a conscientious effort to record them in the depositions, even when, as with some of the examples already quoted, this required the recording of very coarse language. Where the defamatory words were spoken in Welsh,[49] or in a foreign language,[50] the actual words were usually given, with a translation into English. Even the precise words, however, could not include the tone of voice, or the emphasis placed on particular words, which might in some circumstances be crucial.[51]

Witnesses were produced in court, or before a surrogate, to be sworn, in advance of their examination. Special forms of oath were used for Jewish witnesses. In a London case of 1825 the witnesses were 'Louis Norton, John Harris, James Lewin and Levi Cohen, respectively of the Jewish persuasion, who were severally sworn on the Old Testament and admonished as usual.'[52] In a case in the following year, one witness was sworn 'as usual,' and 'Joseph Davis (who declared himself to be a Jew) on the Pentateuch.'[53] These cases suggest flexibility in the forms used: it is probable that the term 'Jew' (rather than 'of Jewish persuasion') and the use of the Pentateuch (rather than the 'Old Testament') in the second case were chosen by the witness. In the same diocese, in 1840, a Quaker witness was permitted to affirm.[54]

### Reliability

Very commonly the interrogatories called upon the examiner to remind witnesses of the dangers (spiritual and temporal) of perjury, and the examiner recorded that the witness was reminded of the punishment due to a false witness. Often these reminders must have been merely formal, but a Chester case of 1826 went a little further than usual in requiring the examiner to introduce the questions with the allocution, 'As you hope to save your soul from eternal perdition, with truth declare ...'[55]

The degree to which witnesses were impressed with these solemnities cannot be estimated from the court records with any degree of accuracy. The frequency of allegations of bribery and coaching, discussed below, suggest that perjury sometimes occurred. Certainly the lawyers involved were not always convinced of the efficacy of the oath. In two York cases of 1826, a suit and counter-suit, a scuffle had taken place in the house of Mary Ann Garside between her and Mary Ripley. One of Garside's witnesses said,

> Mary Ann Garside then took the said Mary Ripley by the shoulders and tried to put her out of the house but she said she would not go away without Thomas Nightingale who was then in the house and to whom the said Mary Ripley was housekeeper; ... this deponent did not hear the said Mary Ann Garside abuse the said Mary Ripley in any way ...[56]

The same incident appears very differently in the deposition of one of Ripley's witnesses:

> Mary Ann Garside seized the said Mary Ripley, knocked her down, tore the cap off her head, and tore her gown; ... when the said Mary Ripley got up the said Mary Ann Garside said to her ... 'You have been Nightingale's kept mistress many years; there he sits and he can't deny it.'[57]

Garside's attorney wrote to Askwith, 'I am satisfied that Ripley's witnesses are grossly perjured.'[58] When the depositions were published, Askwith commented, in sending copies to the attorney, 'You will find some *tight* swearing,'[59] by which he meant to say that the witnesses had been economical with the truth. The judge evidently agreed with the attorney, as Garside's case succeeded (with costs), while Ripley's was dismissed, though without costs.[60] Askwith was satisfied with the result: 'I think we have no great reason to complain.'[61]

## Two Witnesses Essential

The two necessary witnesses might speak to slanders on different occasions, and the plaintiff could take advantage of the diversity of occasions to suggest that the defendant was engaged in a systematic campaign of slander against the plaintiff.[62] But two witnesses were absolutely essential. However persuasive the evidence of a single witness, the judge was bound to dismiss the case. Despite their lawyers' attempts to prepare them, witnesses sometimes failed their parties in the privacy of the examiner's office. In one case a second witness 'failed in her recollection,' and in another a second witness said that he had not heard the slanderous words. Both cases were dismissed, but with small fixed-sum costs against the plaintiffs.[63]

Frequently the necessary second witness deposed to some comment that the defendant made on the pending suit, and herein lay a trap for unwary defendants. Cases have been mentioned in which the plaintiff's friends called on the defendant demanding an explanation or an apology.[64] In entering into any conversation, the defendant ran the risk of supplying essential evidence to the other side. Discussions aimed at settlement might pose a similar trap. In one case the defendant called at the office of the plaintiff's attorney in response to a demand for an apology. The attorney was out, but the defendant said to his clerk that he did not wish to make a public apology, but would have no objection to a private one, adding that he had been 'a damned fool' for speaking the defamatory words. There were no 'judges' rules' to protect defendants from self-incrimination. The clerk gave evidence of this conversation, and sentence was given against the defendant, though without full costs (£10 was allowed).[65]

Defendants, on receiving the citation, were apt to make rash comments, either by way of defiance to the person serving the citation,[66] or by way of seeking sympathy from friends. One defendant told a friend that 'he had got a summons served upon him for calling the plaintiff a whore,' adding 'she ... is a whore; she has been a whore to me.'[67] Another said, 'I have had a very bad job happen to me. I have been put in the spiritual court in Gloucester through Mrs Jones for calling her a whore ... She is rotten with the pox and she is kept by another man.'[68] These conversations were given in evidence.

## Expenses

Witnesses were entitled to their expenses and to an allowance for loss of time. Travelling expenses varied, of course, with the circumstances. In a draft bill of costs in 1821, the sum of £2.11.6 was allowed for 'coach and horse hire and expences' for a male witness travelling a distance of forty-three miles each way. £3.4.0 was allowed for each of two female witnesses.[69] Probably the larger sum is accounted for by provision of greater comfort for female passengers: in another case the fare for a female witness was specified as coach fare 'inside.'[70] On the other hand, the allowance for loss of time was larger for the male witness, who was an apprentice: 5s. per day,[71] as opposed to 3s. 6d. for the women, one of whom was a servant, and the other a 'widow who keeps a small shop.' Compensation for loss of time was made also to women who were not in paid employment: in 1838 Askwith wrote that he thought it reasonable to allow 5s. per day to a woman who was 'mistress of a family and obliged to get someone in the house during her absence.'[72] Three days and expenses exceeding £5 might be required to produce and examine a witness from a distant part of a diocese. Travel from Barnoldswick to York, for example (about fifty miles), was in three stages: horse and gig to Skipton (£1 return fare), coach from Skipton to Leeds (£1.4.0), coach from Leeds to York (£1.4.0); in addition there were travelling expenses (£1), and allowance for loss of time (15s).[73]

Witnesses, naturally, often asked for larger allowances. In a York case of 1823, a witness asked Askwith for an allowance of 15s. for trouble and loss of time. Askwith thought that 10s. was an ample allowance, and his correspondent, Mr Bromby, after consulting the plaintiff, agreed.[74] Askwith paid him 12s., 'at which he grumbled.'[75] It was a standard question in the interrogatories whether the witness had received or expected to receive any kind of payment or reward for giving evidence, and plaintiffs, and their proctors, had to be careful not to make an excessive allowance lest it should discredit the witness when he came to answer the interrogatories. It is evident in some cases that there was rather loose accounting in this respect. In Payne v. Rowley, the case of the discovered love letters, a witness admitted that she had received some money beyond her travelling expenses, 'one pound or two pounds,' to which she considered she was entitled 'for loss of time.' The witness was a twenty-year-old former servant, and 'one pound or two pounds' indicates both a large sum of money and a high degree of imprecision.[76]

In Spooner v. King, the York case of the Baptist minister, where a witness for the plaintiff had been brought over to York in vain by the improper alteration of a compulsory (subpoena) by the plaintiff's attorney, Askwith, who was acting for the defendant, recommended that the *defendant* should offer to pay the expenses of the necessary second trip to York.[77] It was his advice in this case, as in several others, to rely on interrogatories to the plaintiff's witnesses rather than producing defence witnesses, and so the defence had a particular interest in seeing that the plaintiff's witnesses were well disposed.

**Compulsion**

Witnesses could be compelled to give evidence, and sometimes, as we have seen, they declined to be examined until a compulsory was threatened, or actually issued. A witness who objected very strongly to giving evidence might not assist the plaintiff's case, and a compulsory might be withheld for that reason.[78] Enforcement of compulsories was by imprisonment for contempt, but actual imprisonment was, naturally, very rare. In a York case of 1826, a witness (the plaintiff's son) said that his mother did not wish him to be produced as a witness unless the other person, a woman who was to have come as a witness but refused, could not be compelled to come; ... such woman fell under contempt of court and was to have been compelled to come but in consequence of her being a poor woman, and her punishment might have brought her into great difficulty, his mother begged her off ...[79]

The court records confirm that a significavit was actually issued against a witness in this case;[80] that is, matters had proceeded beyond the issue of the compulsory to the stage where she was liable to immediate imprisonment, a very rare circumstance, pointing to extreme reluctance on her part to give evidence. Quite apart from the motives of sympathy alluded to by the plaintiff's son, there was evidently little to be gained by the plaintiff in actually subjecting the reluctant witness to what might be a prolonged period of imprisonment.

## Discrediting the Witness

One of the objects of the interrogatories was to discredit the witness, either by showing that the witness was generally of bad character or otherwise untrustworthy, or by demonstrating a bias in the particular dispute. As we have seen, proctors relied on their clients, or on their clients' attorneys, to supply damaging information about the witnesses. It must be remembered that suggestions in interrogatories were not required to be proved, and that defensive and exceptive allegations were not always proved, and it may be assumed that not all were true. Nevertheless the suggestions and allegations, and the replies to them, reflect contemporary opinion of what was discreditable, and of what might amount to a mitigating explanation.

### (a) Untrustworthy Character

In general, respectability was desirable. In a Norwich case, for instance, the defendant's proctor argued, in support of his theory that the plaintiff's evidence was concocted, that 'the situation in life of complainant's witnesses is inferior to that of defendant's witnesses.' Judges were not unduly influenced by such arguments, as is shown by the many cases in which sentence was given on the evidence of witnesses of low social status. The Norwich case itself is an illustration; sentence with costs was given for the plaintiff, whose witnesses were described as a miller, a shoemaker, a singlewoman, a widow, and a coalheaver and his wife, the judge commenting that (except in respect of the coalheaver) 'there is nothing to impeach the credit of the depositions on the part of the plaintiff.'[81]

Proof of actual crime was an effective way of discrediting witnesses, and accusations were common. A parish clerk was accused of embezzling the sacrament money, wine, and bell metal, and of fighting with the bell-ringers; he denied the embezzlement, and offered a lengthy explanation of the circumstances of his dispute with the ringers.[82] Accusations of theft were commonly made in the interrogatories, and were usually denied, or explained, by the witnesses in their answers.[83] Convictions might be proved by affidavits or by formal certificates.[84] Witnesses were often asked whether they had not been convicted of assault,[85] or bound over to keep the peace for quarrelsome or threatening behaviour;[86] usually it was admitted, in answer, that there had been some such process, but a mitigating explanation was given.[87] In a York case of 1826 a witness was asked whether he had not been indicted for an assault, evidently of a sexual nature, upon the defendant:

Did you not for some time pay your addresses to Mary Ann Garside the ministrant, and upon her refusing to accept you as a suitor did you not quarrel with and assault her, and was not an indictment preferred against you for such assault?

In answer, the witness admitted that he had been indicted at the assizes for rape, but added that he was innocent, and that the grand jury had found 'no bill.'[88]

Accusations against women witnesses of unchastity were common.[89] It was evidently thought to be worth establishing, by way of discredit, that a witness had borne an illegitimate child, even in the distant past, and even where the circumstances might show that she was herself a victim. A set of draft interrogatories at York includes the question, 'Let ... Mary Hesp be asked, have you not had two or more and how many bastard children, and on whom did you filiate the same?' In the margin is a note, probably for the advocate, as follows: 'had two, one she never filiated; ... it is supposed her own father was the father.' In her answer Mary Hesp, then aged forty-eight and unmarried, admitted that she had had two bastard children, one of whom she fathered on Thomas Rickman, and the other 'she did not father on any person,' adding 'that it is eighteen years since she had the last base child which was the one she fathered on Thomas Rickman.'[90] In another York case, the witness said, by way of explanation of two illegitimate children, 'that she was going to be married to the father of her last child, but it was reported he was a married man and therefore she had nothing further to do with him.'[91] In his observations for the use of the advocate, Askwith, reflecting no doubt the attitudes of respectable York, described this witness as 'Elizabeth Sleightholm a washerwoman and a common *whore* admitting that she has had two bastard children to different men.'[92] Though proof of unchastity was relevant to credibility, it was by no means conclusive, and there are several cases in which sentence was given on the evidence of witnesses who admitted having had illegitimate children.[93]

Women were affected by the reputations of their husbands. A York witness was asked, 'Has not your husband been in York Castle and also in the King's Bench or Fleet Prison and been discharged under the Insolvent Debtors Act, and is he not constantly resorted to by persons in the neighbourhood who want to defraud their creditors to advise as to the best manner of its being done?'[94] A marginal note to the draft of this interrogatory, probably written by the attorney, states, 'This is a decent sort of woman but she is entirely under the guidance & control of a wicked bad depraved man, her husband, & dare not but swear as he directs.'[95] Witnesses were accused of keeping bad company,[96] and of drunkenness.[97] Political agitation might be discreditable: in one case a witness, a Baptist minister, denied being a 'Chartist or socialist,' but admitted that 'I once spoke at a meeting.'[98]

It was discreditable to a man that he neglected his family responsibilities. An overseer of the poor deposed of one witness that he was 'a very loose disorderly character' who had been sent to prison for neglect of his family. A constable deposed, of the same witness, that he was addicted to gaming, led a very dissolute life, and neglected his family. A third person said that he had 'left his family and absconded.'[99]

Inquiry was often made into the religious beliefs and practices of the witness. Witnesses were asked whether they believed in God, and if they knew the nature of an oath and the danger of perjury.[100] One witness was asked, 'if he believes in future punishment for misdeeds ... and whether he had not repeatedly said he did not believe in God or Devil.'[101] In a Chester case of 1829, one witness admitted that he had no religion, but said that he believed 'in the existence of a God and of a future state.' In the same case another witness said that he did not go to church or chapel, but 'attended the chapel of a sect called the Dippers [i.e., Baptists] about a month since, and believes in a God and in a state of future rewards and punishments.'[102] Dissent from the Church of England was no disqualification; on the contrary, it might be a sign of moral seriousness. It was said of one witness 'that she is of the methodist religion & as this deponent has always understood & believes is a regular attendant at meeting houses of that connection & that she is a young person of very industrious habits and of blameless conduct and character.'[103] Proof was sometimes offered that witnesses had regularly attended church and received the sacrament, or that they had not.[104] In one case a certificate of non-attendance was produced, signed by the minister and a churchwarden, stating that the plaintiff's witnesses 'are not respectable evidences as they have refrained from coming to Church.' This labour was to little effect, as sentence was given for the plaintiff.[105] Sometimes a kind of examination in religious knowledge was administered by the examiner. One witness was asked, 'Can you repeat the Lord's Prayer, the Belief [i.e., the Apostles' Creed] and the Ninth Commandment [i.e., against bearing false witness].' The witness passed the first test, but failed the second two.[106] In another case the witness (a boy of fourteen) demonstrated to the examiner that he could repeat the Lord's Prayer, and said that he said his prayers every night, but not in the morning 'as he gets up so early that he has no time.'[107]

Catholics were viewed with almost as much suspicion as atheists. In a Somerset case of 1836, where several of the witnesses were Catholics, they were asked whether they believed a Church of England oath to be binding, the question reflecting a widely held suspicion about the Catholic attitude to oaths. One of the witnesses replied that the oath was binding and (perhaps oversimplifying on this point) that he would not obtain absolution in case of perjury.[108]

Several of the witnesses were very young. Youth did not, of course, in itself demonstrate bad character, but it might cast doubt on reliability, and might be combined with other characteristics in order to discredit a witness. In a York case, Askwith, in observations for the defendant's advocate, described the witnesses (two sisters of sixteen and eighteen) as 'young forward impudent sluts, mere children.' The judge, however, was not persuaded by this disparaging slur, if indeed the advocate used it, and gave sentence for the plaintiff.[109] Evidence was quite often accepted from witnesses considerably younger, both boys and girls,[110] in one case from a boy as young as ten years.[111]

*(b) Bias*

It was frequently pointed out, by way of discrediting witnesses, that they were related to the party on whose behalf they were produced. The parties themselves were not competent witnesses, and neither were their spouses,[112] but other near relatives were.[113] It was, of course, preferable to have independent witnesses. Askwith wrote that 'near relations are not the most desirable witnesses in matters of defamation,'[114] but they were better than no witness at all, and there are examples, among the cause papers, of evidence given by parties' sons,[115] daughters,[116] fathers,[117] mothers,[118] brothers,[119] sisters,[120] and other relatives.[121] Where a family dispute was involved, the witnesses might be relatives of both parties, as in a Ripon case where the three witnesses were all related to both parties.[122]

Friends, even intimate friends,[123] of the parties were competent witnesses, though again the ideal witness was one with 'no personal acquaintance,'[124] and witnesses were often asked in interrogatories whether they were not on intimate terms with the plaintiff. In a London case, one of the witnesses had made an offer of marriage to the plaintiff, but her father, who also gave evidence, said that 'the matter at my advice stands over until this suit is settled.' This advice may have been given in order to enhance the credibility of the witness, and perhaps also to support a demonstration that the plaintiff's reputation had suffered from the slander.

In several cases, the other party to the imputed fornication or adultery was produced as a witness. This occurred in a Hereford case against a clergyman where the complaint was that the Revd William Gilpin had accused Elizabeth Roberts of committing adultery with Daniel Bright. Bright, having failed to persuade the parish clerk to accompany him on an evidence-gathering visit to the parson, was himself produced as a witness (without success: the case was dismissed).[125] Even allowing for the 'double standard' of male and female sexual behaviour, such a witness had a strong interest in the result, and his evidence was bound to be viewed with suspicion.

In framing interrogatories, Askwith asked his instructing attorney for useful information 'likely to impeach or throw discredit on the testimony' of opposing witnesses,[126] as 'Pray is Watson related to or in any way under the influence of the plaintiff or her father?'[127] There are many cases in which it was shown, or sought to be shown, that the witness was under the plaintiff's influence in some way – for example, because he was employed by the plaintiff's husband,[128] or rented a house from him.[129] Askwith pointed out in one case that one of the witnesses was 'a young girl aged only 15 years related both to Nightingale [another witness] and Ripley [the plaintiff] and living with them.'[130] These considerations tended to weaken the evidence, but they did not always destroy it. In some cases the plaintiff succeeded on the evidence of her own servant.[131]

Proof of actual bribery was, of course, damaging to credibility, and it was standard practice for the interrogatories to include a question whether the witness had received any fee, reward, or gratuity for giving evidence. The witness usually replied that he expected to receive expenses and a modest allowance for loss of time or wages.[132] As we have seen, there might be some loose accounting in respect of expenses. One witness expected to be paid 'for my trouble,'[133] and another was told by a proctor's clerk that 'she must go to Hereford as often as she should be wanted and she should be well paid for it.'[134]

There were some cases, short of actual bribery, of 'treating' witnesses. This might occur at the preparation stage. One witness was asked 'what were you

& plaintiff's attorney about in the afternoon of Thursday the thirteenth instant at the Globe Inn in Malton ... How much liquor was then drunk ... & who paid for the same?'[135] In a Hereford case, all the defendant's witnesses assembled at her house after the examination for a supper at which tobacco was supplied, and 'plenty of punch – ... a large bowl full like a wash-hand basin – they drank it out of tea cups.'[136] In several cases witnesses received, or expected, a money reward for giving evidence.[137] Witnesses might be encouraged with promises of a pleasant expedition and financial and material reward to boot:

> And now, girls, you will have to go to Lichfield. It will be a nice ride for you. We will make her [defendant's] pocket sweat for there will be five shillings a day and all expenses paid, and we shall be four or five days away, and I will give you a new gown apiece to go.[138]

Promises of reward specifically for a favourable result were alleged in some cases, as where the plaintiff's husband 'was going to put a good pig at each of the witnesses doors after the bustle was over.' A witness in that case expected 'a handsome present' if the plaintiff won.[139] In another case it was suggested that the witness had been offered a guinea a day to prove the plaintiff's case.[140]

Corruption on the part of witnesses was also sometimes alleged. In a York case a witness was alleged to have said to the defendant, 'Mrs Wilson will give me ten shillings a day to go to York with her as a witness, and I am going with her ... but if you will give me more money I will go for you, as I will work for those who will give me the most money.'[141]

Very damaging to the defence was an allegation that the defendant had offered money to a potential witness to refuse to testify.[142] False allegations of attempted bribery must sometimes have occurred, and double-crossing was also sometimes alleged. In a Chester case it was alleged (and sworn) that a witness said that the plaintiff had offered him £5 and a suit of clothes to swear falsely, that he would get all he could from the plaintiff but *not* give false evidence, and that he would then get what he could from the defendant by telling him of what the plaintiff had intended him to do. He said that he had so far received 11s. 6d. from the plaintiff, and 'a round jacket [i.e., a short jacket with circular cut] in part of the suit that had been promised to him but nothing more.'[143]

A standard question in the interrogatories was whether the witness had not been instructed or advised what evidence to give, sometimes with a specific occasion mentioned on which the witness was supposed to have been instructed.[144] It was inevitable that there should be some discussion of a pending case among the witnesses, and between the witnesses and the parties and their legal advisers. Some degree of preparation by the attorneys and proctors was not, as we have seen, improper, and it was common for witnesses to acknowledge that they had been 'examined' in advance of the official examination, by the plaintiff's attorney or by her proctor,[145] but there was a delicate line between preparation and coaching. Occasionally the opposing proctors interviewed witnesses jointly, in order no doubt to avoid accusations of coaching.[146] In one case a defence witness said that the defendant had examined her herself, because 'the proctor was too busy.'[147]

The plaintiff or her husband often was said to have reminded the witness of what he ought to say,[148] and in some cases the witness admitted this. One said that 'he has often been reminded by the promotent and her husband what the words were so as to keep them in his memory, and also by their proctor; that the last time he was reminded was this morning.'[149] Again, there was a delicate line between being reminded and being instructed, and witnesses were often accused of having crossed it.[150] In a Hereford case a witness was asked 'whether she and the other witnesses have not had several meetings to settle which words each witness should depose to when they came to be examined.'[151] It was alleged that the witnesses in a Chester case had been told that they 'must be sure to use the word "shagging."'[152] In a York case the witness was heard to say to the defendant that she did not know what evidence she was going to give 'until Mrs Wilson [the plaintiff] tells me.'[153] Coaching on a larger scale was alleged in a case where the witness was reported as saying that he had had several meetings with the plaintiff and his fellow witness 'at which the plaintiff instructed them both what evidence they were to give, and read over to them at three different times a paper containing the words which they were to make use of.'[154]

After publication, the depositions might reveal similarities that were more than coincidental, and this was a point that could be made to the court in argument. In observations for the advocate in one case where the witnesses were two sisters aged eighteen and sixteen, Askwith commented, on the evidence of the sixteen-year-old, that 'she swears precisely in the same terms and to the same facts as her sister as to the words spoken ... Is this credible !! without concert between these two youngsters and others.'[155] In other cases he commented that there were 'strong internal marks of management,'[156] and that it was evident that the witnesses 'have been thoroughly drilled.'[157]

Occasions were earlier mentioned on which the plaintiff, or her friends, would demand from a person who had spread the slander the name of his 'author,' with the threat that if he did not reveal the name he would himself be subjected to proceedings. In cases where a name was given, the person who gave the name was likely to be produced as a witness, and in such cases the witness had a definite interest in the success of the proceedings, because, if they failed, and if the limitation period had not expired, he might himself be sued. This point was sometimes made to discredit the witness, as by asking him, 'have you not been threatened by ... Joseph England [the plaintiff's husband] ... that unless you came forward as a witness against the defendant ... proceedings would be taken against yourself for the defamation.'[158]

Another situation where a witness's impartiality was brought into question was where the witness was herself accused, as well as the plaintiff. In the York case previously mentioned where the witnesses were the two young sisters, the slander complained of was that the defendant had asserted that a servant and her employer 'were prostitutes and kept by all the men in the parish.' The employer brought a suit in which the servant and her younger sister were the witnesses. The servant, being herself a victim of the alleged slander, had a definite interest in the result and, as Askwith pointed out, by way of further weakening her evidence, she might even be a potential plaintiff in a separate suit: 'in case this suit is ended within six months another might be brought by the servant, in which her mistress might become her witness; this certainly goes most strongly to the credibility of Mary Ann Sawdon [the witness].'[159]

There were many allegations that witnesses were hostile to the adverse party. Commonly, the witness and the defendant had been adversaries in former litigation, or one had committed an assault on the other, or the defendant had informed against the witness, or the witness had some other reason to bear a grudge against the defendant. In one case the witness had, at the time the defamatory words were spoken, called on the defendant to complain of a slander against herself.[160] Frequently it was alleged that a witness had declared hostility to the defendant, as in a York case where the witness was supposed to have said that she 'would fettle [fix] the defendant and ... send the defendant and her four small children to the poorhouse,'[161] and in another case, 'Have you not declared that you will be revenged upon the defendant & that you will have her imprisoned or make her pay expences?'[162] A Hereford witness was proved to have said, 'I am a witness against him ... and I will ruin him if I can for I think I have it in my power.'[163]

The disputes alleged were very varied, often revealing complex hostilities extending over long periods, as in a Gloucester case, where an exceptive allegation was admitted showing that a witness had published an offensive verse ('a song, placard, or libel ... entitled Yorkee Pry') ridiculing the defendant, and the defendant had caused the witness to be prosecuted for not including the printer's name on the broadsheet; the other witnesses had collected money to defray the fine, and had got up a petition to evict the defendant from his residence. The full text of 'Yorkee Pry' is included in one of the depositions on the exceptive allegation: twenty-four lines of rhyming couplets commenting in disagreeable terms on the defendant's physical appearance and his tendency to pry into his neighbours' affairs.[164] There are other examples of this kind of hostility, but it is not possible to explore them in the present context – not because they are tedious: on the contrary, because they are too multifarious and distracting. The writer, like the judge when deciding on admission of an exceptive allegation, must sometimes exclude collateral material, even when it may tend to an elucidation of an aspect of the truth.

A direct financial interest in the result disqualified a witness, and proctors, in preparing their cases, had to be careful that any person financing the suit was not also an essential witness. Witnesses were routinely asked whether they had made themselves liable for the plaintiff's expenses. Generally they answered that they had not, but in a London case, where one of the witnesses was the plaintiff's father, he answered that he was financing the suit and considered himself liable for the plaintiff's expenses. His evidence was rejected, and no costs were allowed for it, though sentence was given for the plaintiff on the evidence of other witnesses.[165] In a York case Askwith advised against proceeding on the evidence of the plaintiff's mother, since her husband 'must I presume be answerable for the costs.'[166] In another York case one of the witnesses was alleged to be the 'paymaster,' i.e. to have promoted the suit at his expense. He denied it, and his fellow witnesses, going a little too far for their own good, said that they had heard him declare expressly that he would not pay a farthing of the costs. Askwith, acting for the other side, commented, 'Now if Nightingale was not expected to pay such costs how did it happen that he made such a declaration? The truth is apparent.'[167]

## (c) Inconsistent Prior Statement

Another question so common in the interrogatories as to be almost routine was whether the witness had not previously admitted that he had not heard the alleged slanderous words, or said that he knew nothing about the matter. This line of questioning was commonly and effectively rebutted by an explanation that if the witness had said, to some questioners, that he knew little or nothing about the matter, it was because he did not wish to become involved in a lawsuit,[168] or simply 'because she did not then think fit to tell [an attorney] what had ... passed.'[169] In one case the witness said that the defendant's husband and his solicitor had so intimidated her by violent language (on the occasion of the alleged inconsistent statement) that she could not remember what she had said to them.[170]

## The Judge's Perception of the Evidence

Generally speaking, the court records do not reveal judges' reasons for admitting exceptive allegations, or for preferring the evidence of one witness to another, but there is one Norwich case that includes reasons for the judicial decision at both stages, and supplies what is usually entirely lacking, namely the judge's perspective on the evidence. Hannah Youngs lived with her married sister and her brother-in-law, Mrs and Mr Jenner. Robert Bailey, a near neighbour, accused Mr Jenner of having slept with Youngs, telling him to 'go in and go to bed with his two wives.' He knew that the three of them slept together, because he had watched the lights in the house when they went to bed at night, and had noticed that no light was carried into Hannah Youngs's room. Five witnesses gave evidence in support of Hannah Youngs, the plaintiff. The defendant's proctor then gave in an exceptive allegation, objecting to the evidence of the witnesses on various grounds. The judge was most reluctant to admit this allegation. He wrote to the defendant's proctor, making an interesting comparison with common law procedure:

> The argument that you use from the practice of the common law courts is totally irrelevant to the proceedings in the ecclesiastical courts, in consequence of the different manner in which causes are considered in the different courts. In the former the defendant is obliged to come into court with all his witnesses before he knows what witnesses will be produced on the part of the plaintiff, or to what they will depose, & must answer immediately on the spur of the occasion. He cannot take the evidence home with him into his closet, weigh all its bearings, & see if he can pick a hole in it. The defendants in our courts therefore have a manifest advantage in this respect, & it is for this reason that they are so properly cautious of admitting exceptive allegations.[171]

Rather surprisingly, however, he went on to say that he would admit the allegation 'as you seem to think a great injury will be done to your client if it be rejected & upon the general principle that when the matter is doubtful it is safer to admit than reject an allegation.'

The allegation was supported by eight witnesses, and, again very unusually, the cause papers include the judge's detailed reasons (twenty manuscript pages) for rejecting the allegation and for accepting the evidence of four of the plaintiff's witnesses. With some of the defence witnesses he found that the evidence was not necessarily contradictory: the words might have been spoken at a time when the defendant's witness was absent. A witness who swore the defendant was elsewhere on the relevant day could not have been sure that he had not returned home at some point during the day. In respect of one defence witness, who swore that she had been at the defendant's house for about fifteen minutes sometime during the summer on a date she could not precisely remember, and had heard a quarrel, but not the defamatory words, the judge commented drily that the evidence 'just goes to prove that there was one quarter of an hour in the course of the summer 1826 when the words deposed to were not heard by the witness.' One of the plaintiff's witnesses, however, was proved to the judge's satisfaction to have contradicted himself, and the judge said, 'I shall pay no attention to any part of his evidence which is not confirmed by other testimony.'

There was one particular matter which the judge said 'may be considered I think as almost conclusive.' This was that the plaintiff's witnesses said that the defendant had claimed to have 'watched the lights' in Jenner's house:

> This seems to me a reason that could not have been invented by any person, and that it must have been given by the defendant himself, and, if so, it is conclusive. This fact is stated not in one deposition only, but in four different ones, & at different times ... Now to me it is quite incomprehensible that four persons should agree in stating this, when it is almost impossible that even one ['should have invented it' struck through] should have known the thing to be possible, as no one could do so, unless he was intimately acquainted with the relative situation of the defendant's & Mr Jenner's windows & sleeping rooms. The most obvious explanation is that this reason was given by the defendant himself & that he had of course used the defamatory words which the witnesses have alleged, & it should seem that he was in the habit of detailing to his friends his sagacity in finding out the secret transactions of his neighbours.

One of the defendant's witnesses said that he had seen a paper with a song on it in which the defendant was described as 'Paul Pry'; evidently the judge was in substantial agreement with the unknown song-writer. Sentence was given for the plaintiff, with costs taxed at the substantial sum of £44.13.6.[172] As in the Gloucester case of the very similar incident of 'Yorkee Pry,' part of the injury complained of, in addition to the slander itself, was invasion of privacy.[173]

## Discrediting the Parties

Interrogatories and exceptive allegations supplied defendants with the means of attacking the plaintiff's reputation and conduct (though not in open court), and these attacks supply a compendious list of the qualities thought least desirable in women:

Is not Ann Hart the wife of Charles Hart very quarrelsome and is she not considered and known to be a very vile abusive woman and an arrant scold?[174]

It was often suggested that the plaintiff was troublesome, quarrelsome, and litigious, the three adjectives being used together as a kind of formula,[175] or abusive,[176] drunk,[177] violent,[178] and a scold,[179] or that she associated with low company,[180] or that she was loose, immoral, abandoned,[181] and unchaste,[182] of light character and incontinent habits,[183] that she had borne a character of levity and instability,[184] or was of indifferent character,[185] or of base character and reputation.[186] The character of a woman's husband was also relevant to her respectability.[187] Such suggestions and allegations, as we have seen, were not defences, but they tended to affect the costs. The answers might also cast doubt on the credibility of the witnesses.

Generally, as might be expected, witnesses produced on the plaintiff's behalf answered that they knew nothing against the plaintiff's character, but occasionally the witnesses admitted that the plaintiff was spoken of 'lightly,'[188] or 'slightly.'[189] The form of the libel in use in York asserted that the plaintiff was 'of good fame and upright life and conversation.' Almost always this was taken by the witness for what it was – a legal formulary – but in one case a witness said she 'is sorry she cannot say she [the plaintiff] is a person of upright life and conversation,' and the other witness in the same case said he 'is sorry to say she is not esteemed by her neighbours.'[190]

The defendant, as well as the plaintiff, might be accused of crime,[191] or, especially if a woman, of being quarrelsome,[192] turbulent,[193] and violent. In a York case there is a reference in this context to the survival of the Skimmington Ride or 'Riding the Stang,' a kind of mock procession used in order to identify and ridicule those who had offended against community norms. Defence witnesses were asked, about the defendant, who was a married woman,

Are you acquainted with the custom called riding the stang? If yea, is it not used (amongst other purposes) to designate and hold out to public contempt notorious scolds and turbulent mischievous characters? ... Has the stang ever been ridden to the best of your knowledge for ... Ann Powell?

Two of the witnesses answered that they knew what riding the stang was, that it was done when a man and his wife were quarrelling, but that they did not know that it had been done for Ann Powell.[194]

The opposite qualities – those most to be admired in women – appear in the deposition of a friendly witness: 'he does not consider her [plaintiff] to be a troublesome quarrelsome or litigious woman – that she is on the contrary a very industrious honest & quiet woman.'[195] Similarly, a York interrogatory asked, 'Is not the defendant a quiet industrious woman ...?'[196] Further up the social scale, industry and quietness give way, as desirable qualities, to propriety and respectability. The Revd Robert Greenwood, for example, said that

> he hath known Mrs Louisa Webber [the plaintiff] from her infancy; ... he and Mrs Greenwood have been in the constant habit of receiving her as a visitor at their house where she hath been for days together previous to her marriage; ... she was particularly correct and chaste in her manners and always conducted herself with the greatest propriety, and never shewed the least tendency to levity, and was considered by him ... and his wife and family as a very virtuous and highly respectable young woman.[197]

It was, however, complimentary to say of a woman that she was 'a woman of high spirit.'[198] In one case a witness (who was a Quaker, and presumably a sober observer of the social scene) described the plaintiff as 'a young woman full of spirits,' though adding, 'but I never saw any thing like boldness or levity in her manner.'[199]

## Exceptive Allegations

An exceptive allegation, as mentioned in the last chapter, might be given in to disprove any facts stated by witnesses, but allegations (which had themselves to be proved by two witnesses) were expensive, and comparatively rare in defamation cases. Admission of exceptive allegations was discretionary, and, as we have seen, judges were reluctant to admit them too readily for fear of diverting the case towards collateral issues. The point about expense might be made in argument to explain why the defendant had not introduced an allegation. In a York case, Askwith, in his brief to the advocate, suggested that the plaintiff's witnesses 'were both men of disreputable character. Yet it was not thought prudent for fear of the expense to plead in defence or exceptive to the testimony of the witnesses.'[200] Some exceptive allegations included elaborate (and therefore expensive) surveys and drawings with the object of showing that witnesses could not have seen or heard what they claimed to have done.[201] Moreover, an allegation of any sort (defensive or exceptive) opened up the possibility of a counter-allegation, with consequent further escalation of costs.[202]

## The Witnesses

The witnesses, as might be expected, were drawn from approximately the same social circles as the parties themselves: small trades and crafts predominate. It will be seen from table 7, below, that, of the 146 depositions at York, 105 are signed by name and 41 are authenticated by mark. Ninety-two of the witnesses were men, and 54 were women. Twenty-seven of the women (50 per cent) signed by name, whereas 78 of the men (85 per cent) did so. Figures for Norwich are comparable, but show a higher proportion of women able to sign.[203] Caution is required in drawing conclusions from these figures about general rates of literacy,[204] as the witnesses do not represent a random sample of the whole population, and because some witnesses may have been able to sign, but not to read or write,[205] and others, while able to read and write, may nevertheless have signed by mark.[206] It has sometimes been suggested that men were considered more worthy of credit as witnesses than women,[207] and the preponderance of men as witnesses lends some support to that view. It is probable that, other things being entirely equal, a man would be preferred as a witness, and a literate man to one who was illiterate. Respectability was desirable, and professional status, office-holding, and proprietorship (badges of respectability) were largely reserved to men. On the other hand, the York cause papers do not give much support to this hypothesis: the disproportion between the sexes of the witnesses is not extremely large, and in York in the period 1815 to 1834 the numbers were equal. The ecclesiastical courts were accustomed to receiving the evidence of women in matrimonial and testamentary cases. It will be recalled that in one case Askwith disparagingly observed, of the plaintiff's witnesses (two sisters), that they were 'young forward impudent sluts, mere children,'[208] but he was stressing their youth rather than their sex, and in any case the judge did not agree, as sentence was given for the plaintiff on their evidence alone. In a Norwich case of 1850, one of the witnesses, Susanna Parr, a schoolmistress, had been among a crowd that had witnessed an altercation in the street. In answer to interrogatories she said, 'I have become a witness in this cause at the request of Mr Gooch the complainant's husband; he noticed me as being there at the first and found me out afterwards. I did not know him.'[209] This shows that Susanna Parr was selected from many possible persons as likely to be an impressive witness, and that her sex was not thought to be a disadvantage.

A reader of the cause papers gains the impression of a consistently honest and conscientious attempt by the officers of the courts to determine the relevant facts, but necessarily fettered at every stage by the limitations inherent in the system of written depositions.

# 6

# Costs

In any kind of litigation costs are important, but in these defamation cases they were crucial, because they were the only financial orders available. To win a case, but without costs, was scarcely a victory, especially as many judges were known to deny costs specifically in order to signify disapproval of the plaintiff's conduct.

In London, as has been mentioned, there was a conventional sum, called 'style of costs,' awarded against a defendant who submitted immediately and confessed the use of the defamatory words. The conventional sum was, in 1816, £3.3.0.[1] In 1830 it had been reduced to £2.[2] Such a low figure had a dual effect: it discouraged defamation suits in the first place, because the plaintiff's proctor would require payment in advance, and it encouraged defendants to give an immediate affirmative issue (i.e., to confess the words and concede the case). A firm of London proctors went so far as to say that 'it seldom happens that a negative issue is given to the libel.'[3] There must have been many defendants who were advised that it was cheaper to settle on these terms than to dispute the case, even if they might have had a defence. In one case a woman sued by her sister-in-law at first appeared in person and stated that she was a minor, evidently with the idea of disputing the case. A month later she withdrew her defence, and confessed the words.[4] A letter to *The Times*, perhaps from her solicitor, explained that her decision was the result of legal advice:

> This affair appears to have arisen from some family quarrel, the action in the ecclesiastical court having been brought against her by her brother[5] for having made use to her sister-in-law Rosetta Cohen of a term contrary as well to this part of our laws as to the usages of society. To avoid expense she had no means to meet, and the consequences thereof, her solicitor advised her to admit her fault and abide the award of the court.[6]

Her subsequent performance of penance led to a little notoriety (which accounts for the letter to the newspaper), and the case will be mentioned again in that context in the next chapter.

In dioceses outside London, some judges awarded fixed-sum costs;[7] the more usual consequence of an affirmative issue was payment of taxed costs (i.e., the proctor's bill as scrutinized and reduced by an officer of the court), which Askwith estimated, in a letter written in 1830, at £7 or £8.[8] Even at this rate there was considerable pressure to concede in order to avoid much higher costs:

> [an affirmative issue] will immediately put an end to the suit & subject defendant to the performance of penance ... and to the payment of taxed costs – say seven or eight pounds. Should we make a shew of resistance and oblige the plaintiff to examine witnesses & she should clearly prove her case the same punishment will follow, but the costs will of course be considerably more – say from 20 to 30£ ... In speaking of the costs I allude to what may be the probable amount of plaintiff's taxed costs, exclusive of defendant's own costs.[9]

Askwith's estimate of the plaintiff's costs in a contested suit is somewhat higher than might be expected in other dioceses, where the employment of an advocate was not essential. In Peterborough, for example, a proctor advising a plaintiff estimated the probable cost of a contested suit at £15.[10] This would have been the estimate for a simple case requiring only two witnesses, without any defensive or exceptive allegations. Any kind of complexity or delay increased the expenses. Four bills of costs in defamation cases in the diocese of St David's were appended to the Report of the Ecclesiastical Courts Commission, at an average amount of about £30.[11]

Where the judge considered that the proceedings had been unnecessarily prolonged, he might provide expressly for restricted costs. In a York case, for example, where there was, in addition to the original libel supported by three witnesses, a defensive allegation supported by two witnesses and a replicatory allegation supported by a further three witnesses on the plaintiff's side, the sentence for the plaintiff was altered to include the proviso that she should recover costs 'so far as is usual in cases of sentence against the defendant where no defensive pleading has been given in; each party in this case to pay their own costs of the additional pleadings given in on both sides.'[12]

The system of taxation (reduction or moderation of the bill) gave the defendant some further protection against excessive charges. The usual rule in York, for example, was that the expenses of two witnesses only were allowable.[13] The procedure for taxation was described as follows (for London):

The complainant's proctor's bill is submitted to the Registrar for taxation and taxed by him, notice being given to the other side of the time fixed for such taxation at least 24 hours previously. The Registrar at the next sitting of the court reports the amount of the bill as taxed; the proctor makes oath that the sum has been or must be necessarily expended on behalf of his party, and the judge then signs the certificate of taxation ...[14]

Many bills of costs were drastically reduced on taxation. It is difficult to conclude very much from this fact alone, because the bills most reduced may have been extravagant in the first place. More persuasive evidence of the efficacy of the system comes from a letter of Askwith's, warning an attorney of the strict attitude of the taxing officer:

I am afraid our Registrar will in his taxation disallow many of the items in your bill, though I think them all fair & reasonable, and will do the best I can to obtain a liberal taxation.[15]

The bill of costs transcribed in appendix A, below, shows that the taxing officer – at any rate the taxing officer at York – was not likely to be unduly impressed by such vague items as 'writing a great number of letters during the dependance of the cause' (claim reduced by one-third) or 'several attendances and other trouble not before charged' (wholly disallowed).

In case of lengthy pleadings and appeal, there was practically no limit to the potential expense. In the notorious case of Russell v. Bentham the estimated costs were between £600 and £700 on each side.[16] The highest taxed bill for a case at the consistory court level appears to be £127, in an Exeter case.[17]

There must have been many cases of plaintiffs who consulted an attorney or a proctor, and were deterred by the fear of costs. Generally such cases left no trace among the court records, because, even if the client wrote a letter on the subject, it would not be part of the official record. However, a few such letters have survived among the cause papers. In a Peterborough case, Thomas Miller, having first instructed his proctor to proceed against John Carter for saying that 'I was a bugger and my wife a whore,' subsequently withdrew:

Sir, I have considered of the thing between John Carter and me, and the more i think on it the more it convince me that the said John Carter will run awa and you say that I must gobble [?] the expence wich it niver will be in my pour for I have noting only what I get by my hand larbor so therefore I must decline it and I thort and my friends it wood be the best way to come over before the thing commence. I ham your servant, Thos Miller.[18]

This letter shows why many plaintiffs were deterred; it also shows why many of limited means were not deterred. If the defendant was not likely to abscond, and if he or his friends could raise £15 or £20, the plaintiff and her proctor had little to lose, so long as there were the two necessary credible witnesses. As we have seen, there were very few defences, and an order against the defendant for costs was enforceable by imprisonment. As long as the court could be relied upon to award costs to a successful plaintiff, the proctor could afford to accept the plaintiff's case without insisting on advance payment.

This calculus changed when the judge could not be relied upon to award costs to the successful plaintiff. The judges were aware that their practice in this respect made a crucial difference to the incentives for litigation. Matthew Marsh, the chancellor of Salisbury, said that defamation causes in his diocese 'used to be very frequent, but I think I have stopped the worst of them, by giving only a nominal sum for costs.'[19] This statement, made to the Ecclesiastical Courts Commission in 1830, influenced the other judges: in Chester, for example, after 1830 nominal awards of costs became frequent, as did cases of refusal of costs altogether.[20] Such special provisions as to costs had occurred before 1830, but they were rare. Granville Vernon, the York chancellor, was also known to be hostile to defamation cases, and William Askwith always warned his clients, and their attorneys, about the unpredictability of the judge's dispositions in respect of costs. The letter quoted above, for example, advising a defendant, went on to say that if it could be shown that there were faults on both sides the judge would probably not condemn in costs, 'but on this point I can say nothing certain, costs being in his discretion.'[21] Practice varied: costs in Norwich, for example, were somewhat more predictable. The Norwich chancellor said that it was the general practice to allow costs to a successful complainant 'unless there were some special circumstances,'[22] and in another case that it was the 'invariable' practice to award costs 'unless there is something in the conduct of the parties to deprive them of costs.'[23] In his speech on the 1855 Bill to abolish the defamation jurisdiction, Lord Brougham quoted the Carlisle chancellor as saying that 'he had no choice allowed him; he must pronounce sentence and order the payment of costs.'[24] It is probably not coincidental that Carlisle had the highest number of defamation suits by population, and they were still comparatively frequent: there had been fifteen cases in the 1850s.[25]

In York, where costs were unpredictable, it was Askwith's practice to insist on advance payment, unless dealing with a reliable attorney who guaranteed his fees. 'In matters of Defamation' he wrote to an attorney who had questioned the practice, where the parties apply to me personally I make it a rule not to prosecute any such suit for them without having money advanced to meet the expences for after the business is ended let the result be what it may I have too often been left unpaid and in cases where Attornies are employed they generally wish to know the amount of the expences and frequently remit for the fees to Counsel, stamps, &c before the cause is ended. There is nothing unreasonable in this & I concluded you could not start [*sic*] an objection to it. Pray do not Attornies on bringing Causes for Trial at the Assizes constantly get their Clients to advance them Money towards their expences fees to Counsel &c before the Issue? At least I have known some very respectable Men do so.[26]

In another case at about the same time, where Askwith was instructed by a clergyman, Askwith asked him to secure an advance from the client:

> As a matter of prudence I think you should require Ann Trattles or her husband Matthew Trattles for her to advance & deposit with you from ten to fifteen pounds towards meeting the expences of this Suit, for it too frequently happens when the Defendant cannot pay the costs, the plaintiff will not in the end pay them without much trouble so that I always in matters of this nature find it best either to have money or satisfactory security before hand for the expences let the event be what it may: it's more easily returned than obtained at the last.[27]

Matthew Trattles paid £10 to Mr Andrew (the clergyman), the suit was commenced, and was met with a counter-suit, whereupon Andrew asked for a further £10. Askwith wrote:

> You did very right in asking for a further advance of Money to meet the expences of both Suits and you may tell Matthew Trattles & his wife that unless they soon comply with your request I shall certainly withdraw from the Suits & desire them to appoint another Proctor. I will not run any risk for them.[28]

Matthew Trattles eventually refused to pay the second £10 and the two suits were settled. Askwith's fees and expenses amounted to £11.5.6 and he wrote to Andrew, 'I conclude from the account which Matthew Trattles gives of his poverty that I must suffer the excess beyond the £10 paid.'[29] After deduction of Andrew's expenses, Askwith actually received only £9. 10s. Andrew forwarded Askwith's bill to Trattles, though without much expectation of success: 'Should he however pay the full amount of your Bills, of which I have little hope, I will take care to remit it to you.'[30] Clearly the attitudes, practices, and expectations of the proctor were crucial: only a very determined plaintiff would be inclined to pay £20 out of pocket in advance. It was not so much that the avidity of lawyers was the primary cause of defamation suits, as Lord Brougham suggested in 1855, as that their caution tended to deter litigation where recovery of costs was doubtful.

When a suit was dismissed, costs could be awarded against the plaintiff, and security might be required by the court at the outset to guarantee payment in that event. Exeter, exceptionally, had a general practice of requiring security from plaintiffs in all defamation cases, which certainly must have created a disincentive to litigate. In other dioceses security might be required when there was a special reason, for example that the plaintiff had gone abroad.[31] In the case of a married woman, it was usual (but not universal) practice for the plaintiff's husband to join in executing the proxy, thereby making himself liable for the costs. The point was argued in a case in the Arches Court, where the defendant objected that the plaintiff's proxy was not signed by her husband, and the plaintiff responded that she had for several years been separated from her husband. The judge gave leave for a proxy to be executed without the husband's signature, but directed security to be given on her behalf 'to answer costs in case she should be condemned therein.'[32]

Where a married woman was the defendant, questions arose about enforcing liability for costs, a married woman in this period generally not owning or controlling property. The ecclesiastical law on the point was that since the suit was against the woman personally, the liability to pay the costs was hers, and hers alone. Askwith wrote on this point to an attorney, 'of course the costs will come out of the husband's pocket, if the wife has no separate estate, but should they not be paid the wife would be the party in contempt.'[33] The attorney was incredulous, and Askwith found it necessary to be more explicit in a second letter:

> You have understood my letter correctly. The husband's lands body or effects are not responsible for the costs. The wife must suffer for the contempt in person by imprisonment until she submits to obey the sentence of the court. How long the duration of such imprisonment would be must depend on herself.[34]

But, it may be observed, not on herself so much as on her husband, whose lack of means, or in some cases neglect, might cause his wife to spend a long period in prison.

In practice it would be expected in most cases that the husband would pay the costs, and the point was made in one case on behalf of a married woman defendant that costs, if awarded, 'must be paid by her inoffending husband, who is a most industrious honest peaceable man.'[35] The plaintiff's advocate

replied, rather crudely, that 'if the husband's pocket was touched, it would perhaps learn him to correct his wife, and teach her to keep a civil tongue in her
head.' The judge steered a middle course, and awarded costs, but of £5 only.[36]

In dioceses where a wide discretion was used, the means of the parties
became relevant. In argument in an Exeter case it was stressed that the defendant 'had ample means of satisfying' an order for costs,[37] and in a York case,
Askwith, acting for a plaintiff, stressed that the defendant, though a minor,
was the son of 'an opulent brewer.'[38] In another case, Askwith's client was
involved in four separate defamation suits, three as plaintiff and one as defendant. 'If money is an object to Mrs Garside,' Askwith wrote to his instructing
attorney,

> it becomes a matter of serious consideration to her (as well as to you and myself)
> to provide & supply the necessary funds for carrying on four causes of defama-
> tion in the ecclesiastical court; her costs alone therein will soon amount to £100
> and when the court finds that she is a *wholesale dealer* I am afraid of the conse-
> quences to her in a pecuniary point of view, let the judgments be what they may,
> especially as the court discountenances suits of this nature as much as possible.[39]

The obligation to pay costs was enforceable by imprisonment, as we have
seen, and a substantial number of persons were imprisoned, but in some cases
the plaintiff did not enforce payment. In a Peterborough case, for example, it
was certified that the defendant 'was in a very ill state of health and unable to
pay the residue of the taxed costs [and] the judge with the consent of ... the
promoter's proctor dismissed the [defendant] from any further attendance.'[40]
In the London case of the man who refused to perform the penance because he
maintained that the words were true, the costs were eventually waived.[41] On
the other hand, imprisonment often induced the defendant's friends, or others,
to pay. In a Llandaff case, where the defendant had been imprisoned, the
parish undertook to pay the costs, presumably in order to avoid having to
maintain his family.[42]

Withholding of costs was regularly used by Granville Vernon, the York
chancellor, to express his disapproval of one or both parties. A case might be
dismissed without costs where the plaintiff had failed to prove her case, but
where the defendant was proved to have used offensive language, as in the
cases earlier mentioned where the plaintiff was said to have 'harboured'
whores,[43] and to have 'gone a-whoring.'[44]

Withholding costs from a successful plaintiff was often seen as a mark of
disapproval of the plaintiff's conduct, and Vernon said of such cases that the
sense was 'that I have felt both parties were equally in fault; that there was

provocation enough to have accounted for the words, though not matter to justify them.'[45] Such an outcome, therefore, scarcely represented a victory for the plaintiff. A more moderate disapprobation of the plaintiff's conduct was sometimes manifested by an award of partial costs, either in the form of a fixed money sum,[46] or in the form of an order to bear a proportion of the taxed costs.[47]

Where costs were to be paid by the opposite side, the proctor annexed the attorney's bill as an item of expense to be taxed, as though it were an expense incurred by the proctor on behalf of the client, no doubt because it was the proctor only who had status to make the claim in the ecclesiastical court.[48] On the other hand, where the bill was to be paid by the client, the proctor sent his bill to the attorney, and the proctor's bill then apppeared as an item of expense in the attorney's bill to the client. Askwith wrote to an attorney:

> I inclose you an account of my charges to the present time amounting to £30.16.2 from which you will deduct for your trouble £5.0.0 and make such other charges to your client as you think right.[49]

As we have seen, in cases where Askwith was instructed by the client personally, or by a clergyman, he did not expect his bill to be paid in full when he had failed to obtain advance payment, and where the client was impecunious.[50] In the case of a professional attorney, however, it may be assumed that the attorney, by instructing a proctor, impliedly undertook to pay the account.

Questions of costs affected the incentives of the parties and of their advisers at every stage. The judges had a high degree of discretion,[51] and different judges used it in different ways, a variation that, together with the other factors mentioned in chapter 4, goes far to explain the differing rates of litigation in the various dioceses.

# 7

# Penance

The sentence of the court was that the defendant should be canonically corrected, and correction took the form of a ceremony variously called penance, retraction, recantation, reclamation, or declaration, in which the defendant asked pardon of God and of the plaintiff, and promised not to offend again. The form of penance, called a 'schedule,' varied quite substantially from one diocese to another. An illustration is given of a printed schedule of penance, as used in Hereford (see plate 8). Most dioceses used a manuscript form, as in the example illustrated from Winchester, witnessed by John Keble (plate 9). In earlier times (apparently until the eighteenth century), the penance in defamation cases had, where the slander itself had been public, been performed in the parish church, during Sunday service, before the congregation.[1] In the nineteenth century, public penance, while not unknown, was highly exceptional.[2] The usual practice was for penance to be performed in the vestry room of the plaintiff's parish church before the clergyman and the churchwardens, and the plaintiff and five or six of her friends if she and they chose to be present. But, as in other points of practice, there were important variations among the dioceses.

By the nineteenth century the whole concept of public penance was widely considered to be obsolete. The chancellor of Oxford, writing to the bishop in 1803, referring to public penance as used (very rarely by this date) in criminal cases, said:

The penance of publick exposure in a white dress is obsolete or nearly so, and I submit to your Lordship whether it would be prudent to attempt that which would probably not only be insignificant in itself at best, but would probably be converted into a sort of triumph by such a man as you describe. The power of the ecclesiastical court is too weak for any great utility; but such as it is we must manage it as we can so as not to expose it to contempt, where we cannot enforce it to good effect.[3]

Penance in defamation cases, normally in private, and not requiring use of a white dress, or white sheet[4] as it was more usually called, did not run quite so large a risk, but the very name 'penance' was associated in the public mind with a ceremony that was obsolete and quaint, not to say ludicrous.[5] In his evidence to Lord Campbell's Committee on defamation in 1843, a Scottish lawyer, John Borthwick, gave examples of public penance for defamation in France and also in Scotland, where the retraction was called a palinode, and the penitent wore sackcloth. Borthwick said that the last Scottish case had been in 1669.[6]

A number of reports mention crowds assembling at churches in the expectation of seeing penance performed in defamation cases.[7] In several cases it was reported that the white sheet was used, but these reports were probably erroneous. The old books of ecclesiastical law stated expressly that the white garment (there called *lineae vestes*, translated by Conset 'linen vestments') was not to be used in defamation cases,[8] and no case was found (except in the Isle of Man) in which it was ordered.[9] In some dioceses it was expressly ordered that the penitent should be 'in his accustomed apparel.'[10] It is clear, however, that many people *expected* a white sheet. The prevalence of erroneous reports can be explained by the association in the public mind between penance and the use of the white sheet: in hearing that the ecclesiastical court had ordered the performance of penance, it was easy to jump to the conclusion that the ceremony involved the white garment, which was still in occasional use in non-defamation cases, and was strongly associated with the idea of penance. For example, in the London case of Cohen v. Cohen,[11] *The Times* reported as fact that 'On Sunday last a woman named Cohen ... stood in a white sheet in the church of St John Clerkenwell for calling her brother's wife a name not to be mentioned "to ears polite."'[12] A letter the next day, evidently from a well-informed source, perhaps the defendant's solicitor, explained that a large and unruly mob had assembled; 'the crowds were however disappointed in seeing this young woman exposed in the open church with the covering of a white sheet etc., the order from the ecclesiastical court only having enjoined her to appear in the vestry room ... after service.'[13] The reporter must have been informed that penance had taken place, and have jumped to the conclusion that the penitent had worn a white sheet in the open church.

There are several other similar cases of crowds assembling in the expectation of seeing a public ceremony, and of going away disappointed.[14] There are some other reports of the use of the white sheet.[15] It is just possible that a defendant might have chosen to wear a sheet, perhaps as a mockery, or that a clergyman with neo-mediaeval ideas might have suggested it, or possibly that an inferior ecclesiastical court might have ordered it, but no such order has been found in the consistory court records. In a Welsh case the draft schedule of penance includes the words 'being bare footed and bare legged having a white sheet about him and a wand in his hand,' but these words are missing from the certified version.[16] The existence of the draft suggests some uncertainty about the matter in the registrar's office.

The widespread expectation among the public of some sort of penitential ceremonial appears from a York case, in which the plaintiff's attorney wrote, to Askwith:

> The defendant ... performed penance in our church this morning but my client is by no means satisfied at the way in which it has been done. She states that the defendant merely walked up the middle aisle to the altar in her usual dress &c without any of the expected marks of penitence. Pray inform me if that is the usual way penance is performed ...[17]

Askwith replied that 'penance appears to have been performed in the usual way required by the court on all similar occasions. The party is not directed to appear otherwise than in his or her ordinary apparel before the minister & church-wardens and acknowledge the offence complained of.'[18]

Penance in defamation cases was not usually in the open church. In a Llandaff case the plaintiff specifically asked for an order that the defendant should 'perform public penance during Divine Service,' but the judge refused, and ordered penance in the vestry room.[19] There were, however, a few instances of public penance. In another case in the same diocese in 1825, penance was ordered to be performed 'at the time of morning prayers and after the Nicene Creed is read.'[20] Sometimes the penance was performed in the body of the church, but not during service,[21] a practice that would permit those who knew of the ceremony to witness it.

A notorious case of public penance occurred in Fen Ditton, near Cambridge, in 1849, which brought the defamation jurisdiction into considerable disrepute. Edward Smith was proved to have said, in a public house in Fen Ditton, 'Mrs James your parson's wife, is a blasted whore and I can prove it.'[22] Martha James instituted a suit in the Arches Court in London, the Ely court (which sat in Cambridge) not having heard any defamation cases for many years. She duly proved her case, but the reason for performance of the penance in public is rather mysterious. The order of the court, as transcribed into the Assignation Book, was that

> Edward Smith shall on Sunday the sixth day of May ... immediately after Divine
> Service and Sermon are ended in the forenoon go into the Vestry Room or Church
> of the said parish of Fen Ditton and in the presence of the Minister or Officiating
> Minister of the said parish & likewise in the presence of the said Martha James
> and five or six of her friends if they be there otherwise in their absence shall with
> audible voice confess and say as follows ...[23]

The word 'or' in the phrase 'Vestry Room or Church' is distinctly odd. The
context would more naturally require 'Vestry Room *of the* Church.' The whole
tenor of the form of words is that the penance should be performed, as was
usual, in the vestry room. After service, Smith was to 'go into' the vestry
room, an expression apt to apply to a member of the congregation then in the
body of the church; it makes little sense to say that he should 'go into the vestry room or church.' Again, it makes no sense to say that the penance shall be
performed in the presence of Martha James 'and five or six of her friends if
they be there' if the penance was to be in the presence of the whole congregation. The use of the word 'or' instead of 'of the' has the appearance of an
attempt to draft the order in a form that would permit public penance, without
drawing attention to the variation from the usual form.

Whatever the intentions of the drafter of the order, it proved to be a disaster
for all concerned in the case. Rumour spread that there was to be public penance, and the village was filled with three thousand persons, and the church
packed with one thousand spectators, 'mostly members of the lower orders,'
who broke pews and windows, interrupted the service with noise, and threw
hassocks, brooms, and pieces of broken pews at the officiating clergyman.
Martha James was present, with her husband (who was, wisely, not officiating). According to a local newspaper, 'it was understood that an unavailing
attempt had been made in the morning to induce Mrs James to absolve Smith
from the penance, but that although the rector added his solicitations to the
other authorities, the lady positively refused, and insisted on the ceremony
being gone through.' Smith pushed, or was pushed, to the centre of the church,
and went through the motions of reading the recantation, though he could not
be heard for the din. Afterwards the windows of the rectory were broken. A
collection was taken to defray Smith's costs, but the proceeds were spent at a
nearby public house (a different one from that in which the slander had been
spoken), and eventually Smith was imprisoned for failure to pay the costs.[24]
The rector had to pay personally for the damage to the church, a requirement
that suggests that he (or his wife) was held responsible for the riot and therefore that it was by their own wish that the penance had been performed in public.[25] The conservative newspaper *John Bull* considered this an instance of an

'obsolete law ... injudiciously put in force,' and thought, evidently with some justification, that such incidents were likely to bring discredit on the church.[26]

It will be recalled that truth was not, strictly speaking, a defence, and the form of the penance, though it varied from diocese to diocese, generally fell short of an actual acknowledgment that the words spoken were untrue. In the forms illustrated (from Hereford and Winchester) the penitent recites that 'I have abused and defamed my neighbour' and that 'I do now recall' the words, and that 'I am heartily sorry for the same,' but this falls short of an express declaration that the words are untrue. In the form used in York, the words were said to be 'defamatory and slanderous' (but not false), and the defendant acknowledged that 'I spoke the said words rashly and unadvisedly and declare that I had no just grounds or reason for speaking the same.' Those present were called upon to 'think no worse of [the plaintiff] by reason of my speaking the ... words.'[27] In London, the form referred to 'scandalous and opprobrious' words 'to the injury and reproach of my neighbour's credit and reputation.'[28] In Norwich, the form commenced with an acknowledgment that 'being transported with passion, I did ...utter several scandalous and defamatory words.'[29] Again, the words were not expressly declared to be false. On the other hand, the form of retraction used in Salisbury included a declaration that the words had been spoken 'unadvisedly, falsely and slanderously,'[30] in Richmond that they were 'contrary to the Truth,'[31] and in Peterborough that 'I believe her life and conversation to be sober chaste and honest,'[32] apparently making no concession to the penitent who might maintain that the words were true. It should be noted, however, that in several dioceses penance was remitted altogether when the words were shown to have been true,[33] and the usual form of words required would here be a relevant consideration.

In some dioceses the form of penance simply referred to 'certain scandalous and opprobrious words' without repeating them, but in many dioceses the actual words proved to have been used were repeated, and the repetition of the word 'whore,' as in the Hereford illustration, is common. Schedules of penance include the phrases 'damned strumpet and soldier's trull,'[34] 'damned flaming bloody whore,'[35] 'nasty stinking whore,'[36] 'Billingsgate whore,'[37] 'damned blasted whore,'[38] 'great fat strumpet,'[39] and 'dirty strumpet.'[40] In some cases the names of third persons were included, thereby causing a repetition of the allegations against them, as in a Norwich case where the schedule of penance required the defendant to confess that he had said, 'You are a whore Miss Banham, a whore of Mr Forrest's and Mr Hatcher's.'[41] Very coarse language might be paraphrased, as in a case in the Arches Court, where the evidence proved that the defendant had said that 'Mr Richards had fucked' the plaintiff: the form of penance recited that he had said that 'Mr Richards had had the carnal use of her body, or to that effect.'[42] In a London case where the words had been spoken in Italian, the Italian words were included in the schedule of penance.[43]

Even with paraphrases, the performance of the ceremony of penance, especially where it did not include an acknowledgment that the words spoken were false, can have done little in most cases to restore the plaintiff's reputation. The effect was more likely to be the reverse, as was the opinion of the Chester registrar.[44] Many plaintiffs did not insist on it,[45] but a surprisingly large number did. In Norwich, of thirty-two cases where the plaintiff obtained sentence, retraction was performed in twenty-three.

It is probable that in many of these cases the facts were not so much that the plaintiff actively desired the performance of penance as that she failed to intervene to prevent it. After sentence had been given, the ordinary course of events would require performance of the penance, and the plaintiff's proctor would have no interest in stopping it, because further proceedings might bring more fees, chargeable to the defendant. In a Carlisle case, where matters had proceeded to a significavit to compel performance of the penance, it is recorded in the Act Book that 'Pearson, the proctor for the complainant being deceased, [the] cause [was] dismissed for want of promotion.'[46] This certainly suggests that the plaintiff had no strong personal interest in compelling performance of the penance, for if she had, she would have engaged a new proctor.

In a number of cases, however, there is evidence that plaintiffs actively desired performance of the penance, in one case even against the express suggestion of the judge. Here, 'the judge strongly recommended to the plaintiffs proctor the propriety of the plaintiff accepting an apology and of avoiding the scandal of compelling the defendant to perform the penance.' The suit had been brought by Mary Willson against William Willson, described as 'gentleman,' so it may be assumed that it was a case of a quarrel within a socially respectable family. The defendant had confessed the slander. The judge's recommendation, however, was not adopted, for performance of the penance was duly certified two weeks later.[47] The judge's reference to the 'scandal' of penance shows that the element of public shame had not entirely disappeared, at least among the socially respectable. Performance of penance in the church would be locally notorious, even if it occurred in the vestry room on a weekday, or when there was no service.[48]

Similarly, in a Norwich case, also at a high social level, the defendant being the wife of a baronet, the plaintiff, having refused a proposal to settle the dispute by arbitration, went on to obtain a sentence, and not only to insist on performance of the penance but to argue strenuously for an order compelling performance of penance in church. However, the judge ordered it to be performed in the clergyman's house (a quite common form of order in Norwich), where, no doubt, it was less conspicuous. The judge is reported as saying:

> By Mr Rackham [plaintiff's proctor] it is contended that retraction should take place in the parish church, and that the court should make no distinction between the rich and the poor. I quite agree in that observation, that there should be no distinction made in consequence of the position of the parties. My impression is that the practice of the court, whenever the defendant has applied, has been to grant that, when the words have not been uttered in public, the retraction should not be made in public.[49]

This is a case in which the plaintiff and her advisers evidently desired to inflict a degree of public humiliation on the defendant.

That penance had a particularly heavy impact on those of high social status is also suggested by the answer of the Exeter chancellor to a question from the Ecclesiastical Courts Commission as to whether he had had occasion to order penance. He replied, 'I have had a case recently of parties in rather a higher situation in life than are usually involved in such suits.' The case referred to is probably Wallis v. Cory (1828), in which the defendant was a clergyman's daughter 'of highly respectable connexion.' She was imprisoned for non-payment of costs, and petitioned, from jail, for further time to be allowed to her for performance of the penance.[50] The case evidently remained in the judge's mind when he gave his evidence to the commission in the following year.

Performance of penance by a man might have an adverse impact on his family. In a Lichfield case of 1830, the defendant's wife, acting independently of her husband and his attorney, consulted a friend, who wrote to the husband's proctor urging him to avoid an order for penance:

> I am sure you will do every thing in your power to settle this matter rather than let the business go to the full extent, for the sake of the defendant's wife who is a very superior woman, & her three little boys as it would be so hurtful to her feelings & degrading to her family, that Mr Hutton should do penance &c.[51]

This shows again that penance was not universally perceived as an empty ceremony, and that it might have a severe social impact on a 'superior' woman and on her family.

In a number of cases, as we have seen, the plaintiff proceeded to the extent of causing the defendant to be imprisoned for non-performance of the penance.[52] In May 1855, near the very end of the court's jurisdiction, a plaintiff threatened enforcement. Her proctor wrote to the defendant:

I beg to intimate that the judge at the last court gave sentence in this cause against you & you were enjoined to perform penance & unless you intimate to me as the proctor for the party complainant that you consent to perform the same between this and Saturday next I shall cause monition to issue to compel the same ...[53]

Penance might be ordered in the clergyman's house, as in the Norwich case of the baronet's wife,[54] or 'privately before the vicar,'[55] or in the house of a churchwarden.[56] In some cases it was ordered to be performed in the 'vestry room or church porch'[57] but I have found no record of actual performance of the ceremony in the porch. Penance, or some equivalent form of apology, might also be performed in the court, either where the plaintiff waived a formal penance,[58] or, in some dioceses, by the general practice of the court, without the plaintiff's agreement.[59] The court might put pressure on the defendant to make an informal apology out of court: in one case a defendant 'was advised to make an apology before next court.'[60] There were cases of penance performed in jail,[61] and in the court under custody.[62] The penance might be remitted altogether,[63] sometimes with the substitution of an admonition to the defendant not to offend again in future,[64] in which case the plaintiff was entitled to a monition (formal order) to this effect, but at her own expense.[65] Granville Vernon, the York chancellor, used his discretion in the matter, ordering performance of penance in cases where he thought the defendant deserved greater censure.[66] In one case Askwith, acting for the defendant, wrote to the instructing attorney to say that his client ought to think himself well off as he had to pay costs only of £5, and 'as he has no penance to perform which the court might have enjoined.'[67]

In a number of cases it is recorded that the plaintiff attended the penance personally,[68] and in a few cases the plaintiff signed the certificate of its performance.[69] The London case of Cohen v. Cohen is interesting in this context, because the parties were Jewish, and it might therefore have been supposed that the plaintiff would not be particularly anxious to enforce or to witness a ceremony of this sort in a Christian church. But the penance was enforced, and some of Rosetta Cohen's (the plaintiff's) friends attended.[70] In a Norwich case also, where the parties were Jewish, performance of penance was enforced.[71] It may be that the plaintiffs in these cases regarded the Church of England simply as part of the secular order; on the other hand it is possible that they wished to cause additional inconvenience and humiliation to the defendants, by compelling participation in a ceremony perceived as alien to their own traditions.

In some of the London cases involving Jews, the form of the penance was altered. The usual form for London contained the phrase 'to the scandal of my

Christian religion.' In Israel v. Barnett (1819) the word 'Christian' was omitted from the manuscript, showing that attention was paid to the matter at the drafting stage; in Salamon v. Benjamin (1821) the word 'Christian' remains, but the word 'my,' though written in the manuscript, is crossed through (by X) and the word 'the' substituted, suggesting a last-minute alteration.[72] The cases were not so common as to have produced a settled practice. In the Norwich case, mentioned above, the standard form of penance for that diocese was used, including a reference to the words having been spoken 'contrary to good manners and the rules of Christian charity,' and a repetition of the Lord's Prayer.[73]

The plaintiff was entitled to notice of the performance of the penance, so that she might attend if she wished,[74] and in several cases plaintiffs complained that they had not received the proper notice,[75] suggesting that witnessing the actual performance of the penance was important to them. In a Llandaff case there was a confusion about the time of the penance, which had been ordered to be performed in a private house (probably the churchwarden's). The plaintiff filed an affidavit that she had attended at the proper time but had been refused admission; a counter-affidavit by the defendant asserted that the plaintiff had not come at the right time. The court ordered a new penance to be performed in the vestry room of the church on twelve hours' notice to the plaintiff.[76]

In most dioceses the plaintiff's friends (in numbers usually stated as five or six) might attend, and sometimes they did so,[77] but in York the form of the order did not refer to friends, and Askwith wrote that it was 'not usual' for them to attend.[78] In one York case, the plaintiff, who was evidently away from home at the time, specifically asked Askwith, her proctor, to write to Mr Bromby (the clergyman instructing Askwith) in Hull, to inform her friends there of the time of the performance of the penance 'according to directions left with' Bromby.[79] This was a plaintiff who had gone to some trouble to have her friends present, though whether they did in fact attend is not recorded.[80]

In a Llandaff case of 1828, the question of due performance of penance was actually carried on appeal to the Arches Court in London. The defendant, having been ordered to do penance in the vestry room, delivered notice of his intention to do so, as the Arches Court said, 'in rather a strange and insulting manner.' The notice was signed 'yours affectionately' and was delivered to the plaintiff in the street by the town crier. The defendant alleged that he had attended at the church at the proper time, and finding no one there, had read the declaration in the presence of a friend. The Llandaff court accepted this, but the plaintiff appealed successfully to the Arches Court, which ordered the penance to be duly performed and certified. The defendant, who had initially confessed the slander, paid a high price for resisting performance of the penance: he was ordered to pay the costs in both courts, amounting (after taxation) to £47.10.4. The plaintiff too had taken a high risk in appealing: her bill of costs in the Arches Court (before taxation) was £53.0.11. No rational considerations could possibly justify these expenses for the sake of a two-minute ceremony. We must here be in the presence of the phenomenon that, when personal feelings run high, litigation can accumulate a momentum of its own.[81]

The motives of plaintiffs in enforcing performance of penance were often mixed, as were their motives for litigating in the first place.[82] They sometimes included a desire to inflict punishment. Enforcement of penance was probably perceived to serve this purpose: it added to the costs, it was personally inconvenient to the defendant, and it included an element of humiliation.

# Part III

# THE CASES

# 8

# The Parties

The great majority of plaintiffs were women, but there were significant variations in this respect from one diocese to another. In Chester and York about 10
per cent of the total number of cases were brought by men, and in Peterborough more than 25 per cent. But in Bath and Wells, with a total number of 237
cases, there was not one brought by a man, and in London, with a total number
of 103 cases, there was only one.[1] One explanation of the discrepancy may be
that a steady stream of cases was, to a degree, self-sustaining. People would
know that this was what men sometimes did, and the proctors would be ready
and willing to undertake suits. But when numbers sank to very low levels there
must have been strong pressure on men, even if aggrieved, not to institute a
suit. At every step the potential plaintiff would have been met with scepticism.
His friends as well as his opponents, and the proctors on both sides, would let
him know that his actions were highly unusual, not to say ridiculous. In a
letter from a London proctor to one at Winchester, about a suit brought there
by a clergyman, the writer said:

> [S]uits of defamation are rarely instituted in ecclesiastical courts unless the party
> defamed is a female – in fact I do not recollect an instance in these courts that
> ever received a judicial determination where the party defamed was a man.[2]

A man contemplating a defamation suit and met with this information
would have had to be very determined to persist, especially since the litigation
offered no prospect of financial advantage. But had the same circumstances
arisen in the diocese of Peterborough the potential plaintiff would probably
have received considerably more encouragement from his proctor.

The defendants were more evenly divided between the sexes, but there was
a consistent predominance of male defendants. The figures for Norwich and

York, given in table 4, below, show that about 65 per cent of the defendants were men. Dr Morris, in her study of the diocese of Bath and Wells, found a similar proportion.[3] Lord Brougham's characterization, mentioned in the introduction, of the defamation cases as squabbles between women is certainly not an accurate overall picture (though there were some cases of the sort he had in mind). On the other hand, the predominance of men as defendants is not so great as to support a conclusion that the defamation jurisdiction was primarily, or even largely, an opportunity for women to redress the wrongs done to them by men (though, again, there were some cases of this sort). One contemporary writer on the rights of women, however, did include a brief treatment of this branch of the law.[4]

It is evident that women were thought just as capable as men of causing damage to reputation, perhaps more capable. Gossip was usually depicted as female (see plate 10), and George Eliot went so far as to write that 'public opinion in these cases is always of the feminine gender.'[5] No easy generalizations can be supported by the evidence in the court records, mainly because the records cannot reveal the frequency with which instances of actual slander led to defamation suits. This is a frequency that may well have varied by sex of slanderer for any of several plausible reasons, not all of them tending in the same direction.

The figures in the table show also the marital status of the women who were parties. It will be seen that, both among plaintiffs and defendants, married women predominate. Suits brought by one married woman against another were quite common. Morris's figures from Bath and Wells are similar. It can be seen, therefore, that the protection of the marriage prospects of single women cannot be identified as a primary function or effect of the defamation jurisdiction (though there were some cases that fell into this category). Perhaps it is not very surprising that a large proportion of the women were married, since most women were married for a large part of their adult lives.

The ages of the parties are not usually given in the court records, unless they were minors. In York, there were five plaintiffs, all unmarried women, who were minors. Three defendants were minors, one woman and two men. Where the plaintiff was a minor, it was necessary for a curator or guardian to be appointed to conduct the litigation in her name. Normally the natural person for this appointment would be her father, but if the father were dead or absent, or if it were necessary for the father to be a witness, some other person would have to be appointed as guardian. The guardian might be a woman, and there are cases where the plaintiff's mother or sister was appointed.[6] The youngest plaintiff seems to have been a fourteen-year-old girl in Norwich, who took her mother's side in a market-place dispute, and was told, 'Go along you young whore for you are as bad as your old bawd of a mother, for she brings you up to nothing but whoring and fortune telling.'[7] The age of adult plaintiffs can be learned occasionally from the depositions: the oldest plaintiff appears to be one in the diocese of Llandaff said to have been 'upwards of seventy years of age,'[8] and the oldest defendant a man in York said to have been 'upwards of eighty years of age.'[9]

Where the defendant was a minor, the case could not proceed until a *curator ad litem* (litigation guardian) had been appointed. Askwith acted for the plaintiff in one such case, earlier mentioned, in which a seventeen-year-old boy had accused the plaintiff of consorting with men for 3s. 6d., and had shouted out at her in the street, 'three and sixpence.' Askwith encountered some procedural difficulties. He obtained an order from the court requiring the defendant to appear by a guardian, but then he heard that this might be resisted:

> I understand the father is advised to refuse being appointed curator ad litem of his son and in case he does much difficulty will arise I fear in getting any other person to act for him under such circumstances.[10]

Eventually, the father did appear for the defendant as guardian, and the case proceeded to proof. The rarity of cases against minors is further shown by difficulties that arose in drafting the sentence. Askwith had to write to proctors in London for advice:

> On the hearing of this cause our judge (Mr Vernon) was satisfied as to the proof of defamation, but felt some difficulty as to the proper sentence to be given against the minor, in consequence of some observations made respecting it by his counsel, and Mr Nicoll the counsel for the plaintiff, for whom I am proctor, is desirous of seeing a draft of sentence in a similar case with which I am not able to supply him from our records. If you should not have a sentence in a defamation cause of which you can send me a copy you perhaps can furnish me with one in some other cause against a minor defendant.[11]

The reply enclosed a draft, including a clause for costs, though the writer had 'doubts whether a minor can be condemned in costs.'[12] In the event, Vernon did not award costs, a decision that Askwith thought to be 'an indulgence in favor of youthful depravity.'[13]

Women are usually described only by their marital status, but sometimes the records reveal that they had independent occupations. In a York case a woman who was involved in a suit and a counter-suit, is described in the records simply as 'widow,' but it appears from a letter of her proctor

(Askwith) mentioned earlier that she was a wholesale dealer, which gave Askwith cause for concern that she would not be sympathetically treated by the court in respect of costs.[14] A Bristol woman defendant is described as a 'shoe binder.'[15] Some of the bills of costs show that women witnesses had independent occupations.[16] Generally occupations are given for men, including the husbands of the women who were parties. These occupations, for York and Norwich, are listed in appendix B, below. This information will not sustain a very refined analysis. Classification in terms of social status is difficult, because the same title may indicate many different things. A clerk in the Foreign Office is 'very different' from a clerk in the Post Office,[17] not to mention a clerk in holy orders. Much discussion could be devoted to the distinctions between a gentleman and an esquire, or between a farmer and a yeoman, or between an innkeeper, a victualler, a beerseller, and an ale draper, or between a shoemaker and a cordwainer. Again, the occupation of clothier might signify trade, craft, or unskilled work. Moreover, there is the question of the reliability of the description (self-description in the case of plaintiffs, and plaintiffs' description in the case of defendants). Plaintiffs may have had an interest, within certain limits, in enhancing their own status, and in reducing in some cases, or perhaps in other cases exaggerating, that of their adversaries.[18] For some historical purposes no doubt such questions must be addressed and resolved, but for present purposes this is neither necessary nor desirable. The numbers are small, and the information has no wide-scale demographic significance. Consequently the occupations have been listed precisely as stated in the records, roughly (but only roughly) grouped under the following headings: gentry, professions, office-holders, farmers, trades, crafts, and unskilled work. So far as possible I have listed related occupations together. In the great majority of the cases both parties in each particular case are from the same walk of life.

Among rural occupations farmers, and among urban occupations small trades and crafts predominate. The very top and the very bottom of the social scale are little represented. In the evidence to the Ecclesiastical Courts Commission several witnesses stated that defamation cases chiefly involved the lower classes.[19] Vernon, the York chancellor, was asked, 'Are your causes of defamation principally or altogether among the lower classes of the people?' and answered 'Entirely.'[20] The chancellor of Salisbury, in reply to the question 'Were ... defamation causes made use of by the lower classes of people to harass one another?' said, 'Just so, in consequence of a little spite of one against the other.'[21] The Chester registrar, when asked 'are these defamation causes used among the lower classes of society?' answered, 'They are.'[22] These answers do not appear entirely consistent with the information in the court records, and they reveal as much about how the respondents defined the 'lower classes' and what ecclesiastical lawyers considered the social purpose of litigation as they do about the actual social status of the litigants in defamation cases. The Norwich registrar perhaps was nearer the mark. When he was asked a similar question, he replied, 'I should say the lower orders, very small tradesmen and mechanics, and people of that kind.'[23] Defamation was evidently not a respectable kind of litigation, compared with testamentary or even matrimonial business. It was accessible to persons of extremely modest means – a feature that might nowadays be considered a merit rather than a reproach – but it did not attract large numbers of the poorest in society, or of the absolutely destitute.

The exclusion of the very poor can be deduced from a letter to a Peterborough proctor written by a parish overseer, advising the proctor not to accept the plaintiff's suit. The proctor had written a preliminary letter to the defendant, threatening a citation unless an apology was forthcoming. The overseer wrote that the defendant considered himself the insulted party (a not uncommon opinion among defendants in defamation cases, as we have seen), and said, 'as neither party has any thing to pay with, being both paupers, perhaps it would be best not to notice it.' He added further discouragement by saying that the proctor's client had 'imposed upon me (as Overseer of the Parish) by obtaining money under a false pretence.'[24] As the case does not appear in the Act Book, it may be presumed that the advice was followed, and that no citation was issued. Unlike some classes of ecclesiastical court business, defamation cases could not be pursued *in forma pauperis*, i.e., with a proctor assigned by the court and without liability for costs.[25]

In a case appealed to the Arches Court from Exeter in 1821, it was argued that defamation cases were so clearly associated with the lower classes that the court ought not to encourage them in respectable social circles. Sir John Nicholl rejected this, being evidently of the opinion that a woman's reputation for chastity was of greater value in higher than in lower social circles:

> I cannot agree that suits of this description between persons in the higher classes of society ought to be discouraged, and less attended to than suits of a similar description between persons in a low condition of life; on the contrary, in the higher classes of society acquiescence would be almost an admission of the charge; and in those classes female reputation is of higher importance and value to the person who possesses it; if an attempt be made to rob any one of that reputation, there is no other remedy, but reference to this Court, to which the law and constitution of the country has placed the cognizance of such offences.[26]

On the other hand, it might be said with equal plausibility that good reputation was particularly important to the poor, just because they had so few other valuable possessions. It was argued on behalf of a publican's wife that

> It need scarcely be added that to a person in the promovent's humble station of life an unblemished reputation is of the first consideration; in its preservation from foul and malignant slander as a wife and mother she cannot be too jealous and in the present instance the character of her house, the only public one in the parish, must stand or fall by the character of its inmates.[27]

Since male plaintiffs form a distinct class, it seems useful to list their professions separately, and this has been done, for England and Wales as a whole (258 cases). The result is included in appendix B. The professions are more heavily represented here (46), especially clergy (34), and this is understandable, because an accusation of unchastity against a clergyman threatened his livelihood.

It will be recalled that the defamation jurisdiction was part of the general English law, and that, like the probate and matrimonial jurisdictions, it governed the whole population, including those not members of the Church of England. In the last chapter, reference was made to several cases where Jewish defendants performed penance. There is no reliable way of estimating the religious affiliations of the parties generally, because these affiliations are not normally included with the parties' descriptions and only come to light when some aspect of the procedure, or a letter or report in a newspaper, happens to identify them. Certainly a number of cases must have involved Protestant dissenters. Seven plaintiffs were dissenting ministers (see appendix B), and at least one was the wife of a dissenting minister.[28] In a Ripon case in 1850, the defendant, who was accompanied to the church by a large crowd when he went there to perform penance, and thereby attracted the attention of the press, was 'an independent in religion and a strenuous opposer of church rates.' The newspaper reporter adds, 'Hence to him this submission to the episcopal church was peculiarly galling.'[29] In a Chester case the defamatory words were spoken as the parties came out of a charity sermon in a dissenting chapel, though this does not establish that they were dissenters.[30] Some of the parties were probably Roman Catholics: in a case in Bath, in 1836, four of the witnesses were Catholics, but the religion of the parties themselves is not stated.[31]

As we have seen,[32] litigation was predominantly among neighbours. Often too it was among close relatives. In a London case of 1840 the parties were doubly related, the defendant having married a sister – an older sister, curiously enough – of his father's second wife. The latter brought a suit against him, so that he was sued by a woman who was both his stepmother and his sister-in-law.[33] There are other cases of suits brought by a sister-in-law against a brother-in-law[34] or against a sister-in-law,[35] and by a brother-in-law against a brother-in-law.[36] There are also cases of suits by sister against brother,[37] sister against sister,[38] mother against son,[39] stepmother against stepson,[40] father against son,[41] niece against uncle,[42] niece against aunt,[43] daughter-in-law against father-in-law,[44] father-in-law against daughter-in-law,[45] and between cousins.[46] Sometimes family disputes, when they had progressed to the stage of a suit in the ecclesiastical court, did not stop at one, but produced multiple suits, and counter-suits.[47]

Usually in family litigation the parties were not residing in the same household, but there is one London case in which they were living under the same roof. Harriet Johnson, the second wife of Charles Johnson, lived alone in rooms on the first floor of the house (i.e., upstairs), refusing to associate with her husband's six daughters by a previous marriage. Charles Johnson took his meals and associated sometimes with his wife, and sometimes with his daughters. On one occasion, according to the evidence of a servant,

> Mr Johnson and his six daughters were at supper in the parlour ... Harriet Johnson called down the stair case from her apartments up stairs 'Mary Johnson you are a damned whore ... I say again, you are a whore.'[48]

One of the other witnesses, the gardener, heard her say to the sisters the next morning that 'they were all whores and damned whores.' He described the household arrangements by saying that Harriet Johnson lived separately 'on account of some family differences' – a rather mild appraisal of the circumstances, it may be thought. Apparently the differences were not resolved, as Harriet Johnson moved out of the house shortly after the incidents mentioned, and no fewer than four suits were commenced in the consistory court, one by Mary Johnson and three by Harriet Johnson (against Charles, Mary, and another daughter). Witnesses were produced only in Mary Johnson's suit, and after four months all the suits were settled.[49]

In view of the wide variety of circumstances that led to defamation suits, it is scarcely appropriate to think in terms of a 'typical' case, but the commonest kind of suit may be said to have been one brought by – or at least in the name of – a married woman of moderate to low social status against a close neighbour.

# 9

# The Injury

We come now to ask, what was the injury complained of? The question is related to wide questions of social and sexual history – such as, what was the harm done by an imputation of unchastity? or, looking at the matter from the other side, how valuable was good sexual reputation? – but it is not the same as those questions. The question addressed here is, what was the injury complained of in defamation suits? – a question on which the court records, together with the surviving proctors' correspondence, constitute the bulk of the available evidence. An examination of this evidence will offer part of an answer to the broader questions, but only part, because on the broader questions there are many other sources of relevant historical evidence, and many reasons for caution in drawing general conclusions from the defamation cause papers alone. The conduct, circumstances, and motives of the six thousand or so persons who were parties to defamation suits in this period are important in the present context, but these persons cannot be thought of as a kind of social sample likely to be representative of the whole population.

## The Nature of the Accusation

The minimum requirement for a successful suit in the ecclesiastical court was that the words proved should impute adultery or fornication. In some dioceses it was usual to give, in the libel, the precise words alleged to have been used by the defendant (an example is transcribed in appendix A), but in others it was generally stated as a matter of form that the defendant had said of the plaintiff 'that she was a whore.' The word 'whore' in this context, equivalent of the Latin 'meretrix,'[1] did not imply payment for sexual services. It amounted merely to an assertion that the defendant had accused the plaintiff of the necessary ecclesiastical law crime: the use of the actual word did not have to be proved, even when it was stated in the libel. As we have seen, the word 'whore' was in common general use, and there also it did not necessarily imply financial dealings, as when a man said of a woman that he remembered the date 'when I made her a whore.'[2] The word might describe a mere irregular marriage, as where one man accused another of living with a woman (ostensibly his wife) 'as rogue and whore.'[3] In a Bristol case a woman said, 'There was never a whore without a rogue.'[4] Interrogatories in another case suggest that the plaintiff had asked the defendant, by way of seeking advice, whether she (the plaintiff) should not marry the man she was living with 'as they had lived whore and rogue together long enough.'[5] The witnesses denied hearing the words, but the question shows that it was not implausible that the phrase might be applied in a semi-jocular manner by a woman to herself. Even the expression 'common prostitute' sometimes was used to imply no more than sexual misconduct or an irregular marriage.[6]

In some cases, however, there was an accusation of actual prostitution: 'she is a common prostitute; we will have her indicted for a nuisance';[7] 'you have been walking the streets, and that's the way you get your living, whore.'[8] In a Hereford case the defendant said to the plaintiff that she was a 'damned blasted whore & that she was kept for the use of other people.'[9] Plaintiffs were accused in several cases of being a man's 'kept mistress,'[10] or of permitting their husbands to receive money for their own sexual favours to others: 'thy man lives by thy whoring';[11] 'you are Sir George's whore; your husband has received money for it.'[12] A slightly less severe accusation was that the plaintiff had received some indirect benefit in return for sexual favours, such as employment for herself,[13] or for her husband: 'If you were not whore to the master your husband would have been off the ground long ago.'[14] In two Exeter cases, the plaintiffs' proctor argued that the slander was not of the 'common and almost usual stamp and to be considered merely words of heat, such as "whores,"' but specifically implied that the plaintiffs (two sisters) had received benefits in exchange for sexual favours:

'You are two damnation whores and live by whoring and have fine rooms kept up by gentlemen for you ...' [and to one of the sisters] 'Thou ... art George Hako-wole's whore and hast thirty pounds a year of him.'[15]

An accusation of irregular marriage could do serious harm. In London in 1831 Thomas Rose, a porter at Symonds Inn (a place of residential accommodation for lawyers), stood to lose his position on account of such an accusation, and he was willing to run the very high risk of actually suborning false evidence in an attempt to prove the validity of the marriage. He and his associate were arrested and charged with the crime, and the defamation case was brought to an end shortly afterwards by the death of his wife, Catherine.[16] In a St David's case in 1849, a man complained, in a letter to his proctor, that a former servant had 'given circulation to a report that Mrs Phillips ... was not a married woman, that all Swansea knew it and that in consequence no respectable person would associate with her.'[17] In the diocese of Chester Sarah Whitehead instituted no fewer than five defamation suits in an attempt to quash rumours that 'she is not mistress Whitehead but is kept by Mr Whitehead as a kept mistress, and her husband is living in London.'[18] Two of the defendants were imprisoned in Lancaster Castle for non-appearance, where they spent four and five months respectively.[19] A Gloucester case also demonstrates the damage to good reputation caused by such allegations. The libel alleged the following conversation between Elizabeth Short and Charlotte Pumnell:

> CP: 'You are a bloody whore and are living along with a married man.' ES: 'I am not, I have been a decent wife for many years.' CP: 'You cannot call yourself a decent wife to be living with a married man. Fetch out your bully; you are not married; you are a bloody bunting whore.'

Charlotte Pumnell appeared in court, admitted calling the plaintiff a whore, and was admonished and ordered to pay 40s. costs.[20] The comparatively lenient disposition shows that the judge did not regard this as a particularly egregious case, but the fact that such insults were in use and that Short complained of them shows that they were capable of causing damage; the amount of the costs, viewed, as the judge probably did view it, as a penalty, is large enough to signify definite judicial disapproval.

An aggravated form of accusation was that the plaintiff had borne an illegitimate child,[21] sometimes many years previously.[22] It might be alleged that particular children, reputedly related to the plaintiff in other ways, were really her illegitimate children,[23] or, more commonly, that the plaintiff's own undoubted children were not her husband's.[24] Sometimes a reference to 'bastards' was a way of adding insult to what was in substance no more than an allegation of irregular marriage: 'Go your ways in and mind your six bastards; the parson was never paid his fees yet for marrying thee.'[25] Several cases involved imputations of incest, three with a brother,[26] one with a father,[27] one with an uncle,[28] and one with a son-in-law (probably meaning stepson).[29]

There were some accusations of miscarriage from illegitimate pregnancy,[30] and of abortion, and attempted abortion. A clergyman's wife was accused of saying of the plaintiff that she was with child and 'had slipt it' and that she 'had gone off in the family way by old Tongue, had been put to bed, and come back a maid.'[31] One defendant was reported to have said, 'Why, damn it, she's worse than one of those who stand the road because she's destroyed it,' and, to another person,

> [Did you not hear] she was in the family way? ... She was then, for that was what she went to Dr Kerr for, and Dr Kerr said if she'd stopt any longer she'd stopt too long, he couldn't a'done any thing for her.[32]

In a Carlisle case of 1839, the defendant said that Isabella Storey, a house-maid,

> came into the kitchen weeping, and demanded of the defendant whether he could either prove or swear that she was with child to Thomas Coats and had taken some stuff to put the child back.

The defendant said that they all knew that she and Coats kept company together, and added that

> she ... had asked him [defendant] to make her some steel filings to clean grates with, and that he could not make them but had got Robert Studholme (a black-smith) to make them for her, and she knew best what use she had put them to.[33]

In a London case, the defendant said, 'They say she has had some medicine ... They say she has had a miscarriage ... [by] somebody who knows some-thing about medicine.'[34] One case involved an allegation that the plaintiff was the mother of a baby whose body had been found in a hay loft,[35] and three cases include actual allegations of infanticide.[36] Infanticide was a crime at common law (murder), and procuring an abortion was a crime by statute,[37] so these allegations were technically beyond the jurisdiction of the ecclesiastical courts.

Pre-marital sexual intercourse, though very common,[38] was not legitimated even by subsequent marriage between the parties, was disreputable at all lev-els of society, and had a long-lasting effect both on women themselves and on their families. In a York case an eighteen-year-old woman was accosted in the street and called a bastard, the fact being, as her attorney explained, that she 'is an illegitimate daughter of Mr Joseph Smith ... but by his present wife & immediately previous to their marriage.'[39] 'I was not married with a big belly if you was,' a woman was accused of saying in one case.[40] Another said, 'Jack Barker meddled on thee before he had thee.'[41] In one of the comparatively few cases involving the upper gentry, the wife of a baronet had accused the plaintiff of living with her husband before their marriage (though, it must be added, not only in sin but also in adultery, as the plaintiff was then separated from a former husband still living).[42]

Some accusations impute multiple lovers to a plaintiff, employing, in some cases, extravagant exaggeration. 'Get away you nasty whore, you have been rode by all Cheltenham,' one woman was supposed to have said, 'thereby meaning and implying,' as the libel prosaically explains, 'that the said Charlotte Matthews had committed adultery or had had criminal intercourse with a great number of persons residing in Cheltenham.'[43] Scarcely less extravagant was the accusation that 'all the crofters at Dunstead have shag'd thee; thou would fit a regiment of soldiers thou great whore; be off with thee.'[44] Other cases demonstrate the injurious effect on a woman's reputation of undiscriminating sexual activity: 'She'll lie under the hedge with any one,'[45] 'she would lay down to any dog,'[46] or, in an urban environment, 'she is common to every fellow in the street.'[47]

An aggravating feature of an accusation was an imputation that the plaintiff had voracious sexual desires. 'Hot-arsed' and similar phrases occur in the cause papers several times.[48] In a York case one woman said of another 'that she was like a salty bitch ready for any body.'[49] One woman complained that a man had said, 'I would not be a nine inch prick in your way, for you would not refuse it.'[50] A more moderate imputation of sexual desire underlay the assertion that 'old Hogg [the plaintiff's husband] is got so fat he cannot do it for her & it is a deed of charity for some one to do something for the woman.'[51]

Many cases, as we have seen, included a claim by the defendant, often expressed in coarse language, to have been a partner in the alleged misconduct: 'I've fucked thee twice in thy own bed';[52] 'I have shagged her twice and have cut off hair from her cunt and here it is.'[53] In a York case, the defendant was alleged to have attacked the plaintiff with deliberate attempt to cause serious damage to her reputation. Addressing her in the presence of her father and brother, he said,

> There's your Susy ... wants to whore and nobody know it; I've fuck'd her in Fenton Mistal, and I've fuck'd her in Dick Burly's, and whatever company she's in I'll tell her out [i.e., denounce her], and if ever she gets married I'll tell her out.[54]

This appears to be a case of an amorous relationship turned sour, for one of the witnesses in an associated case said that they 'have been considered sweethearts.'[55] In another York case the defendant, who had fathered the plaintiff's illegitimate child, attempted to impede her marriage to another man, telling him that 'he should not have her; if he did he would make a Cuckold of him.'[56]

Women rarely accused themselves of unchastity, though there are exceptions even here. In a Winchester case a woman was proved to have said to a man, 'Get thee home to that good for nothing strumpet of thine ... which I have no doubt has been the same to thee as I have been myself.' The suit was brought by the woman referred to as a strumpet, but the defendant's accusation was principally aimed at the man, who was the reputed father of her two illegitimate children, and who, she said, 'had used her very ill.'[57]

A man might use words implying his own sexual attractions: 'Thou laid at our back door with thy coats up and wanted me to come out and meddle with thee,'[58] 'You have inveigled me to lay with you above a hundred times,'[59] 'She asked me to go with her three times before I would go with her.'[60] Much attention has been given to the question of women's sexual desire in the nineteenth century.[61] The defamation cause papers, as we have seen, contain numerous references to it. On the whole, considering that the number of cases is quite small and that the parties to defamation causes are not necessarily representative of the general population, they cannot be considered strong evidence of the general attitudes and practices of women, though they tend to modify any easy generalizations. The papers are, however, somewhat stronger evidence of what men might boast of, and still stronger evidence that manifestation of high sexual desire in women was considered by both sexes to be disreputable.

## The Circumstances of the Accusation

Many of the defamation cases involved not only a disparagement of the plaintiff's character but a direct personal insult, often in language of coarse abuse. At an earlier period in the history of the ecclesiastical courts, it had been supposed, or at least hoped, by some practitioners that the jurisdiction of the courts might be enlarged so as to extend to abusive or insulting words, even if they did not impute an ecclesiastical crime. In the late fifteenth century, defamation causes began to be called causes 'diffamationis sive convicii,'[62] an expression regularly rendered in the nineteenth-century papers as 'defamation or reproach,' and the practitioners' books advised that both should be pleaded.[63] Whether this device ever did result in an enlargement of the courts' jurisdiction is doubtful.[64] By the nineteenth century, certainly, the plaintiff had in every case to establish (by the evidence of two witnesses) the imputation of fornication or adultery. Nevertheless it can still be seen in many cases that the plaintiff was in reality complaining of two distinct injuries: the loss of reputation, and also the immediate hurt of the insult. So a plaintiff might complain, as one did to her proctor, of 'a gross insult and a very great scandal upon my character.'[65] The distinction, derived from the Roman civil law, remains in modern Scottish law, where defamation (injury to reputation) is distinguished from convicium (insult or abuse).[66]

Abusive words addressed directly to the plaintiff took many forms. Words of angry abuse were common, as where one woman said to another, 'Bess, you are a bloody thundering whore.'[67] Many cases involved more or less general insults of this sort, often arising out of a collateral quarrel that originally had nothing to do with the plaintiff's reputation.[68] In other cases the words were more reasoned, specific, or conversational, though not for these reasons necessarily less offensive. In a York case, for example, one woman was alleged to have said to another, 'You have been his [Thomas Nightingale's] kept mistress for many years, and there he is and can't deny it.'[69]

Sometimes, in a conversation between women, the defendant compared her own moral conduct with that of the plaintiff, to the latter's disadvantage, as in the case where the defendant supposedly said, 'I was not married with a big belly if you was.'[70] Similarly, in a Chester case, the defendant was proved to have said to the plaintiff, 'I never went a-shagging for apples or oranges ... You did ... with Peter Smollett.'[71] Again, in a Gloucester case, 'My arse was never done over by a son in law like thine was by James Lord. You nasty stinking rotten old whore.'[72]

The insulting words might be combined with threats of violence,[73] or with actual violence and deliberate intimidation or humiliation. In a York case the plaintiff was attacked by a woman in the parlour of her own house (which was a public house):

> Hannah Wormald said to her, they tell me thou wears breeches, and she then took ... Ann Gartside who is a delicate little woman, and turn[ed] up her clothes all round and laid all bare to see; it was quite shameful to see her; ... Ann Gartside was ashamed and ran out of the room into the kitchen and ... Hannah Wormald after her; ... Hannah Wormald then called ... Ann Gartside a whore and a town's whore, that she was like a salty bitch ready for any body ... and she also struck at her and tore the cap off her head.

When Joseph Gartside, Ann's husband, tried to intervene, he was knocked down by Joshua Wormald, Hannah's husband.[74]

Women's clothing was supposed to have some sort of connexion with moral character,[75] though the supposed link was highly variable. A woman might be accused of overdressing to attract men: one (male) defendant said that 'she used trinkets and curls and paint on purpose to go with men.'[76] Or it might be suggested that she obtained her fine clothes from the proceeds of prostitution:[77] 'you sleep with your lodgers and you get money from them to buy your new caps';[78] 'How do you get your dresses, you stinking whore, by laying on your back';[79] 'Mrs Dee would not have so many fine caps and clothes if Seaborne's money had not supported it.'[80] On the other hand, there was no sure protection from insults to be found in underdressing: one woman was alleged to have said to another, 'You go into the house and mend your stockings you nasty lazy stinking strumpet. ... You are a nasty lazy stinking jade. ... You walk the street by night with fellows.'[81]

The occasion chosen for the speaking of the words might add to the insult, and to the plaintiff's probable distress, as in a Hereford case, where the plaintiff was actually on her way to church to be married, passing the defendant's house, when the defendant ran out and called her a whore.[82] In a Chester case of 1816, the words were spoken in a playhouse; the defendant pointed out the plaintiff, who was standing up in the gallery, and called her 'a damned whore a strumpet and many other names of that kind.'[83] There are numerous cases of accusations in the street.[84] In a York case the defendant accosted the plaintiff in the street, and 'making three low curtsies ... said to [her] "Joe Smith's black bastard, Joe Smith's flounced bastard, Joe Smith's flounced whore, damn her."'[85] Commonly the insulting words were shouted outside the plaintiff's house.[86] The plaintiff might be urged to 'Go in, you whore,'[87] or 'Keep your head in,'[88] if she could be seen; or to 'Come out you old bawd,'[89] 'Turn out, you stinking strumpet,' if she could not.[90]

In one case the defendant put her head out of an upstairs window and shouted to her own husband, as he was leaving the plaintiff's house, 'You have been to see your whore, have you, before you came home.' We have seen that a defamation suit might sometimes function as a kind of shadow matrimonial dispute, and this seems to have been such a case: the defendant thought that if she provoked a lawsuit she would have an opportunity of proving the truth of her husband's adultery.[91]

In a Hereford case the defendant set herself up as a sort of one-woman charivari, and followed the plaintiff about the streets shouting abuse at her and making a noise with a frying pan. One of the witnesses said that she 'is a very troublesome woman and has annoyed the party agent very much by ringing pans at her and other acts of annoyance.'[92] Similarly, in a Norwich case, the defendant 'came into the road clapping her hands and crying after Mrs Church [the plaintiff] "go along you Mrs Church, you strumpet of a whore,"' and that half an hour later when the plaintiff was returning she did the same.[93] Somewhat similar is the York case of the boy shouting out at the plaintiff in the street, 'three and sixpence.'[94] Conduct of this sort could amount to serious harassment. In one case it was said that the plaintiff 'had not liked to shew her-

self much' in consequence of the abuse.[95] In another the plaintiff was sufficiently provoked to come out and remonstrate, 'and asked the defendant what
she had done to him that he could not let her alone in her own premises.'[96]

A doubly hurtful accusation, damaging both to the plaintiff and her family,
was that her children were illegitimate: 'Come out you ... old whore, three of
your children are bastards';[97] 'Go along in and mind your six bastards';[98]
'Look at the bastard within thy arms thou dirty bitch.'[99] As we have seen,
words like these appear quite frequently in the cause papers, both as direct
insults,[100] and in the form of defamatory reports.[101] It was also sometimes
said, as a hurtful insult, that a woman's misconduct had caused damage to her
children: 'It is evident to the eyes of the world that you are a wicked dangerous woman for the judgment of God has fallen upon your children.'[102]

The plaintiff might respond to an insult with outrage, and threaten a lawsuit.
In a York case the plaintiff demanded of the defendant, 'how dared he insult
her in that manner, but the law should take its course.'[103] In another case the
plaintiff responded with direct action: 'she took off her pattens which she had
on and struck the defendant several times.'[104]

There is no doubt that sexual insults were often very hurtful to women, and
were perceived to be so by third parties. The witness who heard the defendant
say 'Bess, you are a bloody thundering whore' considered that 'Mrs Burdon
[the plaintiff] has been very hardly treated and [I] consider it my duty to come
forward and state what I know of the transaction.'[105] In another case a
bystander asked the defendant 'if he was not ashamed of abusing a poor
woman.'[106]

The libel usually asserted that the plaintiff's reputation was 'very much hurt
and injured.'[107] Sometimes this may be passed over as a merely formal recital,
and the statement of witnesses that a plaintiff was 'hurt and aggrieved'[108] or
the assertion of a proctor that his client had been 'grossly wounded'[109] might
be attributed to a strategic desire to assist the plaintiff's cause. But specific
evidence in many cases indicates that the wound was often a real one. It was
reported in various cases that the plaintiff 'cried and was very much hurt,'[110]
that she 'suffered much in her own mind and often cried about it,'[111] or that
she was 'much affected and goes very little out of doors.'[112] One woman was
said to have looked 'pale as death.'[113] The fiancé of another said, in answer to
an interrogatory, 'I have sometimes talked to the producent about the defamatory words, but not much, as it seemed to affect her and I perceived tears come
in her eyes when I spoke of the subject.'[114] In a number of cases the plaintiff
was said to have been made ill by the slander, both in cases of direct insult,[115]
and in cases of rumour: 'the report has injured the plaintiff's health by the
effect it had on her mind.'[116] In a London case there was evidence that the

plaintiff and her husband 'have been so much hurt and affected' by their neighbour's slanderous words that 'they are determined to quit the house ... and have actually removed the greater part of their furniture ... and are trying to let the house.'[117]

The power of words to wound depends on the hearers as well as on the speaker, and it is certainly true that the significance and impact of words vary with their social and linguistic context, but the cases show that sexual insult was painful and damaging to women, and at all levels of society. The parties in many of the cases mentioned here were of modest social status,[118] but in some they belonged to the respectable and reasonably prosperous middle classes.[119]

As we have seen, a woman's reputation affected her family. There are cases in which insult was intended, but where the person primarily insulted was not the plaintiff, but a member of her family, or some other person closely associated with her. Cases are common of insults addressed to the plaintiff's husband, whose own reputation depended in part on that of his wife. 'Who do care for thee?' one man said to another in the course of a public house quarrel, 'What beest thee? ... Thy wife's nothing but a drunken whore,'[120] and 'Go home to thy drunken whore of a wife.'[121] Again, 'Thy wife is a whore to her own brother and had a child by him.'[122] An allegation of an irregular marriage ('you are living together as rogue and whore') might lead to a lawsuit.[123] To say to a man that his wife was a whore was always highly insulting to him, and in most such cases he was probably the moving force behind the ensuing litigation, though the suit had to be brought in his wife's name because she, not he, was the person defamed.

In several cases the word 'cuckold' was used.[124] In some there was express reference to horns, as where the defendant said, 'Are you come out without your horns today?'[125] or in another case where the defendant said, 'you had better put horns on your head you old fool.'[126] To guard against any danger that the speaker's meaning might be mistaken, gestures and sounds could be added: in one case the defendant 'put his fingers on his forehead resembling horns';[127] in another he said, alluding to the supposed connexion between 'cuckold' and 'cuckoo,' 'My brother has made thee – and then whistled so as to imitate the cry of a cuckoo.'[128]

The chastity of a woman even before her marriage was important to her husband's reputation, and a number of cases involve references, by way of insult to the husband, to his wife's pre-marital behaviour, as, 'Who married George Perry's old whore.'[129] In one case the defendant said, 'Your wife was a whore before you married her and has been a whore ever since.'[130] Another said, 'I rode your wife before you knew her. I have had it in her,' making indecent signs with his hands.[131]

Several cases involved allegations that the plaintiff had committed adultery with named or unnamed men.[132] Not infrequently the defendant himself claimed responsibility for this ('I have bull'd thy wife';[133] 'Your wife has been a whore to me'),[134] and the doubly offensive allegation was made triply offensive in a York case where it was combined with an allegation of impotence: 'Yes, damn thee I've fucked her scores of times, and she's fetched me to fuck her when thy pillock wouldn't stand.'[135] Another aggravated form of this kind of insult was that the children of a man's wife were not the man's own. In one case the defendant said, to a husband, 'the child is as much mine as it is yours,'[136] and in another, 'You have no need to be so fond of that child, for it is not yours.'[137]

In most of these cases of insults directly addressed to men, the defendants were also men. There are indeed numerous examples in the cause papers of insults addressed by women to men, usually in the context of provocation, but they do not generally take the form of imputations against the chastity of the man's wife. Probably such insults were in fact less commonly used by women than by men, but this cannot be established beyond doubt from the court records: it may also be the case that when such insults were used, the man insulted, or his wife, was less inclined to institute a lawsuit against a woman than they would have been against a man. However, as everywhere in this study, there are exceptions. In the case last mentioned of the cruel advice that 'you have no need to be so fond of that child, for it is not yours,' the defendant was a woman. In a Gloucester case, a woman was proved to have said, 'I don't go to bed with any man as thy wife does. I don't go to bed with Mr Lloyd for the sake of a glass of gin and water.'[138]

An insult might be directed at a man behind his back, and there are several such cases where the man insulted was not present at the time the words were spoken. In a Gloucester case, the defendant was alleged to have said publicly in a shop that a man was a 'poor contented cuckold,' adding that 'he ought to wear a pair of horns,' and further clarifying her meaning by 'placing her fingers in the shape of horns over her forehead.'[139] An imputation of impotence was sometimes added.[140]

'Contented' in the expression 'poor contented cuckold' added to the insult. Formerly a complacent or conniving husband was called a 'wittol,'[141] and though that word had (so far as the cause papers reveal) dropped out of nineteenth-century usage, the concept remained as a means of insult. In a Norwich case a woman said to a man, 'your wife is Mr Dove's whore and he keeps you and her up and you encourage her in it.'[142] In another case, one man said to another, in the course of a public house quarrel,

You know you sent for my daughter when Yetts and George Palmer were in your little room, and you placed my daughter alongside your wife before the pair of them and said to George Palmer and William Yetts, 'there are two as fine women as the town can produce; take which you please' ... Damme, you know you pulled your wife down in my little room and pulled me on the top of her.[143]

In a number of cases insults were addressed to other persons associated with the plaintiff. One mother was asked, 'Where is the bastard your daughter had in the East Indies?'[144] Another was informed, 'Your platter-faced daughter is nothing but a whore.'[145] The mother's reputation might be damaged by her daughter's supposed behaviour: in one case it was said of the plaintiff that 'she lay in bed with a married man every night and her mother was a she-bawd for suffering it.'[146]

Fathers also might be damaged by an attack on their daughters' behaviour.[147] The attack might be combined with an accusation of incest: 'You blasted old bugger. Go and frig your whore of a daughter,'[148] and a similar statement was addressed to an uncle.[149] To a brother it was said, 'Damn your eyes, you have fucked your sister.'[150] Sons might be insulted and attacked by imputations on their mothers' behaviour,[151] and by use of the word 'whore' in that connexion.[152] Such insults were sometimes combined with calling the son a bastard,[153] though I found no case in which a suit was brought for use of the insulting word standing alone and addressed only to the son.

Other relatives might be similarly insulted: 'Tell thy aunt ... she is a damned whore'[154]; 'thy sister is a whore.'[155] So might dependants, like the servant who, going into a shop on an errand, was addressed by the proprietor's wife: 'Here comes that infernal whore's maid. Your mistress is a brazen-faced whore an infernal strumpet and an impudent strumpet.'[156] Even simple association with a woman of bad reputation might be a cause for insult: 'You keep nothing but a damned whore's company.'[157] In a Carlisle case of 1827 a watchman, who was speaking to the plaintiff at her door about complaints that she had been disturbed, was addressed by the defendant: 'You damned methody rascal, what are you talking to that whore for?'[158]

In some cases the insulting words were addressed to the man alleged to have been the plaintiff's partner in guilt. Men were less frequently insulted than were women by accusations of unchastity, but some such insults were made ('thou art a whoring devil';[159] 'she is thy whore')[160], and some men did object to them. In one case a man called on the defendant with friends, and complained that 'You have been raising an ill and false report about me and Elizabeth Walter.'[161] The man in such a case might support a suit in the woman's name, or, as we shall see later, might bring a suit in his own name. Occasionally citations were issued in the joint names of the man and the woman, but pursued only in the woman's name.[162]

If, as was usual, the suit was brought in the name of the woman, the man was a competent witness, and in several cases evidence was given by men insulted in this way.[163] In one case a group of men in a public house had conducted a mock trial, actually forming what they called a 'jury' to determine the man's guilt.[164] In a Hereford case of 1848, by which date defamation suits were quite rare, Edwin Morris, who was engaged to be married to Sophia Bond (the plaintiff), cared enough about his reputation and hers to report a public house conversation, and to give evidence in the subsequent suit. The conversation was, on Morris's own evidence, of a bantering kind ('Now was you not shagging her, Morris?'), and the innkeeper, who gave his evidence reluctantly 'lest it should injure me in my business to interfere with other persons' broils,' considered that it was a 'very silly affair,' adding, 'I blamed Edwin Morris the most for telling Mr Bond or his daughter anything about it.'[165] The innkeeper's evidence suggests that many men in Morris's position would have overlooked such aspersions; the existence of the cause papers shows that not all were prepared to do so.

The defamatory words were often spoken in public, sometimes addressed directly to the plaintiff, as we have seen, and sometimes addressed to the world at large. At a time when people took a lively interest in their neighbours' affairs, and urban traffic generally proceeded at walking pace, the slightest disturbance in the street was apt to cause an assembly, and to attract the neighbours. In a Somerset case, where the defendant shouted in the street, 'many persons were coming out of their houses to know what the noise was about.'[166] One witness said, in another case, that she 'heard a woman's voice very loud in the street calling some one a whore; that she accordingly went to the door of her house which opens into the street, and looking out she saw Mary Ripley coming along the street and calling ... Mary Ann Garside a whore and a common whore.'[167] In a Norwich case of a doorstep dispute, a crowd estimated by three witnesses at numbers between fifty and eighty assembled in the street.[168] Evidence in other cases shows that crowds – in one case 'a little mob'[169] – assembled to witness quarrels.[170] Such incidents may have been more common in England than elsewhere in Europe. An eminent French visitor to England remarked (of the 1860s), 'Three times in ten minutes I saw crowds collect round doorways, attracted by fights, especially fights between women.'[171]

In a Carlisle case, the defendant actually addressed a congregation that had assembled to hear a Sunday sermon. Frederick Daniel, a dissenting minister, had been preaching to a crowd, estimated at a hundred persons, in the street. When the sermon was over, the defendant, John Ostell, 'stepped forward and asked Daniel if he might say a few words. Daniel replied that it was the Lord's day and he could not allow him.' Frederick Daniel and some of the congregation then left, but 'a great many' remained, to whom Ostell addressed an attack on the morals of Daniel's wife, Louisa, accusing her of having been 'too kind' with a named person, and of having 'tried to entice three young ministers into her company.' On the following Saturday he repeated the allegations to a meeting of 'two hundred persons and upwards.' The sense of that meeting was said by a witness to have been adverse to Ostell: 'the persons there present were much against him.' So was the judge. Sentence was given for Louisa Daniel, and Ostell performed a recantation and paid costs.[172]

A reader of the defamation cause papers must become to some degree inured to offensive words and conduct, but, even so, some cases stand out. Consider the egregious case of Middleton v. Richardson (1851), where the words were calculated to cause in about equal measures insult, distress, and nuisance. The defendant lived next door to the plaintiff, the wife of a schoolmaster, and (in the words of a witness),

> I have often heard him [defendant] speak to the carters going past and ask them if they wanted any twat as there was a bawdy house there. He was alluding to the plaintiff's premises.

Sentence was given for the plaintiff, with penance and costs, showing that the judge also took a serious view.[173]

In one case where both litigants were men, the defendant was supposed to have said to the plaintiff, 'you have seduced my wife,' thereby implicitly accusing his own wife of adultery.[174] The Dean of the Arches (the judge of the Arches Court of Canterbury) thought it incredible that a man, while still living with his wife, should accuse her publicly of adultery. Rather more common are instances of the converse situation, where a wife accuses another woman of committing adultery with her husband. In a Llandaff case of 1850, for example, the defendant said, 'Mrs Asprey ... has had connection with my husband and she is a whore to any one.'[175] There are several other cases of this kind.[176]

## Social Consequences

The slander sometimes led to concerted community action by way of punishment and ridicule. The deliberate assembling of crowds in front of the plaintiff's door may be taken as an example: in a Gloucester case the defendant spoke the offending words 'in the presence of about forty or fifty persons whom he had collected together before the door of ... Ann Draper.'[177] Allusions have already been made to skimmington rides (mock processions) and to 'rough music,' or charivaris,[178] and to the Hereford case in which the defendant annoyed the plaintiff by following her in the streets, banging a frying pan.[179] That seems to have been a one-woman enterprise, but the group charivari was not quite obsolete, as appears from a case in the diocese of London, in the rural parish of Hoddesdon in Hertfordshire at the comparatively late date of 1842. The defendant, a publican, on imparting defamatory information about the plaintiff to his neighbour, a butcher, said, 'We'll have your band out,' alluding, the butcher explained, 'to some rough music that my neighbours once treated me with, tin kettles and so on.' To another witness the defendant said, 'We must have his band out,' which the witness explained as 'butchers' boys with marrow bones and cleavers to make a noise.' A third witness described it as 'tin pots and tin kettles and anything to make a rough noise; cowshorns and cetera.' The custom was evidently well known in the village, but thought to require an explanation at Doctors' Commons. The third witness indicated that there was even a quasi-judicial aspect to this form of community punishment. He said that 'I did not think it would be right to bring out rough music till such time as they could prove it.'[180] In a Chester case of 1834 there was reference to 'wakes week,' the annual village revels, which were evidently an occasion for skimmingtons or rough music.[181] A witness, in response to the question whether she had heard any scandalous reports about the plaintiff, replied, 'O yes, heard, to be sure; we had the best wakes on Friday night before Mr Stannier's door on that account that ever we had in all Hyde wakes week.'[182]

The skimmington usually involved an image of some sort carried in procession, as with the custom of 'riding the stang,' allegedly used against a defendant in Yorkshire in 1819.[183] In several cases there are references to the carrying of images in front of the houses of persons to be held up to opprobrium. In a Llandaff case of 1834 a witness saw 'the son of the ... defendant Mary Williams carrying an image oppposite the house of the party complainant Ann James accompanied by a great many other boys.'[184] In a Gloucester case a similar incident is described, used there against the defendant:

I saw Charles Webb ... with a figure representing a man with one eye out and a long nose, and by pulling a string the figure would be made to kick his legs about. This figure he exhibited on mornings and evenings before the door of defendant's house and attracted a mob round the door ... The defendant has lost one eye and has rather a long nose.[185]

In the Consistory
Court of Llandaff } Roberts v Jones.

Whereas I Charlotte Jones / the wife of
John Jones / of Penydarran in the Parish of Merthyrtidvil
in the County of Glamorgan have unlawfully and contrary
to good manners and the Bond of Christian Charity
publicly and maliciously reported several Scandalous
reproachful and defamatory words tending to the infamy
hurt and diminution of the good name fame and reputation
of Louisa Roberts / the wife of John Roberts of the
Parish of Merthyrtidvil in the said County

Now I the said Charlotte Jones do hereby
retract such Words and any and every thing that I
may have ever said against the good name fame and
reputation of the said Louisa Roberts as I firmly believe
that I had not the least foundation for my doing so,
and for which I am heartily sorry and hereby beg her
forgiveness Witness my hand this Seventh
day of July in the Year of our Lord One thousand
eight hundred and fifty five.

Witnesses

Geo: Garry
Attorneys Clerks Cardiff

James Hasell
Turnkey of Cardiff Gaol

The mark of
Charlotte  ✝  Jones

---

1  Recantation signed by Charlotte Jones (1855), National Library of Wales, LL/CC/G/
2142g. See p. 6. (By permission of the National Library of Wales, and the Bishop of
Llandaff)

2 Two notices among the papers in Bach v. Engstrom (1822), Hereford Record Office, HD4/56. See pp. 24, 145. (By permission of the Hereford Record Office, and the Bishop of Hereford)

3  Love letter from Prudence Payne to Thomas Rowley (1841), Bristol Record Office, EP/J/2/7/5. See p. 38. (By permission of the Bristol Record Office)

4 The Chester Consistory Court. See p. 51. (By permission of the Dean and Chapter)

5 The courtroom at Doctors' Commons. See p. 51. (From Ackermann's *The Microcosm of London*, 1809)

**Granville Venables Vernon,** Master of Arts, Official Principal of the Consistory Court of York, lawfully authorized; To all and singular Clerks and literate Persons, whomsoever and wheresoever within the Diocese of York, Greeting; We do hereby order and charge you jointly and severally, that you or one of you do peremptorily cite *Benjamin Ditty Smith of Skipton in the Diocese of York Hosier*

To appear before Us or our lawful Representative in the Consistory Place within the Cathedral and Metropolitical Church of Saint Peter of York, on *Thursday* being the *second* Day of the Month of *November next ensuing* between the Hours of Eight and Twelve in the Forenoon of the same Day *To Answer Jane Holmes of Skipton aforesaid Spinster in a certain Cause of Defamation or Slander and to obey the Law in all things*

*Extracted by Jno Lawton Proctor York*

And what you or any of you shall do in the Premises, you shall duly certify Us or our lawful Representative at the Time and Place aforesaid, together with these Presents. Given at York under the Seal of our Office this *seventh* Day of the Month of *September* in the Year of our Lord, one Thousand Eight Hundred *and twenty*

*Joseph Buckle*
*Deputy Register.*

6  Citation in a York defamation case (1820), Borthwick Institute of Historical Research, Cons CP 1820/3. See p. 68. (By permission of the Borthwick Institute of Historical Research)

In the Name of God, *Amen*. *Before you the worshipful* and Reverend *Charles Taylor Doctor in Divinity* Vicar General and Official Principal of the Right Reverend Father in God *George Isaac* by Divine Permission, Lord Bishop of Hereford, *lawfully constituted, your Surrogate, or other competent Judge in this Behalf. The Proctor of* allexis ———

*Pellicody Barois* ——————————— *of the Parish of* Whitbourne ——— *in the* County and —— *Diocese of Hereford,* ——— *against* Ann Williams wife of Peter Williams ——— *of the Parish of* Grendon Bishop — *in the* County and Diocese *aforesaid,* ——— *in a certain cause of Defamation or Slander, and against any other Person or Persons lawfully appearing or intervening in Judgment for* her — *by way of Complaint, and hereby complaining to you, doth say, alledge, and in Law propound, in writing, articulately as followeth, that is to say,*

*First.* THAT the said *Ann Williams wife of Peter Williams* the Defendant, was and is of the parish of *Grendon Bishop* in the *County and* ——— Diocese of *Hereford,* and therefore subject to the Jurisdiction of this Court, and the Party proponent doth alledge and propound every Thing in this Article contained, jointly and severally.

*Second.* THAT every Person or Persons who utter, publish, assert, or report or shall have uttered, published, asserted, or reported, reproachful, scandalous, or defamatory Words, to the Hurt and Diminution of the good Name, Fame, and Reputation of another Person, contrary to good Manners and the Bond of Charity, are and ought to be admonished, constrained, and compelled to the reclaiming and retracting of such reproachful, scandalous, and defamatory Words, and to the restoring of the good Name, Fame, and Reputation of the Person thereby injured; and that for the future they refrain from uttering, publishing, or declaring any such reproachful, scandalous, or defamatory Words; and are and ought to be canonically punished and corrected, and doth alledge and propound as before.

*Third.* THAT, notwithstanding the Premises, the said *Ann Williams wife of Peter Williams* the Defendant in this Cause, in the Months of ——— *in January. February. March or April in the year of our Lord One thousand Eight hundred and twenty Six* ———

or in some or one of the said Months *in the said year* ——— and before the commencement of this Suit, within the Parish of *Grendon Bishop* ——— or in some other Parishes or public Places in the Neighbourhood thereof, or near thereunto, in an angry, reproachful, and invidious manner, several times, or at least once, before sundry credible Witnesses, defame, scandalize, and reproach the said *Allexis Pellicody Barois* ——— who was and is a Person of good Reputation and Character; and charged the said *Allexis Pellicody Barois* with having committed the Crime of Adultery, Fornication, or Incontinency, and speaking to or of or meaning or intending the said *Allexis Pellicody Barois* said, affirmed, and published several times, or at least once *that Mrs Barois is not Captain Barois wife but was the wife of another person and that some Gentleman came to Captain Barois, and claimed her as his wife and said he did not want to have any thing to do with her but that he came only to disgrace her meaning and intending thereby that the said Allexis Pellicody Barois had committed Adultery by living with a Person who was not his wife and* did affirm, utter, and publish, words to the same or like effect; and doth alledge and propound as before.

*Fourth.* THAT by reason of the speaking the defamatory Words aforesaid, the good Name, Fame, and Reputation of the said *Allexis Pellicody Barois* is very much hurt and injured amongst *his* Neighbours, acquaintance and others, and this was and is true, public and notorious; and doth alledge and propound as before.

*Fifth.* THAT all and singular the Premises were and are true, public and notorious, and therefore there was and is a public Voice, Fame, and Report, and of which legal Proof being made, the Party proponent prays Right and Justice to be effectually done and administered to his Party in the Premises; and that the said *Ann Williams wife of Peter Williams* for *her* Excess in the Premises be duly forced and compelled to retract and reclaim the defamatory Words aforesaid, and that for the future *she* ——— refrain from uttering such defamatory Words, and that *she* ——— be condemned in the Costs of this Suit, made or to be made on the Part or Behalf of the said *Allexis Pellicody Barois* ——— and compelled to the due Payment thereof by you and your definitive Sentence or final Decree to be given in this Cause; and further to do and decree in the Premises what shall be lawful in this Behalf, the Party proponent not obliging himself to prove all and singular the Premises, or to the Burthen of a superfluous Proof, against which he protests, and prays that so far as he shall prove in the Premises he may obtain his Petition (the Benefit of the Law being always preserved) humbly imploring the Aid of your Office in this Behalf.

7 Libel in a Hereford defamation case (1826), Hereford Record Office, HD4/57. See p. 69. (By permission of the Hereford Record Office)

It is ordered *Extracted out of the Registry of the Consistory Court of Hereford Diocese* by the said Court that *Bertha, otherwise Bythyal, the wife of John Probert of* the Parish of *Eye* in the County *of Court* and Diocese of Hereford who stands convicted by *Sentence on Confession* judicially made *before* her Ordinary of speaking scandalous, reproachful and defamatory Words of and against *Martha the wife of John Williams* of the Parish of *Eye in the said County and Diocese of Hereford* shall make a Reclamation of the said Words before the Minister and Churchwarden of the said Parish *of Eye* the said *Martha Williams and her husband David Martha Williams* shall bring with her and six Persons beside whom on Sunday the *third* Day of *August next* in the Vestry of the Parish Church of *Eye* aforesaid immediately after *Divine* Service due Notice thereof being first given to the said *Martha Williams* and shall repeat after the Minister with an audible Voice the Words following (to wit)

*I Bertha otherwise Bythyal Probert do in the Presence of Almighty God and the Persons here present humbly confess and acknowledge that contrary to the Rules of Christian Charity and good Manners, I have abused and defamed my Neighbour Martha the wife of John Williams by saying that she was a whore and by using other Defamatory words and expressions respecting her which Words I do now recall and promise to bridle my Tongue for the future.*

THE Performance hereof is to be certified under the Hands of the Minister and Churchwarden of the Parish of *Eye* aforesaid, on or before the next Court appointed to be held in the *Cathedral Church of Hereford* on *Thursday* the *Twenty eighth* Day of *August* in the Year of our Lord One Thousand Seven Hundred and *Twenty eight.*

8  Schedule of penance in a Hereford case (1828), Hereford Record Office, HD4/57. See p. 111. (By permission of the Hereford Record Office)

A Schedule of Penance to be performed by
Mary Freemantle of Ampfield in the Parish
of Hursley, in the County of Southampton and
Diocese of Winchester Spinster for certain
Defamatory Words by her Spoken of the
Reverend John Ford of Romsey in the said
County and Diocese Clerk.

The said Mary Freemantle shall be present in the
Vestry Room or Place of the Parish Church of Hursley
or in the Ministers House, if he shall give leave,
on Sunday the sixteenth day of July next immediately
after Divine Service in the morning, when and where
in the presence of the Minister and Churchwardens
of the said Parish and of the said Reverend John
Ford (if he shall think fit to be present) due notice
being given him by the said Mary Freemantle
She the said Mary Freemantle shall make the
following acknowledgment,

"Whereas I Mary Freemantle have rashly and
"contrary to good Manners and Behaviour
"Slandered and defamed the Reverend John
"Ford by speaking and uttering several
"scandalous reproachful and defamatory Words
"and Speeches of and concerning the said John
"Ford, Now I do hereby declare that I am
"heartily sorry for the same, and humbly pray
"Almighty God and desire the said John Ford
"to forgive me my said Offence promising not
"to offend in the like kind again" —

The due performance hereof is to be certified under the hands of the Minister and Churchwardens of Hursley aforesaid to the Consistory Court of Winchester on or before Friday the twenty third day of July next Dated at Winchester the thirtieth day of June one thousand eight hundred and twenty six.

The sixteenth day of July one thousand eight hundred and twenty six.

The within named Mary Freemantle appeared personally in the presence of The Reverend John Keble minister of the Parish and Parish Church of Hursley in the County of Southampton and Diocese of Winchester and William Froslie and Benjamin Bailey Churchwardens of the said Parish of Hursley and then and there duly performed Penance according to the Schedule within written.

John Keble      Minister

William Froslie ⎫
Benj. Bailey    ⎬ Churchwardens

9 Schedule of penance witnessed by John Keble in Ford v. Freemantle (1826), Winchester Record Office, 21M65/C9/302. See p. 111. (By permission of the Hampshire Record Office)

**Mrs. Tittle Tattle Vaux.**

They say I'm often out a little,
    When I indulge in harmless prattle.
The truth, if spoken to a tittle,
    Would put an end to half my tattle.

10  Caricature of a gossip (Lord Brougham), from *Punch* (1844). See p. 124.

# £100 REWARD.

**WHEREAS** a most false, scandalous, and malicious report has been raised, and perseveringly circulated, affecting the character of a Member of a Respectable Family in this Neighbourhood.

# Notice is hereby Given,

that whoever will furnish such information and testimony, as shall lead to the legal conviction and punishment of the person who originated and circulated such report, shall receive upon such conviction the above Reward, by application to H. BURTON, Superintendent of Police.

*Stourbridge, March 17th, 1845.*

J. HEMING, PRINTER.

11 Offer of reward in Bate v. Collis (1845), Lambeth Palace Library, H 694. See pp. 169–70. (By permission of Lambeth Palace Library)

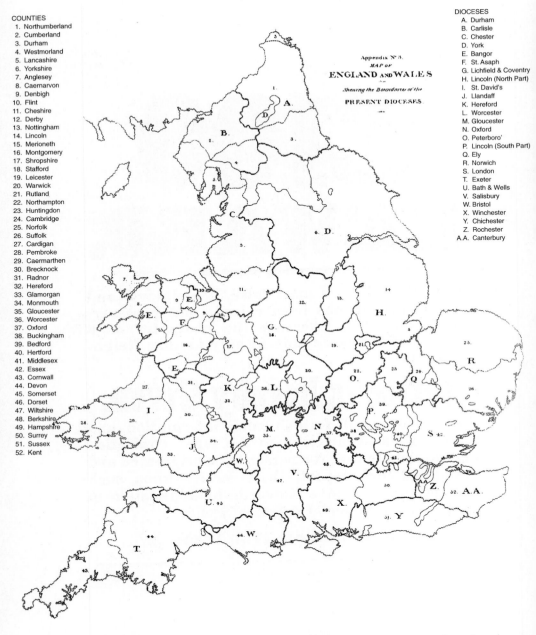

COUNTIES
1. Northumberland
2. Cumberland
3. Durham
4. Westmorland
5. Lancashire
6. Yorkshire
7. Anglesey
8. Caernarvon
9. Denbigh
10. Flint
11. Cheshire
12. Derby
13. Nottingham
14. Lincoln
15. Merioneth
16. Montgomery
17. Shropshire
18. Stafford
19. Leicester
20. Warwick
21. Rutland
22. Northampton
23. Huntingdon
24. Cambridge
25. Norfolk
26. Suffolk
27. Cardigan
28. Pembroke
29. Caermarthen
30. Brecknock
31. Radnor
32. Hereford
33. Glamorgan
34. Monmouth
35. Gloucester
36. Worcester
37. Oxford
38. Buckingham
39. Bedford
40. Hertford
41. Middlesex
42. Essex
43. Cornwall
44. Devon
45. Somerset
46. Dorset
47. Wiltshire
48. Berkshire
49. Hampshire
50. Surrey
51. Sussex
52. Kent

DIOCESES
A. Durham
B. Carlisle
C. Chester
D. York
E. Bangor
F. St. Asaph
G. Lichfield & Coventry
H. Lincoln (North Part)
I. St. David's
J. Llandaff
K. Hereford
L. Worcester
M. Gloucester
N. Oxford
O. Peterboro'
P. Lincoln (South Part)
Q. Ely
R. Norwich
S. London
T. Exeter
U. Bath & Wells
V. Salisbury
W. Bristol
X. Winchester
Y. Chichester
Z. Rochester
A.A. Canterbury

Appendix N° 3.
MAP OF
ENGLAND AND WALES

Shewing the Boundaries of the

PRESENT DIOCESES.

12   The Dioceses in 1835. From appendix 3 of First Report of His Majesty's Commissioners to consider the state of the Established Church ('Ecclesiastical Revenues Commission') PP 1835 xxii

Less elaborate, but equally disagreeable, and probably even more difficult to suppress, was jeering by children in the street. In a York case they 'made Mrs Aaron and her husband so uncomfortable that they have been obliged to leave that neighbourhood.'[186] In a Chester case of 1833, the defendant had said of her son and the plaintiff that 'they had been married by parson prick.' The plaintiff was 'in consequence much affected and goes very little out of doors' and the witness 'has heard her hooted at by boys of the village as having been married by parson prick.'[187] In a Hereford case the plaintiff was walking arm in arm with her fiancé when (according to his evidence) 'a number of boys aged from ten years to fourteen years of age called after us and one of them said, "Who was shagged in the barley field?" and another of the boys answered, "Miss Bond."'[188] In the Llandaff case mentioned above, of the image opposite the plaintiff's house, 'there were a great many boys present and they began to throw stones.'[189]

In several cases defamatory notices were exhibited on papers, or chalked on walls or shutters. The cause papers in one case include the notices (in ink on paper), 'Bach's wife is a whore and he a liar' and 'Bach's wife is a brutal whore and he a liar for ever' (see plate 2).[190] In a Norwich case of 1826 a defamatory notice was placed on a wall near the plaintiff's house, and later tarred over.[191] In a York case, the plaintiff accused the defendant's son of having written 'some scandalous language' on a wall. The defendant objected, and said that 'thou had more need take a wet cloth and wipe off what is written upon the walls, as stand there thou good for nought hussy.' The plaintiff then threatened to prove her allegation by a comparison of handwriting: 'she would go to Mr Headon's (a school master at whose school ... Ann Gee's son learnt) and get the copy book belonging [to] ... Ann Gee's son, and sample it with the writing upon the walls.'[192] In a Somerset case, defamatory expressions were said to be 'publicly written on the walls and shutters of the neighbourhood.'[193]

Proof of offensive notices might be used against the plaintiff's interest. Truth was not generally a complete defence to defamation, but in the Yarmouth case of the florists accusing their employee of adultery the truth of the defamation was allowed to be proved in order to discredit a witness, William Hussey, the man with whom the plaintiff was alleged to have had improper relations. Hussey had sworn that no impropriety had occurred, and said, in the course of his evidence, that the plaintiff's name 'is written in opprobrious terms on the walls near her house.' This evidence was given on the plaintiff's behalf, but to ill effect, for the judge turned the point against her. In his reasons for dismissing the cause he said:

There was a strong impression that there was an improper intimacy existing between Mrs Craske and Hussey; that impression did not only prevail among the defendants, but amongst many of the public, as Mrs Craske's name was chalked on the walls ... He (the Chancellor) was not satisfied with the evidence, and in his opinion Mrs Craske had not made out a case against the defendant.[194]

Community action against women suspected of unchastity occurred at all social levels. Damaging rumours could be circulated at a 'morning visit' in a drawing room[195] just as, at another social level, they might be circulated in a public house.[196] In the Norwich case where the defendant was the wife of a baronet, she sought to show that rumours against the plaintiff were already current in Yarmouth before she had uttered the slander for which the suit was brought. William Yetts, the plaintiff's father, gave evidence, and was asked whether he had not known that

in consequence of the report in Yarmouth ... a party of ladies who assembled to dance at the Bath Rooms, when the complainant was there, had resolved that if she rose to join the dance they would all sit down.

It is hard to imagine a grosser social insult than this, capable of confining a woman to her house just as effectively as the less refined methods employed in other social circles of ringing frying pans or shouting, 'Get in, you whore.' Yetts answered that he had heard of the report about the dance, but not until after the defendant's slander. In any event, as we have seen, prior publication was not a defence, and sentence was given for the plaintiff with penance and full costs.[197]

The libel usually asserted that the plaintiff's good name, fame, and reputation 'is very much hurt and injured amongst her relations friends acquaintance and others.'[198] This was a matter of form, and did not have to be proved, but witnesses examined on the libel usually responded to it. In most cases they said that the plaintiff's reputation was injured, but this is not very strong evidence of actual damage, because it may be supposed that witnesses often answered affirmatively in order to assist the plaintiff's cause, and because words like 'injured' and 'aggrieved' are ambiguous: they may refer to actual damage, or they may mean simply that the plaintiff had suffered a legal injury. So a witness might say that she believed that the plaintiff was injured, but add (possibly under probing from the examiner) that she 'cannot state any particular circumstances,'[199] or that the plaintiff's character was 'much scandalized' but that the witness 'knows not of any particular damage.'[200] One witness said that she 'knows not of any injury [done to the plaintiff] by the words ... but considers the same disgraceful to be spoken of any virtuous woman.'[201] Quite often witnesses said that the plaintiff was not injured by the slander because the words were not credited.[202] One witness cautiously said that the words were believed by some and not by others.[203] In a Gloucester case three witnesses gave three different answers, one saying that the plaintiff was much injured, another saying that she was not, and a third saying that she (the witness) did not know.[204]

Yet, in a substantial number of cases, there is specific evidence of particular damage. In small communities rumours spread quickly: 'in a small town like Thorne such scandal soon spreads all over.'[205] One of Askwith's corresponding attorneys wrote that the defendant

> would continue her abuse which she has done to the great annoyance and injury of Mrs Calvert ever since; indeed in a small village like Scalby such subjects run like wildfire and the consequence is that Mrs Calvert cannot leave her own house without being told by some person or other that Mrs Chapman has been saying this and telling that &c &c.[206]

In another York case it was said that the slander 'has spread over Dewsbury and she [the plaintiff] can go no where without being told of it.' Her fiancé said that 'neither he nor she nor her family could go any where but they were geer'd at.'[207] In other cases it was said that there was 'much talk' against the plaintiff,[208] or 'a great deal of talk about this business for miles round Harling,'[209] or that the slander has been 'very much noised abroad.'[210] In a Chester case it was said that the plaintiff was, on account of the slander, 'often publicly reproached therewith.'[211] Slanderous reports might be a considerable nuisance even if they were not believed. As we see here and elsewhere, the word 'annoyance' was often used in this context. It was an annoyance that might drive the plaintiff out of society. In a Gloucester case, where 'the promoter's character since this abuse has been much talked about,' the witness added, 'She has not liked to shew herself much in consequence.'[212] Slander had, and has, a self-sustaining and escalating effect: 'You are a whore for every body calls you a whore – not only a whore but a damned whore.'[213]

There is ample evidence from non-legal sources of the damage caused to women by loss of good sexual reputation,[214] and this stigma, as it was actually called in some cases,[215] is reflected in the cause papers. 'Several respectable persons are shy of speaking to her,' it was said of one plaintiff.[216] Of others: 'she was very much talked of and slighted';[217] 'she was not so well looked on by her neighbours...much injured, and often publicly reproached';[218] 'she fancies herself an object of observation [i.e., comment],'[219] 'no prudent decent woman will associate with you.'[220] A witness broke off her acquaintance with one plaintiff in consequence of the slander, and heard that a woman had withdrawn her daughter from her care for the same reason.[221] In another case a witness said that she had been advised by her husband to avoid the plaintiff's company.[222] Ordinary help in daily tasks might be denied, as in a Ripon case where 'Mary Goodall refused to help her [the plaintiff] with birling cloth for fear her own character would be affected.'[223] Of another plaintiff it was said that 'no creditable persons ... have had any acquaintance with her and she is looked upon and considered a bad woman.'[224] In a London case the plaintiff's father, who was produced as a witness, said that he and his family had been slighted, particularly by one family, because of the report.[225]

Family relationships might be affected. 'If it were possible that any of her friends were to give credence to the infamous charges which the defendant has made against her,' a proctor asked rhetorically in an Exeter case, 'what must be her fate and what must become of her family?'[226] According to a Chester witness neither the plaintiff's father nor her sister-in-law would speak to the plaintiff or her husband for three months on account of the slander:

> Mary Meakin told this deponent that in consequence of having heard of the said
> defamatory words she was determined to have nothing more to do with her said
> brother or his wife the promovent.[227]

The plaintiff's children might suffer on account of the slander: of one plaintiff it was said, 'her neighbours and others ... have slighted her very much in consequence of it and also her children,'[228] and such treatment might lead the children to turn against their mother. One witness said that he had heard the plaintiff's own children 'upbraid her on account of the slander.'[229]

It was widely expected that a woman who had erred would lose any claim to sympathy, even from friends and relatives. Elizabeth Gaskell's novel *Ruth* (1853), which invites the reader's sympathy for a woman who has been seduced, was fiercely attacked when it was published, and was actually burned by some and forbidden by others as family reading. Gaskell was made ill by the vehemence of the reaction.[230] Almost twenty years later, Anthony Trollope thought it necessary – or at any rate expedient – to apologize, in *The Vicar of Bullhampton* (written 1868, published 1870), for sympathetic treatment of what he called a 'castaway,' and a 'fallen woman.' His justificatory preface to the novel was subsequently reprinted in his *Autobiography* (1876; published 1883), suggesting that Trollope prided himself on a progressive and enlightened view of the matter.

In a London case of 1840 it was suggested, on behalf of the defence, that the plaintiff had left home because of a miscarriage, and that her own father had refused to take leave of her, rather in the manner of the stern father of Victorian melodrama.[231] Suggestions in interrogatories were not required to be proved, and this one was denied. Moreover, there are hints in some of the cases that plaintiffs' witnesses may have been exaggerating the disastrous social consequences of the slander in the expectation that they would thereby assist the plaintiff's cause. Nevertheless, the fact that such social and family ostracisms were perceived as plausible is itself significant.

As we have seen, the protection of prospects of future marriage cannot be accepted as an explanation of the motives of most plaintiffs. However, there are some cases in which this was a motive. In an Isle of Man case of 1821, the plaintiff (a single woman) in her petition said that the slander tended 'to blast her future prospects in life.'[232] In the Gloucester case of Sharpe v. Dauncey (1849), a man who had been engaged to marry the plaintiff said that he had broken off the engagement on account of rumours of her having had an illegitimate child eighteen years earlier. His evidence shows that he took it quite as a matter of course that the facts rumoured, if true, would justify him in terminating the engagement:

> The intended marriage between Sarah Sharpe, the promoter, and myself has not only not taken place but it is not likely to take place; it is not, however, wholly in consequence of the defendant's statements: I have heard things from other quarters quite sufficient to induce me not to marry the promoter whatever my intentions might once have been.[233]

Other cases show the same. In a York case of 1833 the plaintiff's fiancé said that 'he had determined not to marry her till her character was defended.'[234] In the London case mentioned above where the plaintiff's father gave evidence, he said that she had received an offer of marriage, but 'the matter at my advice stands over until this suit is settled.'[235] In a late case (1854) the defendant was the former fiancé himself. He was reported to have said, when asked for an explanation for the breach of the engagement, that 'it was hardly likely that he should marry a girl that had eloped with a married man and had been living with him a week.'[236]

More common is evidence that the slander might damage an existing marriage. A letter written by the stepfather of a plaintiff's husband stated that the plaintiff and her husband 'live very happily together' and added, 'I should be sorry to see their matrimonial felicity endangered by any foul-mouthed slanderers.'[237] In several cases evidence was given that the slander had actually caused 'much anxiety and dispute and quarrel'[238] between husband and wife, or had caused 'much unhappiness' between them,[239] or had the effect of making them live 'very uncomfortably together.'[240] In one of the few cases in which the plaintiff herself gave answers on oath, she said that:

> her and her husband ... have not ... lived happy and comfortably since and have caused frequent quarrels between them, her ... husband declaring that the party promote had some reason for calling her what he did.[241]

Husbands in several cases threatened to turn their wives out: 'I will go home and turn my wife out of doors; I'll not have a whore in the house and know it.'[242] Not all these threats can be taken at face value. The husband may have said something of the sort, or the witness may have reported it, in the expectation that it would supply a satisfactory explanation for instituting the lawsuit. Generally speaking, truth was not a complete defence, but it was nevertheless often asserted that a successful suit would clear the plaintiff's name, a point that will be addressed in the next chapter. In a joint affidavit by husband and wife in a Hereford case, the husband said that he

> could not think of living with his wife had it been true as alleged by the words so spoken by the defendant, and unless she had commenced this suit he should not have been satisfied of the falseness of the words.[243]

As this affidavit is signed by mark (O) and was submitted for the purpose of showing that the suit was commenced by the husband's wish, it may be supposed that it was drawn up by legal advisers, and might therefore be less than conclusive proof of the actual matrimonial relations of Elizabeth and John Roberts (the plaintiff and her husband), but it is reliable evidence of what were respectable motives for commencing defamation suits, and of what husbands might plausibly be expected to think and do in such circumstances. In some cases the defendant threatened to inform the plaintiff's husband of the misconduct alleged,[244] and occasionally witnesses stated that the parties had actually separated in consequence of the slander.[245] In one case a witness heard a husband threaten to beat his wife,[246] and in others it was suggested that a husband had thrashed his wife on account of the slander.[247] Even though the witnesses denied knowledge of the incident, the evidence of the threat and the inclusion of the question in the interrogatories are significant in showing that such conduct, though unlawful, might be sometimes expected.

Loss of business was commonly complained of as a consequence of the slander. In a Chester case of 1829 the plaintiff was a female staymaker, and, according to a witness, 'several females declared they would no longer employ her on account of her bad character.'[248] Two unmarried sisters carrying on business as mantua makers (dressmakers) complained of a slander in Exeter in 1816. Their proctor, in his submission to the court, suggested that their livelihood was threatened:

> If the defendant is not punished ... it may tend as a most serious injury to the promovent[s] by their not receiving that support which has hitherto enabled them to support themselves by their own industry.[249]

A lodging-house keeper complained that she had lost five lodgers.[250] Proof of loss of customers was made by shopkeepers[251] and by keepers of public houses.[252] One witness said he had himself refused credit to the plaintiff in consequence of the slander.[253]

A woman might suffer loss of employment as a consequence of slander, and so might her husband. In the London case where Thomas Rose was the porter at Symonds Inn, the accusation complained of was that his marriage with Catherine Rose was irregular. It is plain from the evidence of several witnesses that this accusation put the husband's job in jeopardy. One of the lessees of the inn told Thomas Rose that 'unless he cleared himself of the charges I should certainly call a meeting of the lessees.'[254] In some cases the plaintiff's own employment was in jeopardy,[255] and this might be so even where the misconduct alleged fell short of sexual intercourse. In a late Chester case (1853) the plaintiff, who was a cook, aged thirty-one, was discovered in the embrace of a fellow servant, a boy of fifteen. The defendant, a 'guest lodger' in the house, purportedly concerned for 'the respectability of the household,' although she did not accuse the plaintiff of 'anything criminal,' told the plaintiff that if she left the house quietly she (the defendant) would not tell the family.[256] In a Somerset case a witness

> intended to have ... Susan Dorney as a nurse, and spoke to her about it; but afterwards [she] heard so notorious a character of [i.e., such ill reports of] ... Dorney that she did not think it was proper to have such a person in her house particularly as she had a young family.[257]

The witness later relented, and did let Dorney live with her for a time, but the passage quoted manifests a common reaction of employers.[258] In a Hereford case the plaintiff was a charwoman; a witness said that 'unless the report had been stopped by these proceedings ... it would have been the means of her losing the whole of her employment and livelihood.'[259]

## Male Plaintiffs

There were substantial variations from one diocese to another in the numbers of male plaintiffs. Overall, male plaintiffs formed about 10 per cent of the total, but in one diocese they constituted over 25 per cent, and in others there were none at all. Dr Gowing's study of the London court between 1572 and 1640 shows that female plaintiffs were then also in a large majority (about 75 per cent overall, and 84.5 per cent in urban areas).[260] An explanation of why male plaintiffs continued to litigate in some dioceses but not in others does not appear from the court records, but it was earlier suggested that the pattern of litigation had a self-sustaining quality: where it was customary for men to sue it was much easier for them to continue to do so than in a diocese where such suits had become rare curiosities.[261]

A man, when insulted, was likely to be called a rogue, villain, rascal, blackguard, thief, or liar, but there was no common word corresponding to the word 'whore.' Thus, a husband and wife might be insulted by saying, 'Tom Sadler is a damnation rogue and his wife is a damnation whore.'[262] No specific allegation was here intended against either, but the variation of insult is significant. It was not generally perceived as particularly insulting to accuse a man of unchastity; indeed, as we have seen, a man might quite often boast of his own misconduct. The words 'whoremaster,'[263] and 'whoremonger,'[264] used for centuries in the ecclesiastical courts,[265] appear in the libels[266] and occasionally in the depositions,[267] but were not, it seems, in common use as everyday insults, though the word 'whoremonger' was familiar from the Bible and in a Peterborough case a Baptist minister was called 'a damned whoremonger.'[268] A number of other expressions involving the necessary accusation of sexual misconduct do have rather more the ring of authentic invective, such as 'whoring devil,'[269] 'whoring bugger,'[270] and 'whoring dog.'[271]

The clergy had a special concern with their sexual reputation for the obvious reason that they were liable to be deprived of their livelihood on proof of sexual misconduct, in the case of Church of England clergy by proceedings in the consistory court itself. Clergy had a strong interest in discouraging rumour of this sort, and in suppressing it when it occurred. In a St David's case of 1838 a clergyman complained that he had been accused of seducing the defendant's servant and that the defendant had said, 'Mr Page and myself should consider it a profanation of religion if we went into a church where Mr Berrington was either in the reading desk or pulpit & did not walk out again.'[272] Such talk could do serious damage. It is not surprising, therefore, to find that clergy constitute a substantial proportion (13 per cent) of the male plaintiffs in defamation cases.[273] Some other professions also had a special interest in good reputation, such as schoolmasters and surgeons, and these too are represented.[274]

In a number of other cases where misconduct of a clergyman was alleged, a suit was brought, but in the woman's name, and these cases may have been brought primarily or partly for the sake of the clergyman's reputation.[275] In a Somerset case of a suit and counter-suit where both parties were committed to prison, the litigation arose out of an insult addressed by Mary Hill to Frederick Board in a public house. Frederick Board and his wife, Jane, were in the employ of a clergyman, Mr Wait, and lived at his house. Mary Hill said to Frederick Board that 'he wouldn't be at the parson's house unless the parson were fonder of his [Board's] wife than of him.' According to one witness, Board knocked her down and called her a whore; she seized a poker, and he knocked her down again.[276] Proceedings followed before the magistrates in which Board was fined 5s. and costs, for assault. This would have been the end of the matter except that the circumstances of the quarrel were revealed at the magistrates' court, and Wait, when he heard of what Hill had said, 'took up the matter and required [Frederick Board] to accompany him to Mr Edmund Davies, a proctor ... for the purpose of instituting a suit.' If, as appears to be the case, it was Wait who insisted on the litigation, largely (it may be supposed) out of concern for his own reputation, it is surprising that he did not also manage to keep Board out of jail, for he was imprisoned for non-appearance to Mary Hill's counter-suit.[277]

Men accused of misconduct who were not clergy appear in some cases to be the moving force behind the suit. In a Salisbury case where a man was accused of improper relations with his housekeeper he brought an action at law, which was said to have been settled on the defendant's making an apology, and the housekeeper brought a suit in the ecclesiastical court.[278] In the Norwich case where the defendant said, addressing the plaintiff's husband, 'your wife is Mr Dove's whore, and he keeps you and her up and you encourage her in it,' both the witnesses said, in answer to interrogatories, that it was Mr Dove who had requested them to give evidence.[279] In the later case in the same diocese where William Hussey had been dismissed from his employment as foreman to a firm of florists in Yarmouth, on account of improper relations with a married woman, suits were brought (unsuccessfully) in her name against two partners of the firm. It appears here that Hussey was the person primarily aggrieved, and he was a witness in both suits. The case shows that men as well as women were liable to lose employment for immoral conduct, even when it occurred off the employer's premises.[280]

In a Chester case of 1833 an altercation arose in spirit vaults, evidently a kind of public house or wine bar, kept by Joseph Lumbers. John Taylor was present in the company of Anne Hooley, who accused Lumbers of neglecting his wife. A violent quarrel ensued in the course of which (according to Taylor's evidence) Lumbers said to Taylor's son, who had been called to intervene in the quarrel, 'Your father ought to be ashamed of himself for bringing his damned whore here.' Taylor remonstrated: 'Surely you don't mean to call this decent elderly woman a whore.' Lumbers replied, 'Yes but I do; what the devil else must she be to be sitting here with you.' In answer to interrogatories Taylor, whose son was an attorney, said that 'at first he had thoughts of proceeding in his own name against the defendant for the language he had used ... and believes he may have said that he should serve him with a citation.' He admitted that he had undertaken at one stage to pay the fees of the plaintiff's proctor 'but has since declared to him that he does not consider himself so responsible.' It is evident here that Taylor was the moving force behind the litigation, and that he did contemplate a suit in his own name, rejecting the idea probably because the evidence that Lumbers had actually imputed misconduct to Taylor was weak, and because Taylor could be a witness in Hooley's suit, but not in his own. The disavowal of liability to pay the fees was probably made on the proctor's advice in order to enable Taylor to be a witness.[281]

In a number of cases the accusation complained of was aggravated in various ways. In several cases men complained that they had been accused of having venereal disease,[282] or of having communicated the disease to their wives.[283] Other cases involve imputations of impotence,[284] incest,[285] seducing a servant,[286] intercourse with a mentally defective girl,[287] and neglecting to provide for an illegitimate child.[288] In one case, according to the libel, the defendant said of a clergyman that he 'entered the bed room of myself and fellow servant, undressed, by force ... got into the bed ... and effected his purpose ... first on me and then on my fellow servant.' The case was technically beyond the court's jurisdiction because the words imputed a common law crime (rape), but the defendant (one of the servants) confessed the words, and sentence was given against her.[289]

As we have seen, a woman sometimes complained that a slanderous allegation had caused her husband to leave her, but there are few cases of the converse situation, where a husband complained that a slanderous allegation of adultery had caused his wife to leave him. In one case evidence was given by a witness to this effect, and this may have been the man's motive for instituting the suit, but the evidence was contradicted by a joint affidavit of the plaintiff's wife and her mother, confirming a separation but denying that it had been caused by anything said by the defendant.[290] In a Welsh case of 1824 a witness said that the accusation had caused 'jarring' between the plaintiff and his wife and 'a stigma upon the name and character of the plaintiff.'[291]

Some cases remain of male plaintiffs in which it does not appear that there was any special reason to institute the suit. These are cases where the plaintiff was said to 'have been caught fucking the girl,'[292] 'caught plump in the act,'[293] caught in bed with the defendant's wife,[294] or that he kept a mistress,[295] had an irregular marriage,[296] was the father of an illegitimate child,[297] or had cuck-olded another man.[298] Though many men – perhaps most men – would not have resented such imputations, some did. In an Exeter case of 1831, the defendant said, 'You have fucked her. ... You keep a prick to fuck fools with.' The plaintiff immediately asked those present to take note as they would be asked to give evidence, and he went on to obtain a sentence and to insist on the performance of penance.[299]

This was a society where accusations of sexual misconduct were capable of causing serious harm. The cause papers, reflecting these social attitudes, contain many examples of the consequent injuries especially, though not exclusively, to women.

# 10

# Motives

Very often the motive for the institution of a lawsuit is obvious, but in the case of a defamation suit in the ecclesiastical court it is not. No monetary award could be made to the plaintiff, except for costs. Truth was not a complete defence, so even a successful suit did not establish that the substance of the slander was false, and did not therefore necessarily vindicate the plaintiff's reputation. The performance of penance, where this occurred, can have done little to assist the plaintiff's interests. In many dioceses the ceremony of penance required the defendant, in retracting the slander, to repeat the very words he had used; even when actual repetition of the opprobrious words was omitted, the ceremony would have served mainly to remind those who heard of it of the slander itself.

The legal formularies asserted that the purpose of the process was 'the restoring the good name, fame, and reputation of the person ... injured,' and the 'restitution' of the plaintiff's good name,[1] but it is not obvious that the proceedings always or even usually had that effect. In his evidence to the Ecclesiastical Courts Commission of 1832, William Ward, the deputy registrar of Chester, was asked whether he thought a defamation suit has 'the effect of restoring the character that is taken away,' and answered, 'No, often the reverse.'[2]

Nevertheless there is much evidence that many plaintiffs and their advisers felt strong pressure, amounting in some cases even to obligation, to institute a defamation suit in response to slander, and it is often stated or implied that the proceedings would 'set up,'[3] or 'clear up,'[4] or lead to the 'vindication'[5] of the plaintiff's character. Although truth was not a complete defence, obtaining a sentence with penance and full costs might be seen as a vindication in dioceses where costs and penance were habitually withheld when the truth of the words was proved. To a degree, also, the very existence of the legal remedy made it necessary to use it, lest failure to do so should be seen as acquiescence. Sir John Nicholl, Dean of the Arches, said in 1821 that defamation suits ought not to be discouraged in the higher classes of society, adding, 'on the contrary, in the higher classes of society acquiescence would be almost an admission of the charge.'[6]

This line of thinking was not confined to the higher classes. In a Chester case of 1827 the plaintiff was the wife of a publican. According to one witness, her customers said they would leave her house 'unless she cleared herself of the scandal,' and another witness heard a customer declare that 'if the plaintiff did not bring the matter of the slander home to the defendant he would leave her house.'[7] One plaintiff's fiancé said that 'he would not marry her till her character was defended.'[8] In another case the plaintiff's father, giving evidence on his daughter's behalf, admitted that he was responsible for the expenses of the suit, and added that 'I consider it my duty to see her character ... protected and set right before the world.'[9]

Perceptions of what was the proper response to slander existed quite independently of the actual remedy obtainable from the court. Many plaintiffs instituted suits mainly because they perceived, or they were told, that this was the proper response to slander. For defamation actionable at law, the bringing of an action or of a prosecution was recognized as the appropriate response of an innocent person wrongly accused. Criminal libel was analogous in some respects to the ecclesiastical process. There also truth was not a complete defence, but private prosecutions were frequently instituted for the purpose of clearing a person's name; indeed, prosecution was in some ways supposed to be preferable for this purpose, as it suggested that the plaintiff was not interested merely in obtaining money.[10] As we have seen, attitudes to defamation tended to carry over from the common law to the ecclesiastical law, and a woman accused of unchastity, or her advisers, might think first of taking appropriate legal action and only later discover that this meant a suit in the ecclesiastical court.

The law of defamation in all courts combined – and indeed still combines – elements of compensation, vindication, punishment, and deterrence, and blurs the lines between the civil and the criminal law. There were deterrent and punitive elements in the common law of civil libel, and there were elements of private satisfaction and vindication of reputation in the law of criminal libel. The 'mixed' civil and criminal nature of a defamation suit was, therefore, by no means peculiar to the ecclesiastical courts. The mixed nature of the suit is indicated by the ambiguous words used to describe the motives of plaintiffs. Mention was made in the last chapter of words like 'injured' and 'aggrieved,' which could refer to actual loss suffered by the plaintiff, or might simply indicate a legal wrong.[11] A similar ambiguity attends the large variety of other words in the cause papers describing the plaintiff's motives. Plaintiffs were said to be seeking redress,[12] satisfaction,[13] amends,[14] justice,[15] reparation,[16] justification,[17] relief,[18] to 'compel atonement for the injury her character has sustained,'[19] 'to bring the matter to a proper hearing,'[20] 'to see herself righted,'[21] or to 'bring the matter home to' the defendant.[22] There was often an element of seeking to 'set straight' the record by an official and public act. One witness was told by the plaintiff that her evidence would be required if the defendant 'did not think fit to make submission to her [the plaintiff].'[23]

'Submission' usually included an apology. Many cases show the importance of apology to the plaintiff and her advisers; it would certainly be an error to suppose that plaintiffs were only interested in costs. Bromby, the clergyman at Hull who instructed Askwith in several cases, wrote in his opening letter of instruction for one case, 'Please to institute such steps as may enable the prosecutor to obtain a recantation from the defamer,'[24] suggesting that this was the plaintiff's principal motive. Again, a letter written by a plaintiff's husband to her proctor stated that the defendant 'has sent to me to know if a compromise can be entered into but refuses to give an apology, consequently the proceedings must take their course.'[25] In a letter instructing a proctor to terminate proceedings, the plaintiff's husband said that he had received an 'ample apology,' and was satisfied.[26] The demand made of Charlotte Jones when she appeared in Mr Huckwell's office in 1854 was for an apology and costs.[27]

The court records do not normally mention settlements made before commencement of legal proceedings, but such settlements must have been common, and there are some references to them among the cause papers. In some cases there was a semi-public aspect to the apology. In a York case, for example, Amos Shires and Timothy Pearson were in a public house with several others. Pearson had made a slanderous comment on a previous occasion about Amos Shires's wife, Mary. She came into the public house for another purpose, in fact to reprimand her husband for neglecting his work, and Amos Shires asked whether she knew Pearson. She said that she did not, and Pearson then said that 'if he had ever said or done any thing against either of them that was wrong, he was sorry for it; that he had no intention so to do, nor could he believe he had ever used the expressions it was said he had done; if he had it was when in liquor and unknown to him and he was sorry for it.' The others present seem to have seen themselves as a sort of adjudicative committee. According to the affidavits of two of them, Mary Shires 'was individually satisfied and had no cause for complaint against ... Timothy Pearson and the company then present expressed their opinion that ... Timothy Pearson stood exculpated from any intention to defame or slander her ... Mary Shires.' One of them added that 'in his opinion ... Timothy Pearson would afterwards be cleared from any charge in any court in England.'[28] A citation was later issued against Pearson, but the incident just described was proved by affidavits, and the case was abandoned.[29] Another quite formal and semi-public apology took place in a public house in a York case of 1837.[30]

When informal settlement failed, and lawyers appeared on the scene, the first step was usually a formal demand for an apology, as, for example:

> Madam, I have received instructions from Thomas Bate Esq. of Hagley to inform you that if you do not, within one week from the present time, make such a *public* apology as I may dictate to you for the very scandalous report which [you] have put into circulation to the injury of the unoffending daughter of that gentleman, Miss Caroline Bate, proceedings will be commenced against you in the ecclesiastical court of Worcester without further notice. I am, Madam, your very obedient humble servant, Henry Clifton, Proctor.[31]

This case was resisted, and eventually found its way to the Arches Court and to the Judicial Committee of the Privy Council.

Not all lawyers' letters were quite so formal. William Askwith, the York proctor, wrote:

> To William Sanderson: A complaint having been made to me that you did on the 1st Inst abuse Ann Duggleby wife of William Duggleby shopkeeper in a most shameful and scandalous manner; this is therefore to give you notice that unless you immediately beg her pardon for such abuse and promise not to offend in like manner in future, I am directed to proceed against you in the Spiritual Court for defamation. I am, yours &c.

Askwith's note on the office copy of the letter adds 'The words a whore, 1st June 1819. Whit Tuesday. About 10 o'clock at night.' Evidently there was no satisfactory response to this letter, as a week later a citation was issued, and a libel was given in.[32] Among Askwith's papers in this case there is also a draft form of apology, indicating what Askwith thought would satisfy the plaintiff:

> I, William Sanderson of Bishop Wilton in the County of York, carpenter, do hereby acknowledge that I have several times unjustly and without any provocation whatsoever, called and abused Ann the wife of William Duggleby of the same place, shopkeeper, for which I am heartily sorry and beg her pardon for the same. As witness my hand this        day of August in the year of our Lord 1819.....Witnesses.

12 August delivered to W Cantley[33]

At the bottom is the note: 'To pay 5/- to poor,' showing that the terms of a settlement were to include a payment to charity; there are some other examples of this, as we shall see. Probably the case was settled, but the records do not reveal on what terms.

Another somewhat different form of apology from the diocese of Peterborough, in this case duly executed by the defendant, read:

> I the within named John Langley, the younger, of Ecton in the county of Northampton, shoemaker, do hereby acknowledge that I have no just grounds whatever for defaming the character of the within named Sarah Langley, the wife of William Langley the younger of Ecton aforesaid, shoemanufacturer, and I promise not to abuse nor defame her again in any manner whatever in consideration of her staying proceedings against me on my making this apology and paying the costs which have been incurred. Witness my hand ... [signed and witnessed][34]

The usual elements of an apology were expression of regret at having uttered the words, acknowledgment that they were untrue, a promise not to repeat them, a plea for pardon, and an undertaking to pay costs. In a Llandaff case, where the plaintiff was a clergyman's wife, the form of apology added an expression of gratitude 'for the amity shown me,'[35] though what form the amity took does not appear, as the defendant had to pay expenses. Not all the elements of an apology were always present, and they might receive differing emphases. The form of apology to Ann Duggleby does not expressly say that the words were untrue, nor does it include an express promise not to repeat them, and that to Sarah Langley does not expressly manifest regret, or beg pardon.[36]

If the defendant refused to apologize, proceedings would probably follow. In a Chester case, 'the defendant was written to to arrange the matter and to sign a private recantation which was drawn up and sent to Mr Walker, attorney, but the defendant treated the same with ridicule and told Mr Soorn [the plaintiff's proctor] to do his worst, and which proposed compromise was ended by the institution of these proceedings by the promovent.'[37]

After the institution of proceedings, apology could be demanded at each stage of the proceedings, as escalating costs raised the stakes. Several proctors' bills of costs include entries such as 'drawing apology in case of her [defendant] relenting.'[38] In a Worcester case a proctor recorded, as an item in his bill, 'attending adverse proctor when it was proposed that the affair should be compromised, but the apology offered not being sufficient the witnesses were ordered by the registrar to attend.'[39]

This last-mentioned case shows that a form of apology might be offered, but rejected by the plaintiff on account of some insufficiency, perhaps the omission of an acknowledgment that the slander was false. In a Peterborough case the plaintiff's attorney wrote:

I have wished the defendant to apologize but he stonily refused on the ground that what he had said was fact. The plaintiff and defendant are brothers in law and I tried all I could to conciliate this matter; perhaps [t]he defendant will when he finds what power the ecclesiastical court has.[40]

Probably an apology was procured, as the case was recorded as settled a month later.[41]

On the other hand, denial of the truth of the slander was not always enough. In a Ripon case, the defendant offered a written 'denial of the scandal charged,' but the plaintiff rejected it and refused to accept 'anything short of a full unqualified apology.'[42] The strength of the plaintiff's position varied, naturally, with the circumstances, and some did have to settle for less than a full apology. In a Peterborough case the apology was very cautiously worded, the defendant undertaking only 'not to circulate any such defamatory reports in future, and that I do not of my own knowledge know such reports to be true.'[43] Apparently the plaintiff was satisfied with this, as there is no record of the issue of a citation.

Where a compromise is recorded it is often stated that the terms included an apology, as where the plaintiff's proctor 'stated that the defendant had made an apology with which the party promovent was satisfied and thereupon alleged the cause to be ended.'[44] In many of the other cases that were settled (two-thirds of all cases), it is likely that an apology of some sort was given.[45] Many plaintiffs desired no more than an apology and costs. In recommending that a plaintiff should settle, Askwith wrote, 'In case the defendant will say that he is sorry for what he has said & pay the expenses of the Citation, Foster should be satisfied.'[46]

If the plaintiff's character were to be 'set right before the world,' an element of publicity was requisite. In the letter quoted above to Ann Collis, the plaintiff's proctor demanded a *public* apology (emphasis in original). The public element was often important to both sides. In the same measure that a public apology was beneficial to the plaintiff, it was painful to the defendant. In a Chester case, the defendant (according to a witness) had declared 'his willingness to go down on his knees to ask pardon of the plaintiff but he would not make any public acknowledgment,'[47] and in another case the defendant unwisely called on the plaintiff's attorney to say that 'he did not wish to make a public apology but would have no objection to a private one,' thereby unluckily supplying evidence against himself of the original slander.[48]

In one case it was proposed that the apology should take place in the presence of the curate,[49] and in another that it should be made in open court,[50] but more usually a public apology in this context meant an apology in writing, with leave to the plaintiff to publish it, rather than words actually spoken in a public forum. In a Gloucester case a proposal for settlement included payment by the defendant of 'the expense of publishing the apology,'[51] and in a Lichfield case a letter on behalf of the defendant said that he 'was willing to sign a paper begging pardon &c but not to have it published in the public papers which the plaintiff insisted should be done.'[52] In the case of apology in a public forum the plaintiff would certainly wish to choose the forum and the occasion. One defendant (it was suggested in interrogatories) had offered to settle, paying the costs, 'and contradicting the report in the public houses he frequented,'[53] not an offer likely to be of great value to the plaintiff, and presumably rejected for that reason.

Plaintiffs were subjected to pressure from various sources. It was alleged in one case that the plaintiff 'barely consents to these proceedings to please her solicitor and has very little to do in the matter further than lending her name.' This was denied by the witness, but the making of the suggestion shows that it was, at the least, plausible. Interestingly, the witness answered not that the plaintiff carried on the suit by her own desire, but that she (the witness) 'believes the present suit has been advised by other friends of the plaintiff rather than by her solicitor.'[54] In a York case there was evidence of pressure on the plaintiff by friends. This was one of the cases in which Askwith was instructed by Mr Bromby, the vicar of Hull. Bromby wrote, in returning the draft libel, 'her friends, she says, will not hear of her relinquishing the suit, provided that her witnesses can be compelled to come forward with their evidence.'[55] After the sentence, which was given for the plaintiff but without costs, she wrote to Bromby to say that no more money was forthcoming, and added, 'I think it very hard of my friends as thay wished me to go on with it for thay know'd that I had nothing,'[56] and in a later letter she wrote, 'I am not to blame for my friends seed every letter that came from you.'[57] It must be borne in mind here that the plaintiff may have had an interest in suggesting that her friends had played a large part in promoting the suit, especially when it came to the reckoning.

Other cases supply convincing evidence of pressure exerted by friends. In an Exeter case the plaintiff's proctor said that he had not recommended a suit: he had suggested that the slander should be treated with 'silent contempt.' But a friend of the plaintiffs (who were two sisters) said that 'if they did not proceed ... they would no longer receive her support.'[58] In the case involving the Jewish community in Ipswich, where it might be thought that the plaintiff would have been reluctant to seek redress from an ecclesiastical tribunal, a witness said that 'her neighbours required it [the slander] to be contradicted.'[59] A plaintiff might be told that she was 'to blame if she did not punish him [defendant] for his conduct.'[60]

Plaintiffs were often told that if they did not institute a lawsuit they endangered their reputations. A witness in a Chester case heard neighbours say that 'they should believe what the defendant said of her if she didn't fetch law.'[61] In a Gloucester case a witness said, 'I have heard Miss Constable and Mrs T. Jenner say that if Harriet Woodhouse did not proceed against Ann Williams and make her know better they should think the defamatory words ... were true.'[62] One witness said that 'many of her (plaintiff's) acquaintance expect her to clear up her character.'[63] Of another plaintiff it was said that 'her motive was not revenge but to set up her character as she has so many respectable friends that she did not like to be held up to be a shame to them.'[64] A witness in a London case said that she [the witness] 'could not sit quiet under such a word [whore]' and that she expected the plaintiff to take action.[65]

Effective pressure could be exerted by an employer, and we have seen examples of this in previous chapters.[66] In a Carlisle case, the defendant told John Hodgson that his housekeeper [the plaintiff] was a common strumpet, and Hodgson gave evidence that 'I told the ... complainant next morning what the ... defendant had said concerning her and that if it was true she must quit my house, and if it was not true she must defend her character and I advised her to apply to Mr Lightfoot attorney in Wigton.' In answer to an interrogatory he added, showing the influence of feminine opinion in such matters, 'My sister spoke to me about it and said the complainant should not be kept in my house if it was true.'[67]

Where the plaintiff was a minor, appointment of a litigation guardian, usually her father, was necessary, and in most such cases he was the moving force behind the proceedings.[68] In a Norwich case where the plaintiff was only fourteen years of age, a letter written to the registrar on behalf of the defendant, praising the defendant's character, added that 'I have also the means of knowing that Mr Russell [the plaintiff's father] has for some time past been endeavouring to persecute these poor people in many different ways.'[69] The plaintiff's consent to the suit was also necessary, but it is impossible to know from the cause papers with what degree of enthusiasm the plaintiffs themselves in these cases contemplated the proceedings. In many cases of adult women also, an active role was played by her father,[70] or by other relatives.[71] In the London case where the plaintiff's father, who was produced as a witness, admitted that he had effectively promoted the suit, he said that he was responsible for the expenses, that he saw his daughter execute the proxy, and that he considered it his duty to see her character 'protected and set right before the world.' The plaintiff succeeded, but her father's evidence was excluded on account of his admitted interest. [72]

In the case of a married woman, her husband's consent was not, as a matter of strict law, necessary, but it was common practice for the husband to join in or ratify the proxy, thus making him liable for costs both to the plaintiff's proctor, and to the other side in case of dismissal with an award of costs against the plaintiff. In the Arches Court, as was mentioned in an earlier chapter, the practice was to demand the husband's signature, but this was not a strict requirement, and was dispensed with in one case, where the plaintiff was separated from her husband, on the plaintiff's giving security for costs.[73] There was a substantial number of cases, however, in the other courts in which husbands did not join and security was not required.

In many cases of married women it is clear that the husband was the moving party, making the initial decision to proceed,[74] instructing the lawyers,[75] asking the witnesses to give evidence,[76] and deciding whether or not to settle.[77] Cases were mentioned in the last chapter where husbands threatened to leave their wives unless proceedings were brought.[78] One plaintiff was said to have brought the suit 'in order to clear herself & to restore peace of mind to her husband.'[79] The husband often assumed that he was in sole charge of the litigation. One headed his letters of instruction to the proctor 'myself v. Bowers.'[80] In a York case where (unusually) the husband gave evidence, he said that he would have overlooked the slander had it not been repeated, but was 'so vexed and angry' by the repetition 'that he did proceed.' Significantly, the word 'he' in the deposition is crossed through and 'his wife' substituted, showing that the witness had temporarily forgotten, perhaps until reminded by the examiner, or until the deposition was read over to him, that the proceedings were in his wife's name, not in his own.[81] Observers of the proceedings often made the same assumption. A friend of one plaintiff was supposed to have said to the defendant's wife, 'Damn your eyes, we have got you, you devils,' adding, to the plaintiff's husband, 'Now stick to them, Ben,' 'meaning and intending,' as the interrogatory laboriously explains – but as the friend probably did not consciously think – 'that the said Benjamin Caswell should cause his wife to carry on and prosecute the present action.'[82] Newspaper reports often referred to 'the plaintiff's wife,' meaning the plaintiff.[83] Even attorneys involved in the case might make the same mistake.[84]

In an interesting Hereford case, the plaintiff, having first instituted a suit, then sought to withdraw, but was overruled by her husband. The defendant was the parish clergyman who had mentioned to the plaintiff that he had heard a report of her misconduct. She said in an affidavit that she did not at all resent his having spoken to her in this way, and that 'she has every wish that there should be no law against him.' But two weeks later she made another affidavit saying that the suit was carried on by her husband's wish, and 'unless she had commenced this suit he should not have been satisfied of the falseness of the words.'[85] Since she signed by mark (O), she may not have appreciated the full effect of the proxy, or indeed of either or both of the later affidavits, which bear the definite appearance of having been drafted respectively by the friends and by the enemies of the clergyman. The second affidavit apparently represented the plaintiff's – or her husband's – settled wish, for the case proceeded to the stage of sentence, when it was dismissed.

The supposition that a married woman was under her husband's control may have had some use as a legal presumption, and may possibly have represented (to some) an ideal, but it was certainly not universally accurate, nor did contemporary observers believe that it was; indeed it was this supposition, as a legal presumption, that led Charles Dickens (in 1837) to make the well-known aphorism that the law is an ass.[86] There are many reminders in the cause papers and in the proctors' correspondence that married women did sometimes act independently. In 1830 Askwith, the York proctor, acting for a defendant in a dispute between two women, cousins of each other, received the following information from his instructing attorney:

The defendant's husband ... will state most positively that the plaintiff was the first aggressor & that she actually struck *him*. He also knows that plaintiff is a notorious scold & has heard her curse & swear upon many occasions & particularly to her own husband who it may be remarked states that he has nothing whatever to do with this suit & wished it to be stopped but states that he cannot guide his wife (the plaintiff).[87]

The attorney was scarcely more flattering to his own client, also a married woman. He said of her, 'we must admit the defendant is not of the most refined of the fair sex; still we believe the plaintiff is equally bad if not worse & if they had each of them what they deserve the Tread Mill would be more suitable than penance in the church.' From what we know of the judge's (Vernon's) attitude to defamation cases, we might predict that the prospects here were not promising for either side, and in fact the suit was settled,[88] in accordance with Askwith's strong advice.[89]

There are some other cases in which it is known that women carried on defamation suits contrary to their husband's wishes. In a Chester case the plaintiff's husband put in a statement that the proceedings were against his wish, and that in his opinion there had been no injury to his character or to his wife's.[90] In a Yorkshire case, where the plaintiff, 'a woman of spirit,'[91] was in open dispute with her husband, the husband sought, unsuccessfully, to stop the proceedings. He wrote to Askwith, who was acting for the plaintiff, that the suit had been instituted 'without my knowledge and directly contrary to my wish.'[92] Askwith explained in a letter to the plaintiff's mother (who was supporting the litigation) that the plaintiff's right to bring the suit could not be removed: 'Mr Harrison [the husband] cannot release his wife's suit, it being brought to recover her fame and character, and it is not in his power to restrain her proceedings.' However, he went on to point out that the husband could release the costs, so requiring the plaintiff to bear the costs even if successful, and preventing the imposition of any financial penalty on the defendant: 'if she succeeds in the action and should recover costs against Leetham, her husband may & probably will release such costs, and in that case the whole expences of the suit would fall upon your daughter to pay out of her own income.'[93] The case did proceed, and was ultimately dismissed. In a London case of 1819 the defendant, who was living apart from his wife, shouted insulting remarks outside her house, saying of the plaintiff, who was a servant of the wife's, 'Look at the young strumpet watching me, or else she is watching her mistress on [sic] from whoring.' It was suggested in the interrogatories that the suit had been promoted by the wife 'to gratify [her] malice against her husband.'[94]

Where husband and wife were living in amity, the husband would, naturally, usually be involved in the institution of the suit, and in its settlement. One York plaintiff said that she was satisfied and that her husband might settle the suit, and she left him to do so.[95] Husbands often took it upon themselves to settle suits on their wives' behalf.[96] As we have seen, this was not effective without the plaintiff's consent, and, where the defendant was a married woman, it appears that her personal consent also was required. In a case in the diocese of St David's in 1835 the defendant's husband, who was a clergyman, agreed to settle, but the defendant then went to see her proctor and told him that 'she had not in any way been party or privy to a settlement ... and that the business of settlement was performed by her ... husband ... without her knowledge and consent.'[97] The outcome of this case is not known. The conduct of the litigation was sometimes managed directly by married women plaintiffs. The plaintiff in a London case went herself to Doctors' Commons to instruct her proctor,[98] and in other cases married women themselves dealt directly with the witnesses.[99]

As we saw in the last chapter, some men accused of adultery or fornication, even where they did not bring a suit in their own names, felt sufficiently aggrieved to encourage a suit in the name of the woman concerned, and in several of these cases the man appears to have been the real promoter of the litigation. In a Gloucester case, where the evidence was that the defendant had said, 'Coote fucked Chavasse's wife,' the witness admitted that he had gone to see the defendant at Coote's request expressly to entrap him into giving the necessary evidence, explaining that 'Coote has expressed to me a desire to punish Harris as a propagator of these reports.'[100] We have seen other examples in earlier chapters.[101]

Among Askwith's correspondence is a letter from an attorney instructing institution of a suit on behalf of a friend of whom it had been said that Ann Wilson was his whore. The attorney wrote that the friend 'is authorized to use the names of Wilson and his wife in this,' and this way of expressing it shows that, in the atttorney's mind, the friend was his real client, Wilson lending her name.[102] Sometimes it was suggested in interrogatories, but denied, that the litigation was promoted by the man accused.[103] If he could be shown to have an independent grudge against the defendant this might discredit the plaintiff's evidence,[104] particularly if the man was himself a witness.[105]

It has been suggested, in reference to the early modern period, that one of the motives for instituting a defamation suit might have been to forestall presentment and punishment by the ecclesiastical court for fornication or adultery.[106] Others have doubted this suggestion.[107] In the nineteenth century this was not a plausible motive, as punishment by the ecclesiastical courts for sexual misconduct was (except in the Isle of Man) virtually obsolete. There are, however, a very few examples of criminal suits. In 1826 a citation was issued against John Brimmell 'to answer certain articles concerning the health of your soul and the reformation of your manners' (the criminal form of suit). The citation was at the promotion of John Rayer and James Dudfield, and it accused Brimmell of adultery with Ann Burlow.[108] She instituted defamation suits against Rayer and Dudfield,[109] all three suits being commenced on the same day.[110] Witnesses were produced and sworn in the two defamation suits, and witnesses were examined on both sides in the criminal suit,[111] but no sentence is recorded in any of the cases, so presumably they were settled. Evidently the cases are connected, but in view of the rarity of criminal suits it is more likely that the defamation cases were started in response to the criminal suit than that they were designed to forestall it. It is also possible that the criminal proceedings were instituted in response to the defamation suits, though in that case it might have been expected that proceedings would have been taken against Burlow instead of, or in addition to, Brimmell.

It might perhaps be supposed that the defamation cases were a survival of the criminal jurisdiction and that the clergy and churchwardens encouraged or supported defamation suits as a means of controlling and punishing defamation, but there is little evidence to support this supposition. Where local clergymen were involved it was generally in the role of peacemakers attempting to effect a settlement. They did not usually perceive ecclesiastical law as an instrument of their own policies, and neither did the ecclesiastical courts consider it their duty to favour the parish clergy. In some cases it is true that clergymen supported plaintiffs,[112] but in others they opposed them. In a Hereford case the clergyman, a churchwarden, and the parish overseer submitted a petition hostile to the plaintiff saying that she had 'a very disreputable character for keeping a bad house & dealing with different men in a very improvident way,' and that in consequence the plaintiff's husband had been served with notice to quit his house 'in order to get rid of them out of the parish.' The court was evidently not impressed by this disparagement, as sentence was given for the plaintiff with costs.[113]

It was often alleged, on the defendant's behalf, that the plaintiff's motive was to obtain money, rather than to clear her character.[114] Evidently obtaining money was a disreputable motive, and it was often alleged and denied.[115] In a York case of 1833 the plaintiff said that 'she did not wish for any money and would not have any.'[116] In several cases there is evidence that the plaintiff did ask for money. A person writing to a Peterborough proctor on the plaintiff's behalf said 'she expects remuneration to herself and clear of any further costs you may have.'[117] In another case in the same diocese the defendant had paid two guineas to the plaintiff herself, and the proctor told the plaintiff that she must return the money if she wished to proceed with the suit. Retaining it, he said, would be 'contrary to the rules of the court.'[118] Presumably these rules, written or unwritten, were to protect defendants from paying money in the expectation that a suit was settled, only to find later that it was not. The apparitor (court officer) wrote to the proctor saying that he hoped he could prevent further proceedings, adding, 'The woman [the plaintiff] is a bad one, I hear.'

A case was earlier mentioned in which the terms of a proposed settlement included the payment of 5s to the poor, and in other cases the plaintiff demanded money to be paid to charity.[119] One proctor, acting on behalf of a plaintiff, stated that he had demanded 'an apology and five pounds to be disposed of as should be thought fit,'[120] perhaps implying charitable disposition. These cases show that, even though no damages could be obtained from the court, the plaintiff was in a position to obtain some money in consideration of a settlement, and that some plaintiffs did so. This appears to have been lawful, but was not considered a very proper use of the process. The amounts obtainable in this way could not have been large, for the defendant had always the option of giving an affirmative issue, confessing the slander, and paying the taxed costs.[121]

Punishment is often mentioned in the cause papers as the plaintiff's avowed motive, or as the avowed motive of others promoting the litigation.[122] 'Dog, I'll make thee pay for calling me a whore,' one Yorkshire plaintiff said,[123] and other plaintiffs expressed similar sentiments in varying language. One said that she 'would work ... Thomas England rarely, that he would be paying about a guinea an hour.'[124] Other such expressions are that 'she would make him smart for it,'[125] that she would 'warm him' or 'trim him,'[126] 'I'll fix you for that,'[127] 'I shall make you know better,'[128] 'I'll pull you up for this,'[129] 'I'll make you pay for that, young man,'[130] 'Recollect you shall suffer for that.'[131] The plaintiff's attorney in a York case said of the defendant, 'He is a very mischievous fellow & has on many occasions boasted of his familiarity with other men's wives in the presence of their husbands. I hope the Court will teach him a salutary lesson at this time.'[132]

The proctors and judges also considered that punishment was one of the proper purposes of a defamation suit. It was recited in the formal documents that the defendant ought to be 'punished and corrected,' the latter word implying punishment inflicted for the offender's own spiritual welfare, as in the ecclesiastical criminal cases which were brought 'for the health of your soul.' In arguments over costs it was often urged on the one side that the defendant's conduct was premeditated, and worthy of punishment, and on the other that he had acted in the heat of the moment and ought not therefore to be severely punished.[133] In a case where the defendant had been imprisoned for non-appearance, her husband and her proctor had come to see Askwith, who was acting for the plaintiff, to effect her release. Askwith wrote to the instructing attorney, manifesting considerable sympathy for the defendant, whom he described as 'the poor woman,' 'I presume you will consider the defendant's incarceration and payment of costs a sufficient punishment for the offence.'[134]

In one Worcester case, where the plaintiff, Caroline Bate, was a fifteen-year-old girl said to have had a child by a footman in her father's household, the father, Thomas Bate, printed and published handbills (see plate 11):

£100
REWARD.

Whereas a most false, scandalous, and malicious report has been raised, and perseveringly circulated, affecting the character of a member of a respectable family in this neighbourhood.

Notice is hereby Given,

that whoever will furnish such information and testimony, as shall lead to the
legal conviction and punishment of the person who originated and circulated such
report, shall receive upon such conviction the above reward, by application to H.
Burton, Superintendent of Police.[135]

The style of this notice, with its reference to wrongdoing, information,
reward, conviction, punishment, and the police, was precisely that in use in
ordinary criminal cases, and indicates punishment as the father's primary
motive. It is an interesting question what immediate effect the circulation of
such a notice would have had upon the reputation of Caroline Bate. It might be
supposed that its main effect would be to cause any who did not already know
of the rumour to find out about it; on the other hand, perhaps everyone who
saw the notice already knew of the rumour, and the offer of such a large
reward may have tended to persuade them that the rumour must be untrue.

An aspect of punishment distinct both from correction and revenge is
denunciation, and this case and some others suggest a determination to use the
formal legal process to denounce the uttering of a slander. A further aspect is
deterrence. Professor Amussen has written, of the early modern period, that
'many defamation cases can be seen as attempts to stop a rumour before it
became "common fame" to the discredit of the victim,'[136] and the same motive
can be discerned in the nineteenth-century cases. One of Thomas Bate's
objects, in publishing the handbill just quoted, and in instituting the suit
against Ann Collis, which he took to two levels of appeal, must have been to
suppress future propagation of the rumour, and if readers of the handbill were
likely already to know of the rumour, perhaps publication of the notice did no
further harm to his daughter and might have done her some good by inhibiting
repetition.[137] In a Welsh case the plaintiff's proctor said that he was willing to
settle, 'provided the party agent was satisfied that she should not in future be
insulted by Mrs Lloyd [the defendant].'[138] In some cases there was an actual
threat by the defendant to propagate a rumour, as in the York case where the
defendant said, 'Whatever company she's in I'll tell her out';[139] in another
case in the same diocese the defendant told the plaintiff that 'he would scandalize her all over the country.'[140] Words of this sort threatened serious harm
and demanded a response.

There is much evidence that plaintiffs, while willing to tolerate a single
instance of slander, felt it necessary to act to prevent repetition. 'If the defendant had not repeated the language in the cool moment of reflection, this suit
would never have been heard of,' said an Exeter proctor in argument, adding

that the plaintiff's motive was 'not revenge but protection of reputation and security from other insults.'[141] In a York case the plaintiff's husband said that if it had not been for a second attack on his wife 'he would have overlooked it, but he was so vexed and angry that his wife did proceed,'[142] and in a London case a man said that 'he would have let it pass, but as the defendant had insulted his wife a second time, he had to act.'[143] An attorney complained on behalf of his client that she had been 'again vilified' and threatened that 'you as well as your husband and daughter will have to be further sued for she is determined not to endure it in the way you are pleased to scandalize her.'[144]

A clergyman, seeking to settle a Winchester case, went to see the defendant, saying that his object was to make peace. He said that he was authorized to inform the defendant that 'if she would refrain from using any such language and contradict the assertions she had already made ... Benjamin Bear and ... Jane Bear [the plaintiff's uncle and the plaintiff] would overlook that had been said by her.' But the defendant refused, threatening to repeat the accusation whenever she met Benjamin Bear, and the clergyman said that 'he was sorry that he could not work any good in her and that she must take the consequences.' The suit proceeded, and sentence was given against the defendant, who eventually performed penance a year later in the presence of the same clergyman, though only after resisting to the point of issue of a significavit to enforce the penance.[145] In the London case where Harriet Johnson lived alone in her own rooms apart from the rest of the family, she had often used abusive words to Mary Johnson, one of her six stepdaughters. Eventually the repetition of the abuse became too much for Mary Johnson, who determined to act: 'she would make her prove her words. She added that she had often threatened to do so, but was then determined to put her threat in execution the next morning.'[146]

Where, as in many of the cases mentioned in the last chapter, the defendant was causing a continuing nuisance, one object of the suit was to restrain the nuisance in the future, as well as to punish the defendant for past misconduct. In a York case Israel Bradley walked backwards and forwards in the street outside Mary Stubbs's house (a public house) calling her a 'bloody thundering whore' and saying that 'he had had connexion with her in every part of the house even in the cellar.' One of the witnesses 'had frequently heard him abuse ... Mary Stubbs in a similar manner.' The initial reaction of the plaintiff and her husband was to ignore Bradley: 'they shut the door and took no notice of him, but let him go on, tho' some respectable persons who were in the house wished much to go out to him, but they would not let them as they said it would be no use.' Here it seems likely that the plaintiff would not have proceeded if she had been assured that the nuisance would cease. The suit was probably effective for her purpose. The judge took a serious view of the case and gave sentence against Bradley with full costs, which led to his subsequent imprisonment for failure to pay them.[147]

Very often there is evidence of a quarrel between the parties, pre-dating the occasion of the slander, that had nothing to do directly with the plaintiff's reputation. These cases of collateral quarrels, common also in earlier periods of the history of the ecclesiastical courts,[148] are well represented in the nineteenth century. A boundary dispute between neighbours might come to high words; high words usually meant low words; and low words, when addressed to women, often included the insult that opened the door of the ecclesiastical court. These cases are not so much evidence of what has been called a plebeian sense of honour[149] (though they are not inconsistent with it) as an indication that those fighting battles will use whatever weapons come to hand.

There might be multiple causes of dispute between the parties. In a Chester case of 1837, for example, there had been a dispute between Mary Chesworth and John Evans, next-door neighbours, over competition in trade – 'a little jealousy,' the plaintiff's proctor called it, 'on account of the promovent beginning to sell milk.' Another cause of dispute was the erection of a shed against the boundary wall. According to a witness who was in the garden with Mary Chesworth and her husband, James,

> John Evans the party promote who was in his own garden adjoining began to abuse ... James Chesworth for erecting a shippen [cattle-shed] against his ... John Evans's wall and on ... Mary Chesworth speaking to him in reply he called her a dirty whore and told her to get in.[150]

It need not be doubted that Mary Chesworth was genuinely insulted by Evans's words, but it may also be suggested that the disputes over the sale of milk and the building of the shed tended to increase the probability of a defamation suit. It will be recalled that, even in dioceses where litigation was comparatively frequent, the absolute number of cases was low. There must have been a vast number of occasions on which the use of the opprobrious word did not result in litigation. Five years earlier the *Law Magazine* had commented that 'considering how freely words of the sort are bandied about by the lower classes, nothing but great prudence on the part of the Ecclesiastical Judges would have prevented the nuisance [of defamation litigation] becoming long ago intolerable.'[151]

The causes of prior disputes were multifarious, and it is not possible in the present context to elaborate upon them. Boundary disputes, disputes over rights of way, disputes over drainage of water, accusations of theft or assault, accusations of informing, claims for various kinds of debt, and the depredations of domestic animals are among the most frequent causes of quarrels. Often previous litigation, civil or criminal, had occurred between the parties or members of their families; in one case the parties had been bound over to keep the peace towards each other on the day before the defamatory words were spoken.[152] Sometimes the dispute arose from a previous slander or alleged slander; cases have been mentioned in earlier chapters of counter-suits to defamation suits. In one such case Askwith commented (on a counter-suit) that 'it seems pretty evident that had not Garside instituted a suit against Ripley no suit would have been brought by Ripley.'[153] In some cases the primary instigator was a friend of the plaintiff seeking to carry on a dispute of his own with the defendant.[154]

In 1838 a scuffle occurred on a highway near Leeds, involving Ellen Hutchinson on the one hand, and a father and son, Jeremiah and Samuel Proctor, on the other. Hutchinson first charged the Proctors with assault and theft, but these charges were dismissed by the magistrates the next morning. She then instituted a defamation suit, complaining that both the Proctors had called her a 'nasty trashy Irish whore.' It seems likely that when the charges before the magistrates were dismissed, Hutchinson took advice and discovered that, if she could prove that she had been called a whore, she might have recourse to another forum – the ecclesiastical court. The judge (Vernon) did not think highly of her motives, as will be seen from a newspaper report of his judgment:

> The CHANCELLOR believed the defamatory expressions had been used, but thought it very unneighbourly and improper to put the defendant to so much expense. He admonished him for his conduct, and left both parties to pay their own costs.[155]

It was very common for defendants to allege that the plaintiff's motive was spite, vengeance, or malice, or that her intention was to ruin the defendant. In a York case the defendant alleged that

> Elizabeth Boyes [the plaintiff] met ... Mary Johnson [the defendant] in the ... yard and said in allusion to the expenses likely to be incurred ... in the threatened suits against ... Mary Johnson and George Johnson (as the witnesses then present understood) 'I will have the shoes off thy fat fellow's feet and the pigs out of thy sty' or words to that effect.[156]

This particular allegation was ruled inadmissible (probably because not sufficiently relevant to the issues before the court), and so we do not know whether it could have been proved. The Salisbury chancellor thought that defamation causes were used by the 'lower classes' of people to harass one another, 'in consequence of a little spite of one against the other.'[157] In a Llandaff case a letter written on the defendant's behalf said that 'I should be very sorry to see him (a poor man) mulcted in costs because a person who may entertain an ill feeling against him has sought to gratify it by citing him to your court.'[158] Usually the plaintiff's witnesses denied such allegations and suggestions,[159] but the frequency with which they were made shows that they were plausible, and in some cases they were proved by witnesses.[160] It is impossible to know in how many cases they were actually true, even if we could establish a criterion of truth in this context: in many cases where hostility ran high the plaintiff herself probably could not have distinguished among mixed motives.

Several cases involved children. In some, one of the parties spoke to, or interrupted the activities of, a child of the other. In a Somerset case of 1851 'Mrs Clack's little boy was playing with a marble or ball and Mrs Baker took it up which caused angry words between [them] and Mrs Baker said ... "you are a jumping or a drunken whore"' (the witness was unsure which word had been used).[161] In a Chester case the defendant's wife told the plaintiff's children to go home and that their mother was 'bringing them up to the gallows.' When the plaintiff remonstrated, she was called (a witness said) a 'nasty dirty bitch of a whore and ... a brimstone faggott with many other very opprobrious and indecent expressions of the like nature.'[162] In other cases the quarrel started among children and was taken up by their parents. In a Norwich case, in the town of Ipswich, where it was proved that Michael Levy had said to Moses Levy, 'your wife is a whore,' it was suggested in the interrogatories that the quarrel had arisen from a dispute among the parties' children. Moses Levy's son Isaac had thrown stones at Michael's son Mier. Another of Michael's sons, also called Isaac, interfered, and one of the boys[163] went home crying. The suggestions continued:

Did not Mrs Levi the complainant say to the defendant's wife on her ... son's going home, 'Look at the bunter how she enjoys it; now her boy has beaten mine.' And did not a quarrel arise between them in consequence? Did not defendant's wife then say ... 'Don't you hear what she has called me? Very nice language she makes use of; my character was always as good as hers.'[164]

Several cases occurred against a background of sexual jealousy. The York cases of Garside v. Ripley and Ripley v. Garside (1826) contain varying accounts of the same incident by opposing witnesses, which Askwith described as *tight* swearing (his emphasis).[165] According to William Page, the attorney instructing Askwith on Garside's behalf, 'the parties are both respect-able, but jealousy has made the breach irreparable.'[166] Thomas Nightingale, 'a man of some property but a drunken dissolute fellow,' had courted Mary Ann Garside, a widow, but had been rejected by her. He had assaulted her, and Page had preferred a bill of indictment against him at the York assizes (Nightingale himself said for rape, but other references are to assault – perhaps it was for attempted rape) 'but did not push the proceedings against him.' Garside (Page said) was willing to let the matter rest 'until provoked by a succession of abuse and of intrusion by him [Nightingale] upon her privicy [sic] under the pretence of wishing to marry her but which she refused.' On 10 June 1826, Nightingale went to Garside's house, and Mary Ripley, his housekeeper, followed him and 'full of rage and jealousy burst in, when she commenced a volley of abuse against Mrs G, who ordered both out, but N would not go and turned upon Ripley calling her everything and that she should not remain in his house another night; much abuse took place in the house and at length a love attack [apparently thus] by Ripley "crying and going to faint" which in part suc-ceeded as N soon left with her.'[167]

Garside promptly instituted a suit against Ripley; and in September Ripley instituted a counter-suit against Garside complaining of slanderous words spo-ken on the same occasion (10 June).[168] The motive for Ripley's counter-suit was said by Page to be jealousy: 'the truth between you and me is, that plain-tiff lives with Nightingale, she is jealous of him & wherever he goes when drunk she follows; that led to the whole affair; Mrs Garside is a marriageable widow and there might be cause for plaintiff's vigilance.'[169] The outcome, with which Askwith was pleased ('I think we have no great reason to com-plain'), was that Garside obtained a sentence with costs, and Ripley's counter-suit was dismissed without costs.[170]

A number of cases were brought against married women, the complaint being that the defendant had alleged adultery by her husband with the plain-tiff. Payne v. Rowley, the Bristol case where the defendant found love letters that had been written to her husband, is a case of this sort.[171] In a Hereford case the defendant was proved to have said that 'Dame Dee was as common a whore as ever went,' adding 'that she is a very bad woman or else she would not inveigle another woman's husband as she did hers.'[172] In a London case the defendant said, addressing her own husband, 'she [the plaintiff] is a whore to you. She has weaned your affections from me and I can prove it.'[173]

Jealousy also (according to an instructing attorney) underlay a York case of 1833:

The defendant is an unmarried man, a farmer, was criminally connected with the plaintiff, tiring of her & becoming in like manner connected with another married woman, the 2 women (tenants of defendant) assaulted each other, were before the magistrates, when defendant espousing the side of plaintiff's antagonist came off successfully before the magistrates, & before them said, certainly such words as the libel contains or nearly so [i.e., that the plaintiff was a whore and that – from the evidence of a witness – 'I have fucked her many times'] & the magistrates believed him. ... The plaintiff was a prostitute in Hull before she was married & her husband knew it, & knows that she has been very common since.[174]

The attorney's account shows the importance of sexual reputation for a woman's credit in the ordinary courts, and the contrasting treatment of men in this respect: it was not supposed that the defendant lost credibility by adverting to his own sexual misconduct. Witnesses were produced to prove the episode in the magistrates' court and, since it tells against the interests of the defendant, it may be assumed that the attorney's account of the episode is substantially accurate, but it is impossible to be certain of the plaintiff's motive for the defamation suit: the gross public insult inflicted on her by the defendant may have been sufficient reason for her to institute the suit, irrespective of any feelings of jealousy. Nor can the attorney's assertion that the defendant tired of the plaintiff's company be accepted without question: one witness said that it was she who had rejected him. The case was eventually settled, and so there was no judicial finding on any of the facts.

The plaintiff's motive for instituting a defamation suit might occasionally be to divert attention from more serious charges. In one of the comparatively rare cases where the plaintiff was a man, the Revd John Spooner, a Baptist minister, had been accused of consorting with prostitutes on a visit to Bradford. He was suspended from his office, but was subsequently reinstated after an investigation. These events divided the congregation. The defendant, Olive King, who was the daughter of a Baptist minister – her father had in fact had been Spooner's predecessor – belonged to the party opposed to Spooner. 'She along with many others thinks the plaintiff guilty and does not scruple to say so.'[175] Spooner did not institute any suit against those speaking of the Bradford incident, but when Olive King said, about a year later, in May 1837, that he 'had gone a-whoring' to Gargrave, he did institute a suit against her. In the opinion of her attorneys, this was an attempt by Spooner to suppress the rumours against him without inviting direct inquiry into the incident at Bradford:

Now Spooner did not put the parties who originated the statement into the Ecclesiastical court. He passed by the numerous persons who repeated the Bradford tale with all its disgusting particularities and which tale really injured him in the estimation of the neighbourhood, & fastened upon an unlucky expression of the defendant which [neither] she nor any other person ever believed or meant to be believed as true & which could not in the least affect his character except so far as it might remind one that he had formerly at Bradford been guilty of the like practices. And why did he so pass by these really hurtful reports & fix with such avidity upon this tho' equally gross comparatively harmless one? Because he wished to stifle inquiry into the Bradford affair yet dare not take it openly.[176]

A feature of all litigation is that it tends to gather a momentum of its own. As the costs mount so may the mutual hostility of the parties and the determination of each to concede nothing to the other. An example is the dispute over performance of penance which was carried to the Arches Court at huge expense.[177] The same phenomenon must have been present in many of the defamation cases that went beyond the initial stages, because no money beyond costs was obtainable from the court, and material considerations would therefore almost always have indicated settlement. In Askwith's correspondence there are several cases where he recommended settlement, but was told that the hostility of the parties made it impossible. In a Gloucester case a clergyman attempted unsuccessfully to effect a settlement. In the words of a witness who was present, 'he at last said that he could not advise Williams [the defendant] to pay any thing but would advise him to go to the end of the cause, when promoter's husband said, "then I will stick to them to the end of the cause also."'[178] Another example is the Somerset case of Dorney v. Webb where a defensive allegation was filed, supported by four witnesses, attacking the plaintiff's prior reputation, and a further replicatory allegation was admitted on the plaintiff's side, supported by seven witnesses, attempting to defend her reputation. No material considerations could have justified the expense of this procedure: truth was in any event not a complete defence, as the case itself demonstrated. Dorney obtained a sentence, but one specially altered to omit from the legal formularies the usual assertions of her good character, showing that the judge did not think highly of her character – so her reputation was scarcely vindicated, she had to pay a large part of her own costs, and the defendant had to pay costs in the substantial amount of £25, as well as her own costs.[179] An early settlement would certainly have been in the interest of both parties.

It is often supposed that the law facilitates the resolution of disputes, but an aspect of litigation that should not be overlooked is that the very existence of a legal remedy may exert pressure on those who are entitled to avail themselves of it to do so, and so far from resolving disputes, legal proceedings may tend to prolong them. This point was made of defamation suits by a seventeenth-century civilian:

> Yet were it not for the sweetness of Revenge, and the encouragement of the Law, such Actions might be better spar'd than what it costs to maintain them; and such ill-scented Suits do favour worse being kept alive in a Tribunal than they would by being buried in Oblivion, specially if the *Defamed* considered, that to forget Injuries is the best use we can make of a bad Memory.[180]

Defamation is not unique in this respect: seldom has any branch of the law in practice conformed in every respect to its ideals.

Pressure on a plaintiff to institute a defamation suit would depend very greatly on the frequency of such suits in her community, and this consideration goes some way to explain the discrepancies in rates of litigation between one diocese and another. In Carlisle, a diocese where litigation was frequent, almost everyone would have known of someone who had been involved in a suit as party, witness, or relative. When a slander was alleged, the parties, their advisers, and potential witnesses would immediately and naturally think of the probable consequence: a defamation suit in the ecclesiastical court. On the other hand, where suits were rare, as in Ely for example, no one would expect a woman who had been slandered to resort to a suit, and consequently no one would think the worse of her if she did not. If she did take legal advice she would receive no encouragement. The litigation had, to this extent, a self-sustaining quality where it was common, and, for the same reasons, it was not likely to be revived where it had become obsolete.

A search for an all-embracing explanation for the institution of defamation suits is unlikely to be fruitful. As we have seen, motives varied widely and were not always worthy of admiration. Moreover the motives of a single plaintiff must often have been mixed: she might be hurt by the accusation, anxious to restore her reputation, apprehensive of repetition of the slander, angry with the defendant, eager to do what the community considered proper, under pressure from friends or relatives to take action, and in dispute with the defendant over collateral matters.

# 11

# Consequences

In one aspect the law reflects the values and attitudes of a society, but in another it influences or determines them. The question addressed in this chapter is, what were the effects of this branch of the law on attitudes and behaviour?

The significance of a branch of the law is not dependent on the frequency of litigation. The importance of matrimonial law, for example, cannot be judged by the number of cases, which was small (fewer than fifty a year in this period). The number of defamation cases in the forty-year period studied here was about three thousand. Evidently those directly involved in the cases were affected; the question is, how many more persons were influenced by the law? This is a question on which the legal records, naturally, cannot give a full answer, but they contain some indications.

Few persons would have been aware of the details of the ecclesiastical law, but many knew that it was not permissible to call a woman a whore. The Ecclesiastical Courts Commission Report of 1832, in recommending abolition of the ecclesiastical jurisdiction, proposed as a substitute the creation of a new criminal offence of sexual slander, punishable by fine or limited imprisonment.[1] In making this proposal the commissioners probably thought that they would not be making much change in practice, or deviating greatly from what many people supposed that the law then was. In practical terms such a supposition would not have been far wrong: most defamation cases were settled on payment by the defendant of the plaintiff's costs, and though this payment was not, strictly speaking, a fine, it must have looked very much like one to most defendants.

The fact that three thousand plaintiffs saw fit to institute suits, and that an additional unknown number threatened to do so, shows that they thought they had something to gain from the process. It is difficult to tell from the records to what degree they were satisfied. Examples have been given of cases that turned out to be very expensive to the plaintiff, and there must have been many plaintiffs, as elsewhere in the law of defamation, who after instituting a suit later came bitterly to regret having had anything to do with the law. In a York case the plaintiff wrote, 'It was not long of me [i.e., by my wish] the business went on. I am very sory it did. I wish I had left the place as I have done know; my mind might have been much more at pece.'[2]

On the other hand, there were some cases of successive suits by the same plaintiff,[3] or by close relatives,[4] showing that one experience of the system did not always deter a second. Plaintiffs were often alleged by defendants to have instituted or to have threatened previous suits, showing that it was at least plausible that a plaintiff might do so: 'has she not brought several pretended actions of defamation in this court?'[5] In another case the plaintiff said to a witness that her evidence would be required 'if the defendant did not see fit to make submission to her,' again suggesting that the plaintiff derived some satisfaction from the prospect.[6]

As we saw in the last chapter, the first step in the process of litigation was a demand by an attorney or a proctor for an apology, and many cases must have been settled at this stage, without the issue of a citation, on payment of a modest sum to cover the plaintiff's costs. The bills of costs found among the cause papers suggest that the expense of an interview, a letter, and drafting and executing an apology might be about 10 or 12s., a sum comparable with a fine imposed by the magistrates for a minor criminal offence.[7] The incentive to pay at this stage must have been considerable, for the issue of the citation would approximately have tripled the expenses. No public record was kept of such cases, but there are incidental references in the cause papers. In one case the defendant objected that the dispute had been settled before the plaintiff's attorney on making a suitable apology and paying expenses of 3 guineas.[8] A witness in a Somerset case said, in answer to an interrogatory, that 'I was made to pay costs and apologize for having defamed ... Maria Ferris [the plaintiff].'[9] In evidence in a related case he said that he had signed the apology 'to avoid the risk of further law expenses which he could not afford to expend.' The apology itself is annexed to the interrogatories and recites that Ferris had 'threatened to commence proceedings against me.'[10] The recital in the apology and the witness's statements suggest that he did not see this event as in any way extraordinary. A person guilty of defamation was expected to apologize: in a York case the judge, in giving sentence against the defendant, observed that 'no proof had been given of any attempt on the part of the defendant to compromise the affair.'[11] In a Llandaff case a person friendly to the defendant protested 'that yesterday as well as frequently before he was pressed to settle while he denies that he said anything which would subject him to punishment.'[12] Attitudes and expectations would have varied from place to place. Defamation cases were fairly frequent in Somerset, Yorkshire, and South Wales; in some other parts of the country no doubt a demand from a lawyer for an apology would have been very unusual.

Some cases were referred to arbitration, before or after the issue of a citation. Askwith, the York proctor, who always encouraged settlement of defamation suits, approved of arbitration: 'I think Mr Winter has acted very properly in offering to refer the matter. Much expense I can assure you may be saved to both parties by that mode of settlement.'[13] The clergy, as we have seen, were often involved in attempts to settle cases, not as officers of the ecclesiastical court (most were not), but as persons with the necessary status, influence, and respect to effect a reconciliation of differences in the parish, and with a proper interest in doing so, one such clergyman being described as the 'spiritual pastor of both these parties, with that anxiety for peace and goodwill for which he is characterized' who had 'kindly interposed his offices for settling matters between them.'[14] These attempts sometimes failed. One defendant refused to undertake to her clergyman not to repeat the slander,[15] and another, having agreed to arbitration, then refused to abide by the clergyman's decision.[16] What was needed to make an arbitration effective was a binding agreement to accept the arbitrator's decision, secured by a bond. Only then would a careful attorney instruct the plaintiff's proctor to discontinue the suit in the ecclesiastical court.[17]

Arbitration had potential advantages to both sides, particularly privacy, substantive and procedural flexibility, and power to select the arbitrator. An advantage to the plaintiff was that the arbitrator might award damages. Although the court had no such power, there was nothing to stop the parties from conferring it on the arbitrator, though probably express words in the reference would have been necessary for this purpose. Askwith wrote on this point that damages depended on the arbitrator's discretion and the terms of the reference.[18] In a brief postscript to a letter on a different matter he mentioned, of the same case, that the 'affair is settled by arbitration and damages of £20.'[19] Probably the sum named was in addition to costs, as witnesses had been examined,[20] and the plaintiff must have incurred considerable expense. Askwith would have used the word 'damages' advisedly, and the party promoting and financing the suit had asked Askwith to submit a liberal bill in anticipation that 'Abbey [the defendant] will have all to pay.'[21]

In the Norwich case where Lady Travers had said in private conversation that Elizabeth Marsh had lived for many years in adultery, Marsh's husband, her father and her brother-in-law called on Lady Travers, who rashly agreed to see them and admitted the conversation, thereby supplying essential evidence against herself. On the evening of the same day the father and brother-in-law called again to find Sir Eaton Travers's solicitor present, and Lady Travers absent (probably by the solicitor's advice). The solicitor made strenuous efforts to settle the case, suggesting that the matter should be referred to 'half a dozen of the principal gentlemen of the town [Yarmouth].' Marsh and her advisers were not, as it turned out, amenable to this suggestion, since they desired actual performance of penance in church, something that a committee of gentlemen could not enforce.[22] The making of the proposal, however, shows that arbitration came readily to mind as an alternative to litigation, especially in social circles where defamation suits in the ecclesiastical courts were disreputable.

It was widely known that a woman had a legal remedy for being called a whore. Several women responded to insults with immediate threats to make the defendant pay,[23] or to 'warm' him,[24] 'trim' him,[25] 'fix' him,[26] or 'make him suffer.'[27] One woman said, 'I shall make you know better,'[28] another, 'I will make you remember that,'[29] and another that if the defendant would not be quiet 'she should be obliged to use means to make her.'[30] In a Chester case a man said, in response to a suggestion by the defendant that 'he has taken us for whores like his sister,' 'you cannot call my sister a whore.'[31]

Often plaintiffs, or their husbands, on the speaking of the offensive words, immediately called on those present to take note, with a view to their being called upon later as witnesses. 'Mr Hinton, didn't you hear Richard Phillips call my wife a whore,' one husband said to an onlooker at a window who had witnessed a street quarrel. The witness replied that 'he certainly did and that there were many others who heard the same.'[32] In a Norwich case the plaintiff's husband desired those present to take down the defendant's words, and he made a note.[33] There are several similar instances.[34]

A woman or her husband sometimes said, in response to the insulting insinuation, 'I'll make you prove your words,'[35] or 'can you prove it?'[36] and, on receiving an affirmative answer, 'well then you shall, and pay for it too.'[37] An announcement that she would make the defendant prove his words meant that she would institute a suit. It can be seen that thinking here was influenced by the common law of defamation, where truth was a defence but had to be proved by the defendant. As we have seen, the ecclesiastical law was more generous to the plaintiff in this respect.

The ecclesiastical law was more generous in another respect also. At common law words were not actionable unless they suggested a serious accusation: mere vituperation was not enough.[38] So, to call a person a rogue, for example, was not actionable if the word was understood in its context as mere general abuse. On the other hand, to call a woman a whore was always punishable in the ecclesiastical court even if the context showed that no serious accusation was intended. There are indications that these two aspects of the ecclesiastical law (truth and 'mere vituperation' as defences) were widely misunderstood. Thus defendants often said, 'You are a whore and I can prove it,' meaning 'Sue me if you dare,' as they could safely have done in case of a provable accusation of theft.[39] Plaintiffs sometimes asked, 'Whose whore am I?'[40] and in an Exeter case the defendant said she thought she could not be hurt unless she said whose whore the plaintiff was – a misunderstanding derived from the common law rule on mere vituperation.[41] In another case in the same diocese the defendant thought that the plaintiff had to prove damage, an accurate understanding, so far as it went, of the common law of slander, but an incomplete understanding of the law as a whole.[42]

In referring to the proceedings, persons concerned usually did not particularly mention ecclesiastical law. One defendant said (according to a suggestion in interrogatories) that 'he had been served with law for calling his son's wife a whore.'[43] Other common words and phrases were 'lawsuit,'[44] 'go to law,'[45] 'go to court about it,'[46] 'threatened with law,'[47] 'at law,'[48] and 'the law should take its course.'[49] But there are some exceptions. A Somerset man employed unusual accuracy when he said, on hearing a woman slander his daughter, that 'he would put her into Wells court,'[50] and a defence witness in two related York cases was asked whether he had not said that he was 'determined to upset the "Parson's ecclesiastical law."'[51] One plaintiff may rather have overestimated her legal power when she said she would 'fetch a warrant' for the defendant.[52]

One defendant told a witness that 'he knew he must not call the complainant a whore.'[53] In a number of other cases there are indications that defendants knew of the legal dangers. In a York case the plaintiff said to the defendant (according to one deposition),

'What, is I a whore?' when ... Robert Kneeshaw said, 'I but I didn't say so,' that ... Sarah Etty then said 'Damn thee did I ever whore with thee?' to which ... Robert Kneeshaw replied, 'Hey but I did not say so'

The word 'Hey' is substituted for 'I' crossed through. Four lines further down, the word 'Hey,' again used by the defendant in repeating the same phrase, is written over an erasure. These amendments suggest doubt about whether the word used three times by the defendant was or was not a form of 'aye' ('yes'), and that the examiner, realizing that the point might be crucial, did his best to record the sound indicated by the witness, and had some difficulty with it. 'Hey' is a Yorkshire form of 'aye.'[54] The other witnesses did not testify to the use of the word, and the case was dismissed without costs,[55] but the conversation suggests that the defendant was aware of legal danger. There are other cases where the defendant on being challenged promptly retracted,[56] and where the defendant expressly said that he would not call the plaintiff a whore so as not to give her a hold over him.[57] In a York case one woman (according to the defendant's attorney) said to another, 'I wish you would call me whore only,' and the other replied, 'No, I shall not do so but I shall go another way to work.'[58] In a London case the defendant studiously avoided naming the plaintiff and the man involved, referring to a 'silversmith's daughter' and a 'tall man with red hair.' A witness 'cautioned him to be very careful in spreading such reports.' The circumlocutions gave no legal immunity to the defendant, but it is significant that he thought to make them.[59]

There is evidence in some cases of friends of the defendant advising an apology. In a Ripon case the defendant said the case was a 'bad job' and, a witness said, 'I and others advised the defendant to make an apology & he said he had already done so by letter.' The defendant, evidently fearful of a suit, had written to the plaintiff's father the day after the slander, saying, 'I am sorry for the insult I gave you last night ... now I beg you will think no more about it. I will make you all the reparation for it that lies in my power.'[60] In a Gloucester case a friend of the defendant said to the plaintiff's husband as soon as the words were spoken, 'I am sorry Halford said it. I hope you won't take any advantage of him for it.'[61] These statements show an understanding of the legal position.

A general knowledge of the law shared by plaintiff, defendant, and witness is well illustrated by a Gloucester case in which the defendant called the plaintiff a 'nasty tawny bitch' and a 'nasty bloody thundering whore.' 'Oh,' said the plaintiff, 'I am a nasty bloody thundering whore, am I?' 'I did not say so,' replied the defendant. 'Yes you did,' said a bystander, 'and I am a witness of it.'[62]

In those social circles where drawing-room gossip was a more probable source of slander than vulgar insult, there is also evidence that people were conscious of legal perils. The fact that words were spoken to friends in private was no sure protection, as several cases show.[63] In a Worcester case of this sort, a witness was asked in interrogatories whether she had not, on an occasion subsequent to the alleged slander, denied any knowledge of the report. In answer she said that 'she did not declare that she had never heard of the report before, nor did she acknowledge to have heard of it, because herself and sister had been desired by the Miss Dixons [relatives and fellow witnesses] if the report was ever mentioned not to admit that they had heard anything about it, because they did not wish us to be the means of circulating such a report.'[64]

Again, this suggests consciousness that spreading rumours had disagreeable legal consequences.

In a number of cases the plaintiff or her friends set out deliberately to entrap the defendant into admitting that he had spoken defamatory words. In one such case the response was, when the plaintiff called with friends, 'I know what you mean ... If I say anything you intend to have your remedy at law.' The defendant here showed a fair knowlege of the substantive legal position, though he was weak on the law of evidence, for the conversation was successfully proved against him.[65]

Another kind of entrapment was to provoke the defendant into a slander. 'Did not [plaintiff] call [defendant] rogue and by many other ... opprobrious names,' an interrogatory suggested, 'on purpose to enrage and provoke him ... to speak some defamatory words with a view intent and design of bringing a suit against him?'[66] In another case in the same diocese (Bath and Wells), the defendant was 'admonished to be cautious as the plaintiff would entrap him.'[67] This was evidently a known danger, at any rate in parts of the country where defamation suits were fairly common.

Another indication is the reaction of bystanders on hearing the defamatory words. In several cases they reproached the defendant, asking him in one case if he was not 'ashamed of abusing a poor woman,'[68] or warned the defendant to be careful.[69] A York defendant was fined 5s. by his club for slandering a woman.[70] One witness said that he had heard the defendant say 'more than he [witness] durst say about any one.'[71] An innkeeper, who might be expected to wish to avoid involvement in litigation with customers, 'told the [defendant] at the time he would come forward [as a witness] his behaviour being so bad.'[72] In a Hereford case where the defendant, in the course of a street brawl with the plaintiff's husband, called the plaintiff a 'blasted whore,' 'many persons who witnessed the proceedings ... cried "shame shame" at the words used by the ... defendant.'[73] A witness in another case said that he thought the plaintiff 'has been very hardly treated [by the slander] & consider it my duty to come forward.'[74] These examples plainly mark sexual slander as antisocial conduct reflecting accurately, though in some cases no doubt indirectly and unconsciously, the position in ecclesiastical law.

Laura Gowing has written, of the early modern period, that 'for married women, the church courts were one of the few jurisdictions where such conflict [arising from defamation] could be fought with a legal agency technically equivalent to that of men,' that 'women ... emerged as legal agents in their own right,' and that 'the church courts were an exception to a legal system that consistently disabled women.'[75] The contrast here alluded to between the ecclesiastical and the common law courts was still a feature of the legal landscape at the middle of the nineteenth century, and it was then still true to say that the ecclesiastical courts gave to women a degree of independent power that was lacking elsewhere, and, moreover, to women of very modest means and social status.

The defamation jurisdiction was not much valued in the nineteenth century by those – mostly men – whose opinions have been recorded and preserved. Writers of pamphlets, speakers in Parliament, members of commissions, authors of reports, and contributors to journals, mostly reflecting the view from London, were almost unanimous for its abolition; the feminist reformers, naturally enough, were concerned with other issues.[76] It is partly for this reason that the cases have been neglected by historians, both legal and social, of the nineteenth century. But the law may exert an influence although those affected are not conscious of it; the cases discussed in this chapter show that this branch of the law did put some limited power into the hands of women, and did have a significant influence on attitudes and behaviour.

# Postscript:

# 'A barbarous state of our law'

The abolition, in 1855, of the defamation jurisdiction of the ecclesiastical courts was not accompanied by any other reform in the law of defamation. The proposal of the Ecclesiastical Courts Commission for a new crime of sexual slander was not implemented, and neither was the common law of slander amended. The consequence was that, for the next thirty-six years, there was no legal remedy for sexual slander unless it caused actual loss.

The legal position was attacked in strong terms on several occasions. In a case in the House of Lords in 1861, Lord Campbell (whose speech was read after his death) wrote,

> I may lament the unsatisfactory state of our law, according to which the imputation by words, however gross, on an occasion however public, upon the chastity of a modest matron or a pure virgin, is not actionable without proof that it has actually produced special temporal damage to her.

Lord Brougham, after reading this speech, added his own view. He considered 'unsatisfactory' too mild a word: 'I think that such a state of things can only be described as a barbarous state of our law in that respect.'[1] Similar criticism appeared elsewhere,[2] and in 1891 English law was amended by the Slander of Women Act,[3] the effect of which was to permit a woman to bring an action at common law for words imputing unchastity, without proof of special damage.

From one point of view the 1891 Act filled a gap left in the law by the abolition of the ecclesiastical jurisdiction thirty-six years earlier, but the position after 1891 differed very radically from that before 1855. A comparison of the two legal positions offers a convenient means of recalling the salient features of the pre-1855 ecclesiastical law.

The 1891 Act applied only to women; the ecclesiastical law, as we have seen, applied to both sexes, though it was used mainly (to the extent of 90 per cent) by women. The discriminatory application of the 1891 Act reflected the assumption that a woman's reputation for chastity was more valuable than a man's, and more worthy of legal protection, an assumption that we saw in practical operation also in the first half of the century even though it was not formally embodied in the ecclesiastical law; this is an assumption that cannot be said, in the social circumstances of the nineteenth century, to have been wholly erroneous.

By the ecclesiastical law, truth was not a defence, and neither was it a defence that the words used were words of mere general abuse and vituperation. The parties could not give evidence, and witnesses were examined in private. At common law, truth was a defence, and mere vituperation was not actionable;[4] the parties could give evidence, and in practice a plaintiff would have to do so in order to rebut a defence of justification and in order to establish her claim for damages; evidence was given in public, and the plaintiff was subject to cross-examination and to defence evidence designed to prove the truth of the slander. Worse, from her point of view, her prior reputation was relevant to damages, and, as the common law of defamation then stood, prior sexual misconduct could be proved for that purpose. In the debate on the bill in 1891, Lord Herschell pointed out this feature of the law by way of answering critics who thought the bill might encourage litigation by a plaintiff who was 'not a modest woman.' Lord Herschell said:

> If a woman be of unchaste life, although not unchaste on the particular occasion, that would clearly be a matter to be considered in regard to damages. I should say that no such action would be likely to succeed.[5]

Thus, from the plaintiff's point of view, the new law had the very disadvantageous effect of exposing her to public cross-examination on her past sexual conduct. There was, it is true, the prospect of damages, but against this had to be set the substantial risk of having to pay the other side's costs if the case were dismissed. Defamation litigation at common law is not for the faint-hearted, nor for the impecunious.

The ecclesiastical court, on the other hand, was in practice as well as in theory open to plaintiffs of very modest means. There the plaintiff could institute a suit with little risk, and leave it in the proctor's hands. She might have to pay a small sum to the proctor at the start – in some dioceses probably not even that – and if there were the two necessary witnesses she could scarcely lose. As we saw there were very few defences, she did not have to appear in court or give evidence, her witnesses did not have to appear in public, and unless the suit was dismissed with costs (a very rare result), there was no financial risk beyond any sum advanced to the proctor.

The practical operation of the ecclesiastical courts in punishing sexual slander as antisocial conduct could not be replicated by the Slander of Women Act: that function could only have been preserved by adopting the suggestion of the Ecclesiastical Courts Commission of 1832 for a new criminal offence of sexual slander, and to this there were grave objections: the enlargement of the criminal law always has costs, and those costs were perceived as particularly high where the criminal law restricted speech. Moreover, the prospect of a proceeding before magistrates, where the complainant and her witnesses would have been subject to public cross-examination, would have been most unattractive, especially if the complainant lacked power to settle or discontinue the case.

The reform of this branch of the law does not readily lend itself to analysis in terms of economic or political interests, or even in terms of vested professional interests. Commenting on the report of the Ecclesiastical Courts Commission in 1832, the *Law Magazine* wrote, '*Defamation*. This branch of jurisdiction is given up by universal consent. The very judges, officers, and practitioners, who profit by it, allow it to be indefensible, and only calculated to excite a prejudice against their courts.'[6] But, despite its many and grave defects, the defamation jurisdiction was, in some of its aspects, and by the reformers' own standards, beneficial to women and to the general interests of society. The commissioners (who included four judges from Doctors' Commons) did not wish to abolish these aspects of the law. On the contrary they wished to preserve them. But no practical means were found of doing so.

# Tables

TABLE 1
Table of all ecclesiastical court business, 1827–30

Province of Canterbury (England)

| Provincial and Diocesan courts | Testamentary | Matrimonial | Tithes | Church rate | Church seat, faculty, &c. | Brawling | Defamation | Miscellaneous, including correction | Appeals | Totals |
|---|---|---|---|---|---|---|---|---|---|---|
| Canterbury (Arches) | 7 | 16 | 2 | 3 | 1 | 2 | – | – | 14 | 45 |
| Ditto (Prerogative) | 410 | – | – | – | – | – | – | – | – | 410 |
| Ditto (Consistory) | 1 | – | – | – | 3 | – | – | – | – | 4 |
| Bath and Wells | 25 | 1 | 43 | 6 | 5 | 2 | 30 | – | – | 112 |
| Bristol (at Bristol) | 6 | – | – | 1 | 1 | – | 11 | – | – | 19 |
| Ditto (at Blandford) | – | – | 1 | – | 1 | 1 | 2 | – | – | 5 |
| Chichester (at Chichester) | – | – | – | 4 | – | – | 5 | – | – | 9 |
| Ely | 3 | – | – | – | 3 | – | – | – | – | 6 |
| Exeter | 8 | 1 | 38 | 15 | 17 | – | 5 | 6 | 3 | 93 |
| Gloucester | 32 | 10 | 1 | – | 26 | 3 | 36 | 10 | – | 118 |
| Hereford | 14 | 3 | 10 | 2 | 8 | 1 | 11 | 8 | – | 57 |
| Lichfield and Coventry | 34 | 2 | 7 | 3 | 14 | – | 20 | 3 | – | 83 |
| Lincoln | 17 | – | – | – | – | 1 | 5 | 2 | – | 25 |
| London | 3 | 42 | – | 1 | – | 3 | 3 | – | – | 52 |
| Norwich | 6 | 5 | 18 | 4 | 19 | 2 | 15 | 3 | – | 72 |
| Oxford | 2 | – | – | – | – | – | – | – | – | 2 |
| Peterborough | 7 | – | – | – | 12 | – | 3 | – | – | 22 |
| Rochester | – | 2 | – | – | 3 | – | 1 | 1 | – | 7 |
| Sarum | – | – | – | – | 1 | 2 | 5 | – | – | 8 |
| Winchester | 5 | 1 | – | – | 9 | – | – | – | – | 15 |
| Worcester | 6 | – | 2 | – | – | – | 5 | – | – | 13 |
| Totals | 586 | 83 | 122 | 39 | 123 | 17 | 157 | 33 | 17 | 1,177 |

TABLE 1 (*concluded*)

| Provincial and Diocesan courts | Testa-mentary | Matri-monial | Tithes | Church rate | Church seat, faculty, &c. | Brawling | Defa-mation | Miscellaneous, including correction | Appeals | Totals |
|---|---|---|---|---|---|---|---|---|---|---|
| **Province of Canterbury (Wales)** | | | | | | | | | | |
| St Asaph | 15 | 1 | 6 | – | 6 | – | 1 | – | – | 29 |
| Bangor | – | – | – | – | 1 | – | – | – | – | 1 |
| St David's | | | | | | | | | | |
| (at Carmarthen) | 45 | – | – | – | 3 | – | 32 | 4 | – | 84 |
| Ditto (at Brecon) | 2 | – | 3 | – | – | – | – | 4 | – | 9 |
| Llandaff | 20 | – | 46 | 3 | 5 | 1 | 35 | 2 | – | 112 |
| Totals | 82 | 1 | 55 | 3 | 15 | 1 | 68 | 10 | – | 235 |
| **Province of York** | | | | | | | | | | |
| York (Exchequer and Prerogative) | 73 | – | – | – | – | – | – | – | – | 73 |
| Ditto (Consistory) | 5 | 8 | 4 | 9 | – | – | 18 | 1 | – | 45 |
| Ditto (Chancery) | – | – | – | – | 25 | 3 | – | 1 | 4 | 33 |
| Carlisle | 36 | – | – | 4 | 5 | – | 23 | 3 | – | 71 |
| Chester | 160 | 9 | 2 | 3 | 22 | – | 62 | – | – | 258 |
| Durham | 5 | – | 1 | – | – | 1 | 3 | 1 | – | 11 |
| Totals | 279 | 17 | 7 | 16 | 52 | 4 | 106 | 6 | 4 | 491 |

From Ecclesiastical Courts Commission Report, PP 1831–2 xxiv, appendix D

TABLE 2

Defamation cases by diocese, 1815–55 (from act books and cause papers) with diocesan populations in 1835

| | Number of defamation cases | Population in 1835 |
|---|---|---|
| Bangor | 41 | 153,344 |
| Bath and Wells | 237 | 403,908 |
| Bristol | 118 | 263,328 |
| Canterbury | | 402,885[1] |
| Carlisle | 165 | 127,701 |
| Chester | 703 | 1,902,354[2] |
| Chichester | 5 | 236,950[3] |
| Durham | 27 | 452,637 |
| Ely | – | 126,316[4] |
| Exeter | 55 | 792,935 |
| Gloucester | 218 | 275,806 |
| Hereford | 84 | 207,451[5] |
| Lichfield | 104 | 983,783 |
| Lincoln | 77 | 855,039 |
| Llandaff | 231 | 183,990 |
| London | 103 | 1,688,899 |
| Norwich | 126 | 692,163 |
| Oxford | 3 | 139,581[6] |
| Peterborough | 105 | 186,193 |
| Ripon | 40[7] | |
| Rochester | 1 | 196,716[8] |
| St Asaph | 39 | 197,392 |
| St David's | 193 | 372,685 |
| Salisbury | 27 | 320,547 |
| Sodor and Man | 11 | 47,985[9] |
| Winchester | 15 | 780,214 |
| Worcester | 39 | 357,548 |
| York | 242 | 1,463,503 |

[1]Act books not found. The Ecclesiastical Courts Commission Report indicates that the business of the consistory court was very small. Two cases from Canterbury were transferred to the Arches Court by letters of request.

[2]Not including cases in the Richmond Commissary Court (see Ripon, below)

[3]The figure reproduced in table 1, above, showing 5 cases in the years 1827–9, appears to be erroneous.

[4]Two cases from Ely were transferred to the Arches Court by letters of request.

[5]Act books not found. The figure (84) is of surviving cause papers.

[6]One case from Oxford was transferred to the Arches Court by letters of request.

[7]Figure includes 27 Richmond cases, in the diocese of Chester until 1836, when the diocese of Ripon was refounded from territory previously part of Chester and York.

[8]Act books not found. The one case is that reported to the Ecclesiastical Courts Commission.

[9]Population figure (for Isle of Man) from 1841 census, PP 1841 (II) ii, 277

TABLE 2 (*Concluded*)

|  | Number of defamation cases |
|---|---|
| Arches Court | 9[10] |
| Chancery (York) | 2[11] |
| Total | 3020 |
| | |
| Apeals: | |
| Arches Court | 9 |
| York Chancery Court | 1 |
| High Court of Delegates | 1 |
| Judicial Committee of Privy Council | 2 |
| Total | 13 |

[10]Original cases transferred by letters of request; appeals are listed below.
[11]Transferred from Manchester (created 1848) by letters of request. Manchester Act Book, Manchester Central Library, M 39/addnl. Consistory Court Act Book, vol. 1
Sources: Act books and cause papers in the various dioceses; population figures from report of Ecclesiastical Revenues Commission, PP 1835 xxii, 12

TABLE 3
Defamation cases by five-year periods, 1815–55, in five dioceses

|  | Bath and Wells | Carlisle | Chester | Norwich | York |
|---|---|---|---|---|---|
| 1815–19 | 15 | 39 | 110 | 13 | 41 |
| 1820–4 | 22 | 31 | 107 | 22 | 51 |
| 1825–9 | 47 | 36 | 176 | 20 | 40 |
| 1830–4 | 52 | 19 | 159 | 24 | 34 |
| 1835–9 | 46 | 10 | 105 | 19 | 42 |
| 1840–4 | 23 | 5 | 26 | 16 | 15 |
| 1845–9 | 17 | 10 | 7 | 10 | 13 |
| 1850–5 | 15 | 15 | 13 | 2 | 6 |
| Totals | 237 | 165 | 703 | 126 | 242 |

Sources: Act books and cause papers

TABLE 4
Defamation cases by sex and marital status of parties (Norwich and York)

| Norwich | | | | | |
|---|---|---|---|---|---|
| | Defendants | | | | |
| | Single woman | Married woman | Widow | Woman (status unknown) | Man | Total |
| Plaintiffs: | | | | | | |
| Single woman | 2 | 8 | – | – | 12 | 22 |
| Married woman | 9 | 27 | 1 | 1 | 52 | 90 |
| Widow | – | 1 | – | – | 3 | 4 |
| Woman (status unknown) | 1 | – | – | – | 4 | 5 |
| Man | 2 | 1 | 2 | – | 1 | 6 |
| Totals | 14 | 37 | 3 | 1 | 72 | 127[1] |

| York | | | | |
|---|---|---|---|---|
| | Defendants | | | |
| | Single woman | Married woman | Widow | Man | Total |
| Plaintiffs: | | | | | |
| Single woman | 4 | 23 | 2 | 32 | 61 |
| Married woman | 4 | 42 | – | 104 | 150 |
| Widow | 1 | 4 | – | 6 | 11 |
| Man | 2 | 6 | – | 12 | 20 |
| Totals | 11 | 75 | 2 | 154 | 242 |

[1]One case of joint defendants, and one case of joint plaintiffs, are counted here as two cases each; one case where the sex of the plaintiff is not indicated is omitted.
Sources: Act books and cause papers

TABLE 5
Population of places of plaintiffs' residence (Norwich)

| Under 500 | 500–1,000 | 1,000–2,000 | 2,000–5,000 | 5,000–10,000 | Over 10,000 |
|---|---|---|---|---|---|
| 23 | 22 | 23 | 9 | – | 47 |

Note: In two cases no parish of residence was stated. (Total number of cases 126)
Sources: Act books and cause papers. Populations from 1841 census, PP 1841 (II) ii, 277

TABLE 6
Disposition of causes at various stages of litigation (Norwich)

| | |
|---|---:|
| Sentence for plaintiff without production of witnesses (affirmative issue) | 3 |
| Sentence for defendant on the pleadings | 6 |
| Discontinued without production of witnesses | 74 |
| Discontinued after production of witnesses | 4 |
| Sentence for plaintiff after proof | 32 |
| Sentence for defendant after proof | 7 |
| Total | 126 |

Sources: Act books and cause papers

TABLE 7
Sex and literacy of witnesses as evidenced by signature (Norwich and York)

| | Male witnesses | | Female witnesses | | |
|---|---|---|---|---|---|
| | Sign | Mark | Sign | Mark | Total |
| *Norwich* | | | | | |
| 1815–19 | 4 | 2 | 2 | – | 8 |
| 1820–4 | 6 | 2 | 5 | 6 | 19 |
| 1825–9 | 12 | 4 | 6 | 1 | 23 |
| 1830–4 | 6 | 1 | – | 1 | 8 |
| 1835–9 | 10 | 2 | 1 | 2 | 15 |
| 1840–4 | 18 | 13[1] | 10[2] | 1 | 42 |
| 1845–50 | 24[3] | 4 | 5 | 3 | 36 |
| Totals | 80 | 28 | 29 | 14 | 151 |
| *York* | | | | | |
| 1815–10 | 14 | 3 | 7 | 9 | 33 |
| 1820–4 | 14 | 4 | 9 | 13 | 40 |
| 1825–9 | 7 | – | 6 | – | 13 |
| 1830–4 | 5 | 1 | – | 4 | 10 |
| 1835–9 | 30[4] | 6[5] | 5 | 1 | 42 |
| 1840–55 | 8 | – | – | – | 8 |
| Totals | 78 | 14 | 27 | 27 | 146 |

[1] Only 7 witnesses: 2 witnesses made four depositions each.
[2] Only 4 witnesses: 2 witnesses made three depositions each in separate suits.
[3] Only 23 witnesses: 1 witness made two depositions.
[4] Only 25 separate witnesses: there are five cases of the same witness giving evidence in two separate suits.
[5] Only 5 witnesses: 1 witness gave evidence in two separate suits.
Source: Cause papers

# Appendix A

# Illustrative Cause Papers

## Citation

Bear v. Bignell (Winchester, 1831), 21M65/C9/70. See 69, above.

William Dealtry, Clerk, D.D. Vicar General and Official Principal of the Right Reverend Father in God Charles Richard by divine permission Lord Bishop of Winchester lawfully appointed, To all and singular clerks and literate persons whomsoever within the County of Southampton and Diocese of Winchester Sendeth Greeting. We do hereby strictly charge enjoin and command ye jointly or separately that ye cite or cause to be cited peremptorily Sarah Bignell of the Parish of Itchen Abbas in the County of Southampton and Diocese of Winchester, Single Woman, that she appear before us or our lawful Surrogate or some other competent Judge in that behalf that shall happen to sit in judgment in the Cathedral Church of the Holy Trinity of Winchester in the Consistory Court there on Friday the twenty fifth day of November instant between the hours of eleven o'clock in the forenoon and one of the Clock in the afternoon of the same day then and there to answer to Jane Bear, Spinster, in a certain Cause of Defamation or reproach And further to do and receive according to Law. And what ye shall do in the premises that ye duly certify to us or our lawful Surrogate together with these presents. Dated at Winchester the Eighteenth day of November in the Year of our Lord one thousand eight hundred and thirty one.
[signed] *Chas Wooldridge Junr*, Proctor

[Affidavit of service of citation attached to above (not transcribed)

Proxies (authorizing proctors to act; not transcribed. The forms of proxy varied considerably from one diocese to another.)]

## Libel

Bear v. Bignell (Winchester, 1831). See 130, above.

In the Name of God, Amen. Before you the Reverend and Worshipful William Dealtry Doctor in Divinity Vicar General and Official Principal of the Right Reverend Father in God Charles Richard by Divine Permission Lord Bishop of Winchester lawfully constituted or your lawful Surrogate or any other competent Judge in that behalf appointed, the Proctor of Jane Bear of the parish of Itchen Abbas in the County of Southampton and Diocese of Winchester, Spinster, against Sarah Bignell of the parish of Itchen Abbas aforesaid in the County and Diocese aforesaid, Single Woman and against any other person whomsoever for her lawfully appearing in Judgment by way of Complaint to you in this behalf complaining to all Effects in the Law saith alledgeth and by these presents in Law propoundeth jointly severally and Articulated [articulately] and of each as followeth

First. That every person and persons who utter publish assert or report or shall have uttered published asserted or reported reproachful scandalous or Defamatory Words to the reproach hurt and diminution of the Good name fame and reputation of another person contrary to Good Manners and the Rule of Charity are and ought to be monished constrained and Compelled to the reclaiming and retracting such reproachful scandalous and defamatory Words and to the restoring of the Good name fame and reputation of the person thereby injured and that for the future they refrain from uttering publishing or declaring any such reproachful scandalous or defamatory Words and are to be canonically corrected and punished and this was and is true public and notorious.

Second. That notwithstanding the premises mentioned in the foregoing articles the said Sarah Bignell did in the Months of September October and November in the Year of our Lord One thousand eight hundred and thirty one or in some one or more of those Months within the parish of Itchen Abbas aforesaid or in some other Parish Parishes or public Places in the Neighbourhood thereof or near thereunto in an angry reproachful and invidious manner several times, [or] at least once, defame the said Jane Bear who was and is a person of good reputation and Character and Charged the said Jane Bear to have committed the Crime of Fornication or Incontinency and speaking to Benjamin Bear who is the uncle of the said Jane Bear (the party Agent in this Cause) and with whom and in whose House at Itchen Abbas aforesaid the said Jane Bear was then and there living and residing as his Housekeeper, affirmed and published several times [or] at the least once these or the like words to Wit, 'Get thee home thee Blackguard to the good for nothing Strumpet' (meaning and intending the said Jane Bear) 'who I have no doubt has been the same to thee as I have been myself, and old Moll' (meaning and intending Mary Bear, the Mother of the said Jane Bear) 'is a good for nothing Old Woman to let her Daughter out to thee as she has done'. And the party proponent doth allege and propound every thing in this Article contained jointly and severally.

Third. That the said Sarah Bignell hath oftentimes [or] at least once since the affirming and uttering the Defamatory Words mentioned in the next foregoing Article owned and confessed that she spoke the said Defamatory Words as in the next preceding Article is set forth and the party proponent doth allege and propound as before.

Fourth. That by reason of the speaking the said Defamatory Words the good name fame and reputation of the said Jane Bear is very much hurt injured and aggrieved amongst her neighbours acquaintance and others and this was and is true public and notorious and the party proponent doth allege and propound as before.

Fifth. That the said Sarah Bignell was and is of the parish of Itchen Abbas in the said County of Southampton and Diocese of Winchester and therefore subject to the Jurisdiction of this Court and the party proponent doth allege and propound as before.

Sixth. That the said Jane Bear the party Agent in this Cause hath rightly and duly complained of the premises to you the Reverend and Worshipful William Dealtry Vicar General and Official Principal of the Right Reverend Father in God Charles Richard by Divine Permission Lord Bishop of Winchester aforesaid and to this Court and the party proponent doth allege and propound as before.

Seventh. That all and singular the premises aforesaid were and are true public and notorious and thereof there was and is a public voice fame and report of which legal proof being made the party proponent prays right and justice to be administered to her [him] and her [his] party in the premises and that the said Sarah Bignell for her Excess in the premises be duly forced and compelled to retract and reclaim the defamatory Words aforesaid and that for the future she refrain from uttering such defamatory Words as aforesaid and that she be condemned in the Costs made or to be made in this Cause on the part and behalf of the said Jane Bear and compelled to the due payment thereof by you and your definitive sentence or final decree to be given in this Cause and further to do and decree in the premises what shall be lawful in this behalf not obliging herself to prove all and singular the Premises, or to the Burthen of a superfluous proof against which the party proponent protests and saving always to herself all benefit of Law prays that so far as she shall prove in the premises so far she may obtain in this her suit humbly imploring the aid of your Office in this behalf.

[signed] *Chas Wooldridge Jr*, Proctor, 20th May 1832

## Depositions

France v. Aaron (York, 1838), Cons CP 1838/4. See 34, 145, above.

*Interrogatories* to be administered to Thomas Overton and Elizabeth Robinson pretended witnesses produced sworn and examined on the part of the promovent

First. Let each of the said pretended witnesses be asked Are you acquainted with the expression of 'putting the Tongs into Bed' or of 'finding the Tongs in Bed' or have you ever heard such expression used. If you have, set forth distinctly what you consider to be the meaning or insinuation intended to be conveyed by such expression.

Second. Have you ever heard that Isabella France the party promovent in the Cause had bore a Bastard Child several years ago. If you have, is such report common and notorious? Do you know such Bastard Child, what is its age, and where does it now reside?

Third. Did you hear the commencement of the Quarrel between the parties? If you did, did not Isabella France begin by taunting Elizabeth Aaron about Tongs being found in her Bed many years ago and did not Elizabeth Aaron then reply that she had not proved herself a whore by having had a Bastard Child like Isabella France? And if you did hear such expressions do you not on your oath believe that Elizabeth Aaron's reply was drawn forth by Isabella France's taunts and was made in heat and passion and not with a deliberate intention to defame and slander the said Isabella France?

Fourth. Let the said Thomas Overton be reminded that he is upon his oath and then let him be asked, Do you not live opposite the House in which the defendant resides and is there not a quarrel arising from a certain cause now existing between you and the defendant? Have you not declared that you will be revenged upon the defendant and that you will have her imprisoned or make her pay expences. Do you not support the party promovent in this cause by having undertaken to be answerable for her costs or for some part thereof or have you not already advanced money for that purpose.

Fifth. Let the said Thomas Overton be further asked was not one Mary Smith a woman of mature age and some other person or persons present during the aforesaid Quarrel besides Elizabeth Robinson the young girl now produced as your fellow witness.

Sixth. Let the Deputy Register examine the said Elizabeth Robinson as to her knowledge of the nature of an oath and the sin and danger of perjury.

Seventh. By whom were you first requested to become a witness in this Cause. Did Mr Thomas Overton your fellow witness ever request you? Have you been told by any one what to say or have you been promised any thing for giving your testimony in this Cause?

Eighth. Have you ever heard Isabella France the party promovent say that she was clear of all the expences of this Cause and did you ever hear her say who was answerable for such expenses?

Ninth. Do you know that a quarrel exists between your fellow witness Thomas Overton and the defendant. Did you ever hear him say that he would be revenged upon her or would send her to prison or fix her for costs and did you ever hear him say that he was answerable for any of Isabella France's Costs?

[signed] *Eust: Strickland* [defendant's advocate]

Depositions on the libel

1. Thomas Overton of Thorne in the County of York Wine Merchant aged fifty two

years or thereabouts a Witness produced admitted and sworn to and upon the Positions and Articles of a Libel given into Court and admitted by and on the part and behalf of Isabella France the Wife of Henry France Ship Carpenter against Elizabeth Aaron the Wife of Mark Aaron doth upon his examination say and depose as follows. Upon the first article of the said Libel. I know and am well acquainted with Isabella France the Wife of Henry France and Elizabeth Aaron the Wife of Mark Aaron, and have so for two or three Years last past. The said Isabella France has always born a good character so far as has come to my knowledge – she has five or six children. I live opposite to her and never observed any thing amiss and should not hesitate to give her a good character. And further to this Article he cannot depose.

Upon the second Article of the said Libel. The said parties live in adjoining houses opposite to where I live, and are the property of my wife's sister for whom I receive the Rents. About three o'clock in the afternoon of Thursday the eighteenth of October last I was in my own house when Elizabeth Aaron came in and begged that I would go and charge the peace and make Isabella France keep the peace as she was quarreling with her and abusing her. I immediately followed her and went after her through her house into the yard behind, which is not divided, but common to her house and that in which Isabella France lives. We no sooner got there than Elizabeth Aaron began using the worst language to Isabella France who was then in her house, I ever heard. The said Elizabeth Aaron called out to her Thou art a whore; thou art a whore; thou art a whore. Thou knows I saw thee come out of thy house yesterday Morning about three o'clock with a man upon thy back. The said Isabella France then came out of her house and said, Mrs Aaron you're a base woman, you're a bad woman, how can you say so, or to that effect. I could not stand the language Elizabeth Aaron made use of. I could do nothing between them. It was in vain trying to stop her tongue so I walked away. And further to this article I cannot depose.

Upon the third article. The business was given into the hands of Mr Hodgkinson the Attorney and Elizabeth Aaron was very quiet ever afterwards till she left the premises.

Upon the fourth article. I should consider that the character of Isabella France is injured by such defamation in a small town like Thorne, such scandal soon spreads all over.

Upon the fifth article of the said libel the said Elizabeth Aaron then was and still is of Thorne in the Diocese of York. And further he cannot depose.

[signed] *Thomas Overton*

The same witness to the interrogatories

To the first interrogatory. I am not acquainted with the expression of 'putting the Tongs into bed' or of 'finding the Tongs in bed' nor have I ever heard such expression used.

To the second. I cannot say that I have heard that Isabella France party in this Cause bore a Bastard Child several years ago.

To the third. I did not hear the commencement of the quarrel between the parties.

To the fourth. I do live opposite the House in which the Defendant resides. I have no quarrel with the Defendant. She has said things disrespectful of my family but I never quarrelled with her at any time. I have never made any declaration or used any expression against the said Defendant as to the expence in this Cause. I do not support the party promovent in this Cause by having undertaken to be answerable for her Costs or for any part thereof, nor have I already advanced money for that purpose.

To the fifth. I do not know that one Mary Smith a woman of mature age was present at the time above deposed to. I don't know a person of that name. Two of the neighbours did come out of their houses when I was there, but they went in again. Elizabeth Robinson I saw standing behind me.

25 March 1839

*Joseph Salvin* (surrogate)                                                     [signed] *Thomas Overton*

2. Elizabeth Robinson of Thorne in the County of York, Spinster aged fifteen years or thereabouts, a witness produced admitted and sworn as before, the daughter of Isaac Robinson of the same place Coal Merchant

Upon the first article of the said libel. I know and am well acquainted with Isabella France the wife of Henry France and Elizabeth Aaron the wife of Mark Aaron parties in this Cause, and have so some years. The said Isabella France is a woman of good character for any thing I know.

Upon the second article of the said libel. On the afternoon of Thursday the eighteenth of last October I had gone to nurse at a neighbour's house which was next door to the said Elizabeth Aaron's, and whilst there, it might be as well as I can recollect about two o'clock in the afternoon, I heard a squabbling in the yard at the back of the house with the said Isabella France and the said Mark Aaron, Elizabeth Aaron's husband, about their children, and I went out to see what was the matter, and I then saw the said Isabella France standing at the back door of her house which opens into a yard common to all the houses in the row, and Elizabeth Aaron was coming out of her own house accompanied by Mr Overton my fellow witness, whom she had been to fetch, that Elizabeth Aaron had then a knife in her hand and she called out to the said Isabella France get in thou damn'd black whore, which she repeated several times, am positive she did so three times, and she then said to Mr Overton, now Mr Overton you see she can't deny it, you see what a bad'un she is, or to that effect, when the said Isabella France replied, you're nothing but a base woman. At such time I did not hear the said Isabella France abuse the said Elizabeth Aaron or give her any cause to abuse her in the manner she did. That I then returned into the neighbours house I was at and heard no more. And further to this article she cannot depose.

Upon the third article. I never heard any abuse among them afterwards.

Upon the fourth article I cannot depose.

Upon the fifth article. Elizabeth Aaron then lived and still lives at Thorne in the Diocese of York. And further she cannot depose.

[signed] *Elizabeth Robinson*

The same witness to the interrogatories.

To the first. I have heard several people when speaking of the said Elizabeth Aaron mention about putting tongs into bed. I don't know what it means, but have heard it related to circumstances respecting Mrs Aaron when she was in place some years before.

To the third. That when all was over at the time above deposed to and Mr Overton was going away the said Isabella France said to the said Elizabeth Aaron what where wast tongs, and how long was they there, and who put 'em there, that when the said Elizabeth Aaron so called the said Isabella France a whore she said can you prove me one, when the said Elizabeth Aaron replied you have proved yourself one. I did not hear her tell the said Isabella France that she had had a bastard child. Mrs Aaron appeared in a passion all the time, but Mrs France did not.

To the second. Mrs France had a child before she was married. I don't know its age, it is now in place, it is a girl.

To the sixth interrogatory. She was fully examined and appeared to understand the nature of an oath.

To the seventh. Mrs France first asked me to become a witness in this cause. Mr Overton has spoken to me about it, and asked if I was coming. I never was told by any person what to say, nor have I been promised any thing for giving my evidence.

To the eighth. I never heard Mrs France say any thing whatever about the Expences in this Cause.

To the ninth. I do not know that there is any quarrel between the said Mr Overton and Mrs Aaron. I never heard him say he would be revenged on her, or would send her to prison for Costs, or any thing of the kind, nor that he was in any way answerable for the Costs.

25 March 1839                                   [signed] *Elizabeth Robinson*

repeated and acknowledged before me
*Joseph Salvin*, surrogate

### Defensive Allegation

France v. Aaron (York, 1838). 30 May 1839. The common form portions are omitted.

[The defendant alleges] ... First. That the said Elizabeth Aaron has been the wife of Mark Aaron (by trade a Waterman) for upwards of twenty four years during the whole of which time she and her said husband have resided in the parish of Thorne aforesaid, that she is the mother of six children by her said husband, two of whom are daughters living at home. And that previous to her marriage she the said Elizabeth Aaron had lived in respectable families as a domestic servant, and she is a woman of upright life and of chaste and decent conversation and for and as such she is commonly called held had named esteemed and reputed within the parish of Thorne aforesaid, and other neighbouring and adjacent places ...

Second. That in the said parish of Thorne and neighbourhood thereof it is a common saying or expression when a female servant has been guilty of an improper connexion with her Master that 'the Tongs have been put into her bed' or that 'the Tongs have been found in her bed' ...

Third. That the said Isabella France, the premises notwithstanding, hath at divers times previous to Thursday the eighteenth day of October last past, and especially on or about the thirteenth day of the month of September last at Thorne aforesaid, when speaking to of or against the said Elizabeth Aaron in the presence and hearing of divers credible witnesses, did say and repeat in a taunting and insulting manner 'Who put the Tongs into bed' 'Who found the Tongs in your bed' or on the said day did, in reference to the said Elizabeth Aaron, use words of the like effect ...

Fourth. That in or about the month of February in the year of our Lord One thousand eight hundred and twenty-one the said Isabella France, who was then called Isabella Easton, then unmarried and a Spinster residing at Sykehouse in the said County of York, bore a bastard female child, which said bastard Child was on or about the eighteenth day of the said month and year baptized in the parish church of Fishlake in the County of York by the name of Jane ...

Fifth. That in part supply of proof of the premises mentioned in the next preceding article, and to all other intents and purposes in the law whatsoever, the party proponent doth exhibit, hereto annex, and prays to be here read and inserted and taken as part and parcel hereof a certain paper writing marked No 1 and doth allege and propound the same to be and contain a true copy of the entry of the baptism of the said female bastard child of the said Isabella France the party proponent in this Cause, formerly Isabella Easton Spinster, mentioned in the next preceding article. That the same has been faithfully extracted from the Register Book of Baptisms kept in and for the said parish of Fishlake for the said year of our Lord one thousand eight hundred and twenty one, and carefully collated with the original entry now remaining therein, and agrees therewith. That all and singular the contents of the said exhibit and of the said original entry were and are true and that Isabella Easton of Sykehouse Spinster therein mentioned as the parent of Jane the child baptized and Isabella France wife of Henry France formerly Isabella Easton Spinster the party promovent in this Cause were and are the same person and not diverse ...

Sixth. Whereas in the second position or article of the pretended libel in this Cause exhibited on the part and behalf of the said Isabella France it is alleged and pleaded as therein contained, now the same is therein falsely and untruly alleged and pleaded, for the truth and fact was and is, and the party proponent doth expressly allege and propound the fact to be, that on Thursday the said eighteenth day of October in the year of our Lord one thousand eight hundred and thirty eight (being the day on which the pretended defamatory words in this Cause mentioned are alleged to have been spoken) the said Isabella France did at Thorne aforesaid while speaking to of or against the said Elizabeth Aaron, in the presence and hearing of divers credible witnesses, use and repeat, in a loud taunting insulting and defamatory manner the aforesaid saying or expression 'Who put the Tongs into Bed' 'Who found the Tongs in your Bed' thereby asserting and meaning and implying (contrary to the fact) that the said Elizabeth Aaron had been incontinent, and, that in such sense the words or expressions then used by the said Isabella France were of and concerning the said Elizabeth Aaron so understood, to the injury of her good name and reputation, that thereupon the said Elizabeth Aaron, being much annoyed excited and irritated did, in a moment of heat, but without any malicious design to defame or slander the said Isabella France, rebuke her for such her language by reminding her of the misfortune into which she herself had fallen, by bearing a bastard child as mentioned in the fourth article of this allegation ...

*Annexed to the allegation* No 1

Page 43

Baptisms solemnized in the Parish of Fishlake in the County of York in the year 1821

| Baptized | Child's Christian name | Names of Parents | | Place of Abode |
| --- | --- | --- | --- | --- |
| | | Christian | Surname | |
| Febry 18th | Jane dr of | Isabella | Easton | Sykehouse |
| Condition &c | By whom ceremony was performed | | | |
| Spinster | Wm Nolbrey, Curate | | | |
| 338 | | | | |

I do hereby certify that the above extract is a true copy from the Register of Baptisms in the Parish of Fishlake in the county and Diocese of York.

April 30th 1839                    *Joseph Arrowsmith*, Vicar of Fishlake

## Personal Answers to the Allegation

France v. Aaron (York, 1838). The common form phrases are omitted.

The personal answers of Isabella France ...

[marginal signature] *W Blanshard* [plaintiff's advocate]

First. To the first position or article of the said allegation this respondent answering saith she admits that the said Elizabeth Aaron may have been the wife of Mark Aaron for upwards of twenty four years that they may have resided in the parish of Thorne during the whole of that period and that the said Elizabeth Aaron is the mother of six children by her said husband two of whom are daughters living at home, but whether the said Elizabeth Aaron previous to her marriage had lived in respectable families as a domestic servant this respondent cannot answer. This respondent further answering saith she denies that the said Elizabeth Aaron is a woman of upright life and of chaste and decent conversation as allegate, or that for and as such she was and is commonly called held had named esteemed and reputed within the Parish of Thorne aforesaid or other neighbouring and adjacent places ...

Second. To the second position or article of the said allegation this respondent answering saith she admits the same to be true

Third. To the third position or article of the said allegation this respondent answering saith she denies the same to be true

Fourth. To the fourth position or article of the said allegation this respondent answering saith she admits the same to be true

Fifth. To the fifth position or article of the said allegation this respondent answering saith she admits the same to be true

Sixth. To the sixth position or article of the said allegation this respondent answering saith she denies that in the second position or article of the libel in this cause exhibited it is falsely and untruly alleged and pleaded or that the truth and fact was and is that on Thursday the eighteenth day of October in the year one thousand eight hundred and thirty eight being the day on which the defamatory words in this Cause mentioned were spoken she this respondent did at Thorne aforesaid either in or out of the presence or hearing of divers or any credible witnesses use or repeat in any manner the saying or expression allegate. And this respondent further answering saith that the said Elizabeth Aaron on the day allegate without any provocation did defame and slander her the said Isabella France as libellate but the defamatory words used had no reference whatever to the circumstance allegate of her having borne a child previous to her marriage ...

On the twenty fourth day of July                                    [signed] *Isabella France*
one thousand eight hundred and
thirty nine the said Isabella France
the respondent herein was duly
sworn to the truth of the above
Before me *Joseph Arrowsmith*, Clerk
Commissioner

[Document appointing commission to receive the plaintiff's personal answers, 23 July 1839, not transcribed]


**Plaintiff's Interrogatories to Witnesses on the Defensive Allegation**

France v. Aaron (York, 1838)

Interrogatories to be administered on the part of the Plaintiff to Mary Smith, Rebecca Goodworth, George Swallow, and John Richardson ...

Let the said Mary Smith be asked In what way do you obtain your livelihood? Do you not occasionally assist your neighbours at the washing Tub and act as Laundress? Have you not frequently been employed by Elizabeth Aaron in such capacity? Do you not generally or occasionally take care of her house during her absence from home? Were you at Elizabeth Aaron's house on the eighteenth day of October one thousand eight hundred and thirty eight? If yea, what were you doing there, and in what part of the house did you stay?

Let the said Rebecca Goodworth be asked Are you not in service with a person of the name of Smith who supplies vessels with provisions at the waterside?

Let the said George Swallow be asked was not Mark Aaron a tenant of yours a few years ago, and did you not give him notice on account of the turbulent conduct of his wife? Did you not express great satisfaction at having got rid of her, and did you not in consequence treat your other tenants in the yard with tea and cakes? Have not Mrs Robinson and Mrs Pattrick your neighbours as well as other persons heard you express satisfaction at having got rid of Elizabeth Aaron from your house? Do you take out a licence for the sale of wine?

Let the said John Richardson be asked, Do you know anything of the private character of Elizabeth Aaron or of her conduct towards her neighbours in her own situation in life? If yea, what is it?

[signed] *W Blanshard* [plaintiff's advocate]


## Depositions on the Allegation

France v. Aaron (York, 1838)

1. George Swallow of Thorne in the county of York Innkeeper aged fifty nine years or thereabouts ...

Upon the first article of the said allegation. I have known and been well acquainted with Elizabeth Aaron one of the parties in this Cause upwards of twenty years last past, her husband Mark Aaron was formerly a seaman, he is now a riverman. My first coming to know her was I was formerly for three years what is called a miller's carrier at Thorne and at that time I used to call at the said Mark Aaron's house at Thorne where they lived ever since I knew them, twice a week for orders. I used to take the order on the day I called and delivered it the day after. I think they have seven children by their marriage but I am not quite certain. I have stood Godfather for some of them. Two of their children are girls at home, and go to school, the eldest will be about seven or eight years old, and the other a year or two younger. I did not know the said Elizabeth Aaron previous to her marriage, nor in what families she lived. I always considered her a woman of very good character. I never heard any thing amiss against her. She and her husband lived as my tenants in a house of mine at Thorne fourteen years but as their family increased my house got too small for them and they left it, but they nearly all the time I have known them lived within about one or two hundred yards of me. And she has always been regard[ed] by her neighbours as a Woman of good Character, and very punctual and honest in all her dealings ...

Upon the second article of the said allegation. There is at Thorne a custom where servants are jealous of their fellow servants acting improperly, of putting Tongs and other things into their beds and by that means discover what has been going on in their beds, but in what it originated I never knew, though I have often heard it used ...

[signed] George Swallow

The same witness to the Interrogatories

The said Mark Aaron was a tenant of mine a few years ago. I never did give him notice to quit, she gave me notice, saying my house was too little. I would let them have a house again if I had one at liberty, any time, she has spoken to me for one of mine and I have promised her to have one when I have one at liberty. They are convenient houses because they are on the canal side. I never did express satisfaction at having got rid of her, nor ever gave tea and cakes to my other tenants in the yard on such occasion. I never did tell Mrs Robinson and Mrs Pattrick nor any of my neighbours nor any other person that I was glad to get rid of Elizabeth Aaron from my house. I do not take out a licence for the sale of wine.

24th October 1839                                         [signed] <i>George Swallow</i>

repeated and acknowledged before me

Joseph Salvin, surrogate

2. Rebecca Goodworth of Doncaster in the County of York Spinster aged eighteen years or thereabouts ...

Upon the second article of the said allegation. I have known and been well acquainted with Elizabeth Aaron the wife of Mark Aaron one of the parties in this Cause about thirteen years, and first became acquainted with her by my living with my father a near neighbour to her at Thorne, next door but one, during that period. I have been living in service at Doncaster nearly a year. I have heard it said many times to the said Elizabeth Aaron when she has had words with her neighbours or others, or differences with them, 'Have you got the Tongs in the bed', and 'who put the Tongs into the bed' by way of aggravating her. I don't know that it is a common expression at Thorne. I never heard it used to any one but the said Elizabeth Aaron ...

Upon the third article of the said allegation. I have known Isabella France the wife of Henry France the other party in this Cause about a year and a half last past, and the first time I knew her to speak to her was in the Gleaning time before this, we were gleaning together in a field near Thorne, the time more particularly I cannot now remember, there were several people gleaning in the same field, but she and I were together separate from the rest. Mrs Aaron and I were very friendly and Isabella France was much against my going there. She was not at this time the subject of our conversation, nor was she in the field with us, when Isabella France began to talk of her and said I can never beat [<i>sic</i>; meet?] Betty Aaron (meaning the said Elizabeth Aaron) without saying to her 'who put the Tongs into bed'. And I then asked her what she mean [*sic*] by it, and she then told me that before Elizabeth Aaron was married, she was in service, and her mistress was jealous of some thing improper betwixt her and her master, that her mistress then went from home and before she went from home she put the best room Tongs into the said Elizabeth Aaron's bed, and when she came home Elizabeth Aaron asked her what she had done with the best room Tongs before she went from home as she could not find them and by this means her mistress knew that she had slept with her master in his bed during her absence and not in her own bed, and she thereupon paid her her wage and turn'd her about her business. And frequently when the said Isabella France has been going in the yard in which she and the said Elizabeth Aaron lived I have heard her call to her 'who put Tongs into bed' ... And further she cannot depose.

[signed] *Rebecca Goodworth*

The same witness to the interrogatories. I am in service at Doncaster with a person of the name of Smithwaite a Butcher who supplies vessels with provisions at the waterside. 24th October 1839

[signed] *Rebecca Goodworth*

repeated and acknowledged
before me
*Joseph Salvin*, surrogate

3. Mary Smith of Thorne in the County of York Spinster aged thirty years or thereabouts ...

Upon the second article of the said allegation. I have known and been well acquainted with Elizabeth Aaron the wife of Mark Aaron one of the parties in this Cause these nine or ten years last past. I gain my livelihood at Thorne by going out washing and nursing and have during that time frequently washed for the said Elizabeth Aaron, and have also nursed her three times she has laid in, and by that means so come to know and be acquainted with her. I do not know that it is a common saying at Thorne when a female servant has been guilty of an improper connexion with her master that 'the Tongs have been put into her bed' and I never heard such expression used by any one except the said Isabella France to the said Elizabeth Aaron ...

Upon the third and sixth articles of the said allegation. I have known the said Isabella France the wife of Henry France the other party in this Cause a year or two. On the afternoon of Thorne fair which was a year since last Thursday I was washing at Elizabeth Aaron's who lives a near neighbour to the said Isabella France the home in which they live being in the same yard, and Elizabeth Aaron's little boy was standing against her house door which was open, and near which I was in the house washing and Isabella France's little boy was standing against her house door which was also open, when he came and spit in Elizabeth Aaron's little boy's face, and the boy said what's that for if thou does that again I'll kick thy bottom, that Isabella France then came out of her house and said to Elizabeth Aaron's little boy wilt thou kick his bottom, and Mrs

Aaron then called her little boy in but he did not come, and her husband then went to the door and said to Isabella France thou had better get in and get thy clean cap on and wash thy face, and Isabella France then called out 'who put tongs into bed', that Mrs Aaron then went to the door and said to the said Isabella France 'I'm not a whore but thou is, thou's proved thyself one by having had a bastard' or to that effect. They then gave over and that was all that passed between 'em. I never heard Isabella France ask Mrs Aaron 'who put tongs into bed' but that once, and Isabella France then began the squabble. That the said Henry France and Mark Aaron were often squabbling and fighting, and the children could not go along the street but they called after them who put Tongs into bed, and they made Mrs Aaron and her husband so uncomfortable they have been obliged to leave that neighbourhood. By the expression which the said Isabella France used as above deposed to, to the said Elizabeth Aaron of 'who put tongs into bed' I supposed she meant that the said Elizabeth Aaron was a whore ...

her<br>
Mary    X    Smith<br>
mark

The same witness to the Interrogatories
I obtain my living by going out washing and charing and nursing. I am but a poor girl. I go out washing among my neighbours and also as laundress. I have frequently been so employed by the said Elizabeth Aaron. And when she has gone from home, I have gone and taken care of her home for a week or a fortnight together. I was at her home on the eighteenth of October last year washing in the kitchen

her<br>
Mary    X    Smith<br>
mark

24th October 1839
repeated and acknowledged
before me
*Joseph Salvin*, surrogate

4. John Richardson of Thorne in the county of York Grocer and Agent of the Banking Company of Sir William Bryan Cooke Baronet aged thirty six years or thereabouts ...
Upon the first article of the said allegation. I have known and been well acquainted with Elizabeth Aaron the wife of Mark Aaron (a Waterman) one of the parties in this Cause upwards of thirteen years last past, during which time she and her husband have resided at Thorne, where they still reside. I think they have several children by their marriage, but what number I cannot say, and I think that they have either two or three of them living at home. I did not know her previous to her marriage. I came to know the said Elizabeth Aaron in consequence of my going to live at Thorne to open a grocer's shop there in the year one thousand eight hundred and twenty six when she became a customer of mine, and has continued so ever since, and by that means I have had con-

stant opportunities of seeing her, and knowing her character, and so far I have so known her she has always born a very excellent character, and in all her transactions with me I have always found her punctual and honest in all her dealings, and so far as I know, she is a person esteemed and respected amongst her neighbours and others ...

[signed] *Jno Richardson*

The same witness to the Interrogatories, answering says, I know nothing of the private character of Elizabeth Aaron or of her conduct towards her neighbours in her own situation in life. What I know of her is being a customer of mine so many years, when I never observed any thing in her conduct but what was highly respectable, and very punctual and honest – very much so.

5th November 1839

[signed] *Jno Richardson*

repeated and acknowledged
before me
*Joseph Salvin*, surrogate

## Sentence

Form for London from H. Coote, *The Practice of the Ecclesiastical Courts* (London 1847), 270–2

In the Name of God Amen. We, Stephen Lushington, Doctor of Laws, Vicar-General of the Right Reverend Father in God, Charles James, by Divine Permission, Lord Bishop of London, and Official Principal of the Consistorial and Episcopal Court of London, lawfully constituted, rightly and duly proceeding, having heard, seen, and understood, and fully and maturely discussed, the merits and circumstances of a certain cause of defamation or slander, which is controverted and remains undetermined before us in judgment, between C.D., of the parish of      in the county of     , and diocese of London, aforesaid, widow, the party agent, and complainant, on the one part, and A.B., of the same parish, in the county and diocese aforesaid, the party accused and complained of on the other part; and the parties aforesaid having lawfully appeared before us in judgment, by their proctors respectively, and the proctor of the said C.D., praying sentence to be given and justice to be done to his party; and the proctor of the said A.B. also praying justice to be done to his party, and having first carefully and diligently searched into and considered the whole proceedings had and done before us in this cause; and having observed all and singular the matters and things that by law, in this behalf, ought to be observed, we have thought fit, and do thus think fit to proceed to the giving our definitive sentence or final decree in this cause, in manner and form following, to wit – for as much as by the acts enacted, deduced, alleged, exhibited, propounded, proved, and confessed in this cause, we have found, and it doth evidently appear unto us, that the proctor for the said C.D. hath fully and sufficiently founded and proved his intention deduced in a certain libel and other pleadings and exhibits, given in, exhibited and admitted on her behalf, and now remaining in the registry of this court (which libel, other pleadings, and exhibits we take and will have taken as if here read and inserted) for us to pronounce as hereinafter is pronounced; and that nothing, at least effectual, hath on the part of the said A.B. been excepted, deduced, exhibited, propounded, proved, or confessed in this cause which may or ought in anywise to defeat, prejudice, or weaken the intention of the said C.D. Therefore we, Stephen Lushington, Doctor of Laws, the judge aforesaid, having first called upon the name of Christ, and having God alone before our eyes, and having heard counsel thereupon, do pronounce, decree, and declare that the said A.B. did, in the year, months and place in the said libel mentioned, or some or one of them, contrary to good manners and the bond of Christian charity, publicly and maliciously say, publish, and report several scandalous, reproachful and defamatory words, in the said libel mentioned, tending to the infamy, hurt, and diminution of the estate, good name, fame, and reputation of the said C.D., wherefore we do pronounce decree and declare that the said A.B. ought to be duly and canonically corrected and punished, according to the law in that behalf provided, for this so great excess and temerity in the premises, and to be forced and compelled to reclaim and retract such defamatory words, and to the restitution of the good name, fame, and reputation of the said C.D., and to cease and desist from such defamatory words for the future; and we do also pronounce, decree, and declare the said A.B. to be enjoined and compelled to perform a salutary and suitable penance according to his demerit, for his excess aforesaid; and we do also pronounce, decree, and declare that the said A.B. be condemned in lawful costs and we do condemn him accordingly.

## Bill of Costs

Robinson v. Sharp (York, 1824), Cons CP 1824/3. The taxing officer's notes are transcribed *in italic script;* figures in the left margin indicate amounts disallowed. Note that expenses were allowed for two witnesses only.

In the Consistory Court of York
A Bill of expences made on the part and behalf of Ellen Robinson Spinster in a certain Cause of Defamation or Slander prosecuted by her against Thomas Sharp
1824

| | |
|---|---|
| Easter Term. Retainer to Proctor | 0.5.0 |
| Attending Mr Sinclair & retaining him as Advocate | 0.6.8 |
| Paid him his retainer and his Clerk | 1.3.6 |
| Miss Robinson being a Minor, drawing and ingrossing Proxy from her electing her Father her Guardian (5 Fol) | 0.7.6 |
| Drawing and ingrossing Proxy from Mr Robinson accepting of the Guardianship of his Daughter (5 Fol) | 0.7.6 |

| | | |
|---|---|---:|
| | Instructions to execute | 0.5.0 |
| 8th May. | Appearance for Miss Robinson on exhibiting her Proxy | 0.7.10 |
| | Exhibition special Act and Attendance | 0.8.0 |
| | Appearance for Mr Robinson on exhibiting his proxy | 0.7.10 |
| | Exhibition special Act and Attendance | 0.8.0 |
| | Drawing Allegation and Petition for a Citation against the Defendant and fair copy | 0.8.8 |
| | Exhibiting before a Surrogate & praying Citation | 0.7.10 |
| | Special Act thereon, Surrogate's Fee and attendance | 0.8.0 |
| | Warrant to prosecute and Stamp Duty | 0.8.7 |
| | Attending the Registry to file same | 0.3.6 |
| | Citation under Seal of Court Stamp Duty and Extracting | 0.12.5 |
| | Note for service | 0.2.6 |
| | Instructions to execute | 0.5.0 |
| 20th | Entering the Citation in Court Book & attendance thereon | 0.3.6 |
| | Appearance in Court & Fee | 0.7.10 |
| 0. 2. 8 | Act of Court and Copy thereon and on an appearance being entered for the Defendants | 0.2.8 |
| | Certificate and Call | 0.1.8 |
| Trinity Term. | Proctor's Term Fee | 0.5.0 |
| | Drawing Libel    (12 Fol) | 0.12.0 |
| | Fair copy for Advocate to peruse & settle | 0.6.0 |
| | Attending him therewith & afterwards for the same | 0.6.8 |
| | Ingrossing two parts of the Libel | 0.12.0 |
| | Stamps thereon | 0.10.2 |
| | Attending Advocate to sign the Libel | 0.3.6 |
| | Paid him for settling and signing it | 1.1.0 |
| 0. 2. 8 | Act of Court & copy on exhibiting the Libel | 0.2.8 |
| | Fair copy of the Libel as exhibited sent to Client | 0.6.0 |
| 2d July | Act of Court & copy on the Libel being admitted and on the | |
| 0. 2. 8 | Defendant's Proctor contesting Suit negatively | 0.2.8 |
| | Advocate and Proctors' Fees on contestation of Suit | 0.15.6 |
| | Attending the Register & adverse Proctor & getting a time fixed for the examination of Witnesses | 0.6.8 |
| 29th | Mary Rayner, Charlotte Stephenson & John Lund having come | |
| 0. 3. 4 | to York to be examined as Witnesses, attending them previous to their examinations | 0.10.0 |

*The general*
*rule has been*
*only to allow*
*for two*

*Witnesses in*
*Defamation*

| | | |
|---|---|---|
| | Ticketing them & making fair copies for the Register and adverse Proctor | 0.9.0 |
| | Special Act Oath & attendance on their being produced & Sworn | 0.8.0 |
| | Act of Court thereon and Copy | 0.2.8 |
| 0. 8.10 | Paid for their examination & Stamps used thereon | 1.6.6 |
| | Attending them during their stay in York | 0.13.4 |
| 30th | Act of Court and Copy on both Proctors propounding all | |
| 0. 2. 8 | Acts & being assigned to conclude | 0.2.8 |
| Michs Term. | Advocate & Proctors Term Fees | 0.15.6 |
| 0. 2. 8 | Act of Court and copy on the Defendant's Proctor exhibiting an Affidavit of the Plaintiff being of age & on being assigned to exhibit a Proxy from her | 0.2.8 |
| | Drawing & ingrossing special Proxy | 0.10.0 |
| | Instructions to execute | 0.3.6 |
| 11th Novr | Act of Court & Copy on both Proctors exhibiting special | |
| 0. 2. 8 | proxies from their Clients & on the Cause being assigned for sentence | 0.2.8 |
| 0. 6. 8 | Attending in the Registry perusing the Depositions of the Witnesses & ordering office copies thereof | 0.6.8 |
| 0. 9. 2 | Office Copies of the Depositions & Answers to Interrogatories & Extracting | 1.7.6 |
| | Office Copy of the Defendant's Interrogatories & Extracting | 0.9.3 |
| 0. 6. 0 | Fair copies of the Interrogatories Depositions and Answers to Interrogatories for Client (46 Fol) | 1.3.0 |
| 1825 | | |
| 27th Jany | The Defendant's Proctor having proposed an amicable | |
| 0. 6. 8 | arrangement of the Suit, making fair copy of his Note & writing therewith to Client | 0.6.8 |
| 0. 3. 4 | Writing to Defendant's Proctor with Client's answer to his proposal | 0.3.6 |
| Hilary Term. | Advocate & Proctors Term Fees | 0.15.6 |
| 0. 5. 4 | Acts of Court and Copies on the Cause being further assigned for Sentence | 0.5.4 |
| 0. 6. 0 | Making fair copies of all the Proceedings in the Cause for the use of Advocate (78 Fol) | 1.19.0 |
| 0. 6. 8 | Perusing and considering the same & making observations thereon | 0.13.4 |
| | Attending Advocate with his Brief | 0.6.8 |
| | Paid him extra therewith | 1.1.0 |

|  | | |
|---|---|---|
| | And to his Clerk | 0.2.6 |
| | Attendance on getting a day fixed for hearing the Cause | 0.6.8 |
| | Drawing & ingrossing Sentence | 0.13.6 |
| | Attending Advocate to sign same | 0.3.6 |
| | The Cause coming on to be heard Advocate and Proctors Information fees | 0.15.6 |
| 0. 4. 6 | Drawing Petition at the Acts of Court, preparing Sentence to be read & fair copy | 0.4.6 |
| 0. 2. 8 | Act of Court & Copy on Sentence being given | 0.2.8 |
| | Paid for Decree of Court | 0.10.0 |
| 0. 6. 8 | Attending the hearing of the Cause | 0.6.8 |
| | Appearance in Court for Miss Robinson after Sentence | 0.7.10 |
| | Allegation at the Acts of Court alleging Sentence given and no appeal and praying Citation why Sentence & to extract Declaration | 0.3.4 |
| | Instructions to the Registry for Citation why Sentence | 0.3.6 |
| 0. 5. 0 | Citation under Seal of Court Stamp Duty & Extracting | 0.12.5 |
| | Note for Service | 0.2.6 |
| | Instructions to execute | 0.5.0 |
| | Easter Term. Proctor's Term Fee | 0.5.0 |
| | Fee on introducing the Citation why Sentence into Court | 0.5.0 |
| 0. 2. 8 | Act of Court thereon and copy | 0.2.8 |
| | Certificate and Call | 0.1.8 |
| | Attending Defendant's Proctor on getting a time fixed for the performance of the Declaration | 0.6.8 |
| | Paid for Declaration | 0.3.4 |
| 0. 2. 8 | Act of Court and copy on the Declaration being returned duly certified &c. | 0.2.8 |
| 0.10. 6 | Writing a great number of letters during the dependance of the Cause | 1.11.6 |
| | Paid for Postages | 0.11.0 |
| 0. 4. 0 | Drawing bill of Costs & fair Copy | 0.8.8 |
| 0.13. 4 | Several attendances and other trouble not before charged | 0.13.4 |
| | | 37.4.4 |
| | Mr Smith's Bill (Miss Robinson's Solicitor) as per Particulars annexed | 13.15.1 |
| | £  s  d | £ 50.19.5 |
| | 43.13.0 | |

*13th May 1825. We tax this Bill at the Sum of Forty three Pounds thirteen shillings     Henry John Dickens, NP*

**Monition for Costs**

Bear v. Bignell (Winchester, 1831). See 76, above.

William Dealtry, Clerk, Doctor in Divinity Vicar General and Official Principal of the Right Reverend Father in God Charles Richard by divine permission Lord Bishop of Winchester lawfully appointed, To all and singular Clerks and literate persons whomsoever within the County of Southampton and Diocese of Winchester Greeting. Whereas We rightly and duly proceeding in a Certain Cause of Defamation or Reproach which came before us in Judgement between Jane Bear of the Parish of Itchen Abbas in the County and Diocese aforesaid Spinster the Party Agent and Complainant of the one Part and Sarah Bignell of the same Parish Singlewoman the Party accused or complained of on the other Part have read and promulged a certain definitive Sentence in Writing on the Part and behalf of the said Jane Bear and against the said Sarah Bignell by which Sentence We have condemned the said Sarah Bignell in the lawful Charges and Expences expended and laid out by and on the Part and behalf of the said Jane Bear in the prosecution and by reason and means of the said Cause which Charges and expences We did moderate and tax at the Sum of Sixteen pounds fourteen shillings and ninepence of lawful money of Great Britain and have at the Petition of the Proctor of the said Jane Bear decreed the said Sarah Bignell to be cited and monished to pay the said Sum of Sixteen pounds fourteen shillings and ninepence being the amount of the Costs taxed by us as aforesaid besides the Expences of this Monition and the Service thereof and the Costs accrued since the said Sentence was promulged (Justice so requiring), We therefore authorize and hereby strictly enjoin and command you jointly or seperately [sic] peremptorily to monish or cause to be monished the aforesaid Sarah Bignell to pay the said Sum of Sixteen pounds fourteen shillings and ninepence, the Costs taxed by us as aforesaid together with the Costs of this Monition and the Service thereof and also the Costs accrued since the publishing or promulging the said Sentence on or before the twenty-first day of December Instant, otherwise to appear Personally before us or our lawful Surrogate or some other competent judge in this behalf in the Cathedral church of the Holy Trinity of Winchester aforesaid and Place of judicature there on Friday, the eighteenth day of January between the Hours of eleven and twelve of the Clock in the Forenoon being the usual time of hearing Causes and doing Justice there, then and there to see and hear herself excommunicated for not paying the said Sum of Sixteen pounds fourteen shillings and ninepence the Costs taxed by us as aforesaid besides the Costs of this Monition and the Service thereof and the subsequent Costs accrued as before mentioned. And further to do and receive according to Law and Justice under Pain of the Law and contempt thereof. And what you shall do or cause to be done in the Premises you shall duly certify to us or our Surrogate or some other competent Judge in this behalf together with these presents. Dated at Winchester the seventh day of December in the Year of our Lord One thousand eight hundred and thirty two.

**Draft Significavit**

Bear v. Bignell (Winchester, 1831). See 76, above.

To His Most Excellent Majesty and our Sovereign Lord William the Fourth by the
Grace of God of the United Kingdom of Great Britain and Ireland King, Defender of
the Faith, William Dealtry Clerk D.D. Vicar General of the Right Reverend Father in
God Charles Richard by Divine Permission Lord Bishop of Winchester and Official
Principal of the Consistory Court of Winchester lawfully constituted, health in him by
whom Kings and Princes rule and govern.

We hereby notify and signify unto your Majesty that one Sarah Bignell of the Parish of
Itchen Abbas in the County of Southampton and Diocese of Winchester hath been duly
pronounced guilty of manifest contumacy and contempt of the Law and Jurisdiction
Ecclesiastical in not having obeyed our Order or Decree to wit to extract or cause to be
extracted from the Registry of the Consistory Court of Winchester aforesaid a schedule
of penance and to do or perform the said penance according to the tenor and purport of
the said Schedule in the Parish Church of Itchen Abbas aforesaid on a day now long
past duly made in a certain cause of defamation which was lately depending in judgment before Us in the Court aforesaid between Jane Bear of the parish of Itchen Abbas
in the said County of Southampton and diocese of Winchester Spinster the Party Agent
or Complainant on the one part and the said Sarah Bignell of the same Parish single
Woman the party accused or complained of on the other part. And we hereby further
notify and signify unto your said Majesty that the said Sarah Bignell hath also been
duly pronounced guilty of manifest contumacy and contempt of the Law and Jurisdiction Ecclesiastical in not having paid or caused to be paid to the said Jane Bear or her
Proctor the sum of £16.14.9 lawful money of Great Britain being the amount of certain
costs taxed against her together with such other costs as were due by Law in the Cause
aforesaid on a certain day now also long past, in obedience [to] our Monition issued
under Seal of the Consistory Court of Winchester aforesaid and duly and personally
served on her the said Sarah Bignell. We therefore humbly implore and entreat your
said Most Excellent Majesty would vouchsafe to command the body of the said Sarah
Bignell to be taken and imprisoned for such contumacy and contempt. Given under the
Seal of the said Consistory Court of Winchester the      day of

AB Registrar or Deputy Registrar

**Extract from Act Book**

Norwich, 1843

The next Court is on Monday 3rd July 1843 [marginal note]
Acts had made done and expedited before the Worshipful Charles Evans Esquire Mas-
ter of Arts Surrogate duly appointed of the Worshipful William Yonge Clerk Master of
Arts Vicar General in Spirituals of the Right Reverend Father in God Edward by divine

permission Lord Bishop of Norwich lawfully constituted Judicially sitting in the Cathedral Church of the Holy and Undivided Trinity of Norwich at the place of Judicature there on Monday the twelfth day of June in the year of our Lord One thousand eight hundred and forty three at the usual hours of hearing there.

Present [signed] J Kitson Noty Pub. Acty [notary public, actuary]

| | |
|---|---|
| Waterson | It is assigned to hear the Judges pleasure touching the |
| agst | admissibility of Rackhams alledged allegation this day |
| Annison | [these words entered in advance] |
| Skipper   Rackham | On which day Rackham prayed and the Judge at his petition admitted the Allegation present Skipper who gave a negative issue thereto. And the Judge at the further petition of Rackham assigned him a Term Probatory to the third next and decreed for Witnesses the next Court day. [added after the session] |
| | |
| Rush | For Sentence this day [these words entered in advance] |
| agst | Same to the next [added afterwards] |
| Woodcock | |
| Skipper   Steward | |
| | |
| Hall | Term assigned to propound all acts this day [these words |
| agst | entered in advance] |
| Roddwell | On which day the defendant being thrice called and not |
| Rackham | appearing Rackham propounded all acts and prayed and the Judge at his petition assigned him a term to conclude the next Court day. [added afterwards] |

# Appendix B

# Occupations of Parties

**Occupations of Parties and Parties' Husbands (Norwich)**

Gentry: 6
   Gentleman 3, esquire 2, knight 1
Professions: 6
   Clergyman 2, schoolmaster 1, surgeon 1, veterinary surgeon 1, banker 1
Office-holders: 2
   Sheriff's officer 1, tollgate keeper 1
Farmers: 16
   Farmer 14, farmer and jobber 1, yeoman 1
Trades: 43
   Cattle dealer 1, butcher 8, butcher and publican 1, publican 5, innkeeper 6, beerseller 1, miller and baker 1, grocer 1, grocer and draper 2, kiddier (hawker) 1, kiddier and, shopkeeper 1, hawker and husbandman 1, pawnbroker 1, broker 2, shopkeeper 1, shopkeeper and tailor 1, fishmonger 1, auctioneer 1, dealer in jewellery 2, baker 1, timber merchant, 2, florist 2
Crafts: 50
   Carpenter 4, house carpenter 1, shipjoiner 2, silk dyer 1, weaver 3, bricklayer 5, ropemaker 1, builder 1, blacksmith 4, whitesmith 2, painter and glazier 1, engineer 1, shoemaker 3, cordwainer 5, plasterer 1, hatter 1, tailor 7, tinplate worker, 1, currier 1, brickmaker 1, master mariner 1, cooper, 1, millwright 1, fustian weaver 1
Unskilled: 25
   Mariner 1, mariner and innkeeper 1, gamekeeper 1, labourer 11, husbandman 3, gardener 3, fisherman 3, boatman 1, coachguard, 1
Occupation not stated: 104

   [Figure includes 42 single women, where statement of occupation would not be expected.]
Total for Norwich: 252

## Occupations of Parties and Parties' Husbands (York)

Gentry: 7
   Gentleman 5, esquire 2
Professions: 10
   Clergyman 2, dissenting minister 2, schoolmaster 1, surgeon 4, veterinary surgeon 1
Office-holders: 4
   Excise officer 2, police officer 1, agent 1
Farmers: 56
   Farmer 41, farmer and cow jobber 1, yeoman 14
Trades: 101
   Innkeeper 23, innholder 1, publican 5, publican and farmer 1, victualler 2, aledraper
   2, cotton manufacturer 1, lace manufacturer 1, man-mercer, hatter, and hosier 1,
   merchant 1, iron merchant 1, hawker 1, grocer 5, teazle dealer 1, spirit merchant 2,
   wine merchant 1, linen draper 1, butcher 13, baker 2, medicine vendor 1, miller 6,
   hackney coach proprietor 1, shopkeeper 13, stone merchant 1, maltster 3, sheep jobber 1, cattle jobber 1, milk seller 1, confectioner 1, horse dealer 3, fishmonger 2,
   manufacturer 2
Crafts: 91
   Tailor 2, tailor and draper 1, tailor and beerseller 1, carpet weaver 1, nail manufacturer 1, trimmer and harness-maker 1, turner 1, ropemaker 2, shoemaker 9, cordwainer 4, clothier 16, woollen clothier 1, cloth maker 2, cloth manufacturer 3, cloth
   dresser 2, dyer 1, blanket maker 1, hosier 1, carpenter 1, joiner 2, cabinet maker 3,
   joiner and cabinetmaker 2, ship's carpenter 1, skinner 1, master mariner, 1, whitesmith 1, blacksmith 3, farrier 1, stonemason 6, silk throwster 1, plumber and glazier
   1, builder 2, bricklayer 1, card case maker 1, clock maker 1, machine maker 2,
   wheelwright 5, cartwright 2, tinplate worker 1, coal leader 1, bell hanger 1
Unskilled: 39
   Labourer 10, mariner 8, waterman 5, ostler 1, gardener 3, cowkeeper 1, servant 2,
   farmer's assistant 1, coach guard 1, warehouseman 1, bath keeper 1, miner 1, collier
   1, truckman 1, mechanic 1, gamekeeper 1
Occupation not stated: 176

   [Figure includes 83 single women, where statement of occupation would not be
   expected.]
Total for York: 484

## Occupations of Male Plaintiffs (England and Wales)

Gentry: 18
  Gentleman 16, esquire 2
Professions: 46
  Clergyman 27, dissenting minister 7, schoolmaster 4, surgeon 6, surgeon and apothecary 1, banker 1
Office-holders: 8
  Exciseman 1, supervisor of excise 1, inspector of police 1, sergeant 1, clerk 4
Farmers: 55
  Farmer 33, yeoman 21, grazier 1
Trades: 32
  Innkeeper 1, publican 3, victualler 2, victualler and builder 1, manufacturer 1, merchant 3, draper 2, miller 1, shopkeeper 3, butcher 7, shopkeeper and retailer of beer 1, timber merchant 1, barge owner 1, broker 1, hatter 1, stationer 1, flour dealer 1, liquor dealer 1
Crafts: 33
  Cardmaker 1, tailor and draper 2, hoopmaker 1, shoemaker 4, clothier 1, cloth spinner 1, warp dresser 1, carpenter 1, cabinetmaker and upholsterer 1, carpenter and wheelwright 1, wheelwright 3, blacksmith 2, smith 1, stonemason 2, mason 1, plumber and glazier 1, builder 3, brickburner and farmer 1, brickmaker 2, slater 1, painter and plasterer 1, ironmaster 1
Unskilled: 13
  Labourer 3, mariner 1, waterman 1, ferryman 1, gardener 2, currier 1, servant 1, carrier 1, miner 1, gamekeeper 1
Occupation not stated: 54

Total: 259
  Sources: Act books and cause papers

# Notes

Archival classmarks are given for documents quoted in the text.

## Introduction

1 John Roberts (Louisa Roberts's husband) to J. Huckwell (her proctor), 10 March 1855 (spelling irregular), Roberts v. Jones (Llandaff, 1853), LL/CC/G/2142t

2 Ibid.

3 The events mentioned in this paragraph are from a signed statement of Huckwell, n.d., LL/CC/G/2142e.

4 LL/CC/G/2142

5 *Star of Gwent*, 3 March 1855, 2d and e

6 Ibid. Simons had corresponded with the bishop, who had said (as might be expected) that he did not exercise judicial jurisdiction personally, and that he had confidence in his chancellor. Simons reproduced the correspondence in his pamphlet.

7 *Star of Gwent*, 3 March 1855, 4 a–b

8 *Cardiff and Merthyr Guardian*, 7 April 1855, 3f. In the *Newspaper Press Directory*, ed. Charles Mitchell (1857), 55 and 69, the *Star* and the *Guardian* are described respectively as 'liberal' and 'conservative.'

9 *Star of Gwent*, 21 April 1855, 2b–c

10 Note 1, above

11 HO 107/2459, f. 421, sch. 273

12 Formal documents were signed by mark (X). Two letters from Cardiff jail, one to her husband and one to Huckwell, are in different hands: LL/CC/G/2142x and u. Huckwell's statement that the circumstances were explained to Jones in the English and Welsh languages may imply that Welsh was her first language, or it may have been the general practice of the office.

13 LL/CC/G/2142e

14 Charlotte Jones to her husband, 12 March 1855, LL/CC/G/2142u

15 Ibid. The letter bears marks of being written 'for the record,' and this would account for its being preserved with the court papers.

16 Ibid.

17 Royal assent, *Parliamentary Debates*, 3rd ser. 139, 111 (26 June 1855)

18 LL/CC/G/2142g. The Bill of Costs includes the item 'Attending exon [execution of recantation] at Cardiff Gaol.' LL/CC/G/2142i

19 The next items in the Bill of Costs (n.d.) are 'Drawing dfdt liberate,' 'Engrossing same,' and 'Liberate under seal and extracting Bill and Copy.'

20 *Parliamentary Debates*, 3rd ser. 137, 1375 (30 March 1855)

21 Phillimore was recommended by the bishop as the best person in the House of Commons to receive a counter-statement in response to Jones's petition. Hugh Williams to Huckwell, 7 March 1855, LL/CC/G/2142

22 Robert Phillimore, *The Practice and Courts of Civil and Ecclesiastical Law, and the statements in Mr Bouverie's speech on the subject, examined, with observations on the value of the study of Civil and International Law in this country; in a letter to the Right Hon W.E. Gladstone* (London 1848), 61–2

23 18 & 19 Vic. c. 41

24 *Parliamentary Debates*, 3rd ser. 137, 1373–4 (20 March 1855)

25 See 79–85, below.

26 Sharpe v. Dauncey (Gloucester, 1849) B4/1/2318

27 See 123, 152–5, below.

28 Act Book, 10 October 1850, GDR 364. See chapter 2, below.

29 See chapter 6, below.

30 On 3 January 1851, Sharpe's proctor sought an order for performance of the penance. The order was made on 13 February, but meanwhile Dauncey had revoked his proctor's proxy (authorization to act for him). The judge ordered the proctor to extract a schedule of penance (i.e., to prepare the necessary documents – the formal apology and the certificate of its performance) on pain of suspension. The proctor did so under protest, but could not find his client. On 8 April, Sharpe's proctor died; she appointed another proctor who did eventually effect service of the order. Dauncey's imprisonment is recorded on 17 September. Cause papers, B4/1/2318, and Act Book, GDR 364

31 See 75–6, below.

32 A statement of the grounds on which habeas corpus was sought is among the papers. It alleges three: want of jurisdiction, failure to serve the relevant documents, and failure by the judge whose order was disobeyed to signify the contempt to the Court of Chancery, B4/1/2318. See chapter 4, below.

33  But T. Starkie, *A Treatise on the Law of Slander and Libel*, 2nd ed. (London 1830), says that this was not a ground for a prohibition, citing Evans v. Brown (1704) 2 Ld Raym 1101.

34  See 18–20, 76, below.

35  See A.H. Manchester, 'The Reform of the Ecclesiastical Courts,' *American Journal of Legal History*, 10 (1966), 51

36  Ecclesiastical Courts Commission Report, PP 1831–2 xxiv

37  See H. Arthurs, *Without the Law: Administrative Justice and Legal Pluralism in Nineteenth-Century England* (Toronto 1985).

38  See *The Times*, 1 February 1848, 4d ('an oyster bed where every oyster is called Jenner'); id., 7 Februrary, 5e ('the court of the Jenners'). Charles Dickens also commented on the family connections in Doctors' Commons, *David Copperfield*, chapters 23 and 26.

39  Ecclesiastical Courts Commission Report, appendix A, 175 (evidence of William Ward, deputy registrar of Chester)

40  See Manchester, 'Reform of the Ecclesiastical Courts,' 55.

41  E. Muscott, *The History and Power of Ecclesiastical Courts* (London 1846), 3

42  Ecclesiastical Courts Commission Report, 63

43  Id., appendix D, no. 12

44  Id., 63

45  *Yorkshire Gazette*, 9 February 1833, 4b

46  *Parliamentary Debates*, 3rd ser. 99, 109 (Bouverie, 30 May 1848)

47  See W.L. Mathieson, *English Church Reform, 1815–40* (London 1923), 158–61; Manchester, 'Reform of the Ecclesiastical Courts,' 70–5.

48  Divorce and Matrimonial Causes Act, 1857, 20 & 21 Vic. c. 85, Court of Probate Act, 1857, 20 & 21 Vic. c. 77

49  23 & 24 Vic. c. 32

50  31 & 32 Vic. c. 109

## 1: The Common Law

1  J. Spencer, 'Criminal Libel' [1977] Crim LR 383, 465, estimates about twenty-four cases a year.

2  T. Starkie, *A Treatise on the Law of Slander and Libel*, 2nd ed. (London 1830); G.W. Cooke, *A Treatise on the Law of Defamation* (London 1844)

3  Slander of Women Act, 1891, 54 & 55 Vic. c. 51

4  See Auctoritate Dei Patris (Council of Oxford, 1222), in W. Lyndwood, *Provinciale* (1430), printed edition (Oxford 1679): 'Excommunicamus omnes illos qui gratia lucri, odii, vel favoris, vel alia quacunque de causa, alicui malitiose crimen impo-

nunt unde infamatus sit apud bonos et graves, ut sic saltem ei purgatio indicatur vel alio modo gravatur.' Lyndwood, at p. 347, glosses 'crimen' to include 'homicidium, adulterium, aut aliqua immunditia fornicationis, furtum, vel fraus quando inest ei dolus, sacrilegium, & caetera huiusmodi.' See also R.H. Helmholz, *Select Cases on Defamation to 1600* (London 1985), xxx–xxxiv. T. Oughton, *Ordo Judiciorum* (London 1728), title IV, xxii (p. 12), tr. J.T. Law, *Forms of Ecclesiastical Law* (London 1831), 46, gives examples of general insulting words as within the jurisdiction of the ecclesiastical court, but J. Ayliffe, *Parergon Juris Canonici Anglicani* (London 1726), 214 says that a prohibition would lie in the case of vague general insults.

5  Note (probably by judge) among papers in Sharpe v. Dauncey (Gloucester, 1849), B4/1/2318, referring to Evans v. Gwyn (1844), 5 QB 844

6  But not in the Isle of Man. There were a few cases instituted in England and Wales after 1815. See 167–8, below.

7  Dix v. Scarse (Peterborough, 1838), X 953. For an account of Dr Lushington's career, see S.M. Waddams, *Law, Politics, and the Church of England: The Career of Stephen Lushington 1782–1873* (Cambridge 1992).

8  Act Book, 22 September 1838, ML 718

9  Harvey v. Campling (Norwich, 1834), libel dated 3 June 1834, DN/CON/130

10  Note of judge's reasons, ibid.

11  Roe v. Mills (Chichester, 1817) (accusation of theft), Kerley v. Kewsley (Sodor and Man, 1820) (man called 'thief, damned bugger and rascal')

12  Askwith to Stockton, 25 January 1820 (copy), in Etty v. Kneeshaw (York, 1819), PP

13  Same to same, 4 November 1820 (copy), PP

14  E. Baines, *History Directory and Gazetteer of the County of York*, vol. 2 (East and North Ridings) (York 1823), 530

15  Page to Askwith, 28 April 1825, in Calvert v. Chapman (York, 1825), PP

16  Askwith to Page, 29 April 1825 (copy), PP

17  Ellis v. Barker (York, 1835). One witness said for 'upwards of an hour'; the other said 'upwards of a quarter of an hour.' Cons CP 1835/9

18  Craik v. Bell (Carlisle, 1832) DRC/3/50 f. 20 and DRC/3/29 entry for 13 April 1832, Booth v. Gordon (Chester, 1820)

19  See Evans v. Gwyn (1844), 5 QB 845.

20  Gwyn v. Evans (St David's, 1841)

21  Starkie, *Slander and Libel*, 119, citing Clerk v. Price (1709), 11 Mod 208

22  See, for the early modern period, L. Gowing, *Domestic Dangers: Women, Words and Sex in Early Modern London* (Oxford 1996), 109, 129.

23  Stead v. Powell (Lincoln, 1825), court papers, box 70. See Kerley v. Kewsley, note 11, above.

24  Act Book, 1 December 1825, Cj 49

25  Swaffer v. Swaffer (Arches Court by letters of request from Canterbury, 1846),
LPL, H 690a, Assignation Book, 22 May 1846, Aaa 47; also Miller v. Carter
(Peterborough, 1820) (proxy given but subsequently withdrawn). In Terry v. Gray
(Chichester, 1821) the plaintiff, a woman, was called (the libel stated) 'a buggering
whore.' EPI/15/1 & 3 (1820–9)

26  Townley v. Reeve (Norwich, 1840), DN/CON/133

27  Starkie, *Slander and Libel*, 122

28  In Routledge v. A. Tomlinson and Routledge v. J. Tomlinson (Chester, 1817), a
man was called a bastard, and his mother a whore.

29  Starkie said that a prohibition would lie in such a case (*Slander and Libel*, 122),
and see R.H. Helmholz, *Roman Canon Law in Reformation England* (Cambridge
1990), 57, for the early modern period.

30  Kelly v. Batty (York, 1816), PP. The common law case is Grimes v. Lovel (1699),
1 Ld Raym 446. Askwith did announce his intention to appeal, but the defendant
died, and the suit abated. Act Book, Cons AB 106, 16 May and 20 June 1816

31  Wardrop v. Bulman (Carlisle, 1853), DRC 3/51 f. 28a, Birkett v. Heron (Durham,
1824)

32  Keelan v. Asprey (Llandaff, 1850), LL/CC/G/2131c, Price v. Thomings (Lichfield,
1824), Bowen v. Duckfield (St David's, 1835) ('damned poxy whore'), Hinder v.
Harper (Gloucester, 1823) ('damned poxy whore'), Rich v. Pugh (Llandaff, 1822)

33  Price v. Rudge (Hereford, 1819), HD4/53

34  Smart v. Heath (Gloucester, 1846), B4/1/1207, Edmunds v. Drew (Gloucester, 1841)

35  Edelstone v. Ellison (Chester, 1818) ('Thy daughter is a whore and she will marry
with the pox'), Kirkby v. Thompson (York, 1820) ('had given a young man the bad
disorder'), Hinder v. Harper (Gloucester, 1823) ('thee hast got it [the pox]'),
Boucher v. Forty (Gloucester, 1828) ('foul distemper'), Jones v. Townsend (Gloucester, 1835) ('Mrs Jones has got the pox in her throat'), Nash v. Jones (Gloucester,
1839) ('pull the handkerchief off thy face and show the holes in thy neck'), Hardcastle v. Willis (Gloucester, 1846) ('thee hast got the pox ... didn't I ... make up
some pills for thee'), Smart v. Heath (Gloucester, 1846) ('You are a nasty pox'd
arsed whore and the marks of it are in your face now and your children's faces'),
Hodges v. Baird (Gloucester 1849) ('rotten with the pox. She pulled up her clothes
and showed me her thighs. They were black and blue'), Philips v. Jones (St
David's, 1834) ('He gave you the pox and you gave it to your husband'), Rush v.
Woodcock (Norwich, 1842) ('she has been rode so often she has been poxed these
eight or ten years').

36  An altercation between Matilda Harper and Joseph Cooke in 1852 led to a suit and
counter-suit. Witnesses deposed to the following conversation: [Cooke:] 'I have
whored with you forty times. Damn my eyes to hell if I haven't. [Harper: What did
you ever give me for it?] I never gave you any thing for it, I had it upon tick.

[Harper: Was it at the time you had the bad disorder that you had to do with me?] It was, at the very time. [Harper: Then I suppose I stand a fairish chance of having it myself.] Damn thee didsn't have it? And it took me an hour and a half to scratch the scurf off your cunt before I could do it again. [Harper: Is it off your mother's face that you mean?] No – off thy cunt.' Harper was proved to have said, in reply to Cooke's assertion that he had whored with her twenty (or, according to another witness, forty) times, 'Aye and damn thee gave me the pox and it cost me twenty pounds to have it cured, and you went to London to have it cured and when you came back you had not got a prick bigger than my little finger.' Harper v. Cooke; Cooke v. Harper (Hereford, 1852), HD4/64

37  Dorney v. Webb (Bath and Wells, 1832). An extensive, accurate, and interesting account of this case appears in Polly Morris, 'Defamation and Sexual Reputation in Somerset 1733–1850,' unpublished PhD thesis (Warwick 1985), 459–95.

38  D/D/Cp 1832. Morris points out that the disease is often asymptomatic. 'Defamation and Sexual Reputation,' 482n41

39  Sentence D/D/Cp 1832 and Act Book, 7 July 1835, D/D/Ca 453. The case is further discussed at 37, below, from the point of view of truth as a justification.

40  Browne v. Fairhurst (Bath and Wells, 1850), D/D/Cp 1850. Salivation was an effect of mercury treatment, commonly given for syphilis. Perhaps 'wet sheets' also alludes to the effect of treatment.

41  Hill v. Prescott, Prescott v. Hill (Chester, 1823), EDC 5 (1824–5)

42  Sewell v. Lawrence (Lincoln, 1823), libels, box 59/11; also Balls v. Bailey (Norwich, 1841) (libel admitted after argument, but defendant ultimately dismissed: Act Book, 15 September 1841 and 28 February 1842)

43  Gregory v. David (Llandaff, 1852), LL/CC/G/2134c

44  Burdon v. Poole (Lichfield, 1838), B/C/5/1838

45  Castletine v. Dugdale (York, 1841)

46  Eldret v. Hare (Lincoln, 1821), cause papers, box 59/1, Act Book, 7 March 1822, Cj 49

47  Bach v. Engstrom (Hereford, 1822), HD4/56

**2: The Ecclesiastical Law**

1  Auctoritate Dei Patris (Council of Oxford, 1222), glossed by W. Lyndwood, *Provinciale* (1430), printed edition (Oxford 1679), ch. 1, note 1, above. See R.H. Helmholz, *Select Cases on Defamation to 1600* (London 1985), xxvi–xli, discussing (at xxxiv–xxxv) an alternative reading of the text; F.M. Powicke and C.R. Cheney, *Councils and Synods with Other Documents Relating to the English Church, II, AD 1205–1313*, 2 vols. (Oxford 1964), 1:107. This Constitution provides for excommunication, not for the 'mixed' civil and criminal suit brought by

the plaintiff in her own name, which was the only kind of suit in operation in the nineteenth century. See B.E. Ferme, 'William Lyndwood and the Provinciale: Canon Law in an Undivided Western Church' (1997), 4 Eccles LJ 615. Purgation is a process requiring a person accused to clear himself or herself by oath (his or her own or others').

2 Circumspecte agatis, 13 Edw. I c. 4, Powicke and Cheney, *Councils and Synods,* 2:974–5. See also Articuli cleri, 9 Edw. II c. 4.

3 Chaucer, *Canterbury Tales,* Friar's Tale, line 6

4 E. Gibson, *Codex Juris Ecclesiastici Anglicani* ... (London 1713). Abridgment by R. Grey, *A System of English Ecclesiastical Law,* 4th ed. (London 1743)

5 *Praxis Francisci Clerke,* 2nd ed. (London 1684), contains twelve articles dealing directly with defamation. See R.H. Helmholz, *Roman Canon Law in Reformation England* (Cambridge 1990), 128–31.

6 T. Oughton, *Ordo Judiciorum* (London 1728), J.T. Law, *Forms of Ecclesiastical Law* (London 1831), H. Conset, *Practice of the Spiritual or Ecclesiastical Courts,* 2nd ed. (London 1700), R. Burn, *Ecclesiastical Law,* 9th ed., by R. Phillimore (London 1842). Also Godolphin, *Repertorium Canonicum,* 3rd ed. (London 1683), J. Ayliffe, *Parergon Canonici Anglicani* (London 1726). Of lesser importance, W. Cockburn, *The Clerk's Assistant in the Practice of the Ecclesiastical Courts* (London 1800), P. Floyer, *The Proctor's Practice in the Ecclesiastical Courts* (London 1816), A. Browne, *A Compendious View of the Ecclesiastical Law of Ireland,* 2nd ed. (Dublin 1803), F.N. Rogers, *A Practical Arrangement of Ecclesiastical Law* (London 1849)

7 See J.H. Baker, *Monuments of Endlesse Labours* (London 1998), 75.

8 A. Waddilove, *A Digest of Cases Decided* ... (London 1849), and E. Maddy, *Digest of Cases Argued and Determined in the Arches and Prerogative Courts of Canterbury* (London 1835)

9 Askwith to Edmondson & Cowburn, 27 July 1837 (copy), in Spooner v. King (York, 1837), PP

10 Edmondson & Cowburn to Askwith, 30 January 1838, PP

11 Lack of precision and local variation were features of the law in earlier periods also; see Helmholz, *Select Cases on Defamation,* xxv, and *Roman Canon Law in Reformation England,* 18–19.

12 See 32, 56–7, 106, below.

13 For example, on truth as a justification. See 33–9, below.

14 Pilling v. Bradley: citation issued in Chester 15 January 1829 (Citation Book) and in York 2 April 1829 (Act Book). Askwith to Jenner, Bush & Jenner, Doctors' Commons, 11 April 1829, PCB. A copy of the reply is in Precedent Book P 39.

15 There is reference to the older practice in Prankard v. Deacle (1828), 1 Hag Ecc 169, 191–2, referring to a defamation case of 1732 in criminal form.

16  Ecclesiastical Courts Commission Report, PP 1831–2 xxiv, 13

17  Crompton v. Butler (1790), 1 Hag Con 460, a decision of Sir William Scott (later Lord Stowell) in the London Consistory Court, was almost always cited in this context. He said the same in Smith v. Watkins (1792), 1 Hag Con 467, though rejecting the libel in that case. For the early modern period, see Helmholz, *Roman Canon Law in Reformation England*, 67–9.

18  Porter v. Dent (Norwich, 1848), DN/CON/136

19  Harvey v. Campling (Norwich 1834), DN/CON/130

20  Asprey v. Keelan (Llandaff, 1850) defendant's interrogatory, LL/CC/G/2130b

21  Askwith to William Page, 18 November 1826 (copy), in Garside v. Anderson and Garside v. Beswick, PP

22  Daniel v. Ostell (Carlisle, 1844), where the plaintiff obtained sentence

23  Knaggs v. Dickinson (York, 1831), *Yorkshire Gazette*, 19 November 1831, 3b

24  Spooner v. King (York, 1837)

25  Askwith to Edmondson & Cowburn, 12 September 1837 (copy), advising that there was no defence. The argument that eventually succeeded is not mentioned in Askwith's notes for counsel. PP

26  Belk v. Messenger (Salisbury, 1816). But in Wetherherd v. Mason (York, 1817) a libel was admitted alleging the words, 'she is nothing better than a common prostitute.' The disposition of this case is unknown.

27  Ley v. Thomas (Bath and Wells, 1852), D/D/Cp 1852. 1851 census returns, 32b Bath, 6 Lansdown, 1B, pp. 20, 21, show that there were four daughters, aged sixteen, fifteen, nine, and five on 30 March 1851. The citation was issued on 13 January 1852. The defendant was curate at Trinity Church, Bath. *Clergy List* (London 1850)

28  See Helmholz, *Select Cases on Defamation*, xcii, and Smith v. Watkins (1792), 1 Hag Con 467, 468 (argument of Dr Swabey).

29  Wallis v. Cory (Exeter, 1828) ('worse than a strumpet' and named man 'romping with her when her husband was absent'), Derges v. Scott (Exeter, 1830) ('damned hell-fire wench' combined with references to specific man and occasion), Clayton v. Marshall (Richmond, 1819) ('she's thy fancy and she's Andrew's fancy')

30  'Fuck' and 'shag' are common.

31  Sheard v. Ramsden (Ripon, 1852), RD/AC/1/13

32  Pearson v. Purvis (York, 1825), notes for advocate and endorsement on advocate's brief, PP

33  Garside v. Ripley (York, 1826), PP

34  Taylor v. Davis (Chester, 1853), EDC 1 196, EDC 5 (1854–5). To similar effect are Orme v. Gibbon (Chester, 1818) ('her hand in a man's breeches' or – according to another witness – 'small clothes'), and Taylor v. Holt (Chester, 1836) ('kissing'), Bentley v. North (Ripon, 1848) (letting man 'touch that grand cock of hers'). A

copy of the Bill of Costs showing the disposition of this last case is in the Precedent Book P 35, ff. 136–44, Borthwick Institute, York.

35 Leatt v. Pearson (London, 1819), Pickering v. Bird (Worcester, 1828), Crosby v. England (York, 1820), Paul v. Forth (York, 1822), Robinson v. Sharp (York, 1824), Cheadle v. Spencer (York, 1826), Williams v. Hill (Gloucester, 1825), Cope v. Jackson (Hereford, 1834), Gooch v. Morley (Norwich, 1850), Crosbie v. Cooper (Lichfield, 1820), Gibson v. Stockbridge (Carlisle, 1843), Pattinson v. Hayton (Carlisle, 1839)

36 Moss v. Elleman (Hereford, 1831), Llewellin v. Eckley (Hereford, 1832), Balls v. Bailey (Norwich, 1841)

37 Roles v. Tuck (London, 1819), Guildhall 12,185/1, W. Blackstone, *Commentaries on the Laws of England*, 15th ed., vol. 3 (London 1809), 125, Thorley v. Kerry (1812), 4 Taunt 355, 365, Barnett v. Allen (1858), 1 F & F 125, 127, 3 H & N 376

38 Fortune v. Roberts (Exeter, 1820), CC 81

39 Swindley v. Kinsey (Chester, 1838)

40 Notes, probably for the use of counsel, by William Askwith, Harrison v. Leetham (Selby, 1821), PP. Selby was a peculiar (outside episcopal jurisdiction); the judge was one of the York advocates, Robert Sinclair.

41 Askwith to Parker, 24 May 1821, Draft Bill of Costs, PP

42 Harriet Johnson v. Charles Johnson (London, 1820). See discussion of Mary Johnson v. Harriet Johnson, 129, below.

43 After the introduction of oral evidence in 1854 such a defence was easier, and the defence did succeed in Carrick v. Beaty (Carlisle, 1854). See Deposition Book DRC/3/51 ff. 30 to 34, and Act Book, 8 November 1854, DRC/3/32.

44 Stephen Lushington, judge of the London Consistory Court, said in his capacity as Admiralty Court judge that this was his practice in salvage cases: The *Martha* (1859), Swab 489, 490.

45 There were some such cases, e.g., Livie v. MacIntosh (London, 1820), Craske v. Youell (Norwich, 1847).

46 Tocker v. Ayre (1821), 3 Phil 539, 541–2 (Arches Court on appeal from Exeter). The decision was affirmed by the High Court of Delegates, and was often cited in the courts of both provinces.

47 Askwith to Wilcock, 20 October 1827 (copy), in Wharton v. Winter (York, 1826), PP. Witnesses for the plaintiff gave evidence, and Askwith drafted a defensive allegation, but the defendant died before the case was disposed of, and the suit abated. Askwith gave similar advice in Ripley v. Garside (York, 1826), Askwith to William Page, 12 February 1827 (copy), PP. Defence witnesses were not produced, and Garside was admonished, but not ordered to pay costs, a result with which Askwith was pleased. Askwith to Page, 21 May 1827 (copy), PP. See Cons CP 1826/4, and Cons Abs Bk 25 May 1827.

48  Hauxwell v. Scott (York, 1835), Cons CP 1835/10 (defensive allegation). No costs were allowed: Cons Abs Bk 3 November 1836.

49  But there are several examples of the converse situation, i.e., accusations by a wife against her husband. See notes 80 and 82 below.

50  Hampden v. Eyton (1846), 4 Notes of Cases 549, 553. The case was appealed to Privy Council, and later compromised. Id., 555

51  Dickinson v. Hancock (Bristol, 1851), EP/J/2/7/12, judgment signed 'Joseph Phillimore'

52  See above, note 14.

53  27 Geo. III c. 44. The suit was dismissed on this ground in Coole v. Mountain (Bristol, 1830).

54  H. Coote, *The Practice of the Ecclesiastical Courts* (London 1847), 269

55  This is explained by Askwith in letters of 20 July 1826 in Garside v. Ripley (York, 1826), and 23 June 1830 (copies), in Kinder v. Dyson (York, 1830), PP.

56  Taylor v. Millard (Bath and Wells, 1835)

57  But admission of defensive allegations was discretionary; an allegation asserting that the plaintiff had defamed the defendant was rejected in Hall v. Daw (Gloucester, 1834), Act Book, 6 November 1834, GDR 356, and cause papers, B4/1/539.

58  Askwith to Hudson, 19 November 1832 (copy), PCB, in Briggs v. Dickinson (York, 1832). He said the same in almost identical language in Kinder v. Dyson (York, 1830), letter of 28 June 1830 (copy), PP.

59  Undated and unsigned. Cause papers in Twiddy v. Dawson (Norwich, 1820), DN/CON/125

60  Act Book, 11 July 1820, DN/ACT/105

61  Granville Vernon, the York chancellor, commented adversely on this aspect of Sodor and Man procedure (not referring to defamation cases in particular), Ecclesiastical Courts Commission Report, appendix A, 117–18.

62  Creer v. Christian (Sodor and Man, 1821), First Book of Petitions, 1821, Manx Museum. On penitential habit in the Isle of Man see 112, below.

63  Christian v. Creer (Sodor and Man, 1821), Second Book of Petitions, 1821

64  Ibid. The sentence, dated 22 June 1821, was rescinded on 21 September 1821.

65  See *Parliamentary Debates*, 26, 705 (1813), where attackers and defenders of the ecclesiastical courts both assumed that truth was no defence. For earlier periods see J.A. Brundage, *Medieval Canon Law* (London 1995), 91, R.H. Helmholz, *Select Cases on Defamation to 1600* (London 1985), xxx–xxxii, and *Roman Canon Law in Reformation England*, 64. Lyndwood, writing in the fifteenth century, said that truth was not a defence where the words were spoken maliciously (*Provinciale*, 346, gloss on 'malitiose'; malice was generally presumed without proof). Where the defendant reported facts that had been actually decided by a common law court

in bastardy proceedings, it was said that there might be a defence of justification: see Starkie, *Slander and Libel*, 124–5, Burn, *Ecclesiastical Law*, 136, citing two seventeenth-century cases.

66 Hampden v. Eyton (1846), 4 Notes of Cases 549n, 552 (Arches Court)

67 Abstract Book, Borthwick Institute, entries for 19 January 1840, and 30 June 1839 (plaintiff's costs exceeded £30); see also appendix A, below.

68 T. & C. Walker to Askwith, 28 December 1833, PP. See 43, below.

69 Askwith to T. & C. Walker, 30 December 1833 (copy), in Humble v. Gypson (York, 1833), PP. He made similar comments in a letter about Garside v. Ripley (York, 1826), qualified by a comment on costs: Askwith to Page, 31 January 1827 (copy), PP, and also Askwith to Garbutt, 5 September 1823 (copy), in Pearson v. Purvis, PP; also proctor's observations in Dobbins v. Hughes (Gloucester, 1826) ('does not lessen the offence but mitigates the punishment & instead of ordering penance the courts usually admonish not to offend the like again & condemn in taxed costs').

70 Askwith to T. & C. Walker, 30 December 1833 (copy). A qualification concerning costs follows.

71 6 & 7 Vic. c. 96; J. Spencer, 'Criminal Libel' [1977], Crim LR 383, 465

72 J. Borthwick, *A Treatise on the Law of Libel and Slander as Applied in Scotland in Criminal Prosecutions and in Actions of Damages* (Edinburgh 1826)

73 Report of Select Committee, House of Lords, on the Law of Defamation, HL Papers 1843, Sess. Pap. 18, reprinted PP 1843 v, 259

74 Libel Act, 1843, 6 & 7 Vic. c. 96, s. 6

75 Lord Brougham, over-egging the pudding, as he sometimes did, supposed a defendant blackmailing the plaintiff for his own sexual purposes. Report of Select Committee, supra note 73, p. 15

76 France v. Aaron (York, 1838; depositions transcribed in appendix A, below), Smith v. Whitter (Chester, 1817)

77 See also chapter 9, below.

78 Joseph Phillimore to John Clifton, 17 September 1844, in Challingworth v. Bowers (Worcester, 1844), 797.69/2631

79 Dorney v. Webb (Bath and Wells, 1832), D/D/Cp 1832. Salkeld v. Pattinson (Carlisle, 1854), DRC/3/51 ff. 41–2 (Deposition Book)

80 Richards v. Clark (London, 1824), Guildhall, 12,185/2

81 Penance was waived by the plaintiff. Assignation Book, 11 June 1825, X19/185

82 Other cases of accusations by a wife against her husband are Llewellyn v. Richards (Llandaff, 1815), Jones v. Watkins (Llandaff, 1819), Asprey v. Keelan (Llandaff, 1850), Moss v. Winkworth (Salisbury, 1827), Pilling v. Bradley (York, 1820),

Dauncey v. French (Gloucester, 1815), Powell v. Probert (Hereford, 1816), Pask v. Presely (Lincoln, 1823), and see 29–30, above, and 143, 175, below.

83 *Mirror of Parliament*, 1835, 309b (12 March 1835)

84 Roberts v. Cornell (London, 1834), cause papers, Guildhall, 12,185/3, Assignation Book, GLRO, X19/188, 22 May 1835. See also Fitzjohn v. Hayes (Peterborough, 1830) (refusal to apologize on ground that words true), King v. Hall (London, 1830) ('there is no harm in telling the truth I hope').

85 Attacks on the plaintiff's reputation were made, for example, in France v. Aaron (York, 1838) (baptismal certificate of illegitimate child attached; see appendix A, below), Smith v. James Whitter (Chester, 1817), Hadley v. Whittaker (Chester, 1825), Dobbins v. Hughes (Gloucester, 1827), Sharpe v. Dauncey (Gloucester, 1849), Bannister v. Tillett (London, 1840), Keelan v. Asprey (Llandaff, 1850), Spooner v. King (York, 1837), Foster v. Sixsmith (Chester, 1834) (nominal costs), Swindley v. Kinsey (Chester, 1838) (nominal costs), Wickham v. Lockyer (Bath and Wells, 1836), Burroughs v. Dutton (Gloucester 1825), Green v. Green (Gloucester 1837) (no costs), Hodges v. Baird (Gloucester, 1849), and Powell v. Probert (Hereford, 1816). Defensive allegations of prior unchastity were rejected in Clayton v. Marshall (Richmond, 1819), Wright v. Williams (St Asaph, 1838), and Biffen v. Lawley (Bath and Wells, 1835).

86 Askwith to T. & C. Walker, 30 December 1833 (copy), PP

87 Dorney v. Webb (Bath and Wells, 1832)

88 This was the 'old' bastardy law, which worked very effectively, from the mother's point of view, as the depositions in several defamation cases demonstrate. See U. Henriques, 'Bastardy and the New Poor Law,' *Past and Present*, 37 (1967), 103–29.

89 Françoise Barret-Ducrocq, *Love in the Time of Victoria* (1989; Harmondsworth 1992), in her study of the petitions of women seeking admission for illegitimate children to the Foundling Hospital, shows that seduction under promise of marriage was considered the most respectable explanation of the circumstances.

90 Dorney v. Webb (Bath and Wells, 1832), D/D/Cp 1832. See Polly Morris, 'Defamation and Sexual Reputation in Somerset 1733–1850,' unpublished PhD thesis (Warwick 1985), 483.

91 Payne v. Rowley (Bristol, 1842), Act Book, 21 December 1842, EP/J/1/44. Payne's witnesses said that Rowley had said that her husband had 'cohabited' with this man's sister; the interrogatories suggested, not without some plausibility, that she had said 'corresponded.' Cause papers, EP/J/2/7/5

92 Other cases of this sort are discussed at 175, below.

93 Craske v. Henry Youell (Norwich, 1846). A separate suit, also unsuccessful, was brought by Craske against William Youell (Norwich, 1846), DN/CON/137.

94 W. White, *History Gazetteer and Directory of Norfolk* (Norwich 1845), under

headings 'Yarmouth,' 'Gardeners &c,' 'Youell & Co., (nurserymen and florists to Her Majesty)'

95 *Norwich Mercury*, 17 July 1847, 3a

96 Ibid.

97 Lyndwood took the same view in the fifteenth century. See Helmholz, *Select Cases on Defamation*, xxxv.

98 Tocker v. Ayre (1821), 3 Phil 539, 541 (Arches Court on appeal from Exeter; Sir J. Nicholl)

99 Bonwell v. Kent (Winchester, 1824), cause papers, 21M65/C9/73

100 Marsh v. Travers (Norwich, 1846), DN/CON/137

101 Lord Northhampton's Case (1613), 12 Co Rep 132, McGregor v. Thwaites (1824), 3 B & C 24, Starkie, *Slander and Libel*, 329–40 (recognizing the rule while disapproving it). The contrary decision in McPherson v. Daniels (1829), 10 B & C 263 was later taken to have altered the law on the point (Odgers, *Libel*, 6th ed., 145), but the rule was thought by Jenner Fust still to be the law in 1846. See Collis v. Bate, below.

102 Kirkby v. Thompson (York, 1820), Roberts v. Gilpin (Hereford, 1828), Bannister v. Tillett (London, 1840), Marsh v. Travers (Norwich, 1846)

103 Kirkby v. Thompson, supra (defendant's and attorney's affidavits to this effect), Browning v. Mitchell (Gloucester, 1838) (defendant expected release from suit on giving up author), Burch v. Brown (Peterborough, 1831) ('I will sooner lie in gaol and rot than give up my author')

104 The census return shows that Caroline Bate was twenty-one in 1851. HO 107, 2047, f. 530

105 Collis v. Bate (1846), 4 Notes of Cases 540, 546 (Arches Court), LPL H 694. A further appeal to the Privy Council was abandoned. Arches Assignation Book, LPL, Aaa 47, and *Return of All Appeals in Ecclesiastical Causes 1832 to Present*, PP 1866 lv, 51, 63. In Bannister v. Tillett (London, 1840) an assertion in the libel, that the defendant had falsely named an informant, was rejected. Assignation Book, 2 June 1840, X19/190, and cause papers, Guildhall, 12,185/5

106 Wooldridge to instructing attorney, addressee not named, n.d. (copy), in Morton v. Christie (Winchester, 1830), 21M65/C9/579

107 Act Book, 17 June 1831, 21M65/C2/109

108 Ecclesiastical Courts Commission Report, appendix A, 61 (evidence of William Pulley)

109 Russell v. Bentham (1812), 4 Notes of Cases 547n

110 Hampden v. Eyton (letters of request from Lichfield, 1846), 4 Notes of Cases 549n, 552–3

111 'ut quia vocat quis aliquem latronem, perjurum, homicidam, vel adulterum, & hoc dicit in judicio per viam accusationis, vel denunciationis, & id probaverit, non

incidit in hanc poenam. ... In his enim casibus non est praesumenda malitia.'
Lyndwood, *Provinciale*, 346, Auctoritate Dei Patris, gloss on 'malitiose.' See
Helmholz, *Select Cases on Defamation*, xxxiv.

112 She said that after she saw the father and daughter in bed 'she went down and
went after her work.' The time was 6.30 a.m.

113 Todd v. Freeman (Norwich, 1820), cause papers, DN/CON/125, Act Book,
10 July 1821, DN/ACT/105

114 See Helmholz, *Roman Canon Law*, 66n.

115 Canon 115, *Constitutions and Canons Ecclesiastical* (reprinted London 1908)

116 Roberts v. Gilpin (Hereford), Dismissory Sentence 29 October 1829 (the omission
of costs may suggest that the words were proved, but another possibility is that the
defendant did not demand costs: there is no deletion of words in the sentence as
was common where costs were asked for but refused), cause papers, HD4/58,
Bishop's Act Book, 1827, HD4/1, 17 September 1829

117 Daveney v. Taylor (Norwich, 1842), cause papers, DN/CON/135, Act Book,
22 August 1842, ACT 106. See also Ley v. Thomas (Bath and Wells, 1852), 28,
above, where two suits against a clergyman were dismissed, primarily on the
ground that the words used were not defamatory, but perhaps secondarily because
they were spoken to the plaintiffs' father by way of admonition.

118 Bates v. Williams (Hereford, 1825), HD4/57

119 Stroud v. Churches (Bath and Wells, 1834), cause papers, D/D/Cp 1834, Act
Book, 20 January 1835, D/D/Ca 453

120 Humble v. Gypson (York, 1833), Cons CP 1833/2. The case was settled, Abstract
Book, 12 June 1834.

121 Lowthian v. Crook (Chester, 1815), Defensive Allegation and Sentence, cause
papers, EDC 5 (1816–17)

122 See 38–9, above.

123 Craske v. William Youell (Norwich, 1846), cause papers, DN/CON/137

124 *Norwich Mercury*, 17 July 1847, 3a

125 E.g., Bastow v. Bakes (York, 1817), Cons CP 1817/1

126 H.C. Coote, *The Practice of the Ecclesiastical Courts* (London 1847), 271 (form
of sentence transcribed in appendix A, below)

127 Lyndwood, *Provinciale*, 346 (gloss on 'malitiose': 'An autem malitia praesuma-
tur'). See Helmholz, *Select Cases on Defamation*, xxxiv.

128 Collis v. Bate (1846), 4 Notes of Cases 540, 541 (Arches Court)

129 Payne v. Rowley (Bristol, 1841). See 37–8, above.

130 Brief to advocate in Briggs v. Dickinson (York, 1832), PCB

131 Askwith to Hudson, 2 February 1833 (copy), PCB

132 Southwood v. Halford (Gloucester, 1848), B4/1/114, Act Book 19 September
1849, GDR 364

133  Stubbs v. Bradley (York, 1841), *Yorkshire Gazette*, 30 July 1842, *York Courant*, 4 August 1842

134  Ecclesiastical Courts Commission Report, appendix A, 127

135  See counsel's argument in Hampden v. Eyton (1846), 4 Notes of Cases 549n, 551: 'There is no precedent for such a defence as that set up in this Allegation, "I was provoked". If provocation were proved, it will not protect a party using defamatory words.'

136  Askwith to Hudson, 19 November 1832, in Briggs v. Dickinson, PCB. Almost identical language appears in a letter of 28 June 1830 (copy) in Kinder v. Dyson (York, 1830), PP, and very similar language in a letter of 10 May 1833 (copy) in Forster v. Creaser (York, 1833), PCB.

137  Askwith to Garbutt, 2 August 1825 (copy), in Pearson v. Purvis (York, 1825), PP

138  Ellis v. Stead (York, 1821), Wharton v. Winter (York, 1826), Kinder v. Dyson (York, 1826), Biffen v. Lawley (Bath and Wells, 1835), Morton v. Christie Winchester, 1830)

139  France v. Aaron (York, 1838)

140  Taylor v. Millard (Bath and Wells, 1835), Act Book, 12 July 1836, D/D/Ca 454, and cause papers, D/D/Cp 1835. An account of the case appears in Morris, 'Defamation and Sexual Reputation,' 566–72.

141  Edmunds v. Drew (Gloucester, 1841) (theft), Allpress v. Reeve, Townley v. Reeve, Whittaker v. Reeve (Norwich, 1840) ('thief, robber, and bugger'), Holmes v. Smith (York, 1820), Brook v. Sykes (York, 1824), Etty v. Kneeshaw (York, 1838), Bateman v. Winn (York, 1840) ('hypocrite and liar')

142  Jones v. Davies (St David's, 1850)

143  Taylor v. Grace (Chester, 1815) ('whoremaster'), and see 152–5, below.

144  Allpress v. Reeve, etc. (Norwich, 1840), Dickinson v. Hancock (Bristol, 1851), Jenkins v. Middleton (Gloucester, 1828), Boothman v. Duxbury (Chester, 1821)

145  Briggs v. Dickinson (York, 1832) (defendant's wife insulted), Crosby v. England (York, 1820)

146  Crosby v. England (York, 1820), Cons CP 1820/8, Southwood v. Halford (Gloucester, 1838)

147  Robinson v. Sharp (York, 1824), Cons CP 1824/3

148  Watkins v. Melling (Hereford, 1819)

149  Hooley v. Lumbers (Chester, 1833); also Ireland v. Jones (Gloucester, 1829)

150  Bastow v. Bakes (York, 1817), Triggs v. Cowmeadow (Gloucester, 1826), Bunce v. Pennington (Chester, 1833), Southwood v. Halford (Gloucester, 1838)

151  Whittle v. West (Bath and Wells, 1831), D/D/Cp 1831. See 185, below.

152  Harper v. Cooke (Hereford, 1853), HD 4/64

153  Humble v. Gypson (York, 1833), Cons CP 1833/2

154 See also Etty v. Kneeshaw (York, 1819), Aspinall v. Bell (York, 1838) ('kiss my arse').

155 Wadley v. Matthews (Worcester, 1815), 797.69/2625

156 Haigh v. Willett (Chester, 1827)

157 Binnington v. Watson (York, 1816) (plaintiff took off her pattens and assaulted defendant), Ellis v. Stead (York, 1821) (defendant's husband doused with water), Kinder v. Dyson (York, 1826) (striking defendant's husband), Simpson v. Bullimore (Norwich, 1824) (threat to throw water on defendant), Aspinall v. Bell (York, 1838) (striking defendant with poker), Hutchinson v. Jeremiah Proctor (York, 1838) (scratching faces of defendant and his son), Othick v. Ellison (York Dean and Chapter, 1829) (plaintiff convicted of assault), Smith v. Jane Whitter (Chester, 1817) (striking defendant, tearing her cap and bruising her face, and dousing defendant's child with water), Burroughs v. Dutton (Gloucester, 1826) (beating defendant's children)

## 3: The Courts and Their Officers

1 Ecclesiastical Courts Commission Report, appendix D, PP 1831–2 xxiv, 567

2 Office of the judge promoted by Betsy Beales v. Sarah Wallis (Norwich, 1824), Act Book, 2 February 1825, DN/ACT 105, and DN/CON/126

3 Ecclesiastical Courts Commission Report, 552 and 564

4 Id., appendix D, 556, 561

5 Id., appendix D, 554–61

6 Id., appendix D, no. 6, 552

7 E.g., Harrison v. Leetham (Selby peculiar, 1820), where a York advocate was judge, and York proctors participated. See Askwith's correspondence in PP.

8 Of the 298 significavits in defamation cases for the period 1815–39, preserved at the PRO, 25 were issued by archidiaconal or peculiar courts. PRO C207/6–11

9 *Returns of all Courts Empowered to grant Probate of Wills ...*, PP 1828 xx, 751

10 These hypotheses are confirmed by the surviving significavits. In the period 1815–29, 18 of 171 were issued by inferior courts; in the period 1830–9, 7 of 127. The significavits after 1839 are not uniformly preserved. PRO C207/6–11

11 In the Isle of Man the bishop still acted personally in some cases.

12 Dr Lushington was chancellor both of London and Rochester, and is counted here twice.

13 *The Clerical Guide and Ecclesiastical Directory* (London 1836), n.p. Ripon, refounded in that year, is not included in the list.

14 *Clergy List* (London 1848), 234–45

15 As in Chester in 1830, where the chancellor was eighty-five years old and 'incapable of attending personally.' Ecclesiastical Courts Commission Report, appendix C, 176 (evidence of W. Ward)

16 Canon 128, *Constitutions and Canons Ecclesiastical* (reprinted London 1908), required that surrogates should be clergy or graduates and 'favourers of true religion.' In London they were the advocates in Doctors' Commons. In Chester they were exclusively clergymen. Ecclesiastical Courts Commission Report, appendix C, 185 (evidence of W. Ward)

17 J.T. Law, *Forms of Ecclesiastical Law* (London 1831), preface. James Thomas Law, 1790–1876 (*DNB*)

18 See 35–6, above.

19 Phillimore to John Clifton, 21 February 1846, Act Book, 794. 011/2495. The case referred to is Bate v. Collis (Worcester 1845), Phillimore's objection being to admission of a defensive allegation after publication of the depositions. On this aspect of the procedure, see 70, below.

20 Act Book, 26 July 1818, Cons AB 106

21 Ecclesiastical Courts Commission Report, appendix A, 185, q. 275 (evidence of W. Ward)

22 Southwood v. Halford (Gloucester, 1848), bill of costs (£12 was alleged to have been wasted) and aggrieved letter from plaintiff's solicitor (James Smith) to the proctor (Smallridge), 14 May 1849, B4/1/114

23 Canon 127, *Constitutions and Canons Ecclesiastical*

24 Oughton, Cockburn, and Browne. See chapter 2, note 6, above.

25 Ecclesiastical Courts Commission, appendix A, 176–8

26 Law, *Forms of Ecclesiastical Law*, preface

27 Id., 6

28 Ecclesiastical Courts Commission Report, appendix A, 133 (evidence of G. Vernon)

29 Ecclesiastical Courts Commission Report, appendix A, 57 (evidence of J.W. Freshfield), 122 (evidence of G.V. Vernon), 143 (evidence of W. Adams)

30 Tocker v. Ayre (1821), 3 Phil 539 (Arches Court), Courtail v. Homfray (1828), 2 Hag Ecc 1 (Arches Court), Collis v. Bate (1846), 4 Notes of Cases 540 (Arches Court), and Hampden v. Eyton (Arches Court, 1846), 4 Notes of Cases 549n

31 Canon 127, *Constitutions and Canons Ecclesiastical*

32 Charles Dickens, *David Copperfield*, chapter 23

33 *Returns respecting Jurisdiction, Records, Emoluments and Fees of Ecclesiastical Courts in England and Wales*, PP 1830 xix, 186. See also *Comparative Statement of the Salaries etc.*, PP 1843 xxx, 409.

34 Ibid. York is shown at £2,191, which probably included Vernon's income from the prerogative court.

35 *Returns of all Courts Empowered to grant Probate of Wills ...*, PP 1828 xx, 751, 834

36 Askwith, letter of 19 November 1832, in Briggs v. Dickinson (York, 1832), PP

37 Askwith, letter of 18 November 1826, in Garside v. Ripley (York, 1826), PP; letter

of 28 June 1830, in Kinder v. Dyson (York, 1830); letter of 10 May 1833, in Forster v. Creaser (York, 1833)

38  *Yorkshire Gazette*, 19 November 1831 (Smith v. Day, York, 1831)

39  *Yorkshire Gazette*, 9 February 1833, 4b (Briggs v. Dickinson, York, 1832)

40  Ecclesiastical Courts Commission Report, appendix A, 127

41  Hutchinson v. J. and S. Proctor (York, 1838), *York Courant*, 2 August 1838, 4d, *Yorkshire Gazette*, 28 July 1838, 8d

42  Ecclesiastical Courts Commission Report, appendix A, 172 (evidence of William Ward)

43  Id. at 113 (evidence of Matthew Marsh)

44  Acquisition List, Borthwick Institute, York

45  *Yorkshire Gazette*, 3 February 1838, 3c

46  Hutchinson v. Proctor (York, 1838), Cons CP 1838/6 and 7

47  Letter of 2 April 1830 (copy), in Pilling v. Bradley (York, 1829), PP. Similarly in Etty v. Kneeshaw (York, 1819) 'the reason assigned by Mr Vernon the Chancellor ... was that Kneeshaw certainly did not come into Court with very pure hands.' Askwith to Stockton, 4 November 1820 (copy), PP. See 19, above.

48  Askwith to Bromby, 14 October 1824 (copy), in Foster v. Stubbing (York, 1823), PP

49  Foster v. Stubbing (York, 1823), Cons CP 1823/2

50  The defendant's father was 'an opulent brewer.' Askwith sought to take advantage of this consideration when acting for married women as defendants: in Forster v. Creaser (York, 1833), he said that the burden of costs, if awarded, would fall on the 'inoffending husband.' Remarks for Advocate, PCB. See 108–9, below.

51  Askwith to Bromby, 22 December 1824, PP, Abstract Book, 9 December 1824

52  *Returns respecting Jurisdiction, Records, Emoluments and Fees of Ecclesiastical Courts in England and Wales*, PP 1830 xix, 186

53  *Returns of all Courts Empowered to grant Probate of Wills ...*, PP 1828 xx, 751, 834 (15s. in one case)

54  Ecclesiastical Courts Commission Report, appendix A, 118 (evidence of G. Vernon)

55  In London advocates were required; see Ecclesiastical Courts Commission Report, appendix A, 142 (evidence of W. Adams).

56  Milden to Charles Wooldridge, 11 March 1825, in Bonwell v. Kent (Winchester, 1824), 21M65/C9/73

57  Robinson v. Sharp (York, 1824), Cons CP 1824/3

58  Tomlinson v. Newton (York, 1825), PP (£3.0.8 in bill of £7.18.0)

59  Letter of 17 February 1830 (copy), in Pilling v. Bradley (York, 1829), PP

60  Askwith to Messrs T. & C. Walker, 15 July 1833 (copy), in Forster v. Creaser (York, 1833), PCB

61  Letter of 29 November 1833 (copy), in Humble v. Gypson (York, 1833), PP

62  Letter of 30 December 1833 (copy), PP

63  Humble v. Gypson (York, 1833), PP (draft allegation with Strickland's comments), and Cons CP 1833/2, and Abstract Book, 12 June 1834

64  Ecclesiastical Courts Commission Report, appendix A, 133 (evidence of G. Vernon)

65  Youngs v. Bailey (Norwich, 1826), Bill of Costs – two opinions on separate points

66  Hall v. Daw (Gloucester, 1834)

67  Pearson v. Purvis (York, 1825), Bear v. Bignell (Winchester, 1824), Bannister v. Tillett (London, 1840)

68  William Moore to Charles Wooldridge, 4 November 1824, in Bonwell v. Kent (Winchester, 1824), 21M65/C9/73

69  Ecclesiastical Courts Commission Report, appendix A, 186–7 (evidence of W. Ward)

70  *Abstract Returns of the Number of Proctors now practising etc.*, PP 1843 xl, 179. In 1830, there were four proctors at Salisbury, three at Oxford, and five at Chester. Ecclesiastical Courts Commission Report, appendix A (evidence of Marsh, Phillimore, and Ward)

71  Canon 129, *Constitutions and Canons Ecclesiastical*

72  E.g., Campbell v. Barrow (Bristol, 1838), Act Book, 6 October 1838 EP/J/1/44 (proctors heard on both sides on admission of libel), Bate v. Collis (Worcester, 1845), Act Book, 5 March 1846 (admission of allegation)

73  Ecclesiastical Courts Commission Report, appendix A, 87–8 (evidence of George Martin, chancellor of Exeter). In Chester written arguments were not offered, and viva voce argument was admitted 'to a certain degree,' 178 (evidence of W. Ward).

74  Ibid., 187 (evidence of W. Ward)

75  Wallis v. Cory (Exeter, 1828), CC 81/81A

76  Ecclesiastical Courts Commission Report, appendix A, 97 (evidence of George Martin, chancellor of Exeter)

77  Askwith to Hudson, 23 November 1832 (copy), in Briggs v. Dickinson (York, 1832), PCB

78  Askwith, letter of 23 July 1823 (copy), in Foster v. Stubbing (York, 1823), PP. Similar advice is given in Wharton v. Winter (York, 1826), Garside v. Ripley (York, 1826), Wilson v. Bowness (York, 1826), Briggs v. Dickinson (York, 1823), Kinder v. Dyson (York, 1839), and Humble v. Gypson (York, 1832), PP.

79  Pearson v. Purvis (York, 1825), Spooner v. King (York, 1837)

80  Wharton v. Winter (York, 1826), Garside v. Ripley (York, 1826), Humble v. Gypson (York, 1833), Forster v. Creaser (York, 1833), PP

81  Askwith to Stockton, 18 October 1820 (copy), in Etty v. Kneeshaw (York, 1820), PP

82  Askwith to Page, 28 April 1827 (copy), in Garside v. Ripley (York, 1826), PP
83  Askwith to [addressee unnamed], 26 May 1827 (copy), in Wilson v. Bowness (York, 1826), PP
84  Askwith to Andrew, 2 April 1827 (copy), in Trattles v. Trattles (York 1827), PP. To the same effect is a letter to Bromby, 22 December 1824 (copy), in Foster v. Stubbing (York, 1824), PP.
85  Calvert v. Chapman (York, 1825), Abstract Book, 9 June 1825
86  Askwith to Page, n.d. (copy), in Calvert v. Chapman (York, 1825), PP
87  Letter from James Walker, addressee not named, 2 February 1825 (copy), in Stredder v. Rowell (Peterborough, 1825), X953
88  Interrogatory in Cheadle v. Spencer (York, 1826), Cons CP 1826/3
89  Chesworth v. Evans (Chester, 1838), EDC 5 (1838–9)
90  Askwith to Edmondson & Cowburn, 1 February 1838 (copy), in Spooner v. King (York, 1837), PP
91  Edmondson & Cowburn to Askwith, 27 January 1838, in Spooner v. King
92  Same to same, 30 January 1838, in Spooner v. King
93  Same to same, 8 February 1838, in Spooner v. King
94  John Robinson to Askwith, 29 January 1827, and other correspondence in Wilson v. Bowness (York, 1826), PP
95  J.H. Bromby, of Hull, in Musgrave v. Abbey (York, 1819), and Foster v. Stubbings (York, 1823), and J. Andrew, of Whitby, in Trattles v. Trattles (York, 1827), PP
96  Bromby to Askwith, 31 May 1823, in Foster v. Stubbings (York, 1823), PP
97  Page to Askwith, 28 April 1825, in Calvert v. Chapman (York, 1825), PP
98  Askwith to Andrew, 2 April 1827 (copy), in Trattles v. Trattles (York, 1827), PP
99  Bromby to Askwith, 11 January 1820, in Musgrave v. Abbey (York, 1819), PP
100 Humble v. Gypson (York, 1833), Pilling v. Bradley (York, 1829), Briggs v. Dickinson (York, 1832), Spooner v. King (York, 1837), Harrison v. Leetham (Selby peculiar, 1820), Etty v. Kneeshaw (York, 1819), PP

## 4: Patterns of Litigation

1  See 113–15, below.
2  James v. Smith (Arches Court, 1848)
3  Cooper v. Gunton (Arches Court, 1852), LPL, H 795
4  Ecclesiastical Courts Commission Report, PP 1831–2 xxiv, 63
5  Roberts v. Jones (Llandaff, 1853), LL/C/G/2142e. The volume of defamation litigation in Llandaff had dropped sharply after 1834 (ten cases in 1834; five in each of the two following years, and fewer than two annually thereafter).
6  Askwith to Hudson, 19 November 1832 (copy), in Briggs v. Dickinson (York, 1832), PCB. See 32, above.

7  See H.W. Arthurs, *Without the Law: Administrative Justice and Legal Pluralism in Nineteenth-Century England* (Toronto, 1985).

8  Enumeration abstracts for populations of Norwich, Yarmouth, and Ipswich in 1841; Ecclesiastical Revenues Commission Report, PP 1835 xxi, 12 for population of dioceses in 1835

9  Polly Morris, 'Defamation and Sexual Reputation in Somerset, 1733–1850,' unpublished PhD thesis (Warwick, 1985), table V, D

10  There are a number of cases in which clergy attempted to settle defamation disputes: J. Crosley to Askwith, 17 February 1819, in Bastow v. Bakes (York, 1818), PP, Bear v. Bignell (Winchester, 1831), Browning v. Mitchell (Gloucester, 1838), Woodhouse v. Williams (Gloucester, 1845), Mosley v. Mosley (Peterborough, 1836). Woodforde, *Diary of a Country Parson* (London 1924–31), entry for 17 November 1794, considered a defamation suit 'a foolish kind of affair between the parties, and the expenses of which to both must be high,' showing that his inclination was to settle it if he could.

11  Norwich, cause papers. Morris similarly found that in Bath and Wells, over a longer period, in 87 per cent of the cases the litigants were from the same parish. 'Defamation and Sexual Reputation in Somerset 1733–1850,' 312

12  Prankard v. Deacle (1828), 1 Hag Ecc 169, 189

13  R.H. Helmholz, *Roman Canon Law in Reformation England* (Cambridge 1990), 18–19

14  Weight v. Hills (Gloucester, 1835). The citation was immediately thrown into the street. Act Book, 12 March 1835, GDR 356

15  Webb v. Smith (Gloucester, 1834)

16  Leverett v. Davy (Norwich, 1822), DN/CON/126

17  Act Book, 10 June 1822, Norwich, DN/ACT/105

18  Askwith to Garbutt, 4 May 1821 (copy), in Smith v. Wardle (York, 1821), PP

19  E.g., Hall v. Fenn (Norwich, 1817), Act Book, 23 December 1817, 24 February 1818, and succeeding entries. DN/ACT/104

20  E.g., Norwich: 3 of 126. See table 6, below.

21  See 1 Hag Con 171n, Ecclesiastical Courts Commission Report, appendix A, 177 (evidence of W. Ward), Moxham v. Hely (Salisbury, 1825), Act Book, 20 October 1825, D1/39/1/75, Shephard & Isherwood to L. Dally, 15 August 1816 (copy of extract of letter describing London practice), Chichester, Ep1/15/1.

22  Rules and Orders, at beginning of Act Book, Norwich, DN/ACT/105

23  Askwith to Page, 24 November 1826 (copy), in Garside v. Anderson (York, 1826), PP, and Abstract Book, and Act Book, Cons AB 106 (dismissed with costs of 8s. 4d.), Askwith to Iveson & Kidd, 28 June 1830 (copy), in Kinder v. Dyson (York, 1830), PP

24  Askwith to Garbutt, 5 September 1825 (copy), in Pearson v. Purvis (York, 1825),

PP. Similar advice was given in Kinder v. Dyson, mentioning figures of £7 or £8 in case of an affirmative issue, and £20 or £30 otherwise (York, 1830), PP.

25 See 158–60, 180–1, below.

26 Act Books, Carlisle, DRC/3/26 to 32. Dismissal meant termination of the suit, not necessarily a decision favourable to the defendant.

27 Letter to J. Huckwell, 9 July 1852, in Gregory v. David (Llandaff, 1852), LL/CC/G/2134j

28 John Bush to Edward Davies, 26 January 1823, in Vigar v. Glass (Salisbury, 1827), D1/41/4/11

29 Act Book, 28 January 1828, 15 March 1828, D1/39/1/75

30 Weed v. Knight (Peterborough, 1823), Act Book, 16 October 1823, Wood v. Sanwell (Peterborough, 1825), Act Book, 4 August 1825, ML 718

31 Askwith to J. Wilcock, 24 October 1827 (copy), in Wharton v. Winter (York, 1827), PP

32 Askwith to T. & C. Walker, 19 March 1834, in Humble v. Gypson (York, 1833), PP

33 Same to same, 2 April 1834 (copy), PP. Similar advice was given in Wharton v. Winter (York, 1826), PP.

34 Same to same, 2 May 1834 (copy), PP

35 T. & C. Walker to Askwith, 7 May 1834, PP

36 Askwith to Edmondson & Cowburn, 9 February 1838 (copy), in Spooner v. King (York, 1837), PP

37 Gates to Atkinson, 24 November 1826 (copy), estimated five or six months (Peterborough), X953 (names of prospective parties not recorded).

38 Askwith to Bromby, 6 January 1824, in Foster v. Stubbing (York, 1823), PP

39 Abstract Book, Borthwick Institute, York

40 Askwith to T. & C. Walker, 14 April 1834 (copy), in Humble v. Gypson (York, 1833), PP

41 Bardsley the elder v. Bardsley the younger, Bardsley the elder v. Anna Maria Bardsley (Chester, 1829), EDC 5 (1828–9)

42 Dorney v. Webb (Bath and Wells, 1832), Waterson v. Anison (Norwich, 1842), Shreve v. Wright (Norwich, 1849), Craske v. Henry Youell, Craske v. William Youell (allegations rejected) (Norwich, 1846)

43 Extensive allegations occur in Bardsley the elder v. Bardsley the younger, Bardsley the elder v. Anna Maria Bardsley (Chester, 1829), Ferris v. Wickham and Wickham v. Lockyer (Bath and Wells, 1836), Cope v. Jackson (Hereford, 1834), Dorney v. Webb (Bath and Wells, 1832).

44 See comments of Dr Lushington in a matrimonial case, Davidson v. Davidson (1856), Deane 132, 167.

45 The Chancery Examiners' Office was also there. H. Horwitz, *Chancery Equity Records and Proceedings 1600–1800* (London 1995), 18

46  Rose v. Knight (London, 1831), Assignation Book, GLR. X 19/187, cause papers, Guildhall, 12,185/3, *The Times*, 30 April 1832, 3f, 8 June 1832, 4d

47  Margaret Latham v. Charlotte Meakin (Chester, 1825), Margaret Latham v. Joseph Meakin (Chester, 1825), Charlotte Meakin v. Robert Latham (Chester, 1826). A citation was also issued against Richard Latham, but this was probably an error for 'Robert.'

48  Whittaker v. Reeve, Townley v. Reeve, Allpress v. Reeve, Reeve v. Allpress (Norwich, 1841)

49  Hudson v. Aspinall (Chester, 1827); Aspinall v. Hudson (Chester, 1828), Marshall v. Joynes; Joynes v. Marshall (Chester, 1830), Fisher v. Tozer; Tozer v. Fisher (Bath and Wells, 1828), Savory v. Spoor; Spoor v. Savory (Norwich, 1828 and 1829)

50  Healey v. Keeling; Keeling v. Healey (Chester, 1816), Bardsley v. Bardsley (Chester, 1829 – three cases), Board v. Hill; Hill v. Board (Bath and Wells, 1843), Leach v. Spurr; Spurr v. Leach (Chester, 1826), Jenkins v. Priest; Priest v. Jenkins (Gloucester, 1848)

51  Also Reeves v. Scanlon; Scanlon v. Reeves (Gloucester, 1826)

52  Elizabeth Russell v. Judith Wigg; Sarah Wigg v. James Russell (Norwich, 1826 and 1827), Wickham v. Lockyer; Ferris v. Wickham (Bath and Wells, 1836)

53  Bardsley the elder v. Bardsley the younger; Bardsley the elder v. Anna Maria Bardsley (Chester, 1829), Cooke v. Harper (Hereford, 1852)

54  Keelan v. Asprey (Llandaff, 1850), LL/CC/G/2131c

55  William Moore to Charles Wooldridge, 4 November 1824, in Bonwell v. Kent (Winchester, 1824), 21M65/C9/73. In Jones v. Townsend (Gloucester, 1835) the prayer was that 'the defendant be assigned to exhibit personal answers to all such matters as are not of a criminal nature,' Act Book, 14 January 1836, GDR 356

56  Ormrod v. Wallwork (Chester, 1829), Chesworth v. Evans (Chester, 1837), Ayre v. Tocker (Exeter, 1819), Webber v. Penn (Exeter, 1817)

57  Examples are Jones v. Davies (St David's, 1850), SD/CCm(G)/593C, where the defendant took the opportunity to swear to provocative words used by the plaintiff, and France v. Aaron (York, 1838), appendix A, below, where the plaintiff denied use of provocative words.

58  Jones v. Townsend (Gloucester, 1835) ('this respondent answering saith she submits to the law and the judgment of this court')

59  17 & 18 Vic. c. 47, applied in Smith v. Barrett (Gloucester, 1854)

60  A Bill of Costs (Hawkes v. Dawes, 1831) includes the comment, 'at this Court it was arranged that this Cause should be heard summarily,' suggesting agreement of the proctors. In Brindle v. Matthews (Gloucester, 1834) the case was first decreed to be heard summarily, and subsequently assigned to proceed plenarily. Act Book, 10 and 24 April 1834, GDR 356

61  In Merryman v. Pidgeon (Gloucester, 1834) the libel occupies a full page of the Act Book, 2 February 1834, GDR 356.

62  See 40–1, above.

63  LPL, Court of Arches, 'H' series, typed handlist, and Assignation Books, Aaa 40–8

64  Boyes v. Johnston (York Deanery, 1842), Chanc AB 51

65  Ayre v. Tocker (Exeter, 1819 and Arches Court, 1821), affd by HCD 1 December 1823, Ecclesiastical Courts Commission Report, appendix C part I, 356

66  Hampden v. Eyton (Arches, 1844) (appeal dismissed) and Bate v. Collis (Worcester, 1845, and Arches Court, 1846) (appeal abandoned), *Return of all Appeals in Ecclesiastical Causes made to the Queen in Council ...*, PP 1866 lv, 51

67  53 Geo. III c. 127. By section 2 power to excommunicate as a spiritual censure was preserved, and by section 3 the court in such a case could imprison for up to six months. This power was very rarely used in defamation cases but there is one instance where the defendant was excommunicated and sentenced to three months' imprisonment for failure to perform penance and pay costs: Leeson v. Wills (Peterborough, 1833), X953. The effect of the statute was discussed by Dr Lushington in Hoile v. Scales (1829), 2 Hag Ecc 566 (brawling).

68  But in Carlisle the old practice of excommunication continued until 1817, e.g., Crean v. Gordon (Carlisle, 1815), Act Book, 21 February 1817, DRC/3/27, and reference to excommunication sometimes continued to appear in monitions, e.g., the monition in Bear v. Bignell (Winchester, 1831), in appendix A, below.

69  An example is in appendix A, below.

70  An example is in appendix A, below.

71  The name 'cursitor' implies process 'as of course.' The precise steps are detailed in a Bill of Costs in Heath v. Backhouse (Richmond, 1824). See also Hamerton v. Hamerton (1827), 1 Hag Ecc 23, 24n (Vice-Chancellor's Court) (officer 'authorized and required' to grant writ).

72  *Canterbury Tales*, General Prologue, 660–2 (the Summoner)

73  Ecclesiastical Courts Commission Report, appendix D, 569–71

74  There were 298 significavits for the twenty-five-year period. Not every significavit led to actual imprisonment, since imprisonment might be avoided by immediate compliance and payment of the sheriff's fee, as in the Chester case mentioned below. Some, but comparatively few, significavits seem to have been lost: 3 out of 34 are missing for the period 1827–9 covered by the Ecclesiastical Courts Commission Report. Significavits are not uniformly preserved for the period after 1839. PRO C/207/6–11

75  See Sharpe v. Dauncey, discussed at 10, above.

76  The monition is transcribed in appendix A, below. The form of monition in H. Coote, *The Practice of the Ecclesiastical Courts* (London 1847), 826, includes the

words 'pay or cause to be paid to [the plaintiff] or to his proctor, for his use, the said sum ...'

77  Opinion of J. Addams in Bear v. Bignell (Winchester, 1831), 21M65/C9/70. The contempt was signified on 22 March 1833, Act Book, AB21M65/C2/109. On 13 June 1833 the plaintiff gave instructions to release the defendant from jail on payment of £10 and performance of penance. 21M65/C9/70

78  Burch v. Brown (Peterborough, 1831). The rule for habeas corpus was discharged with costs (King's Bench, 11 May 1832), X 953, and Act Book, 22 December 1831 and 8 August 1832, ML 718.

79  This was the practice in Worcester, Lichfield, and Llandaff.

80  Bear v. Bignell (Winchester, 1831), opinion of J. Addams dated 9 March 1833, 21M65/C9/70. The Act Book shows that the issue of the monition itself had been delayed 'to afford time to Sarah Bignell to perform the decree of the court voluntarily,' so the judge was probably satisfied that she had received informal notice. 21M65/C2/109

81  Woods v. Lowe (Chester, 1833) (petition to judge) EDC 5 (1833)

82  Askwith to W. Page, 29 June 1826 (copy), in Garside v. Ripley (York, 1826), PP. In Norwich the rules expressly provided that 'no person shall be deemed to be excommunicated for not appearing on the day the citation ... is returnable but the certificate of such citation shall be continued to the next court day and if the person cited does not then appear he may then be deemed to be excommunicated ...' Rules and Orders in Act Book, DN/ACT/105

83  Bennett v. Jenkins (Bristol, 1817), Act Book, 28 June 1817, EP/J/1/43

84  Fox v. Saick (London, 1821), Assignation Book, 3 January 1822, X19/183

85  Sessions of the court were held in the castle on 18 July 1815, 14 December 1830, 3 April 1832, 1 January 1838, and 6 May 1843. Act Books, DN/ACT/104, 105, 106

86  See 36, above.

87  Smith v. Wardle (York, 1822), Abstract Book, 14 February 1822, and letter of Askwith to Garbutt, 15 February 1822 (copy), PP

88  Her name (Elspeth Wardle) appears in the document of Gaol Assignment, 4 March 1824, York Castle Archives.

89  The Abstract Book entry says 'defendant' but this must be an error.

90  Hodgson v. Jackson (York, 1853), Abstract Book, 2 November 1854, 8 December 1854, 18 January 1855

91  Act Book, 4 and 18 July 1843, 1 August 1843, 21 November 1843, 22 October 1844, Board v. Hill and Hill v. Board (Bath and Wells, 1843), D/D/Ca 459, and D/D/Cp 1843. Costs would have been owed not only to each other (which could have been mutually released), but to the sheriff. Frederick Board had first addressed a petition to the home secretary, whose secretary (S.M. Phillips) replied (11 October 1844), suggesting a petition to the judge. Phillips also wrote to the visiting magis-

trates of Taunton Gaol (same date), who wrote a letter to the judge accompanying the joint petition and saying 'we recommend their case to your favourable consideration' (15 October 1844).

92 5 & 6 Vic. c. 116, am. by 7 & 8 Vic. c. 96

93 Holden v. Osbourn (Lichfield, 1832, and Arches Court), Act Book, 7 October 1834, B/C/2/1832–6

94 Moore v. Claque (Sodor and Man, 1814, renewed against Qualthough, 1823), Liber Causarum, 1823, France v. Robinson (Sodor and Man, 1818), Liber Causarum, 1818

## 5: Evidence

1 See 74, above.

2 17 & 18 Vic. c. 47, applied in Smith v. Barrett (Gloucester, 1854), and in several cases in Carlisle

3 This point was made by Samuel Sweet in his evidence to the Ecclesiastical Courts Commission, appendix A, PP 1831–2 xxiv, 19.

4 E.g., Benton v. Ridcoat (Chester, 1820)

5 Ecclesiastical Courts Commission Report, appendix A, 144 (evidence of W. Adams)

6 Id., 199 (evidence of J. Shepherd). John Campbell KC, in his evidence to the Commission, denied that witnesses were embarrassed by the common law procedure, because 'that which is necessary is not immodest' (227).

7 Brisco v. Brisco (HCD, 1815), quoted in G.I.O. Duncan, *The High Court of Delegates* (Cambridge 1986), 114–15 (note)

8 Ecclesiastical Courts Commission Report, appendix A, 37 (evidence of J.W. Freshfield)

9 Id., 147 (evidence of W. Adams)

10 Id., 67, 177 (evidence of Charles Bowdler, William Ward)

11 Id., 54, 67 (evidence of J.W. Freshfield, Charles Bowdler)

12 Williams v. King (London, 1842), Guildhall, 12,185/7

13 Ecclesiastical Courts Commission Report, 184 (evidence of William Ward). In Hodges v. Baird (Gloucester, 1849), one witness admitted that he had heard the libel read that morning by the proctor, while another witness denied having heard it read.

14 Ecclesiastical Courts Commission Report, 26 (evidence of Samuel Sweet)

15 A point stressed by Campbell in his evidence to the Commission, note 6, above. But in some dioceses judges did sometimes examine witnesses themselves, e.g., Charles Evans in Norwich, and Walter Fletcher and William Jackson in Carlisle.

16 Ecclesiastical Courts Commission Report, 18 (evidence of Samuel Sweet)

17 Interrogatory in Bate v. Collis (Worcester, 1846, and Arches Court), LPL, H694
18 Brief for the advocate in Briggs v. Dickinson (York, 1832), PP
19 Ecclesiastical Courts Commission Report, 55 (evidence of Freshfield)
20 W. Denny to Matthew Rackham, 10 April 1842, in Mann v. Groves (Norwich, testamentary, 1842), DN/CON/133
21 Orme v. Gibbon (Chester, 1818), EDC 5 (1818–19)
22 Haigh v. Willett (Chester, 1827), EDC (1828)
23 Harper v. Cooke (Hereford, 1852), HD4/64
24 Jeremy Bentham, *Rationale of Judicial Evidence from the Manuscripts of Jeremy Bentham* (London 1827), 1:594–5
25 Marsh v. Travers (Norwich, 1846), DN/CON/137
26 Alexander v. Moore (Norwich, 1844), DN/CON/136
27 Act Book, 22 March 1844, DN/ACT 106, *Norfolk News*, 29 March 1845, 4f. Similar events occurred in Church v. Matthew Halls (Norwich, 1821), and in Bannister v. Tillett (London, 1840).
28 Roberts v. Gilpin (Hereford, 1828), affidavit of Samuel Woodcock, assistant overseer and parish clerk; he gave evidence for the defendant on an exceptive allegation. HD4/58
29 Etty v. Kneeshaw (York, 1819), 'I should wish all six ... to be here by nine o'clock that they may be examined and return home on the same day.' Askwith to Stockton, 19 May 1820 (copy), in Smith v. Wardle (York, 1821), PP
30 Woodhouse v. Williams (Gloucester, 1845) B4/1/1364. The York Bill of Costs, in appendix A, uses the same phrase.
31 E.g., Johnson v. Goodier (Chester, 1817)
32 Foster v. Stubbing (York, 1823), 'Observations' for counsel, PP and PCB
33 Wardle to Askwith, 7 November 1829, Pilling v. Bradley (York, 1829) Askwith to Bromby, 15 January 1824 (copy), Foster v. Stubbing (York, 1823), PP
34 These features of the system are evidenced in Askwith's correspondence in several cases, e.g., Pilling v. Bradley (York, 1829), Briggs v. Dickinson (York, 1832), Humble v. Gypson (York, 1833), Forster v. Creaser (York, 1833), PP.
35 Askwith to Wardle, 11 December 1829 (copy), in Pilling v. Bradley (York, 1829), PP. See 58, above.
36 See 58, above.
37 Askwith to Bromby, 10 March 1824 (copy), PP
38 Same to same, 19 March 1824 (copy), PP
39 Same to same, 10 March 1824 (copy), PP (emphasis in original)
40 Hawkes v. Dawes (Gloucester, 1831), Foster v. Stubbing (York, 1823), Sawkill v. Knaggs (York, 1829), Pilling v. Bradley (York, 1829), Williams v. King (London, 1842), Higgs v. Higgs (London 1840), Bannister v. Tillett (London, 1840)
41 Bond v. Mapp (Hereford, 1848), HD4/61

42  Richards v. Clark (London, 1824), Guildhall, 12,185/1

43  Declaration of Theophilus Lane, deputy registrar, 16 September 1826, in Fowler v. Hall (Hereford, 1826), HD4/57. Sentence was given for the plaintiff with penance and costs. Another case in which the witness returned to alter her evidence after seeing the proctor is Harrison v. Knibb (Gloucester, 1821).

44  Hutchinson v. Jeremiah and Samuel Proctor (York, 1838), Cons CP 1838/6 and 7

45  Parbery v. Gross (Peterborough, 1816), Waite v. Slaymaker (Peterborough, 1828), Waite v. Foster (Peterborough, 1828), X 954. The last two cases were dismissed: Act Book, 21 January 1830, ML 718.

46  Fitzjohn v. Hayes (Peterborough, 1830), X 954

47  Ecclesiastical Courts Commission Report, appendix A, 183 (evidence of William Ward)

48  Crabtree v. Hardy (Chester, 1824), EDC 5 (1824–5). The examiner was a surrogate, the Revd William Harrison.

49  Many cases in the four Welsh dioceses

50  Barnaschino v. Gironimo (London, 1834) (Italian: 'Ella ... va puttanegiando ... Andò ad un bordello ... Era tanto communale come una vecchia vacca e davvero niente altro che una communale puttana')

51  Wallis v. Cory (Exeter, 1828) (question of whether the words 'It is said that old Mrs Wallis is a whore but she's ten times worse' were spoken with stress on *she's*, so as to imply reference to young Mrs Wallis). CC 81/81A

52  Harris v. Levy (London, 1825), Assignation Book, 4 July 1825, X19/185

53  Romanel v. Emanuel (London, 1826), Assignation Book, 5 December 1826, X19/185

54  Bannister v. Tillett (London, 1840), Guildhall, 12,185/5

55  Williams v. Parry (Chester, 1826), EDC 5 (1826). A similar formula occurs in Anna Maria Bardsley v. Bardsley the elder (Chester, 1829).

56  Deposition of Mary Stelling in Garside v. Ripley (York, 1826), Cons CP 1826/4

57  Deposition of Jane Nightingale in Ripley v. Garside (York, 1826), Cons CP 1826/4

58  Page to Askwith, 14 February 1827, in Ripley v. Garside (York, 1826), PP

59  Askwith to Page, 24 February 1827 (copy), in Garside v. Ripley; Ripley v. Garside (York, 1826), PP

60  Abstract Book, 25 May 1827

61  Askwith to Page, 21 May 1827 (copy), PP

62  Askwith to Garbutt, 14 September 1821 (copy), in Smith v. Wardle (York, 1821), Foster v. Stubbing (York, 1823), observations for counsel, PP and PCB

63  Harris v. Heale (Bath and Wells, 1834) (£1.10.0), Act Book, 6 May 1834, D/D/Ca 453, Green v. Tiddy (Norwich, 1824) (£4), Act Book, 1 February 1825, DN/ACT/105 and cause papers, DN/CON/126

64  See 81–2, above.

65  Southwood v. Halford (Gloucester, 1848), B4/1/114, and Act Book, 19 November 1849, GDR 364, similarly Browning v. Mitchell (Gloucester, 1838), Sheard v. Ramsden (Ripon, 1852)

66  Craik v. Bell (Carlisle, 1832), Robinson v. Johnston (Carlisle, 1832)

67  Hall v. Roddwell (Norwich, 1843), DN/CON/133

68  Jones v. Townsend (Gloucester, 1835), B4/1/542; also Thacker v. Carr (Norwich, 1837)

69  Smith v. Wardle (York, 1821), PP

70  Spooner v. King (York, 1837), PP

71  An allowance in this range was common, as in Stone v. Andrews (Chichester, 1818) (5s. 6d.).

72  Spooner v. King (York, 1837), PP. In Josling v. Price (St David's, 1828) 5s. per day was claimed for each of two women witnesses but on taxation only 2s.6d. per day was allowed. The bill of costs is reproduced as an appendix to the Ecclesiastical Courts Commission Report, appendix C, 468.

73  Spooner v. King (York, 1837), PP

74  Foster v. Stubbing (York, 1823)

75  Askwith to Bromby (copy), 13 May 1824

76  Payne v. Rowley (Bristol, 1841), EP/J/2/7/5, Stephens v. Ridgeway (Hereford, 1828) (5s. offered, but unclear whether or not in addition to expenses)

77  Spooner v. King (York, 1837), PP

78  Askwith to Wardle, 16 July 1829 (copy), in Pilling v. Bradley (York, 1829), PP

79  Cheadle v. Spencer (York, 1826), Cons CP 1826/3

80  Abstract Book, 22 March 1827

81  Youngs v. Bailey (Norwich, 1826)

82  Wharton v. Winter (York, 1826), Cons CP 1826/1

83  E.g., Etty v. Kneeshaw (York, 1819) (deposition of Hannah Appleby), Cons CP 1819/4, Chesworth v. Evans (Chester, 1837), Dewhurst v. Isherwood (Chester, 1839), Stinton v. Humpherson (Hereford, 1832)

84  E.g., Cooke v. Thomas (Hereford, 1824)

85  Ferris v. Wickham (Bath and Wells, 1836)

86  Stinton v. Humpherson (Hereford, 1832)

87  E.g., Etty v. Kneeshaw (York, 1819) (deposition of Mary Hesp), Cons CP 1819/4

88  Ripley v. Garside (York, 1826) (deposition of Thomas Nightingale), Cons CP 1826/4

89  E.g., Chesworth v. Evans (Chester, 1837) (deposition of Elizabeth Fletcher), EDC 5 (1838–9), Wickham v. Lockyer (Bath and Wells, 1836) (irregular marriage), Harper v. Cooke (Hereford, 1853)

90  Etty v. Kneeshaw (York, 1819) (deposition of Mary Hesp), Cons CP 1819/4

91  Ripley v. Garside (York, 1826) (deposition of Elizabeth Sleightholm), Cons CP 1826/4

92  Id., PCB (emphasis in original)
93  E.g., Williams v. Probert (Hereford, 1827)
94  Humble v. Gypson (York, 1833), Cons CP 1833/2
95  Humble v. Gypson (York, 1833), PP
96  Dewhurst v. Isherwood (Chester, 1839), Prissick v. Parry (Chester, 1845)
97  Briggs v. Dickinson (York, 1832)
98  Hodges v. Baird (Gloucester, 1849)
99  Bardsley the elder v. Bardsley the younger; Bardsley the elder v. Anna Maria Bardsley (Chester, 1829), EDC 5 (1828–9)
100 Whittle v. West (Bath and Wells, 1831)
101 Ferris v. Wickham (Bath and Wells, 1836), D/D/Cp 1836
102 Bardsley the elder v. Anna Maria Bardsley (Chester, 1829), EDC 5 (1828–9). This was the test also at common law: R v. Taylor (1790), Peake 14, C. Allen, *The Law of Evidence in Victorian England* (Cambridge 1997), 52.
103 Ormrod v. Wallwork (Chester, 1829), EDC 5 (1830–1)
104 Ormrod v. Wallwork (Chester, 1829), Powell v. Probert (Hereford, 1816), Fowler v. Hall (Hereford, 1825), Bates v. Williams (Hereford, 1825)
105 Powell v. Probert (Hereford, 1816), HD4/53
106 Attersall v. Last (Exeter, 1816), CC 80
107 Stephens v. Ridgeway (Hereford, 1829), HD4/58
108 Ferris v. Wickham (Bath and Wells, 1836)
109 Forster v. Creaser (York, 1833), Cons CP 1833/4
110 Tranter v. Edmonds (Hereford, 1821) (age fourteen), Tranter v. Butcher (Hereford, 1821) (age fourteen), Owen v. Mitchell (Hereford, 1825) (age fourteen), Stephens v. Ridgeway (Hereford, 1829) (age fourteen), Moss v. Elleman (Hereford, 1831) (two witnesses aged thirteen), Routledge v. John and Alice Tomlinson (Chester, 1817) (age fourteen), Poole v. Latham (Chester, 1823) (age thirteen), Bennett v. Thomas (Chester, 1828) (age thirteen), Waterson v. Annison (Norwich, 1842) (age fourteen), Biffin v. Lawley (Bath and Wells, 1834) (age thirteen), Davies v. Thomas (Llandaff, 1815) (age fourteen), Ellis v. Somers (Bath and Wells, 1829) (ages fourteen and fifteen), Taylor v. Millard (Bath and Wells, 1835) (age fourteen), Hall v. Roddwell (Norwich, 1843) (age thirteen), Atkinson v. Graham (Carlisle, 1830) (ages thirteen and eleven), Cambridge v. Young (Gloucester, 1852) (age fourteen), Smith v. Barrett (Gloucester, 1854) (age twelve), Cope v. Jackson (Hereford, 1834) (witnesses aged twelve, thirteen, fourteen, fifteen, and sixteen), and many cases of witnesses aged fifteen
111 Stevens v. Leturge (Bath and Wells, 1831)
112 This is expressly stated to be the law by Askwith in a letter of 29 October 1830 (copy), to Iveson & Kidd, in Kinder v. Dyson (York, 1830), PP. It was the rule also at common law (C. Allen, *Law of Evidence in Victorian England*, 98). But in

Buckler v. Briggs (Peterborough, 1816), and Binnington v. Watson (York, 1816), the plaintiff's husband gave evidence. In Wallis v. Cory (Exeter, 1828), the plaintiff's husband, who was a proctor, addressed 'observations' to the court.

113 But there may have been some doubt on the point, since objections were raised to near relatives as witnesses in Webber v. Penn (Exeter, 1816), Boucher v. Forty (Gloucester, 1828), Webb v. Smith (Gloucester, 1834), Peart v. Roberts (Gloucester, 1834), and Brindle v. Matthews (Gloucester, 1834).

114 Askwith to Earnshaw, 24 November 1826 (copy), in Wilson v. Bowness (York, 1826), PP. He wrote to similar effect to Hodgson, 20 October 1827 (copy), in Wharton v. Winter (York, 1827), PP.

115 Peart v. Roberts (Gloucester, 1834), Cheadle v. Spencer (York, 1826), Gregory v. David (Llandaff, 1852), Simpson v. Jacobs (Norwich, 1818), Hutchinson v. Jeremiah Proctor (York, 1838), Chamberlain v. Watkins (Hereford, 1834), Poole v. Latham (Chester, 1823)

116 Whittle v. West (Bath and Wells, 1831), Vowles v. White (Bath and Wells, 1832), Smith v. Powell (Bath and Wells, 1846), Keelan v. Asprey (Llandaff, 1850), Crosby v. England (York, 1820), Brearey v. Bakewell (Lichfield, 1818), Ellis v. Somers, Ellis v. Michell, Ellis v. Ellis (Bath and Wells, 1829), Hudson v. Aspinall (Chester, 1827), Taylor v. Hazlehurst (Chester, 1822), Gregory v. David (Llandaff, 1852)

117 Hutchinson v. Samuel Proctor (York, 1838), Bannister v. Tillett (London, 1840), Marsh v. Travers (Norwich, 1846), Wharton v. Winter (York, 1826), Harper v. Cooke (Hereford, 1853)

118 James v. Miles (London, 1835), Morgan v. Hodges (Hereford, 1824), Smith v. Whitter (Chester, 1817), Parry v. Hall (Chester, 1820)

119 Lockwood v. Sheldon (Chester, 1839), Gittins v. Featherstone (Worcester, 1822), Ingles v. Cooke (Hereford, 1816), Stephens v. Ridgeway (Hereford, 1829), Bond v. Mapp (Hereford, 1848), Harrison v. Mayall (Chester, 1822) (both witnesses), Craske v. W. Youell; Craske v. H. Youell (Norwich, 1846)

120 Crosby v. England (York, 1820)

121 Barnes v. Haslem (Chester, 1817) (niece), Orme v. Gibbon (Chester 1818) (sister-in-law), Hazlehurst v. Alberston (Chester, 1818) (stepdaughter), Chesworth v. Evans (Chester, 1837) (mother-in-law and sister-in-law), Daveney v. Taylor (Norwich, 1842) (uncle), Gooch v. Morley (Norwich, 1850) (stepfather), Rose v. Knight (London, 1831) (aunt), Llewellin v. Eckley (Hereford, 1832) (nephew), King v. Hall (London, 1830) (niece), Etty v. Kneeshaw (York, 1819) (niece), Peart v. Roberts (Gloucester, 1834) (sister-in-law)

122 Bentley v. North (Ripon, 1849). Another such case is Priest v. Jenkins (Gloucester, 1848), where the parties were brother and sister and the witnesses were their father, sister, and great-niece spanning ages from seventy-three to fifteen.

123 Webber v. Penn (Exeter, 1816) (party's fiancée), Bond v. Mapp (Hereford, 1848) (fiancé)

124 Tocker v. Ayre (1821), 3 Phil 539, at 542 (Arches Court on appeal from Exeter)

125 Roberts v. Gilpin (Hereford, 1828); see 82, above. The man accused gave evidence also in Paginton v. Kayns (Salisbury, 1830), Gooch v. Morley (Norwich, 1850), Viner v. Clack (Bath and Wells, 1836), and Bear v. Bignell (Winchester, 1831).

126 Askwith to T. & C. Walker, 11 May 1834 (copy), in Humble v. Gypson (York, 1833), PP

127 Askwith to Hodgson, 10 October 1827 (copy), in Wharton v. Winter (York, 1827), PP

128 Milner v. Welborn (York, Deanery Court, 1826), DY CP 1826/1

129 Paul v. Forth (York, 1822)

130 Ripley v. Garside (York, 1826), observations for advocate, PCB

131 Forster v. Creaser (York, 1833), Gittins v. Featherstone (Worcester, 1822)

132 E.g., Craik v. Bell (Carlisle, 1832), Deposition Book DRC/3/50, f. 60

133 Tidmarsh v. Smart (Gloucester, 1848), B4/1/1128

134 Mutlow v. Bowen (Hereford, 1817), HD4/53

135 Humble v. Gypson (York, 1833). The answer was that the witness paid for his own beer. Cons CP 1833/2

136 Cope v. Jackson (Hereford, 1834), deposition of Ann Hackford. HD4/61

137 Bates v. Williams (Hereford, 1825), Middleton v. Richardson (Ripon, 1851)

138 Cooper v. Rutland (Lichfield, 1833) (words allegedly spoken by plaintiff), B/C/5/1833

139 Watkins v. Melling (Hereford, 1819), HD4/53

140 Linton v. Bastin (Exeter, 1815)

141 Wilson v. Gee (York, 1817), Cons CP 1817/8

142 Heald v. Jepson (Chester, 1819)

143 Bardsley the elder v. Bardsley the younger (Chester, 1829), EDC 5 (1828–9)

144 Humble v. Gypson (York, 1833), Cons CP 1833/2 ('What were you and the plaintiff's attorney about in the afternoon of Thursday the thirteenth ...?')

145 Bastow v. Bakes (York, 1817), Burdon v. Poole (Lichfield, 1836)

146 Cambridge v. Young (Gloucester, 1852)

147 Cope v. Jackson (Hereford, 1834), HD4/61

148 Ellis v. Stead (York, 1821)

149 Jones v. Williams (Bangor, 1815), B/CC/G/393b

150 Fowler v. Hall (Hereford, 1825)

151 Stinton v. Humpherson (Hereford, 1832), HD4/59

152 Ormrod v. Wallwork (Chester, 1829), EDC 5 (1830–1)

153  Wilson v. Gee (York, 1817), Cons CP 1817/8

154  Bardsley the elder v. Bardsley the younger (Chester, 1829)

155  Forster v. Creaser (York, 1833), PCB

156  Etty v. Kneeshaw (York, 1819), PCB

157  Briggs v. Dickinson (York, 1832), PP

158  England v. Sampson (Lichfield, 1851), B/C/5/1852. Similarly Williams v. King (London, 1842)

159  Forster v. Creaser (York, 1833), remarks for advocate, PCB. A similar point was made in Etty v. Kneeshaw (York, 1816), PP.

160  Asprey v. Keelan (Llandaff, 1850)

161  Dennison v. Haigh (York, 1816), Cons CP 1816/4

162  France v. Aaron (York, 1838), Cons CP 1838/4

163  Cooke v. Thomas (Hereford, 1824), HD4/56

164  Webb v. Smith (Gloucester, 1834), B4/1/544. The case was dismissed with costs taxed at £18. 17s. Bill of Costs and Act Book, 18 May 1835, GDR 356

165  Bannister v. Tillett (London, 1840), Guildhall, 12,185/5, Assignation Book, 5 May 1840, p. 184, X19/190

166  Askwith to Garbutt, 18 June 1821 (copy), in Smith v. Wardle (York, 1821), PP

167  Observations for advocate in Ripley v. Garside (York, 1826), PP

168  Chesworth v. Evans (Chester, 1837), Groves v. Lonsdale (York, 1825), Cons CP 1825/6 (sentence for plaintiff), Southwood v. Halford (Gloucester, 1848)

169  Holmes v. Smith (York, 1820), Cons CP 1820/3 (sentence for plaintiff)

170  Garner v. Williams (Chester, 1825), EDC 5 (1824–5)

171  Yonge to Skipper, 22 October 1827 in Youngs v. Bailey (Norwich, 1826), DN/CON/127

172  Act Book, 1 January 1828, DN/ACT/105, and cause papers, DN/CON/127

173  See chapter 9, below.

174  Interrogatory in Hart v. Cockshaw (York, Dean and Chapter, 1835), D/C 1835/1

175  Mary Ann Watkins v. David Smith (Gloucester, 1837), Lucas v. Lawrence (Gloucester, 1847), Faulkes v. Bowdler (Gloucester, 1848), Southwood v. Halford (Gloucester, 1848), Humble v. Gypson (York, 1833), Boothman v. Duxbury (Chester, 1821), Taylor v. Fletcher (Chester, 1827), Edmunds v. Drew (Gloucester, 1841), Price v. Parry (Gloucester, 1841), Jenny Watkins v. John Smith (Gloucester, 1837), Ingles v. Cooke (Hereford, 1816), Hoby v. Bythell (Hereford, 1817)

176  Crosby v. England (York, 1820), Brook v. Sykes (York, 1824), Garside v. Ripley (York, 1826), Kinder v. Dyson (York, 1826), Edmunds v. Drew (Gloucester, 1841)

177  Rose v. Knight (London, 1831), Hutchinson v. J. Proctor; Hutchinson v. S. Proctor (York, 1838)

178  Smith v. Jane Whitter (Chester, 1817), Brook v. Sykes (York, 1824), Llewellin v. Eckley (Hereford, 1832), Green v. Green (Gloucester, 1837)

179 Brook v. Sykes (York, 1824); also Ellis v. Stead (York, 1821) ('scolding')
180 Aspinall v. Bell (York, 1838), Grovenor v. Wright (Gloucester, 1834)
181 Dewhurst v. Isherwood (Chester, 1819)
182 Cogswell v. Danson (Chester, 1833), Idle v. Crawshay (York, 1833), Hauxwell v. Scott (York, 1835), Johnson v. Goodier (Chester, 1817), Green v. Green (Gloucester, 1837)
183 Stubbs v. Bradley (York, 1841)
184 Hadley v. Whittaker (Chester, 1825)
185 Taylor v. Fletcher (Chester, 1827)
186 Batten v. Adams (Bath and Wells, 1830), Jenny Watkins v. John Smith (Gloucester, 1837), Southwood v. Halford (Gloucester, 1848)
187 The defendant's bill of costs in Smith v. Evans (Gloucester, 1847), refers to 'material facts attending the Character of Promoter's Husband.'
188 Hauxwell v. Scott (York, 1835), Cons CP 1835/10
189 Foster v. Sixsmith (Chester, 1834), EDC 5 (1835)
190 Othick v. Ellison (York, Dean and Chapter, 1829), D/C 1829/11. Sentence was for the plaintiff, without costs. Witnesses in Paginton v. Kayns (Salisbury, 1830), said they had heard that the plaintiff was not of good character.
191 Etty v. Kneeshaw (York, 1819)
192 Ellis v. Stead (York, 1821)
193 France v. Aaron (York, 1838). See appendix A.
194 Noble v. Powell (York, 1819), Cons CP 1819/5. The defendant resided in the village of Walton, Yorks.
195 Roberts v. Gilpin (Hereford, 1828), HD4/58
196 Cheadle v. Spencer (York, 1826), Cons CP 1826/3
197 Webber v. Penn (Exeter, 1816), CC 79a/80
198 Page to Askwith, 20 September 1826, in Garside v. Ripley (York, 1826); also Harrison v. Leetham (Selby peculiar, 1820), PP; see 30, above.
199 Bannister v. Tillett (London, 1840), Guildhall, 12,185/5
200 Briggs v. Dickinson (York, 1832), PP. Sentence was for the plaintiff but with small costs.
201 Craske v. Youell (Norwich, 1846), Edelstone v. Ellison (Chester, 1818)
202 See chapter 4, above, and King v. Hall (London, 1830) (plaintiff's replicatory allegation with expert evidence to prove that it was possible for the witnesses to have heard what they claimed).
203 This is in accord with D. Vincent, *Literacy and Popular Culture* (Cambridge 1989), 25, where Norfolk and Suffolk, but not Yorkshire, are shown as counties where, in 1864, women were more literate than men.
204 L. Stone, 'Literacy and Education in England, 1660–1900,' *Past and Present*, 42

(1969), 69, 104, 120, shows the adult male literacy rate in Yorkshire in 1831–7 at 70 per cent, and in England and Wales in 1840 at 66 per cent.

205  Stone, 'Literacy and Education,' 98, 119. In some cases depositions were prepared for authentication by mark with the words 'the mark of ...' but then signed by the witness; e.g., Morgan v. Hodges (Hereford, 1824).

206  L. Gowing, *Domestic Dangers: Women, Words and Sex in Early Modern London* (Oxford 1996), 53

207  Id., 49–51

208  Forster v. Creaser (York, 1833), PP; see 92, above.

209  Gooch v. Morley (Norwich, 1850), DN/CON/137

## 6: Costs

1  Shephard & Isherwood to Richard Dally, 15 May 1816 (copy of extract from letter), Chichester, Ep1/15/1&3

2  Ecclesiastical Courts Commission Report, appendix A, PP 1831–2 xxiv, 201 (evidence of J. Shephard, deputy registrar)

3  Shephard & Isherwood to Richard Dally, 15 May 1816 (copy of extract from letter), Chichester, Ep1/15/1&3. See 69, above.

4  Cohen v. Cohen (London, 1839), Assignation Book, 7 November and 6 December 1839, GLRO, X19/190

5  This was a common error, even among lawyers; see 164, below. The suit was of course brought by Rosetta Cohen, not by her husband, though perhaps by the husband's wish and at his expense.

6  *The Times*, 19 December 1839 (letter signed 'W')

7  Maggs v. Vorryard (Bristol, 1821) (£3.3.0), Taylor v. Acutt (Gloucester, 1831) (£2.2.0), Billett v. Burnett (Salisbury, 1831) (£1.10.0), Blatch v. Clough (Salisbury, 1838) (£2)

8  For Norwich, the cost was estimated at 'from three to four guineas.' Ecclesiastical Courts Commission Report, appendix A, 216 (evidence of J. Kitson)

9  Askwith to Iveson & Kidd, 28 June 1830 (copy), in Kinder v. Dyson (York, 1830), PP

10  Gates to Atkinson, 24 November 1826 (potential parties not named), Peterborough, X953

11  Ecclesiastical Courts Commission Report, appendix C, part VI, 465–74

12  Ellis v. Stead (York, 1821), Cons CP 1821/4

13  Robinson v. Sharp (York, 1824), Cons CP 1824/3 (marginal note by taxing officer; the bill of costs is transcribed in appendix A, below), Askwith to Page, 24 November 1826 (copy), in Garside v. Ripley (York, 1826), PP

14  Shephard, Bedford, & Middleton to J. Huckwell, 23 July 1855 in Morgan v. Morgan (Llandaff, 1855), LL/CC/G/2143p

15  Askwith to Page, 14 December 1825 (copy), in Tomlinson v. Newton (York, 1825), PP

16  See 40–1, above.

17  Webber v. Penn (Exeter, 1816), Act Book, 13 February 1818, 8282 (reduced on taxation from £152)

18  Thomas Miller to Gates, 23 May 1825, in Miller v. Carter (Peterborough, not found in Act Book), X 953

19  Ecclesiastical Courts Commission Report, appendix A, 113 (22 May, 1830)

20  Cheers (or Edge) v. Edwards (Chester, 1831) (£10 substituted for 'lawful costs'), Hadfield v. Harrop (Chester, 1831) (£5), Woods v. Lowe (Chester, 1833) (£3), Williams v. Fleetcroft (Chester, 1834) (£5), Jane Clayton v. Taylor (Chester, 1834) (£5), Foster v. Sixsmith (Chester, 1834) (£5), Maddock v. Simpson (Chester, 1836) (25s.), Leftwich v. Edge (Chester, 1834) (no costs), Blagden v. Ellson (Chester, 1833) (no costs), Bunce v. Pennington (Chester, 1833) (no costs), Goodbody v. Cooper (Chester, 1834) (25s.), Hooley v. Lumbers (Chester, 1833) (no costs), Cogswell v. Dawson (Chester, 1833) (no costs). The Chester registrar, who was a fellow witness before the Commission, must have known immediately of Marsh's statement.

21  Askwith to Iveson & Kidd, 28 June 1830 (copy), in Kinder v. Dyson (York, 1830), PP

22  Norfolk News, 29 March 1845 4f (Alexander v. Moore)

23  Norwich Mercury, 5 June 1847, 3d (Marsh v. Travers)

24  Parliamentary Debates, 3rd ser. 139, 1374 (30 November 1855)

25  Act Books, DRC/3/32. See table 3, below.

26  Askwith to Page, 28 April 1827 (copy), in Garside v. Ripley (York, 1826), PP

27  Askwith to Revd James Andrew, 13 February 1827 (copy), in Trattles v. Trattles (York, 1827), PP

28  Same to same, 8 March 1827 (copy), PP

29  Same to same, 2 April 1827 (copy), PP. See chapter 3, above.

30  Andrew to Askwith, 10 April 1827, PP

31  Dagger v. Evans (Bath and Wells, 1836)

32  Shew v. Webb (Arches Court by letters of request from Bath and Wells, 1835), Assignation Book, 27 November 1835, LPL, Aaa 45

33  Askwith to Edmondson & Cowburn, 10 June 1837 (copy), in Spooner v. King (York, 1837), PP

34  Same to same, 22 June 1837 (copy)

35  Observations for advocate in Forster v. Creaser (York, 1833), PP

36  Forster v. Creaser, Yorkshire Gazette, 27 July 1833, 2f

37  Proctor's observations in Derges v. Scott (Exeter, 1830), CC 81/81A
38  Foster v. Stubbing (York, 1823), PP and PCB (observations for advocate). Costs were refused; see 125, below.
39  Askwith to Page, 18 November 1826 (copy), in Garside v. Ripley, and three other suits (York, 1826) PP (emphasis in original)
40  Gibbs v. Austin (Peterborough, 1831), Act Book, 13 June 1834, ML 718
41  See 36, above (Roberts v. Cornell).
42  French v. James (Llandaff, 1825), LL/CC/G/1912
43  Etty v. Kneeshaw (York, 1819), 19, above.
44  Spooner v. King (York, 1837), 28, above.
45  Ecclesiastical Courts Commission Report, appendix A, 127 (evidence of G. Vernon)
46  Briggs v. Dickinson (York, 1832) (£5), Forster v. Creaser (York, 1833) (£5), Dorney v. Webb (Bath and Wells, 1832) (£25), Foster v. Sixsmith (Chester, 1834) (£5), Sharpe v. Dauncey (Gloucester, 1849) (£12)
47  Ferris v. Wickham (Bath and Wells, 1836) (two-thirds), Baines v. Lawley (Bath and Wells, 1837) (one-half)
48  As in Robinson v. Sharp (York, 1824), Cons CP 1824/3 (attorney's bill, £13.15.1; total allowed, £43.13.0). The bill is transcribed in appendix A, below.
49  Askwith to Stockton, 5 August 1820, in Etty v. Kneeshaw (York, 1819), PP
50  See 62–3, 107, above.
51  This is evidenced by frequent comments to this effect by Askwith in his correspondence, and by the fact that no appeal from an award of costs by a consistory court judge was allowed during the period under study. One appeal was allowed from the York Deanery Court in Boyes v. Johnson (York, 1842).

## 7: Penance

1  T. Oughton, *Ordo Judiciorum* (London 1728), 392, title 268, vi
2  Public punishments of all kinds were in steep decline. See J.M. Beattie, *Crime and the Courts in England, 1660–1800* (Princeton 1986), 613–16.
3  Letter quoted in R.E. Rodes, *This House I Have Built: A Study of the Legal History of Establishment in England*, vol. 2 (Notre Dame 1991), 23
4  In fairly common use in the early modern period; see L. Gowing, *Domestic Dangers: Women, Words and Sex in Early Modern England* (Oxford 1996), 105. An order for penance for fornication, in 1798, among the Worcester cause papers, 795.02/2123, provides: 'At the tolling of the second bell to Morning Service, having a white sheet over her wearing apparel and holding a white rod of about an ell [1 1/4 yards] long in her hand after the manner of a penitent sinner; she shall stand in the porch of the said Church and shall ask forgiveness of all that pass by

her; and when the second lesson is ended she shall be brought into the said Church
and placed in the middle alley of the same near to the Minister's reading desk,
where she shall stand, arrayed as before, all the time of divine service and sermon.
And when the Nicene Creed is ended she shall make a humble acknowledgement
of her crime saying after the Minister with an audible voice, "I Esther Scott do in
the presence of Almighty God and this congregation humbly confess and acknowledge that not having the fear of God before my eyes but being seduced by the devil
and my own unlawful desires I have been guilty of committing the sin of fornication.'" The phrase 'white sheet' was still in metaphorical use in the nineteenth
century (*OED*).

5  There are several references in the evidence given to the Ecclesiastical Courts
   Commission of the danger of ridicule attaching to performance of penance, e.g.,
   evidence of George Martin, chancellor of Exeter, Ecclesiastical Courts Commission Report, appendix A, PP 1831–2 xxiv, 100.

6  *Report of Select Committee of the House of Lords on Defamation*, HL Papers 1843,
   Sess. Pap. 18, reprinted PP 1843 v, 259 (evidence of John Borthwick), 143 (q 584)

7  *Gloucestershire Notes and Queries*, 1:170 (1881), *Law Times*, 10:61 (1847), referring to Lucas v. Lawrence (Gloucester, 1847), Ecclesiastical Courts Commission
   Report, appendix A, 114 (evidence of Matthew Marsh)

8  F. Clerke, *Praxis* (London 1684), 362 ('sed non indutis lineis vestibus'), Oughton,
   *Ordo Judiciorum*, 392 ('non indutis linteis vestibus'), H. Conset, *Practice of the
   Spiritual or Ecclesiastical Courts*, 2nd ed. (London 1700), 343–4 ('linnen vest-
   ments must not be put on')

9  That the white sheet was still in regular use in the Isle of Man appears from a case
   of 1823 where two men were charged with performing a mock ceremony in a public house involving a horse covered with a white sheet. A witness said that 'William
   Christian who sat on the horse was not sober and had performed penance at Church
   that sabbath day [for what offence is not stated]. The horse had no sheet on it.'
   (Sodor and Man), Precedent Book, 10 June 1823

10  Stevenson v. Dempster (Richmond, 1835), Forsyth v. Chisholm (Durham, 1831)

11  See 103–4, above.

12  *The Times*, 18 December 1839, 2e

13  *The Times*, 19 December 1839 (letter signed 'W')

14  *The Times*, 15 December 1829 (two cases, not identified)

15  *Guardian*, 1 September 1847, 545c, referring to Duffett v. Evans (Bristol, 1845);
    (the schedule of penance is among the cause papers and contains no reference to a
    sheet), EP/J/2/7/11, *Notes and Queries*, 5th ser. 1 (1874), 16, and 12 (1879), 58,
    referring to Newton v. Hutton (Chester, 1840)

16  French v. James (Llandaff, 1825), LL/CC/G/1912

17  Page to Askwith, 21 December 1825, in Tomlinson v. Newton (York, 1825), PP

18  Askwith to Page, 22 December 1825 (copy)
19  Courtail v. Homfray (Llandaff and Arches Court, 1828), LPL, J 24/8
20  French v. James (Llandaff, 1825), LL/CC/G/1912
21  Miles v. Williams (St Asaph, 1824), Act Book, 3 June 1824, SA/CB/28, *The Times*,
    20 December 1826 (case not identified), 13 December 1838
22  James v. Smith (Arches Court, 1848), LPL, H 753
23  Assignation Book, 24 April 1849, Aas 48 f. 222
24  *Cambridge Chronicle*, 12 May 1849, 2f, 2g, 2 July 1849, 2d, *Cambridge Adver-
    tiser*, 9 May 1849, 3c, 3d, *John Bull*, 12 May 1849, 293
25  *Cambridge Chronicle*, 14 July 1849, 2d
26  *John Bull*, 12 May 1849, 293
27  E.g., Bastow v. Bakes (York, 1816), Cons CP 1817/1
28  H.C. Coote, *The Practice of the Ecclesiastical Courts* (London 1847), 272
29  Form of Retraction in Hall v. Roddwell (Norwich, 1843), DN/CON/133; similarly
    in Durham
30  Schedule of Penance in Iles v. Plank (Salisbury, 1828), D1/41/4/11; also Act
    Book entry for 7 November 1827 in Moss v. Winkworth (Salisbury, 1827), D1/39/
    175
31  Stevenson v. Dempster (Richmond, 1835), RD/AC/1/9
32  Mercer v. Crompton (Peterborough, 1823), X951
33  See 34, 37, above.
34  Crosbie v. Cooper (Lichfield, 1820), B/C/5/1820
35  Houldcroft v. Horton (Lichfield, 1828), B/C/5/1829
36  Bentley v. Foster (Exeter, 1815), CC 80
37  Mercer v. Crompton (Peterborough, 1823), X951
38  Dymond v. Heath (Exeter, 1818), CC 80
39  Wallis v. Cory (Exeter, 1828), CC 81/81A
40  Burnett v. Edwards (Exeter, 1834), CC 82
41  Banham v. Freeman (Norwich, 1815), DN/CON/124
42  Stephens v. Davies (Arches Court by Letters of Request from St David's, 1851),
    LPL, H 778
43  Barnaschino v. Gironimo (London, 1834), Guildhall, 12,185/4
44  Ecclesiastical Courts Commission Report, appendix A, 178 (evidence of W. Ward)
45  Penance was expressly waived in Houldcroft v. Horton (Lichfield, 1829), and Cope
    v. Jackson (Hereford, 1834).
46  Robinson v. Johnston (Carlisle, 1833), Act Book, 20 December 1833, DRC/3/30
47  Willson v. Willson (Lichfield, 1836), Act Book, 31 January and 28 February 1837,
    B/C/2 1836–41 and cause papers, B/C/5/1837. In Bear v. Bignell (Winchester,
    1831), performance of penance was expressly stipulated as a condition of the defen-
    dant's release from prison. Instructions to proctor, 13 June 1833, 21M65/C9/70.

48  In Willson v. Willson it was ordered to be performed between 8 and 9 on a Sunday morning.

49  Marsh v. Travers (Norwich, 1846), *Norwich Mercury*, 5 June 1847, 3d, 3e

50  Ecclesiastical Courts Commission Report, appendix A, 100 (evidence of George Martin). Wallis v. Cory (Exeter, 1828), Act Book, 15 May 1829, 853m, and cause papers, CC 81/81A

51  Richard Hutchinson to John Mott, 18 March 1830, in Slagg v. Hutton (Lichfield, 1830), B/C/5/1830. The defendant gave an affirmative issue and penance was ordered, but the Act Book does not record its actual performance, suggesting that the plaintiff did not insist. B/C/2 1829–32, entries for 6 July and 2 November 1830

52  Twiddy v. Dawson (Norwich, 1820), King v. Hall (London, 1830), Roberts v. Cornell (London, 1834), Sparrow v. Raw (London, 1820), French v. James (Llandaff, 1825), Burch v. Brown (Peterborough, 1831), Nowell v. Gowen (Bath and Wells, 1835), Sharpe v. Dauncey (Gloucester, 1850); see 10, above.

53  J. Huckwell to Charlotte Morgan, 24 May 1855, in Morgan v. Morgan (Llandaff, 1854), LL/CC/G/2143p

54  Also Mercer v. Crompton (Peterborough, 1823), Pearson v. Purvis (York, 1825)

55  Wright v. Wright (Peterborough, 1826), Act Book, 20 July 1826, ML 718

56  Summerfield v. Williams (Llandaff, 1819), Stradling v. Williams (Llandaff, 1823), Ann Collins v. Llewellyn (Llandaff, 1826), Evans v. Jones (Llandaff, 1832), Thomas v. Earle (Llandaff, 1831)

57  Matthews v. Fielding (Gloucester, 1846), Act Book, 24 May 1847, GDR 364

58  Brown v. Nash (Salisbury, 1820)

59  Collett v. Tarring (Bath and Wells, 1822), over the plaintiff's objection. Act Book, 11 March 1823, D/D/Ca 451. Penance in court was also used in Carlisle, Salisbury, and Peterborough.

60  Hill v. Davis (Gloucester, 1824), Act Book, 29 December 1824, GDR 349

61  Russell v. Wigg (Norwich, 1826) (in Norwich Castle), Rudd v. Brett (Norwich, 1837) (in chapel of jail certified by minister and magistrate), Cross v. Cross (Worcester, 1823) (in the jail of the City of Worcester), Evans v. Latham (Chester, 1839) (in chapel of Chester Castle)

62  Smith v. Gibbs (Worcester, 1820), Nowell v. Gowen (Bath and Wells, 1835)

63  Robertson v. Milner (Bristol, 1840), Coulstring v. Frost (Bristol, 1841), Clayton v. Gale (Gloucester, 1821), Price v. Parry (Gloucester, 1841)

64  Scanlon v. Reeves (Gloucester, 1826), Greenhalf v. Geeves (Gloucester, 1851), Southwood v. Halford (Gloucester, 1848), and many cases in York

65  Askwith to Wardle, 2 April 1830 and 6 May 1830 (copies), in Pilling v. Bradley (York, 1829), advising against incurring the expense. Presumably a person could not be found in contempt without proof that the monition had been infringed.

66  Ecclesiastical Courts Commission Report, appendix A, 127 (evidence of G. Vernon)

67  Askwith to Hudson, 2 February 1833, in Briggs v. Dickinson (York, 1832), PP and PCB. See 44, above.

68  Lucas v. Laurence (Gloucester, 1847), 10 *Law Times* 61, quoting *Cheltenham Journal*. In Griffiths v. Goode (Chester, 1823), the court specifically ordered that the recantation should be performed in the presence of the plaintiff. Act Book, entry for 4 November 1823, EDC 1/194

69  Hinton v. Povey (Chester, 1836), Whitehead v. Massey (Chester, 1837)

70  *The Times*, 19 December 1839. The letter (signed 'W') states that Deborah Cohen, the defendant, was 'a young woman of the Jewish persuasion.'

71  Levy v. Levy (Norwich, 1831)

72  Israel v. Barnett (London, 1819), Salamon v. Benjamin (London, 1821), Guildhall, 12,185/1

73  Levy v. Levy (Norwich, 1831), DN/CON/128. The depositions are in DN/CON/129. The parties, and some members of their families, are mentioned in C. Roth, *The Rise of Provincial Jewry ... 1740–1840* (London 1950), 71–4.

74  In Pearson v. Purvis (York, 1825), Askwith sent a form of notice to the defendant's attorney for delivery to the plaintiff; it stated the time and place and that 'you may attend if you think proper.' Askwith to Garbutt, 5 October 1825 (copy), PP

75  Chesworth v. Evans (Chester, 1837), Newton v. Hutton (Chester, 1839)

76  Jane Collins v. Llewellyn (Llandaff, 1826), LL/CC/G/1938

77  Wells v. Vince (London, 1830), *The Times*, 8 March 1830, 4d

78  Askwith to Page, 14 December 1825 (copy), in Tomlinson v. Newton (York, 1825), PP

79  Askwith to Bromby, 12 November 1824 (copy), in Foster v. Stubbing (York, 1823)

80  Performance of the penance was duly certified, Abstract Book, 9 December 1824. A letter from Askwith to Bromby, 22 December 1824 (copy), mentions that penance has been certified, but not who was present.

81  Courtail v. Homfray (Llandaff and Arches Court, 1828), LPL, J 24/8, reported in the Arches Court at 2 Hag Ecc 1

82  See 156–78, below.

## 8: The Parties

1  Ninety-five per cent of London cases were brought by women in the first half of the eighteenth century. T. Meldrum, 'A Women's Court in London: Defamation at the Bishop of London's Consistory Court, 1700–1745,' *London Journal*, 19 (1994), 6

2  W. Moore to C. Wooldridge, 4 November 1824, in Bonwell v. Kent (Winchester, 1824), 21M65/C9/73

3  In the period 1822 to 1850, 160 of a total of 269. P. Morris, 'Defamation and Sexual Reputation in Somerset,' unpublished PhD thesis (Warwick 1985), table V, A.

In earlier periods women were in the majority. R.M. Karras, *Common Women, Prostitution, and Sexuality in Medieval England* (Oxford 1996), 139 (diocese of London)

4  J.S. Wharton, *An exposition of the laws relating to the women of England, showing their rights, remedies and responsibilities in every position of life* (London 1853). The reformers were more interested in suffrage, divorce, child custody, and property rights than in retaining the ecclesiastical law of defamation.

5  George Eliot, *The Mill on the Floss* (1860), book 7, chapter 1, when Maggie Tulliver has been condemned by public opinion for eloping with a lover. See also E. Trudgill, *Madonnas and Magdalenes: The Origin and Development of Victorian Sexual Attitudes* (London 1976), 105–6: 'Women were especially censorious against unchaste women.'

6  Walkden v. Oldham (Chester, 1826), Cole v. Fuller (London, 1825)

7  Russell v. Wigg (Norwich, 1826), DN/CON/127

8  Davies v. Thomas (Llandaff, 1815), LL/CC/G/1780c. Estimates of age were not necessarily accurate: in King v. Hall (London, 1830), one witness said she thought the plaintiff was upwards of seventy years but another said she thought she was less than sixty.

9  Groves v. Lonsdale (York, 1825), Cons CP 1825/6

10  Askwith to Bromby, 23 July 1823 (copy), in Foster v. Stubbing (York, 1823), PP

11  Askwith to Jenner, Bush, & Jenner (copy), 30 September 1824

12  Jenner, Bush, & Jenner to Askwith (copy), 6 October 1824, Precedent Book (York), P 39, ff. 233–4

13  Askwith to Bromby, 14 October 1824 (copy), PP

14  Askwith to Page, 18 November 1826, in Garside v. Anderson (York, 1826), PP

15  Brook v. Read (Bristol, 1835), EP/J/44

16  See 87, above, and 150–1, below.

17  Anthony Trollope, *Marion Fay* (1882), chapter 9

18  In Hauxwell v. Scott (York, 1835), the defendant is described as 'gentleman' in the libel, but appears from the depositions to be a tailor. Cons CP 1835/10

19  See also *Parliamentary Debates* 3rd ser. 99, 100 (Bouverie, 30 May 1848).

20  Ecclesiatical Courts Commission Report, appendix A, PP 1831–2 xxiv, 127

21  Id., 113 (evidence of Matthew Marsh)

22  Id., 177 (evidence of W. Ward)

23  Id., 216 (evidence of J. Kitson)

24  Billins to Title, 5 August 1833, in Kidsley v. King (Peterborough), X 953

25  See T. Oughton, *Ordo Judiciorum* (London 1728), VIII, I, (b), 23, and Rose v. Knight (London, 1831), reported on this point in *The Times*, 29 March 1832, 3e.

26  Tocker v. Ayre (1821), 3 Phil 539, at 539–40

27  Proctor's observations on behalf of the plaintiff in Derges v. Scott (Exeter, 1830), CC 81/81A
28  Daniel v. Ostell (Carlisle, 1843)
29  Fernandez v. Horner (Ripon, 1850), *Bury and Norwich Post*, 11 September 1850, 4d
30  Kinsey v. Williams (Chester, 1833); also Smith v. Wardle (York, 1821)
31  Ferris v. Wickham (Bath and Wells, 1836)
32  See 68, above.
33  Higgs v. Higgs (London, 1840)
34  Vigar v. Glass (Salisbury, 1827), Slagg v. Hutton (Lichfield, 1830)
35  Richards v. Clark (London, 1824), Bentley v. North (Ripon, 1849), Cohen v. Cohen (London, 1839)
36  Fitzjohn v. Hayes (Peterborough, 1830)
37  Pitcher v. Pitcher (Gloucester, 1847), Priest v. Jenkins (Gloucester, 1848)
38  Leather v. Maskery (Chester, 1855)
39  Lees v. Lees (Lichfield, 1828)
40  Robson v. Robson (Durham, 1827)
41  Bardsley the elder v. Bardsley the younger (Chester, 1829)
42  James v. Miles (London, 1835)
43  Johnson v. White (London, 1826)
44  Anna Maria Bardsley v. Bardsley the elder (Chester, 1829), Green v. Green (Gloucester, 1837)
45  Bardsley the elder v. Anna Maria Bardsley (Chester, 1829)
46  Kinder v. Dyson (York, 1830)
47  Jenkins v. Priest; Priest v. Jenkins (Gloucester, 1848), Bardsley v. Bardsley (Chester, 1829) (three suits), Sarah Higgs v. Alfred Higgs; Sarah Higgs v. Maria Higgs (London, 1840)
48  Mary Johnson v. Harriet Johnson (London, 1819), GLRO Ac 73.11 box 40
49  Assignation Book, 25 March 1820, X19/182

## 9: The Injury

1  R.M. Karras, 'The Latin Vocabulary of Illicit Sex in English Ecclesiastical Court Records,' *Journal of Medieval Latin*, 2 (1992), 6. See also Karras, *Common Women: Prostitution and Sexuality in Medieval England* (Oxford 1996), 27 and 29.
2  Sharpe v. Dauncey (Gloucester, 1849). See 9, above.
3  Pope v. Richards (Gloucester 1833), Act Book, 7 November 1833, GDR 356
4  Dickinson v. Hancock (Bristol, 1851), EP/J/2/7/12
5  Keelan v. Asprey (Llandaff, 1850), LL/CC/G/2131
6  Smith v. Burroughs (Norwich, 1936), Hall v. Daw (Gloucester, 1834); also Rose v.

Knight (London, 1831) ('state of prostitution'). Bracebridge Hemyng wrote that 'literally every woman who yields to her passion and loses her virtue is a prostitute.' 'Prostitution in London' in H. Mayhew, *London Labour and the London Poor* (London 1861; reprinted 1968), 215

7  Willan v. Brown (Carlisle, 1827), DRC/3/50, f. 26

8  Stevenson v. Dempster (Richmond, 1835), RD/AC/1/9, Hardcastle v. Willis (Gloucester, 1846)

9  Shenton v. Sheppard (Hereford, 1815), HD4/53

10  Stanway v. Barney (Lichfield, 1826), B/C/5/1826; also Hinton v. Pearce (Bath and Wells, 1831), Lloyd v. Lloyd (Llandaff, 1829)

11  Lucas v. Lawrence (Gloucester, 1847), B4/1/556, Ham v. Maughfling (London, 1819)

12  Harrison v. Knibbs (Gloucester, 1821), B4/1/1474

13  Crabtree v. Hardy (Chester, 1824). See 84, above.

14  Evans v. Evans (Hereford, 1848), HD4/64; also Board v. Hill (Bath and Wells, 1846)

15  Grace Scanes v. Ford; Mary Scanes v. Ford (Exeter, 1816), CC 83

16  Rose v. Knight (London, 1831); see 72–3, above.

17  Phillips v. Luke (St David's, 1849), SD/CC/G/589

18  Whitehead v. Mary Smith, Whitehead v. James Smith, Whitehead v. Brown, Whitehead v. Yates, Whitehead v. Marshall (Chester, 1827), EDC 5 (1828)

19  Jane Marshall and Eleanor Yates; see Ecclesiastical Courts Commission Report, PP 1831–2 xxiv, appendix C, part VII, 529, and appendix D, no. 12, 570–1

20  Short v. Pumnell (Gloucester, 1853), B4/1/1351, Act Book, 12 August and 7 October 1853, GDR 364; irregular marriage was also alleged in Johnson v. Goodier (Chester, 1817).

21  Webber v. Penn (Exeter, 1816), Wigan v. Clarke (Chester, 1829)

22  France v. Aaron (York, 1838) (seventeen years)

23  Watkins v. Fleming (Sodor and Man, 1821) (reputed brother), Sharpe v. Dauncey (Gloucester, 1849) (reputed niece)

24  Simonette v. Metcalfe (Richmond, 1817), Noble v. Powell (Gloucester, 1819), Dewhurst v. Isherwood (Chester, 1839), Curry v. Overthrow (Gloucester, 1821), Jones v. Ladkin (Lichfield, 1815), John v. Prichard (Landaff, 1827), Billett v. Burnett (Salisbury, 1831), Gore v. Stratford (Gloucester, 1847), Forrest v. Gommershall (Chester, 1820), Bragg v. Rumney (Carlisle, 1837), Thomas v. Thomas (St David's, 1834), Morgan v. Charles (St David's, 1841), Fowles v. Knight (Salisbury, 1830), Taylor v. Hazlehurst (Chester, 1822), Morgan v. Morgan (Llandaff, 1854)

25  Hall v. Daw (Gloucester, 1834), B4/1/539

26  Vowles v. White (Bath and Wells, 1832), Churchward v. Churchward (Exeter, 1815), Jephcott v. Tibbitts (Lichfield, 1831)

27  Mary Johnson v. Harriet Johnson (London, 1819)

28  Bear v. Bignell (Winchester, 1831)

29  Sparks v. Thornell (Gloucester, 1854)

30  Triggs v. Cowmeadow (Gloucester, 1825), Sharpe v. Dauncey (Gloucester, 1849), Highland v. Steel (Carlisle, 1850)

31  Bates v. Williams (Hereford, 1825), HD4/57

32  Ayres v. Bliss (Peterborough, 1839) (proctor's notes of evidence), X 953

33  Storey v. Moffatt (Carlisle, 1839), Deposition Book, DRC/3/50, f. 91

34  Bannister v. Tillett (London, 1840), Guildhall, 12,185/5

35  Young v. Stollard (Bath and Wells, 1839)

36  Kewley v. Teare (Sodor and Man, 1818), Triggs v. Cowmeadow (Gloucester, 1825), Bastard and Coltering v. Howlett (Norwich, 1833)

37  43 Geo. III c. 58, ss. 1 and 2

38  It has been estimated, for the eighteenth century, that more than one-third of women were pregnant at their marriages. P.E.H. Hair, 'Bridal Pregnancy in Rural England in Earlier Centuries,' *Population Studies*, 20:2 (1966), R.C. Newman, *A Hampshire Parish: Bramshott and Liphook* (Petersfield 1976), 98–9, and J. Skinner, *Journal of a Somerset Rector, 1802–1834*, ed. H. and P. Coombs (Bath 1971), 409

39  William Garbutt to Askwith, 27 April 1821, in Smith v. Wardle (York, 1821), PP

40  Walker v. Clarke (Peterborough, 1818), X951

41  Barker v. Buxton (Lichfield, 1827), B/C/5/1827; also Hodges v. Baird (Gloucester, 1849), Clayton v. Marshall (Richmond, 1819)

42  Marsh v. Travers (Norwich, 1846)

43  White v. Matthews; counter-citation (Gloucester, 1845), Act Book, 8 October 1845, GDR 356

44  Newbold v. Newbold (Chester, 1825), EDC 5 (1824–5); also Forster v. Creaser (York, 1833) ('kept by all the fellows in the parish')

45  Owen v. Mitchell (Hereford, 1825), HD4/57

46  Bean v. Swann (Norwich, 1821), DN/CON/125

47  Dunning v. Waters (London, 1826), GLRO (libel), Acc 2865 box 4; similarly Price v. Rudge (Hereford, 1819)

48  Protheroe v. Price (Hereford, 1815), HD4/53, Slater v. Wills (Gloucester, 1819), Watkins v. Powell (Gloucester, 1840), Binnington v. Watson (York, 1815) ('Mrs Stab Arse')

49  Gartside v. Wormald (York, 1835), Cons CP 1835/6. Also Hogg v. Crook (Gloucester, 1838)

50  Taylor v. Tongue (Hereford, 1839), HD4/61

51  Hogg v. Crook (Gloucester, 1838), B4/1/1402

52  Wood v. Butterworth (York, 1836), Cons CP 1836/10; also Butterworth v. Wood

(York, 1836), Hall v. Roddwell (Norwich, 1843), Phillips v. Bowen (St David's, 1836), Harper v. Cooke (Hereford, 1853)

53  Batten v. Adams (Bath and Wells, 1830), D/D/Cp 1830; also Andrews v. Adams (Bath and Wells, 1832) (same defendant in both cases), Duffett v. Evans (Bristol, 1847), Simonette v. Metcalf (Richmond, 1817) (words addressed to defendant's wife), Payne v. Marsh (Worcester, 1822)

54  Butterworth v. Wood (York, 1836), Cons CP 1836/10A

55  Wood v. Butterworth (York, 1836), Cons CP 1836/10

56  Idle v. Crawshay (York, 1833), and see below. Cons CP 1833/3

57  Bear v. Bignell (Winchester, 1831), 21M65/C9/70; see 76, above, and appendix A, below.

58  Boothman v. Duxbury (Chester, 1821), EDC 5 (1822–3)

59  Harrison v. Knibbs (Gloucester, 1821), B4/1/1474

60  Brown v. Stephens (Gloucester, 1844), B4/1/633

61  Often quoted is the statement that 'if the passions of women were ready, strong, and spontaneous, in a degree even remotely approaching the form they assume in the coarser sex, there can be little doubt that sexual irregularities would reach a height, of which, at present, we have happily no conception ... No! Nature has laid many heavy burdens on the shoulders of the weaker sex: let us rejoice that this at least is spared them.' [W.R. Greg], 'Prostitution,' *Westminster Review*, 53 (1850), 457. A statement of this sort may reveal more about the commentator than about the matter commented upon and raises difficulties about who is being assessed and by whom and for what purposes. Modern discussions are numerous.

62  R.H. Helmholz, *Select Cases on Defamation to 1600* (London 1985), xxix

63  H. Conset, *The Practice of the Spiritual or Ecclesiastical Courts* (London 1700), 335; T. Oughton, *Ordo Judiciorum* (London 1728), title IV, xxv and xxvi; Law, *Forms of Ecclesiastical Law* (London 1831), 47

64  Helmholz, *Select Cases on Defamation*, xxx. See 17, note 4, above.

65  Johnson v. Bulliman (Peterborough, 1821), X 955

66  D.M. Walker, *Principles of Scottish Private Law*, 4th ed., vol. 2, book 4 (Oxford 1988), 26–7

67  Burdon v. Poole (Lichfield, 1836), B/C/5/1838

68  Settle v. Tempest (Chester, 1822), Griffiths v. Goode (Chester, 1823), Stevenson v. Dempster (Richmond, 1835)

69  Ripley v. Garside (York, 1826), Cons CP 1826/4; see 86, above, and 174–5, below.

70  Walker v. Clarke (Peterborough, 1818), X951

71  Binks v. Barker (Chester, 1824), EDC 5 (1824–5)

72  Sparks v. Thornell (Gloucester, 1854), B4/1/2231

73  Routledge v. Richardson (Carlisle, 1850)

74  Gartside v. Wormald (York, 1835), Cons CP 1835/6

75 See Mariana Valverde, 'The Love of Finery: Fashion and the Fallen Woman in Nineteenth Century Social Discourse,' *Victorian Studies*, 32 (1969), 169.
76 Harrison v. Taylor (Chester, 1828), EDC 5 (1828). See J.L. Matus, *Unstable Bodies* (Manchester 1995), 72.
77 Harrison v. Taylor (Chester, 1828)
78 Mackay v. Fleetwood (Carlisle, 1852), DRC/3/51, f. 26
79 Browne v. Fairhurst (Bath and Wells, 1850), D/D/Cp 1850
80 Dee v. Seaborne (Hereford, 1831), HD4/59
81 Libel in Pritchard v. James (Gloucester, 1853), B4/1/1129
82 Ingles v. Cooke (Hereford, 1816)
83 Preston v. Edge (Chester, 1816), EDC 5 (1816–17)
84 Routledge v. John Tomlinson (Chester, 1817), Verrey v. Yarnold (Worcester, 1816), Hadley v. Whittaker (Chester, 1825)
85 Smith v. Wardle (York, 1821), Cons CP 1821/3
86 Booth v. Gordon (Chester, 1820), Tranter v. Edmunds; Tranter v. Butcher (Hereford, 1821), Whitehead v. James Smith (Chester, 1827), Dennison v. Haigh (York, 1816), Garside v. Ripley (York, 1827), Stubbs v. Bradley (York, 1841), Ellis v. Barker (York, 1835), Hart v. Cockshaw (York, Dean and Chapter, 1835)
87 Biffen v. Lawley (Bath and Wells, 1834), D/D/Cp 1834, Robinson v. Sharp (York, 1824), Stone v. Andrews (Chichester, 1818), Hall v. Daw (Gloucester, 1834), Powell v. Probert (Hereford, 1816), Smith v. Powell (Bath and Wells, 1846)
88 Highland v. Steel (Carlisle, 1850), DRC/3/51, f. 9
89 Edmunds v. Drew (Gloucester, 1841), B4/1/2161
90 Cope v. Jackson (Hereford, 1834), HD4/61
91 Richards v. Clark (London, 1825), Guildhall, 12,185/2. See 36, above, and 175, below.
92 Williams v. Probert (Hereford, 1827), HD4/57
93 Church v. Elizabeth Halls (Norwich, 1821), DN/CDN/125
94 Foster v. Stubbing (York, 1823); see 58, above.
95 Edmunds v. Drew (Gloucester, 1841), B4/1/2161
96 Morgan v. Hodges (Hereford, 1824), HD4/56
97 Edmunds v. Drew (Gloucester, 1841), B4/1/2161
98 Hall v. Daw (Gloucester, 1834), B4/1/539
99 Taylor v. Hazlehurst (Chester, 1822), EDC 5 (1822–3)
100 Dewhurst v. Isherwood (Chester, 1839), Curry v. Overthrow (Gloucester, 1821), Jones v. Ladkin (Lichfield, 1815), John v. Prichard (Landaff, 1827), Billett v. Burnett (Salisbury, 1831), Gore v. Stratford (Gloucester, 1847)
101 Forrest v. Gommershall (Chester, 1820), Bragg v. Rumney (Carlisle, 1837), Thomas v. Thomas (St David's, 1834), Morgan v. Charles (St David's, 1841), Fowles v. Knight (Salisbury, 1830), Wigan v. Clarke (Chester, 1829)

102 Milkinch v. Trevor (Chester, 1821), EDC 5 (1820–1). Some physical defect is apparently alluded to here. The defendant also said, 'You breed nothing but mules.'

103 Holmes v. Smith (York, 1820), Cons CP 1820/3

104 Binnington v. Watson (York, 1816), Cons CP 1816/3

105 Burdon v. Poole (Lichfield, 1836), B/C/5/1838

106 Barlow v. Hobson (Chester, 1823), EDC 5 (1822–3)

107 H.C. Coote, *The Practice of the Ecclesiastical Courts* (London 1847), 267, appendix A, below, and plate 7

108 Milner v. Welborn (York, Deanery Court, 1826), DY CP 1826/1

109 Harrison v. Leetham (York, Peculiar, 1820), Askwith's note (n.d.), PP

110 Crosby v. England (York, 1820), Smith v. Wardle (York, 1821), Cons CP 1821/3, Pilling v. Bradley (York, 1829), Humble v. Gypson (York, 1833), Barlow v. Hobson (Chester, 1823), Faulkes v. Bowdler (Gloucester, 1848), King v. Hall (London, 1829)

111 Dewhurst v. Isherwood (Chester, 1839), EDC 5 (1838–9)

112 Kinsey v. Williams (Chester, 1833), EDC 5 (1834)

113 Crosby v. England (York, 1820), Cons CP 1820/8

114 Bond v. Mapp (Hereford, 1848), HD4/64

115 Claxton v. Simpson (Norwich, 1837), Bannister v. Tillett (London, 1840), Keelan v. Asprey (Llandaff, 1850)

116 Webber v. Penn (Exeter, 1816), CC 79A/80

117 Livie v. Mackintosh (London, 1820), LPL, H326A

118 In Burdon v. Poole, the words were spoken in the course of a street quarrel following a violent altercation in the plaintiff's house; the defendant was the wife of a butcher, who, like her husband, signed her proxy by mark (X).

119 In Bannister v. Tillett, the plaintiff's father kept a jewellery shop.

120 Southwood v. Halford (Gloucester, 1848), B4/1/114; also Milner v. Welborn (York, Deanery Court, 1826), Leverett v. Davy (Norwich, 1822), Watson v. Allen (Lincoln, 1824), Higham v. Howe (Lichfield, 1828), Willson v. Willson (Lichfield, 1836), Nowell v. Gowan (Bath and Wells, 1835), Fortune v. Roberts (Exeter, 1820), Hill v. Salter (Exeter, 1820), Board v. Hill (Bath and Wells, 1846)

121 Higham v. John Howe (Lichfield, 1828), B/C/5/1829; also King v. Hall (London, 1830), Garner v. Williams (Chester, 1825)

122 Vowles v. White (Bath and Wells, 1832), D/D/Cp 1832

123 Pope v. Richards (Gloucester, 1833), note 3, above

124 Williams v. Parry (Chester, 1826), Bennett v. Chatworthy (Llandaff, 1828), Binnington v. Watson (York, 1816), Middleton v. Richardson (Ripon, 1851), Anna Maria Bardsley v. Bardsley the elder (Chester, 1829)

125 Dix v. Scarse (Peterborough, 1838), X953; see 18–19, above.

126  Viner v. Clack (Bath and Wells, 1836), D/D/Cp 1836

127  Webb v. Smith (Gloucester, 1834), B4/1/544; also Weight v. Hulls (Gloucester, 1835)

128  Barrow v. Barrow (Chester, 1832), EDC 5 (1832); also Webb v. Smith (Gloucester, 1834)

129  Welshman v. Love (Bath and Wells, 1850), D/D/Cp 1850

130  Caswell v. Halford (Hereford, 1845), HD4/64; also Meakin v. Robert Latham (Chester, 1826), Leach v. Spurr (Chester, 1826)

131  Garrett v. Smith (Lichfield, 1819), B/C/5/1819

132  Sawkill v. Knaggs (York, 1829), Dent v. Dodd (Peterborough, 1816), Williams v. Watts (St David's, 1831), Morris v. Lewis (St David's, 1832)

133  Newall v. Hutchinson (York, 1835), Cons CP 1835/7

134  Deykes v. Phillips (Hereford, 1827), HD4/57; also Smith v. Burroughs (Norwich, 1836), Jane Clayton v. Taylor (Chester, 1834), Wyman v. Butler (Gloucester, 1838), Brennan v. Whiting (Peterborough, 1823), Stubbs v. Bradley (York, 1841)

135  Bastow v. Bakes (York, 1817), Cons CP 1817/1

136  Mills v. Freeman (York, 1834), Cons CP 1834/2

137  Morgan v. Charles (St David's, 1841), SD/CCCm (G)/573

138  Seabourne v. Munger (Gloucester, 1827), B4/1/2918; also Simpson v. Jacobs (Norwich, 1818)

139  Weight v. Hulls (Gloucester, 1835), B4/1/1027

140  Hogg v. Crook (Gloucester, 1838), quoted above

141  F.N. Rogers, *A Practical Arrangement of Ecclesiastical Law*, 2nd ed. (London 1849), 331, citing Rolle's *Abridgement* (1668). The word appears in defamation causes of an earlier period: L. Gowing, *Domestic Dangers: Women, Words and Sex in Early Modern London* (Oxford 1996), 96, 106, 129.

142  Simpson v. Jacobs (Norwich, 1818), DN/CON/124

143  Linken v. Prior (Norwich, 1832), DN/CON/129

144  Morton v. Christie (Winchester, 1830), 21M65/C9/579

145  James v. Miles (London, 1835), Guildhall, 12,185/4

146  Clayton v. Gale (Gloucester, 1821), B4/1/1122; also Bear v. Bignell (Winchester, 1831)

147  Edelstone v. Ellison (Chester, 1818), Lay v. Cox (Oxford, 1817), Sheard v. Ramsden (Ripon, 1852)

148  Willimont v. Willimont (Norwich, 1836), DN/CON/131

149  Bear v. Bignell (Winchester, 1831)

150  Churchward v. Churchward (Exeter, 1815), CC 80

151  Bridgwood v. Barker (Lichfield, 1816), Draper v. Birt (Gloucester, 1819)

152  Dauncey v. French (Gloucester, 1815), Coaker v. Pinson (Exeter, 1827), Hinder v. Harper (Gloucester, 1824)

153 Routledge v. John and Alice Tomlinson (Chester, 1817)

154 Barnes v. Haslam (Chester, 1817), EDC 5 (1818–19)

155 Stephens v. Ridgeway (Hereford, 1829), HD4/58, Lockwood v. Sheldon (Chester, 1839)

156 Doughty v. Campling (Norwich, 1834), DN/CON/130

157 Greenhalgh v. Clough (Chester, 1822), EDC 5 (1822–3)

158 Willan v. Brown (Carlisle, 1827), DRC/3/50, f. 26

159 Heald v. Jepson (Chester, 1819), EDC 5 (1818–19)

160 Clayton v. Marshall (Richmond, (1819), RD/AC/1/10

161 Walter v. Taylor (Bath and Wells, 1817), D/D/Cp 1817

162 Blanning and Toogood v. Penny; Blanning and Toogood v. White (Bath and Wells, 1819)

163 Heald v. Jepson (Chester, 1819)

164 Paginton v. Kayns (Salisbury, 1830)

165 Bond v. Mapp (Hereford, 1848), HD4/64

166 Dorney v. Webb (Bath and Wells, 1832), D/D/Cp 1832

167 Garside v. Ripley (York, 1827), Cons CP 1826/4

168 Gooch v. Morley (Norwich, 1851)

169 Higgs v. Higgs (London, 1840), Guildhall, 12,185/5

170 Milkinch v. Trevor (Chester, 1821), Goodbody v. Cooper (Chester, 1834), Draper v. Birt (Gloucester, 1819), Leatt v. Pearson (London, 1819), Booth v. Gordon (Chester, 1820), Halliwell v. Tempest (Chester, 1832), Claxton v. Simpson (Norwich, 1837), Mackay v. Fleetwood (Carlisle, 1852), Asprey v. Keelan (Llandaff, 1850)

171 Hippolyte Taine, *Notes on England, 1860–70*, tr. E. Hyams (1957), quoted in R. Pearsall, *The Worm in the Bud: The World of Victorian Sexuality* (London 1969), 341–2

172 Daniel v. Ostell (Carlisle, 1845), Act Book, 25 April 1845, 25 July 1845, DRC/3/31, Deposition Book, DRC/3/50 pp. 230–6

173 Middleton v. Richardson (Ripon, 1851), cause papers, RD/AC/1/12

174 Hampden v. Eyton (Arches Court, 1846, by letters of request). See 31, above.

175 Asprey v. Keelan (Llandaff, 1850), LL/CC/G/2130

176 Powell v. Probert (Hereford, 1816), Jones v. Watkins (Llandaff, 1819), Pilling v. Bradley (York, 1829), Pask v. Presely (Lincoln, 1823), Moss v. Winkworth (Salisbury, 1827), Dauncey v. French (Gloucester, 1815), Richards v. Clark (London, 1824). See 29–30, 36–8, above, and 175, below.

177 Draper v. Birt (Gloucester, 1819), B4/1/1343

178 For the seventeenth century, see M. Ingram, 'Ridings, Rough Music, and the Reform of Popular Culture in Early Modern England,' *Past and Present*, 105 (1984), 79.

179 Williams v. Probert (Hereford, 1827)

180 Williams v. King (London, 1842), Guildhall, 12,185/7

181 D. Underdown, *Revels, Riots, and Rebellion: Popular Politics and Culture in England, 1603–1660* (Oxford 1985), associates skimmingtons with village revels in the seventeeth century. See also Ingram, 'Ridings,' 94.

182 Stannier v. Precious (Chester, 1834), EDC 5 (1835–6)

183 Noble v. Powell (York, 1819), Cons CP 1819/5. See 100, above.

184 James v. Williams (Llandaff, 1834), LL/CC/G/2082

185 Webb v. Smith (Gloucester, 1834), B4/1/544

186 France v. Aaron (York, 1838), Cons CP 1838/4, depositions transcribed in appendix A, below; also Ellis v. Stead (York, 1821)

187 Kinsey v. Williams (Chester, 1833), EDC 5 (1834)

188 Bond v. Mapp (Hereford, 1848), HD4/64

189 James v. Williams (Llandaff, 1834), LL/CC/G/2082

190 Bach v. Engstrom (Hereford, 1822), HD4/56

191 Youngs v. Bailey (Norwich, 1826)

192 Wilson v. Gee (York, 1817), Cons CP 1817/8

193 Biffen v. Lawley (Bath and Wells, 1825), D/D/Cp 1825

194 Craske v. Henry Youell (Norwich, 1847), DN/CON/137, and *Norwich Mercury*, 17 July 1847, 3a; see 38–9, 43, above.

195 Ayre v. Hambly (Exeter, 1819), Ayre v. Tocker (Exeter, 1819, and Arches Court LPL, H310), Bate v. Collis (Worcester, 1846, and Arches Court), Marsh v. Travers (Norwich, 1846)

196 Smith v. Day (York, 1831)

197 Marsh v. Travers (Norwich, 1846), DN/CON/137, Act Book, 31 May 1847, DN/ACT 106

198 Coote, *The Practice of the Ecclesiastical Courts*, 267

199 Hadfield v. Harrup (Chester, 1831), EDC 5 (1833)

200 Briscoe v. Briscoe (Chester, 1831), EDC 5 (1832)

201 Collett v. Tarring (Bath and Wells, 1822), D/D/Cp 1822

202 Peart v. Roberts (Gloucester, 1834), Goodbody v. Cooper (Chester, 1834), Leather v. Maskery (Chester, 1855), Pitcher v. Pitcher (Gloucester, 1847), Cambridge v. Young (Gloucester, 1852), Pow v. Osbourn (Bath and Wells, 1832), Stroud v. Churches (Bath and Wells, 1834), James v. Miles (London, 1835), Priest v. Jenkins (Gloucester, 1848)

203 Potter v. Huey (Chester, 1821)

204 Hall v. Daw (Gloucester, 1834)

205 France v. Aaron (York, 1838), Cons CP 1838/4; see appendix A.

206 Page to Askwith, 30 April 1825, in Calvert v. Chapman (York, 1825), PP

207 Idle v. Crawshay (York, 1833), Cons CP 1833/3

208 Dewhurst v. Isherwood (Chester, 1839), EDC 5 (1838–9)

209 Rush v. Woodcock (Norwich, 1842), DN/CON/133

210 Bunce v. Pennington (Chester, 1833), EDC 5 (1834); also Powell v. Probert (Hereford, 1816), Brewer v. Stark (Exeter, 1819), Chesworth v. Evans (Chester, 1837), James v. Barker (Carlisle, 1844), Middleton v. Richardson (Ripon, 1851)

211 Howarth v. Bannister (Chester, 1816), EDC 5 (1816–17)

212 Edmunds v. Drew (Gloucester, 1841), B4/1/2161

213 Milkinch v. Trevor (Chester, 1821), EDC 5 (1820–1)

214 In *The Mill on the Floss* (1860), Maggie Tulliver is mistakenly, though not altogether unreasonably, suspected of having eloped with a lover. She is turned away from the door by her brother; she finds it impossible to obtain employment; no one will speak to her in the street, and the kindly and sympathetic rector advises her to leave town. George Eliot wrote that she has been condemned by public opinion (book 7, chapters 1 and 2).

215 Leatt v. Pearson (London, 1819), Marsh v. Travers (Norwich, 1846)

216 Welshman v. Love (Bath and Wells, 1850), D/D/Cp 1850

217 Griffiths v. Goode (Chester, 1823), EDC 5 (1822–3)

218 Howarth v. Bannister (Chester, 1816), EDC 5 (1816–17)

219 Bannister v. Tillett (London, 1840), Guildhall, 12,185/5

220 Claxton v. Simpson (Norwich, 1837), DN/CON/131

221 Webber v. Penn (Exeter, 1816)

222 Aspinall v. Hudson (Chester, 1828)

223 Middleton v. Richardson (Ripon, 1851). 'Birling' is explained by another witness as 'plucking bits of cotton out of the cloth ... & then rolling it up,' an operation that required assistance. RD/AC/1/12

224 Dorney v. Webb (Bath and Wells, 1832) (defence witness), D/D/Cp 1832

225 Bannister v. Tillett (London, 1840)

226 Wallis v. Cory (Exeter, 1828), CC 81/81A

227 Meakin v. Robert Latham (Chester, 1826), EDC 5 (1826)

228 Cheadle v. Spencer (York, 1826), Cons CP 1826/3

229 Foster v. Sixsmith (Chester, 1834), EDC 5 (1835)

230 E. Wright, *Mrs Gaskell: The Basis for Reassessment* (Oxford 1965), 37n, A. Pollard, *Mrs Gaskell: Novelist and Biographer* (Manchester 1965), 86, and M. Ganz, *Elizabeth Gaskell: The Artist in Conflict* (New York 1969), 105–7. But E. Trudgill, *Madonnas and Magdalenes: The Origin and Development of Victorian Sexual Attitudes* (London 1976), 224–5, points out that hostile reviews were in the minority, and sees the incident as a sign of relaxation of an earlier greater prudishness.

231 Bannister v. Tillett (London, 1840)

232 Watkins v. Fleming (Sodor and Man, 1821), Liber Causarum 1821

233  Sharpe v. Dauncey (Gloucester, 1849), B4/1/2318; see 8–10, above.

234  Idle v. Crawshay (York, 1833), Cons CP 1833/3

235  Bannister v. Tillett (London, 1840), Guildhall, 12,185/5

236  Stevens v. Shimmin (Chester, 1854), EDC 5 (1854–5)

237  John Vallance to Revd J.H. Bromby (instructing agent to William Askwith), 16 June 1819, in Musgrave v. Abbey (York, 1819), PP

238  Kewley v. Kewley (Sodor and Man, 1820), Liber Causarum 1820

239  Simpson v. Jacobs (Norwich, 1818), DN/CON/124

240  Dee v. Seaborne (Hereford, 1831), HD4/59; also Merritt v. Long (Gloucester, 1826)

241  Chesworth v. Evans (Chester, 1837), EDC 5 (1838–9)

242  Heald v. Jepson (Chester, 1819), EDC 5 (1818–19); also Forrest v. Gommershall (Chester, 1830), Oakes v. Billings (Chester, 1826), Grimmage v. Edwards (Chester, 1828), Pilling v. Taylor (Chester, 1834), Taylor v. Fletcher (Chester, 1827)

243  Roberts v. Gilpin (Hereford, 1829), HD4/58

244  Payne v. Marsh (Worcester, 1822), Billamy v. Ware (York, 1821) (draft libel), PP

245  Heald v. Jepson (Chester, 1819), Smith v. Powell (Bath and Wells, 1846)

246  Taylor v. Fletcher (Chester, 1827)

247  Dewhurst v. Isherwood (Chester, 1839), Aspinall v. Hudson (Chester, 1828)

248  Anna Maria Bardsley v. Bardsley the elder (Chester, 1829)

249  Grace Scanes v. Ford (Exeter, 1816), CC 83

250  Prissick v. Parry (Chester, 1845); also Stevenson v. Dempster (Richmond, 1835)

251  Johnson v. Goodier (Chester, 1817), Hadfield v. Welsh (Chester, 1831), Hadfield v. Harrup (Chester, 1831), Pilling v. Taylor (Chester, 1834), Stannier v. Precious (Chester, 1834)

252  Derges v. Scott (Exeter, 1830), Beech v. Moore (Chester, 1821), Haigh v. Willett (Chester, 1827), Cogswell v. Dawson (Chester, 1833)

253  Middleton v. Richardson (Ripon, 1851)

254  Rose v. Knight (London, 1831), Guildhall, 12,185/3; see 72–3, 131–2, above.

255  Castletine v. Dugdale (York, 1841)

256  Taylor v. Davis (Chester, 1853), EDC 5 (1854–5); see 29, above.

257  Dorney v. Webb (Bath and Wells, 1832), D/D/Cp 1832; see 22, 37, above. Also Pickering v. Bird (Worcester, 1828), Storey v. Moffatt (Carlisle, 1839)

258  See also Taylor v. Millard (Bath and Wells, 1835), Smith v. Powell (Bath and Wells, 1846)

259  Roberts v. Gilpin (Hereford, 1829), HD4/58

260  Gowing, *Domestic Dangers*, 35

261  See 123, above.

262  Sadler v. Stimpson (Norwich, 1819), DN/CON/125

263  Taylor v. Grace (Chester, 1815), Shone v. Hughes (Chester, 1815), Dutton v.

Hardman (Chester, 1822), Williams v. Evans (Chester, 1823), Ellis v. Barclay (Chester, 1825), Kershaw v. Butterworth (Chester, 1825), Pickles v. Rudd (Chester, 1830), Newton v. Peers (Chester, 1817), Bardsley the elder v. Anna Maria Bardsley (Chester, 1829), Bardsley the elder v. Bardsley the younger (Chester, 1829), Law v. Law (Peterborough, 1819), Locke v. Phillips (Peterborough, 1840), Brown v. Harvey (Exeter, 1818), Heald v. Jepson (Chester, 1819)

264   Brown v. Harvey (Exeter, 1818), Meakin v. Best (Chester, 1845), Chadwick v. Wilde (Chester, 1834), Fitzjohn v. Hayes (Peterborough, 1830), Latham v. Poole (Chester, 1823), Dutton v. Hardman (Chester, 1822), Harrison v. Adams (Chester, 1816)

265   See Helmholz, *Select Cases on Defamation*, 18 (York case of 1593). 'Whoremaster' may correspond to the Latin 'pronuba'; see Karras, 'The Latin Vocabulary of Illicit Sex.' The word was rare in the early modern period. M. Ingram, *Church Courts, Sex, and Marriage in England, 1570–1640* (Cambridge 1987), 302

266   E.g., Eltonhead v. Cooper (Chester, 1816) ('whoremaster or whoremonger'), Brown v. Harvey (Exeter, 1818) ('whoremaster, whoremonger and fornicator')

267   See Taylor v. Grace (Chester, 1815), where the interrogatory suggested that the plaintiff had provoked the defendant by calling him a 'whoremaster.' EDC 5, 1814–15

268   Houlgate v. Sturdy (Lichfield, 1826), B/C/5/1827

269   Heald v. Jepson (Chester, 1819), EDC 5 (1818–19)

270   Smith v. Phillips (Peterborough, 1818), X951

271   Cooke v. Harper (Hereford, 1852), HD4/64

272   Berrington v. Page (St David's, 1838), SD/CCCm (G)/560

273   Appendix B, below.

274   Bennett v. Thomas (Chester, 1828) (surgeon), Alexander v. Moore (Norwich, 1847) (surgeon), George Clayton v. Taylor (Chester, 1834) (schoolmaster)

275   David v. Jones (Llandaff, 1824), Sanday v. Haine (Bath and Wells, 1821), Board v. Hill (Bath and Wells, 1843)

276   Board, in his petition, admitted striking Hill. Another witness said that Board did not knock Hill down, and that she struck him with the poker. D/D/Cp 1843

277   Hill v. Board (Bath and Wells, 1843), Act Book, 21 November 1843, D/D/Ca 459; see 72–8, above.

278   Snell v. Bailey (Salisbury, 1832, and Arches Court, 1832), LPL H 484/9

279   Simpson v. Jacobs (Norwich, 1818), DN/CON/124; see 140, above. Also Walter v. Taylor (Bath and Wells, 1819), Snell v. Bailey (Salisbury, 1832, and Arches Court, 1833), Viner v. Clack (Bath and Wells, 1836)

280   Craske v. F. and H. Youell (Norwich, 1846); see 38–9, 43, above.

281   Hooley v. Lumbers (Chester, 1833), EDC 5 (1834). Sentence was given for the

plaintiff but with costs of 25s. only; Court Book, 10 May 1834 and 6 November 1834, EDC 1/195. See 97, above.

282 Fitzjohn v. Hayes (Peterborough, 1830), Cooke v. Harper (Hereford, 1852)

283 Bateman v. Winn (York, 1840), Kershaw v. Butterworth (Chester, 1825), Parry v. Trevor (Chester, 1845), Law v. Law (Peterborough, 1819), Warner v. Barnes (Norwich Dean and Chapter, 1835)

284 Cooke v. Harper (Hereford, 1852)

285 Knaggs v. Dickinson (York, 1831), Johnson v. Leverett (Worcester, 1823), Todd v. Freeman (Norwich, 1820), Whitehead v. Massey (Chester, 1837)

286 Alexander v. Moore (Norwich, 1847), Latham v. Poole (Chester, 1823), Wells v. Phillips (Arches, 1849)

287 Forrester v. Armstrong (Carlisle, 1854) ('dumb and not quite right')

288 Leeson v. Wills (Peterborough, 1833)

289 Kemp v. Welch (Winchester, 1831), 21M65/C9/484

290 Chadwick v. Wild (Chester, 1834)

291 Jones v. Roberts (Bangor, 1824), B/CC/G/403c

292 Waite v. Slaymaker (Peterborough, 1828), X954

293 Waite v. Foster (Peterborough, 1828), X954, Hirst v. Taylor (Ripon, 1851)

294 Hall v. Ringrose (Peterborough, 1816), Lowis v. Fowkes (Peterborough, 1824) (wife and two daughters)

295 Lowe v. Randall (Peterborough, 1840)

296 Barois v. Williams (Hereford, 1826)

297 Maw v. Rainforth (Lincoln – Archdeaconry Court of Stow, 1829)

298 Eltonhead v. Cooper (Chester, 1816)

299 Phillips v. Cutmore (Exeter, 1831), Act Book, 18 March 1831, 853m, and cause papers CC 83; similarly Jones v. Roberts (Bangor, 1824)

## 10: Motives

1 H.C. Coote, *The Practice of the Ecclesiastical Courts* (London 1847), 266 (libel), 272 (sentence), and see appendix A, below.

2 Ecclesiastical Courts Commission Report, appendix A, PP 1831–2, xxiv, 177 (evidence of W. Ward)

3 King v. Hall (London, 1830), Guildhall, 12,185/3

4 Fisher v. Tozer (Bath and Wells, 1828), D/D/Cp 1828; also Grimmage v. Edwards (Chester, 1828) ('clear herself of the scandal')

5 Edmunds v. Drew (Gloucester, 1841), B4/1/2161; also Hutchinson v. J. Proctor (York, 1838) ('to justify herself before the public')

6 Tocker v. Ayre (1821), 3 Phil 539 (Arches Court on appeal from Exeter)

7 Haigh v. Willett (Chester, 1827), EDC 5 (1828)

8  Idle v. Crawshay (York, 1833), Cons CP 1833/3

9  Bannister v. Tillett (London, 1840), Guildhall, 12,185/6; see 148–9, above.

10  See Report of Select Committee of the House of Lords on the Law of Defamation, HL Papers 1843 Sess. Pap. 18, reprinted PP 1843 v, 259, and Anthony Trollope, *Cousin Henry* (1881).

11  See 138–9, 146, above.

12  Holmes v. Smith (York, 1820), Kirkby v. Thompson (York, 1820), King v. Hall (London, 1830), Challingworth v. Bowers (Worcester, 1844)

13  Pilling v. Bradley (York, 1829), Kirkby v. Thompson (York, 1820), Porter v. Rayson (Peterborough, 1830)

14  Forrester v. Armstrong (Carlisle, 1854) (male plaintiff)

15  Kirkby v. Thompson (York, 1820)

16  Bromby to Askwith, 27 February 1824, in Foster v. Stubbing (York, 1823), PP

17  Hutchinson v. J. Proctor (York, 1838)

18  Harrison v. Leetham (Selby Peculiar, 1820), PP

19  Chater v. Gibbins (Peterborough, 1833), X 955

20  Beech v. Moore (Chester 1821), EDC 5 (1822–3)

21  Townley v. Reeve (Norwich, 1841), DN/CON/133

22  Haigh v. Willett (Chester, 1827), EDC 5 (1828)

23  Holmes v. Smith (York, 1820), Cons CP 1820/3; also Kirkby v. Thompson (York, 1820)

24  Bromby to Askwith, 13 May 1819, in Musgrave v. Abbey (York, 1819), PP

25  William Challingworth to C. Evans, 11 July 1844, in Challingworth v. Bowers (Worcester, 1844), 797.69/2631

26  Rodgers v. Brearley (Lichfield, 1830), B/C/5/1830

27  See 3, above.

28  Shires v. Pearson (York, 1836), Cons CP 1836/8 (affidavits dated 27 April 1836)

29  Abstract Book, 28 April 1836

30  Humble v. Gypson (York, 1837)

31  Henry Clifton to Ann Collis, 29 March 1845, in Bate v. Collis (Worcester, 1845 and Arches Court, 1846), LPL, H694. Also Porter v. Rayson (Peterborough, 1830)

32  Duggleby v. Sanderson (York, Dean and Chapter Court, 1819), Dean and Chapter Court Book, 25 June 1819, Borthwick Institute, D/C AB 21, and D/C CP 1819/1

33  Askwith to Sanderson 18 June 1819 (copy), in Duggleby v. Sanderson (York, Dean and Chapter Court, 1819), PP

34  Langley v. Langley (Peterborough, 1841), X 953

35  Williams v. James (Llandaff, 1831), LL/CC/G/2060

36  Variations of a similar sort appear in Roberts v. Jones (Llandaff, 1853), Jones v. Williams (Llandaff, 1854), Barlow v. Phillips (Llandaff, 1854), Jennings v. Leyshon (Gloucester, 1827).

37  Chesworth v. Evans (Chester, 1837) (proctor's submission to court), EDC 5 (1838–9)

38  Board v. Hill (Bath and Wells, 1843), D/D/Cp 1843; also Edmunds v. Drew (Gloucester, 1841)

39  Payne v. Marsh (Worcester, 1822), 797.69/2631

40  William Robinson to Gates, 7 September 1830, in Fitzjohn v. Hayes (Peterborough, 1830), X 954

41  Act Book, 7 October 1830, ML 718

42  Bentley v. North (Ripon, 1849), Bill of Costs, Borthwick Institute, Proctor's Precedent Book, P 35, f. 139

43  Ward v. Warner (Peterborough, 1837), X953

44  Clark v. Marks (Bath and Wells, 1840), Act Book, 4 August 1840, D/D/Ca 457, Foster v. Hart (Peterborough, 1818), Act Book, 6 November 1818, ML 717, Williams v. Owens (St Asaph, 1839), Act Book, 22 October 1839 SA/CB/28

45  Williams v. James (Llandaff, 1831)

46  Askwith to Bromby, 23 July 1823 (copy), in Foster v. Stubbing (York, 1823), PP

47  Haigh v. Willett (Chester, 1827), EDC 5 (1828)

48  Southwood v. Halford (Gloucester, 1848), B4/1/114; see 87, above.

49  Browning v. Mitchell (Gloucester, 1838)

50  Duffett v. Evans (Bristol, 1847)

51  Southwood v. Halford (Gloucester, 1848), B4/1/114

52  Slagg v. Hutton (Lichfield, 1830)

53  Webb v. Smith (Gloucester, 1834), B4/1/544

54  Cogswell v. Dawson (Chester, 1833), EDC 5 (1834); a similar suggestion was made in Holmes v. Smith (York, 1820).

55  Bromby to Askwith, 6 November 1823, in Foster v. Stubbing (York, 1823), PP

56  Mary Foster to Bromby, 2 January 1825, PP (spelling irregular)

57  Same to same, 25 February 1825, PP

58  Scanes v. Ford (Exeter, 1816) (proctor's argument), CC 80

59  Levy v. Levy (Norwich, 1831), DN/CON/129; see 118, above, and 174, below.

60  Morse v. Morse (Bath and Wells, 1827), D/D/Cp 1827; also Wickham v. Lockyer (Bath and Wells, 1836)

61  Pilling v. Taylor (Chester, 1834), EDC 5 (1835)

62  Woodhouse v. Williams (Gloucester, 1845), B4/1/1364

63  Fisher v. Tozer (Bath and Wells, 1828), D/D/Cp 1828

64  King v. Hall (London, 1830), Guildhall, 12,185/3

65  Richards v. Clark (London, 1824), Guildhall, 12,185/2

66  Board v. Hill (Bath and Wells, 1843); see 153, above.

67  Pattinson v. Hayton (Carlisle, 1839), Deposition Book, DRC/3/50, ff. 93–5; see also 124, above.

68 This is very clear in Bate v. Collis (Worcester, 1845 and Arches Court); see Collis v. Bate (1846), 4 Notes of Cases 540.

69 W. Beart to J. Kitson, 4 February 1827, in Russell v. Wigg (Norwich, 1826), DN/ CON/127. The letter failed in its purpose, for sentence was given against the defendant, and she was imprisoned for non-payment of costs.

70 Dorney v. Webb (Bath and Wells, 1832), Marsh v. Travers (Norwich, 1846), Bannister v. Tillett (London, 1840)

71 Harrison v. Leetham (Selby Peculiar, 1820) (mother), PP, Cole v. Fuller (London, 1825) (sister), Stephens v. Ridgeway (Hereford, 1828) (brother), Lockwood v. Sheldon (Chester, 1839) (brother), Duffett v. Evans (Bristol, 1847) (brother), Musgrave v. Abbey (York, 1819) (husband's stepfather)

72 Bannister v. Tillett (London, 1840), Guildhall, 12,185/5; see 97, above.

73 Shew v. Webb (Arches Court, 1835). See 108, above.

74 Williams v. King (London, 1842), Wilson v. Bowness (York, 1826), PP

75 Welshman v. Love (Bath and Wells, 1850)

76 Briggs v. Dickinson (York, 1832), Gooch v. Morley (Norwich, 1850)

77 Jennings v. Leyshon (Gloucester, 1826), Phillips v. Luke (St David's, 1849).

78 See 150, above.

79 Harper v. Cooke (Hereford, 1853), HD4/64

80 Challingworth v. Bowers (Worcester, 1844), 797.69/2631

81 Binnington v. Watson (York, 1816), Cons CP 1816/3

82 Caswell v. Halford (Hereford, 1845), HD4/64

83 York Courant, 2 August 1838, 4d

84 John Crosley to Askwith, 3 August 1818 and 4 October 1818, and J.L. Lee to Askwith, 29 September 1818, in Bastow v. Bakes (York, 1818), PP; see 103, above.

85 Roberts v. Gilpin (Hereford, 1828), HD4/58

86 Charles Dickens, Oliver Twist (1837), chapter 51

87 Iveson & Kidd to Askwith, 28 October 1830, in Kinder v. Dyson, PP

88 Act Book, 8 November 1830, Cons AB 107

89 Askwith to Iveson and Kidd, n.d. (copy), but replying to letter of 26 June 1830, PP

90 Podmore v. Sutton (Chester, 1836)

91 Askwith's notes, probably for the advocate, in Harrison v. Leetham (Selby Peculiar, 1820), PP

92 John Harrison to Askwith, 25 May 1820, PP

93 Askwith to Sarah Winter, 26 May 1820 (copy), PP

94 Leatt v. Pearson (London, 1819), Guildhall, 12,1851/1. Other defamation cases linked with matrimonial disputes are discussed at 29–30, 36–8, 143, above, and 175, below.

95 Humble v. Gypson (York, 1833)

96 Browning v. Mitchell (Gloucester, 1838)

97 Harries v. Lloyd (St David's, 1835) (affidavit of defendant's proctor), SD/CC/G/ 544a

98 King v. Hall (London, 1829)

99 Wilson v. Gee (York, 1817)

100 Chavasse v. Harris (Gloucester, 1833), B4/1/741

101 Simpson v. Jacobs (Norwich, 1818); see 153, above; also Gooch v. Morley (Norwich, 1850)

102 John Robinson to Askwith, 18 May 1826, in Wilson v. Bowness (York, 1826), PP

103 Castletine v. Dugdale (York, 1841)

104 In Roberts v. Gilpin (Hereford, 1828), the man was alleged to have been in dispute with the defendant, a clergyman, over tithes.

105 As in Roberts v. Gilpin (Hereford, 1828), Heald v. Jepson (Chester, 1819)

106 C.A. Haigh. 'Slander and the Church Courts in the Sixteenth Century,' *Transactions of the Lancashire and Cheshire Antiquarian Society*, 78 (1975), 5

107 J.A. Sharpe, *Defamation and Sexual Slander in Early Modern England: The Church Courts at York*, Borthwick Papers, no. 58, Borthwick Institute (York, 1980), 25–6

108 Rayer and Dudfield v. Brimmell (Gloucester, 1826), B4/1/2558

109 Burlow v. Dudfield, Burlow v. Rayer (Gloucester, 1826), B4/1/2559 and 2560

110 Act Book, 15 June 1826, GDR 352. The cases are listed in the Ecclesiastical Courts Commission Report, appendix C, no. 7, 403.

111 Act Book, 4 February 1827, GDR 352. The depositions are missing.

112 E.g., Webber v. Penn (Exeter, 1816)

113 Powell v. Probert (Hereford, 1816), HD4/53

114 Boothman v. Duxbury (Chester, 1821), Humble v. Gypson (York, 1833), Batten v. Adams (Bath and Wells, 1830), Whittle v. West (Bath and Wells, 1831), Mosley v. Mosley (Peterborough, 1836)

115 Burroughs v. Dutton (Gloucester, 1826), Rose v. Knight (London, 1831), Foster v. Stubbing (York, 1823)

116 Humble v. Gypson (York, 1831), Cons CP 1833/2

117 Chater v. Gibbins (Peterborough, 1833), X955

118 Close v. Dixey (Peterborough, 1833), X955

119 John Crosley to Askwith, 17 February 1819, in Bastow v. Bakes (York, 1818), PP (£5 to Leeds Infirmary), Browning v. Mitchell (Gloucester, 1838), CC 81/81A

120 Derges v. Scott (Exeter, 1830) CC 81/81A

121 See chapter 6, above.

122 Wilson v. Bowness (York, 1826), Taylor v. Brailly (Peterborough, 1825), Linken v. Prior (Norwich, 1832), Marsh v. Travers (Norwich, 1846), Chavasse v. Harris (Gloucester, 1833), Bannister v. Tillett (London, 1840), Livie v. Mackintosh (London, 1820), Phillips v. Luke (St David's, 1849)

123  Harrison v. Leetham (Selby Peculiar, 1820), PP; see 29–30, above.

124  Crosby v. England (York, 1820), Cons CP 1820/8

125  Storey v. Moffatt (Carlisle, 1839), DRC/3/50, f. 87

126  Etty v. Kneeshaw (York, 1819), Cons CP 1819/4

127  Edelstone v. Ellison (Chester, 1818), EDC 5 (1818–19); also Etty v. Kneeshaw (York, 1819)

128  Dorney v. Webb (Bath and Wells, 1832), D/D/Cp 1832; also Woodhouse v. Williams (Gloucester, 1845)

129  Moss v. Elleman (Hereford, 1831), HD4/59

130  Goodson v. Tucker (Bath and Wells, 1847), D/D/Cp 1847; also Robinson v. Sharp (York, 1824), Pilling v. Taylor (Chester, 1834)

131  Lucas v. Lawrence (Gloucester, 1847), B4/1/556

132  John Crosley to Askwith, 17 February 1819, in Bastow v. Bakes (York, 1818), PP

133  See 44, above. Also Wallis v. Cory (Exeter, 1828)

134  Askwith to W. Page, n.d., in Calvert v. Chapman (York, 1825); significavit issued 9 June 1825, Abstract Book and PP; see 62, above.

135  Bate v. Collis (Worcester, 1845, and Arches Court, 1846), LPL, H694

136  Susan D. Amussen, *An Ordered Society: Gender and Class in Early Modern England* (Oxford 1988), 130

137  The census records show that she was still living at home unmarried in 1851 then aged twenty-one, 1851 HO 107/2047 f. 530. Thomas Bate (aged sixty in 1841), died before 1851.

138  Harries v. Lloyd (St David's, 1835), SD/CCCm (G)/544

139  Butterworth v. Wood (York, 1836), Cons CP 1836/10A; see 134, above.

140  Etty v. Kneeshaw (York, 1819), Cons CP 1819/4

141  Derges v. Scott (Exeter, 1830), CC 81/81A; also G. Scanes v. Ford (Exeter, 1816) ('silent contempt' tried but found ineffective)

142  Binnington v. Watson (York, 1816), Cons CP 1816/3. See 164, above.

143  Williams v. King (London, 1842), Guildhall, 12,185/7; also Smith v. Wardle (York, 1821), Foster v. Stubbing (York, 1823)

144  George Swinder to Elizabeth Aspinall, 18 March 1828, in Hudson v. Aspinall (Chester, 1827), EDC 5 (1827)

145  Bear v. Bignell (Winchester, 1832), deposition of Revd Robert Wright, 23 March 1832, Significavit, Schedule of Penance, 16 June 1833, 21M65/C9/70, and Act Book, 22 March 1833, 21M65/C2/109

146  Mary Johnson v. Harriet Johnson (London, 1819), GLRO Ac 73.11 box 14/10+40; see 129, above.

147  Stubbs v. Bradley (York, 1841), Cons CP 1841/3, Abstract Book, 17 November 1842, 2 February, 1843, *Yorkshire Gazette*, 30 July 1842, 8a, *York Courant*, 4 August 1842, 4b

148 Sharpe, *Defamation and Sexual Slander*, 22, L. Gowing, 'Gender and the Language of Insult in Early Modern London,' *History Workshop*, 35 (1993), 18, and *Domestic Dangers: Women, Words and Sex in Early Modern London* (Oxford 1996), 263

149 L. Stone, *The Family, Sex, and Marriage in England 1500–1800* (London 1977), Sharpe, *Defamation and Sexual Slander*, Polly Morris, 'Defamation and Sexual Reputation in Somerset 1733–1850,' unpublished PhD thesis (Warwick 1985)

150 Chesworth v. Evans (Chester, 1837), EDC 5 (1838–9)

151 *Law Magazine*, 7 (1832), 291

152 Anna Maria Bardsley v. Bardsley the elder (Chester, 1829)

153 Observations for the use of advocate in Garside v. Ripley; Ripley v. Garside (York, 1826), PP; also Trattles v. Trattles (York, 1827), Forrest v. Gommershall; Gommershall v. Forrest (Chester, 1821), Russell v. Wigg; Wigg v. Russell (Norwich, 1826 and 1827)

154 This was alleged in the connected cases of Jenny Watkins v. John Smith and Mary Ann Watkins v. David Smith (Gloucester, 1837), and in Butts v. Hollington (Worcester, 1847).

155 Hutchinson v. J. and S. Proctor (York, 1838), Cons CP 1838/6 and 7, *York Courant*, 2 August 1838, 4d; see 57–8, above.

156 Defensive allegation in Boyes v. Johnson (York, Deanery Court, 1841), Borthwick Institute, DY 1841/2

157 Ecclesiastical Courts Commission Report, appendix A, 115 (evidence of Matthew Marsh); see 126–7, above.

158 Samuel Cox to J. Huckwell, 9 July 1852, in Gregory v. David (Llandaff, 1852), LL/CC/G/2134

159 Edelstone v. Ellison (Chester, 1818) (threat of ruination denied, but 'I'll fix you' proved), Hooley v. Lumbers (Chester, 1833), Robson v. Robson (Durham, 1827), King v. Hall (London, 1830)

160 Binnington v. Watson (York, 1816)

161 Clack v. Baker (Bath and Wells, 1851), D/D/Cp 1851; also Smith v. Jane Whitter (Chester, 1817), Hadfield v. Harrup (Chester, 1831), Routledge v. Richardson (Carlisle, 1850)

162 Oakes v. Billings (Chester, 1826), EDC 5 (1826)

163 The interrogatory says it was Michael's second son (who was also called Isaac), but one of the witnesses said he saw Moses' son Isaac come home crying, so perhaps the instructions were misunderstood in drafting the interrogatory.

164 Levy v. Levy (Norwich, 1831), DN/CON/129; The spelling 'Levi' is in the interrogatories, and witnesses were asked whether this was not the proper spelling. Michael Levi, Isaac Levi the elder, Isaac Levi the younger, and Mier Levi (so spelled) are all listed as leading members of the Jewish community in Ipswich in

1841: C. Roth, *The Rise of Provincial Jewry ... 1740–1840* (London 1950), 72.
'Bunter' means a low vulgar woman (*OED*) and sometimes a whore. A witness
said in one case, 'I believe Bunter means a whore in the country language,'
Middleton v. Richardson (Ripon, 1851). In Pitcher v. Pitcher (Gloucester, 1847),
the phrases 'old bunter' and 'bunting whore' were used, and in Linton v. Bastin
(Exeter, 1815), 'bunting whore.' See R. Pearsall, *The Worm in the Bud: The World
of Victorian Sexuality* (London 1969), 502. Bracebridge Hemyng, 'Prostitution in
London,' in H. Mayhew, *London Labour and the London Poor* (London 1861;
reprinted 1968) 223, says that a bunter is a prostitute who defaults on rent. Other
cases of quarrels beginning among children are Hazlehurst v. Alberston (Chester,
1818), Smith v. Powell (Bath and Wells, 1846), and France v. Aaron (York, 1838).

165 See 86, above.
166 Page to Askwith, 17 June 1826, in Garside v. Ripley; Ripley v. Garside (York,
1826), PP; also Hampden v. Eyton (Arches Court, 1846) (dispute between two
men)
167 Page to Askwith, 5 January 1827, PP
168 Act Book, 29 June, 26 October 1826, Borthwick Institute
169 Page to Askwith, 22 November 1826, PP
170 Askwith to Page, 21 May 1827 (copy), PP
171 See 36–8, 143, above.
172 Dee v. Seabourne (Hereford, 1831), HD4/59; also Ormrod v. Wallwork (Chester,
1829), Baker v. Stone (Bath and Wells, 1829), Wright v. Bullen (Gloucester,
1836), Johnson v. Johnson (London, 1819), Richards v. Clark (London, 1824)
173 Richards v. Clark (London, 1824), Guildhall, 12,185/2; see 36, above.
174 T. & C. Walker to Askwith, 28 December 1833, in Humble v. Gypson (York,
1833), PP
175 Edmondson & Cowburn to Askwith, June 7 1837, in Spooner v. King (York,
1837), PP
176 Edmondson & Cowburn to Askwith, October 28, 1837, PP
177 Courtail v. Homfray (Llandaff and Arches Court, 1828); see 119–20, above.
178 Woodhouse v. Williams (Gloucester, 1845), B4/1/1364
179 Dorney v. Webb (Bath and Wells, 1832); see 36, above.
180 J. Godolphin, *Repertorium Canonicum*, 3rd ed. (London 1687), 63

## 11: Consequences

1 Ecclesiastical Courts Commission Report, PP 1831–2 xxiv, 63. See 12, above.
2 Mary Foster to Bromby, 24 February 1825, in Foster v. Stubbing (York, 1823), PP
3 Spoor v. Savory; Spoor v. Ray (Norwich, 1829), Shreve v. Wright (Norwich, 1848
and 1849)

4  Biffen v. Lawley (Bath and Wells, 1835), Baines v. Lawley (Bath and Wells, 1837) (sisters)

5  Edmunds v. Drew (Gloucester, 1841), B4/1/2161; this question was common in Gloucester interrogatories, e.g., Price v. Parry (Gloucester, 1841).

6  Holmes v. Smith (York, 1820), Cons CP 1820/3; see 158, above.

7  See bills of costs in appendix C to the Ecclesiastical Courts Commission Report, 465–74.

8  Hudson v. Aspinall (Chester, 1828)

9  Ferris v. Wickham (Bath and Wells, 1836), D/D/Cp 1836

10  Wickham v. Lockyer (Bath and Wells, 1836), D/D/Cp 1836

11  Forster v. Creaser (York, 1833), *Yorkshire Gazette*, 27 July 1833, 2f

12  Samuel Cox to J. Huckwell, 9 July 1852, in Gregory v. David (Llandaff, 1852), LL/ CC/G/2134j

13  Askwith to J. Wilcock, 25 November 1826 (copy), in Wharton v. Winter (York, 1826), PP

14  John Crosley (attorney) to Askwith, 17 February 1819, in Bastow v. Bakes (York, 1818), PP; see 67–8, above.

15  Bear v. Bignell (Winchester, 1832)

16  Noble v. Powell (York, 1819)

17  Wilcock to Asquith, 5 November 1826, in Wharton v. Winter (York, 1826), PP

18  Askwith to Bromby, 21 December 1819 (copy), in Musgrave v. Abbey (York, 1819), PP

19  Askwith to Thomas Lascelles, 24 January 1820 (copy), PP

20  Depositions are in Cons CP 1819/2.

21  J. Vallance to Askwith, 22 December 1819, PP

22  Marsh v. Travers (Norwich, 1846), DN/CON/137; see also 81, 116–17, above.

23  Goodson v. Tucker (Bath and Wells, 1847), Robinson v. Sharp (York, 1824), Pilling v. Taylor (Chester, 1834), Ellis v. Barker (York, 1835) (plaintiff's sister)

24  Etty v. Kneeshaw (York, 1819), Cons CP 1819/4

25  Etty v. Kneeshaw (York, 1819), Cons CP 1819/4

26  Edelstone v. Ellison (Chester, 1818), EDC 5 (1818–19)

27  Lucas v. Lawrence (Gloucester, 1847), B4/1/556

28  Dorney v. Webb (Bath and Wells, 1832), D/D/Cp 1832; also Storey v. Moffatt (Carlisle, 1839) ('make him recant')

29  Price v. Thomings (Lichfield, 1824), B/C/5/1825

30  Ellis v. Stead (York, 1821), Cons CP 1821/4; and see 169, above.

31  Lockwood v. Sheldon (Chester, 1839), EDC 5 (1840–1)

32  Deykes v. Phillips (Hereford, 1827), HD4/57

33  Linken v. Prior (Norwich, 1832)

34  Pattinson v. Hayton (Carlisle, 1839), Phillips v. Cutmore (Exeter, 1831), Stinton v.

Humpherson (Hereford, 1832), Lucas v. Lawrence (Gloucester, 1843), Price v. Rudge (Hereford, 1819), Johnson v. Johnson (London, 1819), Livie v. Mackintosh (London, 1820), James v. Williams (Llandaff, 1834), Sheard v. Ramsden (Ripon, 1852), Biffen v. Lawley (Bath and Wells, 1834), Rudd v. Brett (Norwich, 1837), Price v. Parry (Gloucester, 1841)

35  Newell v. Hutchinson (York, 1835), Cons CP 1835/7, Wood v. Butterworth (York, 1836)

36  Tidmarsh v. Smart (Gloucester, 1848), B4/1/1128, Atkinson v. Graham (Carlisle, 1830)

37  Robinson v. Sharp (York, 1824), Cons CP 1824/3; similarly, Gore v. Stratford (Gloucester, 1847), Pilling v. Bradley (York, 1829), Milner v. Welborn (York, Deanery, 1826), Bentley v. North (Ripon, 1849), Rowell v. Copeman (Norwich, 1845), Howarth v. Bannister (Chester, 1816), Macklin v. Gunter (Hereford, 1825), Atkinson v. Atkinson (Carlisle, 1825), Brook v. Sykes (York, 1824), Binnington v. Watson (York, 1815)

38  See 29, above.

39  Duffett v. Evans (Bristol, 1847), EP/J/2/7/11 ('she is a whore & I can prove her such'), Musgrave v. Abbey (York, 1819)

40  Hadley v. Whittaker (Chester, 1825), EDC 5 (1824–5), Barnes v. Parker (Chester, 1831), Garbutt v. Johnson (Chester, 1824)

41  Linton v. Bastin (Exeter, 1815)

42  Webber v. Penn (Exeter, 1816)

43  Anna Maria Bardsley v. Bardsley the elder (Chester, 1829), EDC 5 (1828–9)

44  Higgs v. Higgs (London, 1840), Guildhall, 12,185/5

45  Carrick v. Beaty (Carlisle, 1852), DRC/3/51 f. 30

46  King v. Hall (London, 1830), Guildhall, 12,185/3

47  Richards v. Clark (London, 1824), Guildhall, 12,185/2

48  Higgs v. Higgs (London, 1840), Guildhall, 12,185/5

49  Holmes v. Smith (York, 1820), Cons CP 1820/3

50  Dorney v. Webb (Bath and Wells, 1832), D/D/Cp 1832

51  Hutchinson v. J. and S. Proctor (York, 1838), Cons CP 1838/6 and 7

52  Etty v. Kneeshaw (York, 1819), Cons CP 1819/4. But abuse may have been punishable by local courts as a breach of the peace. See Crosby v. England (York, 1820) (referring to Lord Mayor's Court).

53  Shreve v. Wright (Norwich, 1848), DN/CON/137

54  J. Wright, *English Dialect Dictionary* (Oxford 1905), s.v. 'aye.' 'Hey' meaning 'yes' appears in a deposition in Smith v. Wardle (York, 1821). The attorney, in a letter to Askwith referring to the same incident, gives the word as 'aye.' Garbutt to Askwith, 1 September 1821, PP

55  Etty v. Kneeshaw (York, 1819), Abstract Book, 2 November 1820, Cons CP 1819/4

56  Newell v. Hutchinson (York, 1835), Cambridge v. Young (Gloucester, 1852)

57  Crosby v. England (York, 1820), Cons CP 1820/8

58  Ripley v. Garside (York, 1826), Cons CP 1826/4

59  Bannister v. Tillett (London, 1840), Guildhall, 12,185/5

60  Sheard v. Ramsden (Ripon, 1852), RD/AC/1/13

61  Southwood v. Halford (Gloucester, 1848), B4/1/114

62  Cambridge v. Young (Gloucester, 1852), B4/1/1046

63  Ayre v. Tocker (Exeter, 1820), Bate v. Collis (Worcester, 1846), Marsh v. Travers (Norwich, 1846)

64  Bate v. Collis (Worcester, 1846, and Arches Court), LPL, H694

65  Alexander v. Moore (Norwich, 1844), DN/CON/136; see 81–2, above. See also Chavasse v. Harris (Gloucester, 1833), 167, above, Roberts v. Gilpin (Hereford, 1828), 82, above (where the parish clerk refused to be used for this purpose), Price v. Rudge (Hereford, 1819), Carrick v. Beaty (Carlisle, 1854).

66  Whittle v. West (Bath and Wells, 1831), D/D/Cp 1831

67  Biffen v. Lawley (Bath and Wells, 1835), D/D/Cp 1835

68  Barlow v. Hobson (Chester, 1823), EDC 5 (1822–3); also Pilling v. Bradley (York, 1829), Smith v. Day (York, 1831), Humble v. Gypson (York, 1833), Matt v. Leak (Norwich, 1846), James v. Smith (Arches Court, 1849), Foster v. Sixsmith (Chester, 1834)

69  Richards v. Clark (London, 1824)

70  Briggs v. Dickinson (York, 1832)

71  Dee v. Seaborne (Hereford, 1831), HD4/59; also Snell v. Bailey (Salisbury and Arches Court, 1832), LPL H 484/9

72  Attersall v. Last (Exeter, 1816), CC 80

73  Deykes v. Phillips (Hereford, 1827), HD4/57

74  Burdon v. Poole (Lichfield, 1838), B/C/5/1838

75  L. Gowing, *Domestic Dangers: Women, Words and Sex in Early Modern London* (Oxford 1996), 266, 268, 274

76  See 266, note 4, above.

**Postscript**

1  Lynch v. Knight (1861), 9 HLC 577, at 593 and 594

2  Roberts v. Roberts (1864), 5 B & S 384, Speight v. Gosney (1891), 60 LJQB 231, W.B. Odgers, *A Digest of the Law of Libel and Slander* (London 1881), 87

3  54 & 55 Vic. c. 51. The law had been earlier amended to the same effect in Nova Scotia, Rules of Practice, 1884, ord. 19, rule 29, and in Ontario, 52 Vic. c. 14, s. 1 (1889).

4  W. Blackstone, *Commentaries on the Laws of England*, 15th ed., vol. 3 (London

1809), 125, Thorley v. Kerry (1812), 4 Taunt 355, 365, Barnett v. Allen (1858), 1 F & F 125, 127, 3 H & N 376

5 *Parliamentary Debates*, 3rd ser. 354, 1710, 1711 (29 June 1891)

6 *Law Magazine*, 7 (1832), 291

# Bibliography

**Manuscript Sources**

See list of archives at xvi, above.

**Works Cited**

Allen, C. *The Law of Evidence in Victorian England*. Cambridge 1997

Amussen, S.D. *An Ordered Society: Gender and Class in Early Modern England*. Oxford 1988

Arthurs, H. *Without the Law: Administrative Justice and Legal Pluralism in Nineteenth-Century England*. Toronto 1985

Ayliffe, J. *Parergon Juris Canonici Anglicani*. London 1726

Baines, E. *History Directory and Gazetteer of the County of York*. York 1823

Baker, J.H. *Monuments of Endlesse Labours: English Canonists and Their Work, 1300–1900*. London 1998

Barret-Ducrocq, F. *Love in the Time of Victoria*. 1989; Harmondsworth 1992

Beattie, J.M. *Crime and the Courts in England, 1660–1800*. Princeton 1986

Bentham, J. *Rationale of Judicial Evidence from the Manuscripts of Jeremy Bentham*. London 1827

Blackstone, W. *Commentaries on the Laws of England*. 15th ed. London 1809

Borthwick, J. *A Treatise on the Law of Libel and Slander as Applied in Scotland in Criminal Prosecutions and in Actions of Damages*. Edinburgh 1826

Browne, A. *A Compendious View of the Ecclesiastical Law of Ireland*. 2nd ed. Dublin 1803

Brundage, J.A. *Medieval Canon Law*. London 1995

Burn, R. *Ecclesiastical Law*. 9th ed. by R. Phillimore. London 1842

*The Clerical Guide and Ecclesiastical Directory*. London 1836

Clerke, F. *Praxis tam jus dicentibus quam aliis omnibus qui in Foro Ecclesiastico versantur apprime utilis.* 2nd ed. London 1684

Cockburn, W. *The Clerk's Assistant in the Practice of the Ecclesiastical Courts.* London 1800

Conset, H. *The Practice of the Spiritual or Ecclesiastical Courts.* 2nd ed. London 1700

Cooke, G.W. *A Treatise on the Law of Defamation.* London 1844

Coote, H.C. *The Practice of the Ecclesiastical Courts, with Forms and Tables of Costs.* London 1847

Duncan, G.I.O. *The High Court of Delegates.* Cambridge 1986

Ferme, B.E. 'William Lyndwood and the Provinciale: Canon Law in an Undivided Western Church.' (1997) 4 Eccles. LJ 615

Floyer, P. *The Proctor's Practice in the Ecclesiastical Courts.* London 1816

Ganz, M. *Elizabeth Gaskell: The Artist in Conflict.* New York 1969

Gibson, E. *Codex Juris Ecclesiastici Anglicani ... .* London 1713

Godolphin, J. *Repertorium Canonicum, or an Abridgment of the Ecclesiastical Laws of this Realm, consistent with the Temporal.* 3rd ed. London 1687

Gowing, L. 'Gender and the Language of Insult in Early Modern London.' *History Workshop,* 35 (1993), 18

– *Domestic Dangers: Women, Words and Sex in Early Modern London.* Oxford 1996

[Greg, W.R.] 'Prostitution.' *Westminster Review,* 53 (1850), 457

Grey, R. *A System of English Ecclesiastical Law.* 4th ed London 1743

Haigh, C.A. 'Slander and the Church Courts in the Sixteenth Century.' *Transactions of the Lancashire and Cheshire Antiquarian Society,* 78 (1975)

Hair, P.E.H. 'Bridal Pregnancy in Rural England in Earlier Centuries.' *Population Studies,* 20:2 (1966)

Helmholz, R.H. *Select Cases on Defamation to 1600.* London 1985

– *Roman Canon Law in Reformation England.* Cambridge 1990

Hemyng, B. 'Prostitution in London.' In H. Mayhew, *London Labour and the London Poor.* London 1861; reprinted 1968

Henriques, U. 'Bastardy and the New Poor Law.' *Past and Present,* 37 (1967), 103–29

Horwitz, H. *Chancery Equity Records and Proceedings 1600–1800.* London 1995

Ingram, M. 'Ridings, Rough Music, and the Reform of Popular Culture in Early Modern England.' *Past and Present,* 105 (1984), 79

– *Church Courts, Sex, and Marriage in England, 1570–1640.* Cambridge 1987

Karras, R.M. 'The Latin Vocabulary of Illicit Sex in English Ecclesiastical Court Records.' *Journal of Medieval Latin,* 2 (1992), 6

– *Common Women, Prostitution, and Sexuality in Medieval England.* Oxford 1996

Law, J.T. *Forms of Ecclesiastical Law, or the mode of conducting suits in the Consistory Courts: being a translation of the first part of Oughton's Ordo Judiciorum with*

*large additions from Clarke's Praxis, Conset on Practice, Ayliffe's Parergon, &c.*
London 1831

Lyndwood, W. *Provinciale (seu constitutiones Angliae) continens constitutiones provinciales quatuordecim archiepiscopum cantuariensum.* 1430: printed ed. Oxford 1679

Maddy, E. *Digest of Cases Argued and Determined in the Arches and Prerogative Courts of Canterbury.* London 1835

Manchester, A.H. 'The Reform of the Ecclesiastical Courts.' *American Journal of Legal History,* 10 (1966), 51

Mathieson, W.L. *English Church Reform, 1815–40.* London 1923

Matus, J.L. *Unstable Bodies.* Manchester 1995

Meldrum, T. 'A Women's Court in London: Defamation at the Bishop of London's Consistory Court, 1700–1745.' *London Journal,* 19 (1994), 6

Morris, P. 'Defamation and Sexual Reputation in Somerset 1733–1850.' PhD thesis. Warwick 1985

Muscott, E. *The History and Power of Ecclesiastical Courts.* London 1846

Newman, R.C. *A Hampshire Parish: Bramshott and Liphook.* Petersfield 1976

Odgers, W.B. *A Digest of the Law of Libel and Slander.* London 1881

Oughton, T. *Ordo Judiciorum, sive methodus procedendi in negotiis et litibus in foro ecclesiastico-civili Britannico et Hibernico.* London 1728

Pearsall, R. *The Worm in the Bud: The World of Victorian Sexuality.* London 1969

Phillimore, R. *The Practice and Courts of Civil and Ecclesiastical Law, and the statements in Mr Bouverie's speech on the subject, examined, with observations on the value of the study of Civil and International Law in this country; in a letter to the Right Hon W.E. Gladstone.* London 1848

Pollard, A. *Mrs Gaskell: Novelist and Biographer.* Manchester 1965

Powicke, F.M., and C.R. Cheney. *Councils and Synods with Other Documents Relating to the English Church, II, AD 1205–1313.* Oxford 1964

Rodes, R.E. *This House I Have Built: A Study of the Legal History of Establishment in England.* Notre Dame 1991

Rogers, F.N. *A Practical Arrangement of Ecclesiastical Law.* 2nd ed. London 1849

Roth, C. *The Rise of Provincial Jewry ... 1740–1840.* London 1950

Sharpe, J.A. *Defamation and Sexual Slander in Early Modern England: The Church Courts at York.* Borthwick Papers, no. 58. Borthwick Institute. York 1980

Skinner, J. *Journal of a Somerset Rector, 1802–1834.* Ed. H. and P. Coombs. Bath 1971

Spencer, J. 'Criminal Libel' [1977] Crim LR 383

Starkie, T. *A Treatise on the Law of Slander and Libel.* 2nd ed. London 1830

Stone, L. 'Literacy and Education in England, 1660–1900.' *Past and Present,* 42 (1969), 69

– *The Family, Sex, and Marriage in England 1500–1800.* London 1977

Taine, H. *Notes on England, 1860–70*. Tr. E. Hyams. London 1957

Trudgill, E. *Madonnas and Magdalenes: The Origin and Development of Victorian Sexual Attitudes*. London 1976

Underdown, D. *Revels, Riots, and Rebellion: Popular Politics and Culture in England, 1603–1660*. Oxford 1985

Valverde, M. 'The Love of Finery: Fashion and the Fallen Woman in Nineteenth Century Social Discourse.' *Victorian Studies*, 32 (1969), 169

Vincent, D. *Literacy and Popular Culture*. Cambridge 1989

Waddams, S.M. *Law, Politics and the Church of England: The Career of Stephen Lushington 1782–1873*. Cambridge 1992

Waddilove, A. *A Digest of Cases Decided in the Court of Arches, the Prerogative Court of Canterbury, the Consistory Court of London, and on Appeal therefrom to the Judicial Committee of the Privy Council: with references to decisions in the House of Lords and the Courts of Law and Equity and to the several Statutes and Text-Books*. London 1849

Walker, D.M. *Principles of Scottish Private Law*. 4th ed. Oxford 1988

Wharton, J.S. *An exposition of the laws relating to the women of England, showing their rights, remedies and responsibilities in every position of life*. London 1853

White, W. *History Gazetteer and Directory of Norfolk*. Norwich 1845

Woodforde, J. *Diary of a Country Parson*. London 1924–31

Wright, E. *Mrs Gaskell: The Basis for Reassessment*. Oxford 1965

# Table of Cases

# Index